Boston's Black Athletes

SPORT, IDENTITY, AND CULTURE

Series Editor

Gerald R. Gems (North Central College)

The *Sport, Identity, and Culture* series addresses the important role sport plays in social, cultural, and political contexts throughout history. While the series is primarily historical in its focus, it welcomes interdisciplinary projects. It is intentionally broad in its conceptualization, as sport—its organization, practice, and meanings—exists both within and beyond the territorial, cultural, social, ethnic, racial, gender, psychological, and chronological borders that construct and define individual and group identity.

Editorial Board

Linda J. Borish, Western Michigan

Susanna Hedenborg, Malmö University

Jorge Iber, Texas Tech University

Malcolm MacLean, University of Gloucestershire

Patricia Anne Vertinsky, University of British Columbia

Gertrud Pfister, University of Copenhagen

Titles in the Series

Boston's Black Athletes: Identity, Performance, and Activism, edited by Robert Cvornyek and Douglas Stark

Mental Health, Gender, and the Rise of Sport, by Gerald R. Gems

The Statues and Legacies of Combat Athletes in the Americas, edited by C. Nathan Hatton and David M.K. Sheinin

Populism and Professional Wrestling in the Sunbelt South: From Rasslin' to Sports Entertainment, by Christopher L. Stacey

Asians and Pacific Islanders in American Football: Historical and Contemporary Experiences, by Joel S. Franks

The Miami Times *and the Fight for Equality: Race, Sport, and the Black Press, 1948–1958*, by Yanela G. McLeod

The Early Years of Chicago Soccer, 1887–1939, by Gabe Logan

Transnational Sport in the American West: Oaxaca California Basketball, by Bernardo Ramirez Rios

Sport and the Shaping of Civic Identity in Chicago, by Gerald R. Gems

Boston's Black Athletes

Identity, Performance, and Activism

Edited by Robert Cvornyek
and Douglas Stark

LEXINGTON BOOKS
Lanham • Boulder • New York • London

Published by Lexington Books
An imprint of The Rowman & Littlefield Publishing Group, Inc.
4501 Forbes Boulevard, Suite 200, Lanham, Maryland 20706
www.rowman.com

86-90 Paul Street, London EC2A 4NE

Cover image caption: In April 1945, Black baseball stars Jackie Robinson, Sam Jethroe, and Marvin Williams participated in an orchestrated and ill-fated tryout with the Boston Red Sox. Robinson and Jethroe reunited in Boston in 1950 after Robinson shattered the color line in 1947 with the Brooklyn Dodgers and Jethroe integrated major league baseball in Boston in 1950 with the Boston Braves. Both men are pictured in Franklin Field, the Braves home ballpark. Jethroe was the oldest player to win Rookie of the Year honors in 1950. He was 32 years old.

Copyright © 2024 by The Rowman & Littlefield Publishing Group, Inc.

All rights reserved. No part of this book may be reproduced in any form or by any electronic or mechanical means, including information storage and retrieval systems, without written permission from the publisher, except by a reviewer who may quote passages in a review.

British Library Cataloguing in Publication Information Available

Library of Congress Cataloging-in-Publication Data

Names: Cvornyek, Robert, editor. | Stark, Douglas (Douglas Andrew), 1972- editor.
Title: Boston's Black athletes: identity, performance, and activism / Edited by Robert Cvornyek and Douglas Stark.
Description: Lanham, Maryland: Lexington Books, [2024] | Series: Sport, identity, and culture | Includes bibliographical references and index.
Identifiers: LCCN 2024006362 (print) | LCCN 2024006363 (ebook) | ISBN 9781666909043 (cloth) | ISBN 9781666909050 (ebook)
Subjects: LCSH: African-American athletes—Massachusetts—Boston—History. | Racism in sports—Massachusetts—Boston—History. | African American athletes—Massachusetts—Boston—Social conditions. | Sports—Sociological aspects—Massachusetts—Boston. | Boston (Mass.)—Race relations—History.
Classification: LCC GV706.32 .B68 2024 (print) | LCC GV706.32 (ebook) | DDC 796.089/96073—dc23/eng/20240214
LC record available at https://lccn.loc.gov/2024006362
LC ebook record available at https://lccn.loc.gov/2024006363

For Elizabeth and Isabella
"Know this child will be gifted with love, with patience,
and with faith. They'll make their way."

For Ben and Tessa
"Wishing you both long, happy, and peaceful lives."

Contents

Foreword: Representation Matters   ix
   Chanté Bonds

Acknowledgments   xiii

Chapter 1: Frenchy A. Johnson: The Life and Times of America's
   First Black Sports Star   1
   Edward H. Jones

Chapter 2: Black Brahmin Birdies: Golf and the Life of George
   Franklin Grant (1846–1910)   35
   Lane Demas

Chapter 3: Kittie Knox, Boston Cyclist in the 1890s: The War
   between Exclusion and Inclusion   51
   Lorenz J. Finison

Chapter 4: "Under Wraps": The Life and Legacy of Sam Langford   75
   Andrew Smith

Chapter 5: Marshall "Major" Taylor: The Worcester Whirlwind   89
   Lorenz J. Finison and Lynne Tolman

Chapter 6: Louise Mae Stokes Fraser: An Overlooked Legend   109
   Leslie Heaphy

Chapter 7: Lou Montgomery: Tackling Jim Crow   117
   Susan A. Michalczyk

Chapter 8: Constructing Legends: Pumpsie Green, Race, and the
   Boston Red Sox   137
   Robert E. Weir

viii *Contents*

Chapter 9: A Seasoned Rookie: Veteran Sam Jethroe Joins the
    Boston Braves   179
    Stephanie Liscio

Chapter 10: Staying East of the Mississippi: Reengaging with
    Rodeo's Diverse History and the New England Connection   193
    Tracey Owens Patton

Chapter 11: Boom Boom Barbosa to Jair: Boston's Minor-League,
    Major-League Soccer and Black Identity   213
    Steven Apostolov

Chapter 12: Fighting for Recognition: The Almost-Legendary
    Career of Medina Dixon   233
    Donna L. Halper

Afterword: (Re)centering Boston Sport History: A Biographical
    Glimpse of Seven African American Female Athletes Who Are
    Shaping Boston Sport   253
    Eileen Narcotta-Welp

Index   277

About the Editors and Contributors   291

Foreword

Representation Matters

Chanté Bonds

My experience as a collegiate and professional athlete in Boston taught me to appreciate the close connection between sports and community. I was born in Boston and raised in Brockton, where family and friends surrounded me, supported my athletic dreams, and shared their considerable knowledge about basketball and football. When I walked home from school, neighbors offered suggestions on how to improve my game and encouraged me to become a thoughtful and unselfish player. I stayed focused, avoided accolades, and committed to being a team player.

I gravitated toward football, but easier access to basketball kept me running most days. Asphalt courts, complete with rims and nets, were scarce and usually occupied. So, my friends and I hammered milk crates to trees and played in the street. We also engaged in endless hours of "burn" to strengthen our ball-handling and defensive skills. Burn kept two players within a tightly confined space battling each other for possession of the basketball. Parents and friends watched with admiration and jokingly talked trash about our performance. They helped shape our lives as we moved toward our future. At Brockton High School, my basketball future began to surface. I led our team to a state championship and upon graduation accepted an athletic scholarship from Bentley University in nearby Waltham, Massachusetts. Bentley proved a new experience for me, one that opened me to a White world. I learned to navigate the campus's racial terrain, but not without the help of teammates and coaches. They eased the transition. During my four-year career at the University, we achieved a record of 104–28, and, in 2003, we earned an appearance in the final four of the NCAA Division II national basketball championship. Playing led to coaching, and I enjoyed teaching the game to many young collegiate women in Greater Boston and the tristate areas.

Despite my basketball success, my mind often drifted to football, the game I was meant to play. When I attended Winthrop Elementary School in Brockton, I finally had the chance to join my classmates in our own organized football league. My companions and I played an entire football season. We played one game before the bell rang in the morning and another at recess. Back then, I never witnessed a woman, let alone a Black woman, playing football at a highly skilled competitive level. That perception changed in 2009, when I met Adrienne Smith. I was tossing a football on Fire Island in New York when Smith approached and introduced herself as a wide receiver for the New York Sharks of the Women's Football Alliance (WFA). Later that year, I joined Smith as a defensive back for the Sharks. Our lives remained connected as both of us made the move to play for the Boston Militia in 2011 and then the Boston Renegades in 2015. Throughout our careers, we helped Boston win five national WFA championships. I also welcomed the privilege to represent my country as a member of the US Women's National Football Team of the International Federation of American Football (IFAF). In 2022, I received a gold medal at the IFAF Women's World Championship. As co-captain of the team, it was an honor to lead a group of such talented women. The IFAF championship was a personal as well as professional achievement. The following year, I stood shoulder to shoulder with New England Patriot Lawyer Milloy as an honoree of The Tradition gala held in TD Garden. The event, sponsored by The Sports Museum in Boston, acknowledges local athletes for their hometown contributions. As a young girl, I dreamt of playing tackle football as a career. At the Tradition ceremony, being honored alongside a Super Bowl champion and other amazing professional athletes, I realized that dream had become a reality.

As an athlete, I lived in the present and dealt with everyday challenges. I was not aware that I was becoming part of a broader assembly of African American athletes that signified my city, and neighborhood. Distant memories of Black athletes from the Greater Boston area exist, but their accomplishments had been overlooked in traditional narratives that featured legendary White players. The racially selective account of Boston sports obscured the existence and contributions of generations of Black athletic performers. And, in the process, African Americans were denied a representation in sports, a recognition they richly deserved. The contributors to this book remind us that Boston's Black community hosted and supported an enduring tradition in sports. The authors acknowledge and provide scholarly attention to stories that have remained hushed for too long.

Boston's Black Athletes spans one hundred and fifty years of Black athletic participation in Boston sports. The opening chapter on Frenchy Johnson, a

Foreword xi

pioneer rower, begins during the Reconstruction Era, when most Blacks in America recently freed themselves from slavery. Subsequent chapters highlight figures that represent various stages of the Freedom Movement, when African Americans in Boston and throughout the nation battled Jim Crow and struggled to achieve equality on and off the field. The biographies in this book provide a sweeping history that captures the temporal breath of Black athletic performance.

This book highlights characteristic figures who endured the dishonor of segregation and emerged as several of Boston's earliest, but least-known, freedom fighters. It also includes pivotal figures like Pumpsie Green of the Red Sox, who was the last player to integrate a major league baseball team. I was drawn to the women in the book who served as agents of racial and gender change. The historic achievements of Kittie Knox, Louise Stokes, and Medina Dixon must function as examples for every young African American girl interested in sports. I now understand that my journey as an athlete connects with them.

African American athletes in Boston played to be heard and are still playing to be heard. Racial intolerance persists within the city and its sports venues. Throughout the past and present, athletes have used their notoriety and accomplishments to raise the issue of racial awareness in Boston. This book documents the efforts of gifted athletes who directed their talent toward the struggle for social justice. Representation does matter. Black Bostonians need to see themselves represented in all aspects of life, including sports. The athletes in this book represent something larger than themselves and the sport they played. They represent me and others like me.

Acknowledgments

When we began this project during the depths of the pandemic, we could not envision where it would lead. What started out as a one-volume book, quickly blossomed into a multi-volume project spanning 175 years of Boston sports, Black athletes, and community activism. Black athletes representing multiple gender identities playing amateur, semi-professional, and professional levels were included. Many twists and turns occurred; some topics were shelved for lack of research while others were explored and ultimately completed. In the process, each of us expanded our understanding and appreciation of race and sports in Boston. We felt disheartened that many of these stories had been forgotten or erased. As sports fans and historians, we continually learned about new players, teams, and communities that had been overlooked, and in the process, we gained greater insight into the shifting nature of what explains race and sports in Boston. Our sincere hope is that these stories are not the end, but a beginning, a challenge for others to continue researching and sharing these wonderful and inspiring stories.

A book of this nature would not be possible without our contributors. Each one tackled their subject with great enthusiasm, uncovering lost items of information long after they submitted their drafts. Each contributor kept researching, writing, and refining their articles. We extend our heartfelt appreciation for your willingness to contribute your time and knowledge.

We benefited from wonderful conversations with a wide range of individuals, including Dick Johnson at The Sports Museum, Charlie Titus at UMass Boston, Alfreda Harris at the Shelburne Community Center, Jeff Gerson at UMass Lowell, Ted Fay at UMass Boston, and Richard Lapchick at the University of Central Florida. Many other individuals proved equally helpful during this process, too many to name, but know that your assistance, no matter how big or small, was much appreciated.

We wish to express our deepest thanks to Sydney Wedbush at Lexington Press, who joined us midstream but championed our project and facilitated our final manuscript delivery. Many thanks for all your guidance and assistance

xiv   *Acknowledgments*

as we reached the finish line. We also wish to express our sincere thanks to Samuel Withers for his expert proofing and editing of the manuscripts. His attention to detail guided this book throughout the production phase.

We also wish to thank those who helped us secure images, including the Amon Carter Museum of American Art, Boston College Athletics, the Conway Library at Harvard University, Getty Images, the Leslie Jones Collection at the Boston Public Library, National Baseball Hall of Fame and Museum, Old Dominion Athletics, the Smithsonian, Robert Mara, and Steven Apostolov.

To our proofreaders, Eileen and Michelle Moon, an extremely talented mother-daughter editing team, who joined us once again and whose close reading and pinpoint edits and comments ensured that this manuscript was ready for submission. Along the way, I am sure that both learned a great deal about Boston's Black athletes. Kaitlyn Batka provided technical and stylistic expertise at crucial moments in this project, and we remain most grateful. Amy Polick, Elizabeth Crowe, and Tyler Towne, the academic leaders at Florida State University, Panama City, provided support, encouragement, and productive conversation. Their leadership embodies academic integrity at the University. My deepest love and respect, however, found a home in Abbie Reed.

Our manuscript readers did not miss a beat, and our heartfelt thanks goes to Kathryn Leann Harris and Greg Tranter. Again, both Kathryn and Greg joined our project team, and their knowledge of sports and enthusiasm for the subject helped us consider new ways to express our arguments. Your comments proved extremely helpful as we strengthened the overall story.

Chapter 1

Frenchy A. Johnson

The Life and Times of America's First Black Sports Star

Edward H. Jones

Frenchy *Johnson went to Boston,*
where he rowed the Charles.
There he honed his sculling skills,
which won him fame and laurels.[1]

On a warm July afternoon in 1878, a crowd estimated by one account at forty thousand gathered along the banks of Boston's Charles River.[2] This crowd reportedly extended to the housetops and along the city's Mill Dam wall "as far as the eye could reach."[3] They were there to witness some of the nation's best oarsmen of the day display their rowing prowess. Exactly 102 years after America celebrated its independence from Great Britain, Boston was celebrating its annual Fourth of July rowing regatta, as rowing competitions were called. The day was ideal for boat racing, with sunny weather and smooth water. And despite a breeze that provided relief from seven previous days of hot weather, at least some of the competitors likely rowed shirtless to keep cool. As one newspaper colorfully reported, the sun, "because of his native modesty, felt hurt at the primitive attire of the brawny boatmen," and thus "veiled his face behind a mantle of fleecy clouds."[4]

The first rowing race of the afternoon was a three-mile, single-sculls race with a turn for professional oarsmen. This race involved long, narrow, sleek racing boats called shells, consisting of lightweight frames covered by a thin shell of wood, treated paper, or other waterproof material. These boats were designed for a single rower (sculler) who wielded an oar (also known as a scull) in each hand. The term *scull* is also sometimes used to describe a racing shell rowed with sculls. Sculling typically involves one, two, or four rowers, each wielding an oar in each hand. In comparison to sculling, sweep rowing typically involves two, four, or eight rowers in a boat, each pulling on a single oar (also known as a sweep) with both hands. Today, sculls and sweeps are more commonly referred to simply as oars.

In a race with a turn, the competitors had to row to an anchored boat, buoy, post, flag, or other fixed marker (stake) positioned at the race's halfway point, pivot around the stake ("turn the stake"), and row back to the starting point. In addition to providing a challenge for the rowers, races with stake turns, popular at the time, allowed the spectators to view both the start and finish of the race. An example of a two-man (paired-oar) sweep boat turning a stake can be seen in the painting *The Biglin Brothers Turning the Stake* (1873) by Philadelphia artist and amateur sculler Thomas Eakins.[5]

In the single-sculls race this day in Boston, five oarsmen were vying for the first prize of $150,[6] calculated to be equal to well over four thousand dollars in today's currency.[7] The entrants, according to lane assignments, were Jeremiah Driscoll of Brookline, Massachusetts; Evan Morris of Pittsburgh, Pennsylvania; Michael Lynch of Salem, Massachusetts; George Lane of Charlestown, Massachusetts; and Frenchy Johnson of Boston, Massachusetts,[8] dubbed by one source as "Boston's favorite Sculler."[9] As one of the very few Black oarsmen of the era, Johnson was a popular and skilled competitor, as he would demonstrate this day.

At the word "Go," Johnson surged ahead, "soon settled down to his work, and with a stroke [rate] of thirty-six to the minute was cleaving the water with a tremendous pace and fast leaving his opponents." Then, Johnson, still rowing at thirty-six strokes per minute, turned the stake at least eight boat lengths ahead of Morris, his nearest competitor. Johnson, on his way to the finish line, passed Driscoll, who had yet to turn the stake. Johnson easily won, and the *Boston Globe* proclaimed the win with the sub-headline "Frenchy Johnson Again Victorious."[10] The *Boston Evening Transcript* had a more vivid description of Johnson's performance:

> Johnson's rowing was "just splendid," his black back swinging back and forth with all the regularity and seemingly with all the ease of a well-greased pendulum. But hold! here they come, Johnson a dozen lengths in the lead, still swaying back and forth, back and forth, and over the line he goes in 21.42 [21 minutes and 42 seconds] amid the yells of the crowd, the shrill whistling of the steamers and the short, sharp "well done" of the signal gun.[11]

When Johnson pulled around to the judges' boat, he was asked whether he had any interest in claiming a foul. "No, nobody near enough to trouble me," he responded.

Boston's annual Fourth of July rowing regatta continued to look favorably on its adopted son. Johnson won the double-sculls in 1880 with boatmate and fellow Bostonian Frank Hill.[12] In Johnson's day, amateur and professional rowing enjoyed a level of popularity among the public that hasn't been seen since.[13] As sports entertainment, rowing events were exciting, accessible, easily understood, and most importantly, free. If a spectator could make their way to a river or lake, they did not have to worry about paying an admission fee as they might if entering a ballpark, racetrack, arena, or stadium. No other Black athlete enjoyed the acclaim that Johnson received during his short rowing career. The popularity of rowing meant that races were constantly in the news. And the telegraph helped race results to be quickly reported throughout the continental United States and beyond.[14]

Before there was the pioneering Black major league baseball player Moses Fleetwood Walker, before there was the Black world champion bicycle racer Marshall "Major" Taylor, and before there was three-time Kentucky Derby–winning Black jockey Isaac Murphy, there was the celebrated Black professional oarsman from Boston, Frenchy Johnson. While other Black athletes may have achieved a degree of prominence during his era, none received the acclaim and adulation of Johnson. He lived an extraordinary life during extraordinary times; this is the story of both.

SOUTHERN DISCOMFORT

The year 1836 saw the passing of Betsy Ross,[15] James Madison,[16] and Aaron Burr,[17] three of the last surviving ties to the American Revolution. At the same time, another revolution was underway, borne of the proposition that all men were created equal. Northern abolitionists were engaged in a fervent struggle to remove the ugly stain of slavery from the fabric of a young America. It was only sixty years earlier that Ross, Madison, and Burr witnessed the birth of a new nation. Now that nation was divided over the issue of slavery. Until the Emancipation Proclamation abolished slavery in 1863, the slave-based economy in the American South would continue unimpeded, as would ancillary benefits to the enslavers. One of those benefits was the use of enslaved individuals as oarsmen in rowing races along the coastal areas of the American South.

The Aquatic Club of Georgia was formally established on January 12, 1836,[18] almost a decade before rowing clubs were established at Yale (1843)[19] and Harvard (1844)[20] Universities, which held their first annual

Harvard-Yale Boat Race in 1852.[21] Rowing races involving the enslaved were a reality in the antebellum American South. In one such regatta in 1839, organized by the Lower Creek Boat Club of Savannah, Georgia, the spectators included large parties of the City's "finest belles." It was noted that the outcome of a race had all been "in the hands of fortune, and the stout arms of the sable crews, the rowers being all men of color."[22] It wasn't clear, though, if these particular oarsmen were free men of color receiving payment for their services or enslaved men hired out by their owners who were intent on profiting from their enslavement. However, an 1849 article in the *Daily Georgian* made it clear when it described a regatta at Georgia's Broughton Island on the Altamaha River. The article stated that "[T]he fact that these races are rowed by the slaves of the owners of these boats, and that these oarsmen feel a pride in the contest utterly inappreciable elsewhere, gives a strong zest" to the event.[23] Another account that appeared in the *Georgia Citizen* in 1852 describes a regatta at Charleston, South Carolina, where the winning boat, the forty-three-foot-long *Becky Sharp*, was rowed by eight "negro oarsmen" belonging to four individuals in equal numbers.[24]

Regardless of how much "pride" or "zest" they may have exhibited, the fact remains that these oarsmen were the property of other human beings. No amount of boat-racing excitement could make up for the fact that these rowers were enslaved. Their lives were not theirs to live as free men until after the Civil War. They were held in bondage, and thus they were the antebellum equivalent of ancient galley slaves rowing at the command of their masters.

The boats used during these so-called slave races were not the sleek racing shells of Frenchy Johnson's day, but instead were dugout canoes fashioned from a single log. Two of the more celebrated boats of the Aquatic Club of Georgia were the *Goddess of Liberty* and the *Devil's Darning Needle*. The *Goddess* was a dugout hewn from a single cypress log and described as a perfect model of symmetry. It was thirty-two feet long and three feet, eleven inches wide. It was a six-oared sweep boat, in which each of the six oarsmen "pulled" a single oar with both hands, with each oar alternately positioned on each side of the boat. The *Devil's Needle* was a six-oared boat also, described as a low, sharp, "wicked looking thing—black as Satan himself." It was thirty-three feet, six inches long and "remarkably narrow," with outriggers of iron to increase the length and leverage of its oars and was steered by a "curiously shaped oar on a pivot."[25]

By his own admission, Frenchy Johnson had been enslaved in his native Virginia. This raises the question of whether he was ever a member of a rowing crew of enslaved men. Nothing in the historical record indicates he was involved in any sort of rowing while enslaved. Nor did any of Johnson's few interviews with the press hint that he ever rowed while enslaved. And even if he had rowed as part of a crew of enslaved men, the experience would have contributed little or nothing to his prowess as a professional sculler. The sheer muscular force required to pull a sweep oar on a thirty-two-foot dugout canoe hewn from an entire cypress log is not the same as the coordination and balance required to finesse the oars of a sleek twenty-eight-foot-long, twelve-and-a-half-inch-wide, thirty-one-pound, paper-hulled, single-sculls racing shell like the boat Johnson rowed at Silver Lake (New York) in 1878.[26] This latter skill set was not something enslaved oarsmen would have had to master. Therefore, it does not seem very likely that as an enslaved teenager in Virginia, Johnson acquired the skills needed to row professionally in later life.

Any inquiry into the life of Johnson inevitably leads to the question "Why was he called Frenchy?" Any thought that Johnson might be French was dispelled in an 1877 article appearing in the *Binghamton (NY) Daily Times*.[27] The article stated that he "is not, as his name might be supposed to indicate, at all Frenchy either in nationality or nature, but is a native of Virginia, having formerly been a slave." Another article announced the results of a sculling race with the headline "Riley Scoops the Frenchman," the Frenchman moniker merely being a play on Johnson's name.[28] In yet a third article, a correspondent for the *New York World* referred to "[o]ne Johnson, who is called 'Frenchy' because he happens to be black," with no explanation as to the statement's meaning.[29] Unfortunately, all three of these articles failed to provide an indication of how Johnson became "Frenchy" or what his middle initial, *A*, stood for. Aside from a few newspaper interviews with Johnson in his twenties, there appears to be no documented information on Johnson's life as a child prior to the abolition of slavery in America. Enslaved individuals were considered property, like a mule or a plow, and thus were not included in census records prior to emancipation in 1863. Nor were they usually included by name in local directories or birth or death records. In addition, rarely were enslaved individuals listed by name on county slave schedules created to keep inventory of local slave populations. Typically, the enslaved were listed only by sex, age, and color—*B* for Black and *M* for Mulatto.[30] Johnson's early life remains a mystery.

There is, however, one item that might shed light on the origin of the name "Frenchy." In 1870, Johnson had an out-of-wedlock child with a formerly enslaved woman named Anna (or Alma) Watts, discussed in more detail later.[31] The child, a son, was named Francis J. Watts, with the "Francis J." possibly a recognition of the child's father, Frenchy Johnson. Further, could Frenchy be a nickname for Francis, a name not unknown among the formerly enslaved?[32] Could it be that Johnson did not want to be Francis, so he became Frenchy? Interestingly, the Latin origin of the name *Francis* means "free man."[33] In the end, however, perhaps the real answer may prove to be the simplest—Johnson liked the name "Frenchy" and decided to adopt it.

The American press has bestowed some colorful monikers on its sports heroes. Some examples include "The Brown Bomber" for heavyweight boxing champ Joe Louis and "The Buckeye Bullet" for Ohio State and Olympic track star Jessie Owens. These tags were not applied only to Black athletes. White athletes were also recipients of such epithets, such as "The Galloping Ghost" for 1920s All-American football star Red Grange and "The Sultan of Swat" for baseball great Babe Ruth. Johnson was not immune from such labels, even if his labels lacked alliteration. Some of the many superlatives he was given include, with capitalizations added: the Celebrated "Frenchy" Johnson;[34] the Colored Knight of the Oar;[35] the Stalwart Oarsman of Ebony Hue;[36] the Colored Phenomenon;[37] the Fastest Sculler in New England;[38] and the Colored Hero of the Spoons,[39] with *spoons* being a colloquialism for oars having curved, spoon-like blades (spoon oars) used by some scullers at the time.[40] Similarly, colloquial expressions for scullers at the time were "willow dippers,"[41] who, when rowing, were said to be "feathering the spruces."[42] However, not all of Johnson's monikers were complimentary, with the names "Ethiopian"[43] and "African"[44] being clearly derogatory references to his race.

Besides the origin of the name *Frenchy*, the date and place of Johnson's birth is uncertain. What is certain is that his parents were Thomas and Harriet Johnson, who almost certainly were enslaved.[45] In an interview in August 1881, Johnson said he would be thirty-two years old on the tenth of October of that year.[46] This would make his birth year 1849. But in another interview four years earlier, published on October 16, 1877, he said he was twenty-seven, making his birth year 1850.[47] A further contradiction appears in the 1880 census schedule recorded in June of that year, which lists his age at thirty-five.[48] Based on the October tenth birth date, his birth year would be 1845. Similarly, in the 1877 interview, he said he was born in Germantown, Virginia,[49] but official records indicate Hampton, Virginia.[50] No doubt growing up in slavery accounts for some, if not all, of these discrepancies. The dates and places of his birth were almost certainly best-guess estimates at the time. The institution of slavery had, in essence, obliterated Johnson's early life from the historical record. When he does appear in the record, it is in 1867, two years after the end of the American Civil War and four years after the end of slavery.

On January 1, 1863, two years into the Civil War, President Abraham Lincoln issued the Emancipation Proclamation, which declared that "all persons held as slaves . . . within any State . . . in rebellion against the United States . . . shall be then, thenceforward, and forever free . . . " The war, however, would continue for another two years, ending on April 9, 1865. In March 1865, as the war neared its end, the US Congress established the Bureau of Refugees, Freedmen, and Abandoned Lands, commonly known as the Freedmen's Bureau. The Freedmen's Bureau was created to address the affairs and needs of the newly emancipated slaves in the former Confederate States. These individuals, who numbered nearly four million in 1860, had been an underclass, with no formal education or independent means of support.[51] The newly freed individuals had to be fed, housed, clothed, and educated so they could eventually be put in a position where they could be self-sufficient. The Freedmen's Bureau was designed to meet those needs. The Freedmen's Bureau also set up special courts to hear legal matters involving the formerly enslaved, including Frenchy Johnson. One such court was located at Fort Monroe, Virginia.[52]

FREEDOM'S FORTRESS

Fort Monroe was a Union stronghold in the Confederate state of Virginia. It was a massive fortification that has also been referred to as "Fortress Monroe" because of its formidable structure. Situated on a peninsula, the Fort was surrounded by a moat and had thick granite walls rising twenty-four feet above the moat's waterline. It provided Union forces with a strategic defensive position at the mouth of the Chesapeake Bay. Today, it exists as a museum that chronicles the Fort's Civil War history.[53] It is not clear exactly when Frenchy Johnson made his way to Fort Monroe. He very well could have arrived prior to the end of the war as an escaped slave seeking sanctuary at the Fort. Slaves who managed to make their way to the Fort could feel safe from the evils of slavery. In May 1861, the commanding officer, Major-General Benjamin Butler, contended that the escaped slaves were considered "contraband of war," and he therefore had no obligation to return them to their owners.[54]

By early August, the number of refugees escaping to the Fort had swollen to two thousand.[55] Enslaved men, women, and children were not the only ones fleeing to the protection of Fort Monroe. Free persons of color also sought refuge at the Fort against marauding parties of rebels who had been rounding up able-bodied Blacks and forcing them to work on the construction of Confederate fortifications in the area.[56] Whether Frenchy Johnson was among the influx of enslaved persons seeking refuge at Fort Monroe is not known. What is known is that official records place him at the Fort in February 1867, almost two years after the end of the Civil War.

STINKING BULL PEN SOLDIERS

The paper trail for Johnson unfortunately has an inauspicious beginning. According to an incident report among the Proceedings of the Freedmen's

Bureau Court, Johnson was involved in an encounter that occurred just outside of the gates of Fort Monroe. The handwritten report captioned *Commonwealth (VA) versus Frenchy Johnson (colored)* described the incident. Johnson, who reportedly was "drunk and hallering [sic]," confronted some soldiers, cursing them and calling them "stinking bull pen soldiers." When the soldiers attempted to subdue Johnson, the incident escalated into a knock-down, drag-out affair, with Johnson being struck with a gun at least twice. The skirmish was punctuated by blows struck, a sword brandished, and an arrest made. Following his arrest, Johnson pled guilty to "drunkenness and disorderly conduct" and was sentenced to "confinement for one month" in military prison, presumably at Fort Monroe.[57] Thus was Johnson's unpropitious debut into the historical record.

Upon completion of his sentence, Johnson next appears on a Freedmen's Bureau "List of Colored Persons Sent North."[58] With so many ex-slaves concentrated in the South, the Freedmen's Bureau sought to relocate many of them to New England, where better opportunities might exist. In Johnson's case, on April 20, 1867, he and other former slaves boarded the wooden-hulled steamer ship *George Appold* bound for Boston, Massachusetts. The passenger list indicates that Johnson was eighteen at the time.[59]

BOSTON STRONG

By 1872, Johnson was living in Boston but had not yet begun his professional rowing career. City tax records show that he was working as a laborer.[60] At the time, he was single and had a relationship with a woman named Anna (or Alma) Watts, as previously mentioned. Like Johnson, Watts had been enslaved in Virginia and was relocated to Boston via steamship from Fort Monroe around the same time as Johnson.[61] In the 1870 US Census, she was listed as a twenty-year-old "Chambermaid,"[62] suggesting she was one of the "colored girl servants" hired to work in the homes of White Bostonians.[63] It is not known if Johnson knew Watts at Fort Monroe, but in Boston, their relationship produced a son—Francis J. Watts. Sadly, however, the infant died at six months of age from infant cholera,[64] a deadly diarrheal disease of children in the nineteenth century referred to then as the "summer complaint."[65] In 1871, the year the infant Watts died, Boston saw 526 child deaths from infant cholera.[66] Sadder still, around the time the infant Watts was born, both mother and son had arrived at the Tewksbury Almshouse, an institution for the "pauper insane" at Tewkesbury, Massachusetts.[67] Intake records show that the infant Watts died at Tewkesbury. The records identify Johnson as the child's father, who had promised to marry Alma Watts (identified as Anna in the 1870 US Census) but had "cleared off," his whereabouts not known.[68] This might explain why the name Frenchy Johnson does not appear in the 1870 US Census. According to that same census, Alma could neither read nor write.[69] In addition, the word "Feeble" was written as a notation in the margin of Alma's intake record, which could explain why she and her infant son were confined to Tewkesbury in the first place.[70]

FRENCHY IN LOVE

It is not known if Johnson ever knew of the death of his child or even the fate of its mother, but by 1873, he had moved on to the next major event of his life. On November 29, 1873, Johnson married Theresa Rickords (or Rickards) in Boston.[71] She was a free-born woman of color from West Chester, Pennsylvania. According to the marriage registration, he was twenty-five, and she was seventeen. The marriage registration lists Johnson's occupation as "Engineer." This could possibly refer to work he might have done at Fort Monroe on breastworks, entrenchments, and other fortification-securing activities under the supervision of military engineers.[72] However, Boston tax records for the same year lists Johnson's occupation as "Laborer."[73] So perhaps "Engineer" was a bit of hyperbole, possibly to impress his new bride. Johnson and Rickords were married by the Reverend William F. Dickerson, pastor of Boston's Anderson Street Church, where the couple most likely were married.[74]

Dickerson was a free-born man of color originally from New Jersey. He was an educated man, having graduated from Lincoln University in Chester County, Pennsylvania, in 1870 with a B.A. degree. Lincoln University was described as "a Collegiate and Theological Institution of Colored Men." Students were required to take a classical course of study that included Latin, Greek, geometry, logic, rhetoric, philosophy, astronomy, Hebrew, Bible, evidence of Christianity, and Constitution of the United States.[75] As one of the very few college-educated Black men at the time, Dickerson certainly must have impressed Johnson. By 1880, Dickerson had risen to become the thirteenth bishop of the African Methodist Episcopal (A.M.E.) Church.[76] Founded in 1816, the A.M.E. Church is America's oldest Black denomination still in existence.[77] As for Johnson, his marriage did not survive, and by 1880, the same year Dickerson was elevated to bishop, Johnson found himself single again, although now his occupation was listed in the 1880 census as "Oarsman."[78] No doubt the life of a professional sculler had put strains on Johnson's marriage.

OARSMAN

It is not known exactly when Johnson began his career as a professional oarsman. But by October 13th of 1875, Johnson, from Boston's West End, had rowed a three-mile race with a turn on Boston's Charles River against Michael Delowry of Boston's North End.[79] The race was for two hundred dollars "a side," which meant that the financial backer(s) of each side (of each competitor) put up two hundred dollars, with the winner taking all four hundred dollars to be shared with his respective backer(s).[80] There was considerable betting on the match, with Delowry favored almost two to one. This was one of Johnson's first, if not *the* first, of his professional rowing races. However, instead of lightweight, sleek racing shells, the competitors rowed forty-five-pound, utilitarian, flat-bottomed, working boats.[81]

The *Boston Journal* reported that both men were well-matched and displayed "pluck and wind, two indispensables in a race on the water." At the start of the race, Delowry had a slight lead and was first to turn the stake. But Johnson "showed himself" in the second half of the race. "He put in some good work on the third mile and passed Delowry in spite of [Delowry's] best efforts." Johnson reached the finish line leading Delowry by a dozen boat lengths—an impressive result for a budding professional rowing career.[82] Today, the four-hundred-dollar prize would be equivalent to over ten thousand dollars.[83]

As to who may have introduced Johnson to the art of sculling, two names top the list—Charles Courtney, a close friend of Johnson and onetime American single-sculls champion, and Tom "T.C." Butler, a fellow Bostonian and Johnson's occasional double-sculls partner. "He [Johnson] did not know anything at all about sculling until he went to Owego [New York] with me [in 1877]," Courtney told a reporter. "There is a chance for wonderful improvement in Frenchy. Any one will have to get up early in the morning to beat him."[84] Courtney further touted Johnson's sculling skills—"Frenchy Johnson has proven himself capable of keeping company with the swiftest oarsmen of the day."[85]

As for Butler's involvement in Johnson's development, an article recalling the glory days of professional sculling stated that Frenchy "was brought out" by Tom Butler, who "took great pains with him." So rapidly did Johnson improve that "within a year after Butler took him in hand was he able to out-scull his tutor" as he "rowed against many a good sculler and generally got a bit of what was offered [in prize money]."[86] Another published reflection recalled that in Johnson and an up-and-coming oarsman named George Hosmer, Tom Butler and his brother Jim had "two green ones in hand about the same time," and that "they turned out well is shown by their records."

However, in comparing the two novices, the article said, "Frenchy was surely the champion of his race and a clever one on the broad field of comparison," while Hosmer was held by [professional oarsman] George Faulkner "to be one of the best all-around men he had ever seen."[87] Such a comparison was typical of the struggle Johnson often faced to be recognized as not just the best "colored" sculler of his day or Boston's best sculler, but one of the *best* scullers, period. Three other Black scullers of note at the time were Robert Berry of Toronto;[88] Burt Brown, referred to in the press as the Union Springs (NY) mulatto;[89] and Frank Hart of Boston, who later became a champion pedestrian (competitive walker).[90] While all three achieved a measure of success, none received the accolades or achieved the popularity of Johnson.

Johnson's sculling prowess was further noted in an 1878 article appearing in *Forest and Stream*. The article begins without reservation, touting Johnson's recent victory on August 18 of that year at the Silver Lake Regatta near Boston. "Of 'Frenchy' Johnson's rowing, only one thing can be said, that with better coaching and a little finer style he will soon be a man to be feared by all who may pull over the same course with him in the future." Unfortunately, the article went on to point out that the absence of several prominent oarsmen from the race, the questionable performance of another, and an illness on the part of yet a third, robbed Johnson's victory of much of its significance. Consequently, Johnson's skill was minimized to being "*Boston's* best man and one who can make away with anybody *but the very best*" [emphasis added]. The article did, however, make note that Johnson had the best time ever made at Silver Lake, his winning time being twenty-one minutes and twenty-one seconds.[91]

Perhaps the best account of Johnson's sculling ability is found in a short item appearing on May 18, 1880, in the Harvard College daily newspaper, the *Harvard Echo*. Professional scullers George Faulkner, Wallace Ross, and Frenchy Johnson were out on the Charles River during Harvard's annual class rowing races—freshmen, sophomore, etc. Johnson's skills were summed up in a single sentence—"The ease with which Frenchy kept ahead of the Junior scullers was a sight to behold."[92]

STRENGTH, ENDURANCE, AND POPULARITY

Regardless of exactly when Johnson learned to scull or who taught him, he entered the sport as a strong, muscular, athletic man in his mid-twenties. At 155 pounds and five feet, ten inches tall, Johnson was described as "well put together—a large chested, big framed, muscled fellow"[93] with "tremendous strength and endurance."[94] Johnson was also described as "seemingly well educated," perhaps a result of attending one of the schools set up by the Freedmen's Bureau to help educate newly freed slaves.[95] He was also described as being "quiet"[96] and conducting himself in a "becoming and gentlemanly manner."[97] As one reporter wrote, "the manly and generous conduct of the colored knight of the oar has won for him many friends."[98] By all accounts, his amiable personality made him a spectator favorite wherever he competed, both on and off the water. This was especially true in and around his hometown of Boston. One instance of his popularity was evidenced at the start of the Silver Lake Regatta in 1878. The *New York Times* noted that as he took up his position, "he was loudly cheered, for he has of late become a decided favorite . . . and is looked upon as one of most promising oarsmen in the country."[99] Moreover, after winning the regatta, he "received an enthusiastic reception and was serenaded by his friends."[100] Similarly, he was featured during an evening of entertainment at the Boston Music Hall in 1879. The event was presented by the city's Shawmut Rowing Club and included an exhibition of hydraulic rowing machines. Johnson, who was billed that night as Boston's favorite sculler, was given a warm welcome the moment he showed himself onstage. As reported in the *Boston Globe,* his quick strokes at the machine "called out storms of applause."[101]

TINKER, TAILOR, BOXER, THIEF

Johnson's popularity made him an idol among many of the young people of Boston. One such fan was Jake Kilrain. He had reportedly been "a great admirer" of several notable oarsmen of the time, including Frenchy Johnson.[102] It was his admiration for these men that led him to take up rowing in his early twenties. Kilrain soon developed into a skilled and successful oarsman in both the amateur and professional ranks. In 1883, rowing under his actual surname, "Killion," he won the junior single-sculls amateur championship on the Passaic River at Newark, New Jersey.[103] However, when race authorities learned that he had also been boxing professionally on the side under the surname "Kilrain," he was stripped of his amateur status as an oarsman and barred from further participation in amateur rowing competitions.[104] He explained his use of the two surnames in an 1888 autobiography: "My name is Joseph John Killion. When I was a lad, my comrades persisted in calling me Kilrain, and the name has stuck to me ever since, so I have bowed to the inevitable, and now write my name 'Kilrain.'"[105] Having lost his amateur status, Kilrain was forced to join the ranks of professional oarsmen. However, the financial rewards of professional rowing evidently were not what he had hoped, so he redirected all his efforts to professional boxing.[106] He quickly rose through the boxing ranks, culminating in an 1889 bout in Richburg, Mississippi, against the then-reigning world bare-knuckle heavyweight champion John L. Sullivan, dubbed "Boston's Big Fellow," by one account.[107] After seventy-five rounds, lasting two hours and eighteen minutes, one of Kilrain's seconds (corner men) conceded the fight and "threw up the sponge" (threw in the towel) as an admission of defeat.[108] Although Kilrain lost, he was acknowledged to be, without a doubt, "a game man and a good fighter."[109]

Having notoriety can also have its drawbacks. In 1876, the Boston press reported on a woman who had appropriated the name "Frenchy Johnson" as an alias to carry out a shoplifting spree in Boston. The woman, whose real name was Mary Wilson, was considered one of the most expert and notorious shoplifters in the country. Eventually, she and two other female shoplifters were arrested in Boston, where detectives were waiting for them upon their arrival by train from New York City.[110] No comment was reported from the "real" Frenchy Johnson.

SCULLING SKULLDUGGERY, OR THE MYSTERIOUS AFFAIR AT CHAUTAUQUA LAKE

Without a doubt, the most scandalous incident in the annals of professional rowing is what has been called the Chautauqua Lake Fizzle.[111] A real-life whodunit, it's a mystery that has remained unsolved for nearly a century and a half. The cast of characters consisted of Charles Courtney, Edward "Ned" Hanlan, and Frenchy Johnson. Courtney and Hanlan, described by the *New York Herald* as "the two greatest oarsmen this world has ever produced," were scheduled to row a five-mile race with a turn at Chautauqua Lake in the western corner of New York State.[112] The winner would pocket six thousand dollars, worth over $170,000 today.[113] For this race, Courtney's friend and rowing rival Frenchy Johnson would serve as Courtney's trainer and assistant.[114] Courtney hailed from Union Springs, New York, near Ithaca, while Hanlan was from Toronto, Canada. It was therefore natural that the race was seen by many as a contest for the sculling supremacy of North America. The race was to take place on the afternoon of October 16, 1879. In the preceding days, spectators, reporters, and betting men poured into the nearby small town of Mayville, New York, the perfect peaceful setting for a mystery. The crowds overflowed the town's accommodations, causing the price of available rooms to climb.[115]

The *Rochester Democrat and Chronicle* reported that the absence of sporting events in other parts of the country had the effect of bringing together "all the rougher element" of society to Mayville, and they all came prepared for business.[116] An account, published six days after the race, noted that the crowd was smaller than anticipated, but a disreputable bunch nonetheless:

The crowd was anything but as large as was anticipated, there being scarcely six thousand people present, two-thirds of which, it is safe to say, were gamblers, pick-pockets, and cut-throats. The gambling den, the prize ring, the thieves' haunts, the low dive, and the groggery (low-class barroom) were all fully represented, and in fact it was by odds the roughest crowd—taken as a whole—that the eyes of a decent person ever beheld. It is a hard matter to find a man who will acknowledge having been to see the race.[117]

Anticipation was high for "what was expected to be one of the greatest boat races ever witnessed."[118] Like any good whodunit, there needed to be an "it"—a misdeed or wrongdoing done by a "who" that disrupted the normal order of things. In this case, on the morning of the big race, it was discovered that Courtney's new racing shell had been sawed nearly in two. When Courtney saw his new boat ruined and disfigured, he reportedly "stood for a moment in silence and then breaking down completely, cried like a child."[119]

It was not long after the incident was discovered that an investigation was made, the race was called off, and accusations began to fly. Amid all the chaos that afternoon, Hanlan, dubbed the Boy in Blue because of his trademark blue racing attire,[120] nonetheless proceeded to row the course alone with false hopes of claiming the six thousand dollars. Even without competition, he turned in the fastest five-mile time on record. He was never awarded the money, however, as the big race never took place.[121]

Of the three principals, now suspects—Courtney, Hanlan, and Johnson—none was immune from accusations of taking part in the boat-sawing incident. All three were vilified by the press. As more details of the incident were revealed, newspapers around the country took aim at all three, with headlines such as "The Chautauqua Fizzle,"[122] "The Hanlan-Courtney Fiasco,"[123] "Sawed In Twain,"[124] "Courtney's Cutter,"[125] and "Frenchy Johnson's Lies."[126] The press also mocked both competing oarsmen with digs such as "Both Hanlan and Courtney are *row-bust* persons" [emphasis added].[127] Courtney called the whole incident "the most villainous scheme ever concocted."[128] As for Frenchy Johnson, Pittsburgh oarsman Eph Morris alleged, with no supporting evidence, that Johnson cut his own boat at a regatta in Pittsburgh and, therefore, believed that Johnson cut Courtney's boat also.[129] Johnson viewed the matter differently:

[W]hen I was in Pittsburgh at the regatta I put my boat up in Eph Morris' boat-house. I went out and rowed my trial heat and won it, and the next day, when I went to row for the final heat, I found my boat with a hole in it. Morris was kind enough to say that either I or George Clark, my backer, put the hole there, and that story, which was a lie, was circulated against me in the press. I never rowed an unfair or dishonest race in my life.[130]

Disgrace, swindle, and miserable farce is how the *New York Herald* described the disappointing events of race day at Chautauqua. "Disappointment and chagrin" were the universal feelings of those in attendance, who departed the scene thoroughly disgusted with the entire affair. The *Herald* called the race "the most miserable end to what promised to be a notable race and will do great harm to boat racing for some years to come."[131] The article would prove prophetic, as the "Great Race Not Rowed" at Chautauqua would sound the death knell for professional rowing in America.[132] As the *Herald* acknowledged—"amateur boating men confidently boasted that the whole affair had given professional rowing its death blow."[133]

As a Black man in nineteenth-century America, Johnson surely recognized that had he engaged in any underhanded or untoward activity related to the Chautauqua race, he would have been the first one to be accused, regardless of his popularity among the rowing crowd. His close association with and access to Courtney and his boats would have made him a prime suspect in what the press called the "Dastardly Deed."[134] He would not have been foolish enough to have put himself in such a seemingly culpable position, knowing full well that fingers would be pointing to him. As one writer proclaimed years after Johnson's death, Frenchy always denied that he was a party to "the deed." The writer strongly believed that Johnson was unjustly the target of accusations and was used by those who were in on the deal.[135] There is no concrete evidence to suggest that Johnson had any part of the scheme. So, unless some new evidence surfaces, the mystery of the Chautauqua Race Fizzle will remain unsolved.

SLIPPING AND SLIDING

On September 20, 1870, U.S. Patent No. 107,439 was granted to Boston's Walter Brown,[136] a onetime American single-sculls champion.[137] The patent was titled "Improvement in Seats for Row Boats." The corresponding invention would become known as the sliding seat and would revolutionize rowing. The sliding seat would eventually be adopted by the best oarsmen of the day, including Johnson. Brown's invention consisted of a seat that slid along a set of tracks, providing a more efficient rowing stroke. With the advent of the sliding seat, rowing was transformed from a back and arm activity to a leg activity. The sliding seat took advantage of the powerful muscles of the calves and thighs to push against a foot plate, called a foot stretcher, to leverage the oars to propel the boat. Instead of the rower pivoting back and forth on a stationary, bench-like seat affixed to the boat, a sliding seat freely slides with the rower along tracks or "guides," as described in Brown's patent.[138] An

1873 article in the *New York Herald* described a modified version of the sliding seat that was being used by English universities. "These seats are simply pieces of board—say a foot square—mounted on small wheels, which travel on rails running fore and aft on the thwart or stationary seat itself," the article explained.[139] This use of friction-reducing wheels on sliding seats is a basic concept still in use today.

A short history of the sliding seat was given by Walter Camp in the 1899 publication, *Yale, Her Campus, Class-Rooms, and Athletics*.[140] Camp is considered the "Father of American Football" for his contributions to the evolution of the early game.[141] The reduction of football squads to eleven men to a side, the establishment of the line of scrimmage, and the creation of the position of quarterback were all introduced by Walter Camp.[142] As an undergraduate at Yale University (1876–1880), Camp starred as a halfback on the football team, played left field and shortstop and pitched on the baseball team, played singles and doubles in intercollegiate tennis tournaments, won the high hurdles in track,[143] and rowed the number-three seat of his class of 1880's six-man crew.[144] At the time, Yale University had club, class, and even professional school (ex., Law School) rowing crews.[145] With Camp's rowing experience at Yale, he could credibly argue in 1899 that:

> The most interesting feature in connection with boat-building of the last thirty years has been the introduction of the sliding seat. . . . It is not absolutely known who invented the sliding seat; but it is certain that the idea came from America, and the invention originated here.[146]

In *Yale*, Camp contended that there are two individuals who have been called the inventors of the sliding seat—Captain J. C. Babcock, an American Civil War veteran and former oarsman, and Walter Brown, the onetime American single-sculls champion and the patentee of the sliding seat in America. However, Camp believed the greatest number of authorities favored Brown, who is claimed to have had the idea of the sliding seat after observing British oarsmen "slipping or sliding" on greased seats when Brown was in training in England in 1869.[147] This slipping and sliding was what the Americans termed the "buckskin and butter plan."[148] British scullers would slide on long, highly polished thwarts (stationary plank seats) by the liberal use of grease or soap, with the scullers sporting "leather patches on their rowing breeches" for durability.[149]

Use of the sliding seat came at a time when Frenchy Johnson was coming into prominence as an oarsman, allowing him to take advantage of this improvement to the sport. Charles Courtney, Johnson's friend and rival oarsman, noted in 1879 that Johnson was improving every day since he had followed Courtney's advice and discarded his nineteen-inch slide and substituted one of twenty-two inches. "It allowed a longer and freer stroke and improved his form perceptibly," Courtney contended, and in another year "he expected great things from Frenchy."[150]

ROUGH AND TUMBLE

In the year following the Chautauqua Lake Fizzle, Johnson was directly involved with his own fizzle. On June 1, 1880, he was scheduled to row against Wallace Ross of New Brunswick, Canada, in a three-mile race on the Charles River. At the word "Go!" Johnson "bounded off with a rattling stroke," while Ross just sat in his boat and did not even "dip his oars," claiming he never heard the starter say "Go!" The one-sided, non-race ended in controversy, and the event was to be rescheduled for later that day, but it never happened. That evening, Johnson encountered Ross, and a fight ensued, whereby Ross knocked Johnson down twice. Johnson, in turn, got Ross in a headlock and was "pummeling" him when the police were called to stop the fight.[151] The *Boston Globe* called the race "Another Fizzle."[152] The *St. John Daily News (New Brunswick)* ran the following item from the *Toronto Daily Mail* lambasting Ross:

> The United States has its Courtney, but Canada has its Ross. Both have done their best to disgrace professional rowing, and both have been eminently successful. . . . Courtney sawed his boats at Chautauqua, Ross turns a deaf ear to the starter at Boston, and follows up with a rough-and-tumble fight with his colored opponent.[153]

Although quiet and gentlemanly, Johnson showed that when needed, he could stand up for himself and not back down. Fortunately for Johnson, this encounter ended more favorably than his skirmish with the soldiers at Fort Monroe, as no arrests were reported in the press.

FRENCHY TAKES AIM

Frenchy Johnson's rowing career was short-lived, lasting only about five years. His last race was the Thames Grove Regatta, a single-sculls, three-mile race with a turn on July 29, 1880, on the Thames River at Norwich, Connecticut. Out of five entrants, Johnson placed fourth.[154] That night he claimed to be sick. He would later admit that he had been sick ever since the incident with Wallace Ross two months earlier. He said he was suffering from the pulmonary ailment then called consumption,[155] now considered to

18　　　　　　　　　　　　　　*Edward H. Jones*

be tuberculosis.[156] Perhaps realizing that his rowing days were numbered, Johnson, the consummate sportsman, had already taken up the sport of competitive shooting. He had become a member of the Lynn (MA) Central Sportsmen's Club. In the same way he had become a skilled oarsman, Johnson earned recognition as an expert marksman, as the following excerpt from the *Boston Globe* attests:

Glass Ball Shooting at Lynn [MA]

Notwithstanding the showers of yesterday, the shooting-house of the Lynn Central club was well-filled by devotees of glass ball shooting. The light was good, but the wind which accompanied the showers was hard to control, and the little blue sphericals were but toys, and "old Boreas" (Greek god of the north wind) tossed them in all directions, to the detriment of the gentleman who gave the word "pull." The shooting was first-class . . . the conditions calling for twenty-five broken balls every week. So far in the match Mr. Frenchy A. Johnson has succeeded in accomplishing the feat, and yesterday's trial places him in the front ranks of all comers with 100 broken balls from the rotary traps, Mr. Johnson having broken twenty-five straight balls at each trial. Considering the weather conditions, this capital shooting is worthy of especial [sic] mention.[157]

In Johnson's day, competition marksmen aimed their shotguns at targets that included clay pigeons, live pigeons, and glass balls that were launched into the air. The glass balls were not unlike modern-day glass Christmas tree ornaments in appearance, only with thicker glass. The glass ball could have a plain smooth surface, an embossed textured surface,[158] or multifaceted flat surfaces, the latter two to prevent shotgun pellets from merely glancing off the ball and not breaking it.[159] Some glass balls were even filled with feathers so that the shot would "make the feathers fly" when the ball was hit, producing the same effect as when actual birds were shot.[160] The glass target balls would be launched into the air by spring-loaded devices called traps.[161] Glass balls eventually fell out of favor, primarily because of the hazards to humans and grazing livestock caused by broken glass covering the ground.[162] Glass ball shooting was eventually replaced by clay pigeon shooting. During Johnson's time, shooting live pigeons was also a normal practice, and Johnson was skilled at the sport. As might be imagined, shooting live pigeons had both its proponents and its detractors.[163] Johnson also set his sights on targets a bit more formidable than pigeons. In 1878, he shot a three-hundred-pound bear during a stay in Canada, prompting the *Boston Globe* to comment that in killing the beast, he "made more of an impression with his gun than with his oar."[164]

Johnson's skill as a marksman made him a natural choice to become a member of an all-Black volunteer militia in Boston, where in 1880 he held the rank of Private.[165] The group was known as the Shaw Guards, named in honor of Colonel Robert Gould Shaw, a White officer who commanded the all-Black Fifty-Fourth Massachusetts Infantry regiment during the American Civil War.[166] Shaw died in 1863 while leading his troops during a failed assault on Fort Wagner in South Carolina,[167] depicted in the 1989 movie *Glory*.[168] Prominent Black citizens of Boston had pledged to keep Shaw's name alive and believed it was the duty of every Black man in the city to "impress on the public the necessity of the colored people having a military company representing their race."[169] The Shaw Guards afforded Johnson a further opportunity to display his shooting skills, such as the time he outshot his fellow guardsmen during a rifle practice outside of Boston in 1880.[170]

Most interesting is the respect given to Johnson the marksman by the *Boston Globe* when it referred to the city's adopted son as *Mr.* Frenchy A. Johnson and *Mr.* F. A. Johnson [emphasis added].[171] In contrast, such respectful forms of address were never shown to Johnson the oarsman, which was possibly an indication of the less-than-lofty esteem the country was beginning to have for the sport of professional rowing.

THE LAST INTERVIEW

By the fall of 1880, Johnson had sold his boats and given up racing, claiming the money just wasn't there.[172] He continued competitive shooting, however. Regarding his health, in the spring of 1881, he said he had been sick but was improving and would "soon be around."[173] But in the fall of that year, he told a reporter from the *Fall River (MA) Daily Herald* that he had left rowing altogether. "I'm troubled, you know, with lung disease," he explained, "and my best hold is to keep out of such active exercise." When asked further about his illness, Johnson acknowledged that he had consumption (tuberculosis). "I have consulted the best doctors in Boston," he said, "[b]ut I feel better today than I have felt in a long time." The reporter noted that although Johnson spoke in a husky voice, he nonetheless looked robust.[174] By December 1882, it had been reported that Johnson, "once well-known as a professional sculler, and the friend and admirer of Charles Courtney," had been sent to Lowell (MA) on account of his consumption by the Lynn (MA) Sportsmen's (Gun) Club, of which he was a member.[175] The Club later arranged for Johnson to relocate to Florida, as he was reportedly "slowly dying" from his lung ailment.[176]

As a final dig at the ailing Johnson and Courtney over the Chautauqua Lake Fizzle, the *Cincinnati Daily Gazette* wrote in 1881 that "Courtney's 'faithful dog,' 'Frenchy' Johnson is dying of consumption, and he says that before he leaves for the other world he will show that the Union Spring[s] athlete [Courtney] knows more about a saw than he does about a boat."[177] But whatever Johnson knew about the Fizzle, he took it with him to his grave. No revelation ever came forth.

In a dispatch dated March 19, 1883, the *New York Clipper* announced the death of Johnson in Florida,[178] reportedly in Jacksonville, according to the *New York Globe*.[179] Based on his age in the interview he had given to the *Fall River (MA) Daily Herald*, he was thirty-three years old when he died. The following obituary appeared in the *Boston Globe Supplement* for March 20, 1883:

Death of Frenchy Johnson

Frenchy A. Johnson, a well-known oarsman of this city, died recently in Florida, where he had been sent by the Lynn Sportsman's Club for the benefit of his health. Johnson was a good oarsman and successfully contested many regattas. His lungs became affected a few years ago, and he abandoned boat racing. While able he shot game for the Boston hotels and the general market. He has won many money prizes and trophies at glass ball and pigeon shooting.[180]

FRENCHY'S LEGACY

Frenchy Johnson transcended the racial prejudices of a post–Civil War America that found amusement and delight in depictions of African Americans as buffoonish, stereotypical caricatures. Typical of such depictions were the inherently racist color lithographs of nineteenth-century printmaker Currier & Ives, a firm thought of by many as a creator of nostalgic, inoffensive, scenes of America. In contrast, the collection of Currier & Ives prints called the Darktown Comic Series were particularly offensive. Two of the prints in this series depicted buffoonish-looking African American scullers engaged in ridiculous, clownish antics on the water.[181] Johnson was reportedly the direct target of such racist images only once. It was an event that mocked Johnson in a way reminiscent of racist blackface minstrel shows. At a masked ball in Wilkes-Barre, Pennsylvania, an attendee was dressed as Johnson, with a black face behind and Courtney's face in front, and with a large boat he'd sawed in two, parodying the Chautauqua Lake Fizzle. The costume was described as "original but awfully awkward," which almost certainly referred to the costume's unwieldiness rather than its insensitivity.[182] This appears to be the only intentionally racist display directed at Johnson reported in the press. Fortunately, Johnson was never the target of overtly racist vitriol spewed by the press which his pugilistic namesake, champion boxer Jack Johnson, experienced in the early twentieth century.[183] There were, however, at least two instances when Johnson was quoted by the press in the stereotypical Black dialect often attributed to persons of color at the time: "He had dun dat long enuff . . . " and "Law! [Lord!] If dey should handicap him [Courtney], and den he beat me, where should I be!"[184]

In 2006, Twentieth Century Fox released a DVD titled *The Boy in Blue* about Canadian sculler Ned Hanlan, starring Nicholas Cage. During a regatta scene, Johnson's name appears written on a chalkboard of entrants scheduled to race, and during the race, an official calling the event through a brass megaphone shouts out, "And here comes Frenchy Johnson." Unfortunately, the scene is intended for comic relief, and Johnson ends up falling out of his shell and into the water for no apparent reason, while Hanlan is too hung over to even make it to the finish line. Moreover, you only see Johnson's back rowing from a distance. You never see his face to determine if he was even accurately depicted as a Black man.[185]

Johnson's skill on the water and his demeanor off the water earned the respect of his rowing contemporaries and made him a favorite among spectators. He had a following among the Black population. When he announced he would not be competing in the 1881 rowing season because of poor health, the *Boston Herald* noted that this would "leave the colored people without a representative in professional events."[186] As to his character, Johnson apparently displayed the integrity, intelligence, and command to have allowed him to have been chosen to referee an amateur single-sculls race at Silver Lake, New York, where the press reported that he "of course performed his duties satisfactorily."[187]

As someone who rose from slavery to become a respected and accomplished participant in two sports (sculling and shooting) that were overwhelmingly White, Johnson triumphed over adversity by his skill, determination, and willingness to brave the indignities that came with being a Black man in late-nineteenth-century America. This little-known athlete deserves to be elevated to his rightful place in the pantheon of American professional scullers. Moreover, let the nation acknowledge Frenchy Johnson as "America's First Black Sports Star."

> *Though Frenchy Johnson's life was short,*
> *he showed both skill and bravery.*
> *He triumphed o'er life's challenges,*
> *having risen up from slavery.*[188]

NOTES

1. Edward H. Jones, from "Frenchy at the Oars" (author's unpublished poem, 2022).

2. "Rowing Regatta on the Charles," *Boston Globe*, July 4, 1878, 6.

3. "The Rowing Regatta," *Boston Evening Transcript*, July 5, 1878, 2.

4. Ibid.

5. Thomas Eakins, *The Biglin Brothers Turning the Stake*, oil on canvas, 1873, from the Cleveland Museum of Art H. B. Hurlbut Collection, https://www.clevelandart.org/art/1927.1984. For an example of a nineteenth-century manual on sculling and sweep rowing (sweeping), see S. W. Barnes, *Instruction and Hints on Rowing* (Galveston, TX: S.W. Barnes, 1891).

6. "The Rowing Regatta," *Boston Evening Transcript*, July 5, 1878, 2.

7. "Inflation Calculator," U.S. Official Inflation Data, https://www.officialdata.org.

8. "Rowing Regatta on the Charles," *Boston Globe*, July 4, 1878, 6.

9. "Boston Music Hall, Grand Athletic Exhibition," *Boston Globe*, January 26, 1879, 3.

10. "Rowing Regatta on the Charles," *Boston Globe*, July 4, 1878, 6.

11. "The Rowing Regatta," *Boston Evening Transcript*, July 5, 1878, 2.

12. "The City Regatta," *Boston Globe*, July, 6, 1880, 1.

13. For a detailed look at the intersection of professional rowing and society in nineteenth-century America, see William Lanouette, *The Triumph of the Amateurs: The Rise, Ruin, and Banishment of Professional Rowing in the Gilded Age* (Guilford, CT: Lyon Press, 2021).

14. For examples of the far-reaching interest in American rowing competitions, see "Champion Scull Race in Montreal," *Hawaiian Gazette (Honolulu, HI)*, November 13, 1878, 5; "Single Sculls," *Cheyenne (WY) Daily Leader*, August 9, 1879, 2; "Latest by Mail," *Daily Press and Dakotaian (Yankton, SD)*, October 21, 1879, 2; "Sporting Summary," *Sporting Chronicle (Lancashire, England)*, April 23, 1880, 2.

15. "Obituary of Elizabeth Claypoole," *Poulson's American Daily Advertiser (Philadelphia, PA)*, February 1, 1836, 3. Elizabeth Claypoole was Betty Ross's married name at the time of her death.

16. "Death of Mr. Madison," *Alexandria (VA) Gazette*, July 2, 1836, 3.

17. "Death of Col. Aaron Burr," *Alexandria Gazette*, September 17, 1836, 2.

18. "Regatta at St. Mary's Georgia," *New York Evening Star*, February 1, 1836, 1.

19. Lyman H. Bagg, *Yale College Annals: I. Boating, 1843–79* (New York: Henry Holt, 1879), 275.

20. Charles A. Peverelly, *The Book of American Pastimes* (New York: self-pub, 1866), 117.

21. "Boat Race at Centre-Harbor," *New Hampshire (Concord) Statesman*, August 7, 1852, 2; "The Regatta at Lake Winnipiseogee," *Boston Semi-Weekly Atlas*, August 7, 1852, 4.

22. "The Savannah Regatta," *Charleston (SC) Courier*, May 13, 1839, 2.

23. "Regatta," *Daily Georgian (Savannah)*, April 23, 1849, 2.

24. "The Charleston Regatta," *Georgia (Macon) Citizen*, November 20, 1852, 2.

25. "Regatta, at St. Mary's," *American Turf Register and Sporting Magazine*, March 1836, 325.

26. "Oar and Paddle," *Forest and Stream*, August 22, 1878, 49.

27. "Frenchy A. Johnson," *Binghamton (NY) Daily Times*, October 18, 1877, 13.

28. "Riley Scoops the 'Frenchman,'" *Cleveland Leader*, July 7, 1879, 2.

29. "Inclined to be Funny," *St. Louis Globe-Democrat*, October 23, 1879, 2.

30. For an example of a typical Virginia Slave Schedule, see "United States Census (Slave Schedule), 1860," database with images, *FamilySearch* (https://familysearch.org/ark:/61903/1:1:W2XG-YGMM: 16 October 2019), Henry Johnston, 1860.

31. "Massachusetts Deaths, 1841–1915, 1921–1924," database with images, *FamilySearch* (https://familysearch.org/ark:/61903/1:1:N7VD-VBV: 2 March 2021), Francis J. Watts, 02 Mar 1871; citing Tewksbury, Massachusetts, v 239 p 225, State Archives, Boston; FHL microfilm 960, 199.

32. For examples of formerly enslaved individuals named Francis, see Elizabeth Cann Kambourian, comp., *The Freedmen's Bureau in Virginia: Names of Destitute Freedmen Dependent Upon the Government in the Military Districts of Virginia* (Westminster, MD: Heritage Books, 2009).

33. Yvonne Navarro, *First Name Reverse Dictionary: Given Names Listed by Meaning* (Jefferson, NC: McFarland, 1993), 81.

34. "Sporting Notes," *Jersey (Jersey City) Journal*, September 25, 1879, 1.

35. "Oar and Paddle," *Forest and Stream*, August 22, 1878, 49.

36. "The Single-Scull Race," *Boston Globe*, June 18, 1878, 1.

37. "The Champion Oarsmen," *Ottawa (Ontario) Daily Citizen*, September 30, 1878, 4.

38. "The Courtney-Riley Race To-Day," *New York Herald*, September 27, 1877, 6.

39. "Rowing Ripples," *Forest and Stream*, May 2, 1878, 241.

40. "Amateur Boating," *Providence (RI) Evening Press*, July 26, 1860, 1. For an example of a spoon-blade oar, see Davis, Michael F., Oar and Scull, U.S. Patent 231,016, filed March 18, 1880, and issued August 10, 1880.

41. "Courtney and Johnson," *Democrat and Chronicle (Rochester, NY)*, July 22, 1879, 4.

42. "New Rowing Club," *Galveston (TX) Tri-Weekly News*, September 26, 1873, 1.

43. "The Great Boat Race Today," *Montreal (Quebec) Daily Witness*, October 16, 1879, 4.

44. "Great Scullers' Race," *New York Herald*, September 27, 1877, 5.

45. "Massachusetts Marriages, 1695–1910, 1921–1924," database, *FamilySearch* (https://www.familysearch.org/ark:/61903/1:1:FH3T-QD6: 28 July 2021), Theresa Rickards in entry for Frenchy A. Johnson, 1873.

46. "Frenchy Johnson," *Fall River (MA) Daily Herald*, August 18, 1881, 4.

47. "Frenchy A. Johnson," *Binghamton (NY) Daily Times*, October 18, 1877, 13.

48. "United States Census, 1880," database with images, *FamilySearch* (https://www.familysearch.org/ark:/61903/1:1:MHXV-NXZ: 14 January 2022), Frenchy Johnson in household of Sarah Johnson, Boston, Suffolk, Massachusetts, United States; citing enumeration district, sheet, NARA microfilm publication T9

(Washington, D.C.: National Archives and Records Administration, n.d.), FHL microfilm.

49. "Frenchy A. Johnson," *Binghamton (NY) Daily Times*, October 18, 1877, 13.

50. "Massachusetts Marriages, 1695–1910, 1921–1924," database, *FamilySearch* (https://www.familysearch.org/ark:/61903/1:1:FH3T-QDN: 28 July 2021), Frenchy A. Johnson, 1873.

51. *Population of the United States in 1860; Compiled From the Original Returns of the Eighth Census*, Joseph C. G. Kennedy, Supt. of Census (Washington, DC: Government Printing Office, 1864), vii–viii.

52. For a brief overview of the Freedmen's Bureau, see Kambourian, *The Freedmen's Bureau in Virginia*, ix–xii.

53. See Fort Monroe National Monument, National Park Service, https://www .nps.gov/fomr/; Casemate Museum at Fort Monroe, Fort Monroe Authority, https: //fort monroe.org/place_to_visit/casemate-museum/. For a detailed history of Fort Monroe, see Richard P. Weinert Jr. and Colonel Robert Arthur, *Defender of the Chesapeake: The Story of Fort Monroe* (Shippensburg, PA: White Mane Publishing, 1989).

54. "Negroes Taking Refuge at Fort Monroe," *Frank Leslie's Illustrated Newspaper*, June 8, 1861, 55, and illustrations, 56–57; "Contraband Negroes," *Pine and Palm*, August 17, 1861, 4; see Edward Lillie Pierce, "The Contrabands at Fortress Monroe," *Atlantic Monthly*, November 1861, 626–40.

55. "Two Thousand Contrabands at Fortress Monroe," *Pine and Palm*, August 10, 1861, 3.

56. "Negroes Taking Refuge at Fort Monroe," *Frank Leslie's Illustrated Newspaper*, June 8, 1861, 55, and illustrations, 56–57.

57. "United States, Freedmen's Bureau, Freedmen's Court Records, 1865–1872," database with images, *FamilySearch* (https://familysearch.org/ark:/61903/1:1:Q234-C5HQ: accessed 25 August 2022), Frenchy Johnson; citing Residence, Virginia, United States, NARA microfilm publication M1913, Records of the Bureau of Refugees, Freedmen, and Abandoned Lands, 1861–1880, RG 105, (Washington, D.C.: National Archives and Records Administration, n.d.), roll 130; FHL microfilm 2,414,528.

58. "United States Freedmen's Bureau, Records of Freedmen, 1865–1872," database with images, *FamilySearch* (https://familysearch.org/ark:/61903/1:1:Q2H5-2K6Y: 9 August 2017), Frenchy Johnson, 20 Apr 1867; citing Virginia, United States, NARA microfilm publication M1913, Records of the Field Offices for the State of Virginia, Bureau of Refugees, Freedmen, and Abandoned Lands, 1865–1872, RG 105. (Washington D.C.: National Archives and Records Administration, 1969–1978), roll 130; FHL microfilm 2,414,528.

59. Ibid. The steamer ship *George Appold* (1864–1889) was named after a Baltimore businessman who was a director at the Merchants and Miners Transportation Co., which owned the vessel. See Edward A. Mueller, *The Queen of Sea Routes: The Merchants and Miners Transportation Company* (Fleischmanns, NY: Purple Mountain Press, 1999), 19.

60. "Massachusetts, Boston Tax Records, 1822–1918," database with images, *FamilySearch* (https://www.familysearch.org/ark:/61903/1:1:68QT-W3TB: 23 August 2021), Frenchy A. Johnson, 1872.

61. Tewksbury Almshouse, "Tewksbury Almshouse Intake Record: Watts, Alma," *Tewksbury Almshouse Intake Records [1854–1884]*, accessed August 25, 2022, https://tewksburyalms.omeka.net/items/show/38839.

62. "United States Census, 1870," database with images, *FamilySearch* (https://www.familysearch.org/ark:/61903/1:1:MD32-F1T: 29 May 2021), Anna Watts in entry for Louisa E. Small, 1870.

63. Elizabeth Hafkin Peck, "Black Migration to Boston in the Late-Nineteenth Century" (PhD dissertation, Brandeis University, 2006), 28.

64. "Massachusetts Deaths, 1841–1915, 1921–1924," database with images, *FamilySearch* (https://familysearch.org/ark:/61903/1:1:N7VD-VBV: 2 March 2021), Francis J. Watts, 02 Mar 1871; citing Tewksbury, Massachusetts, v 239 p 225, State Archives, Boston; FHL microfilm 960, 199.

65. J. Thomas, MD, *A Comprehensive Medical Dictionary* (Philadelphia: J. B. Lippincott, 1875), s.v. "summer complaint."

66. "The Harvest of Death," *Daily Evening Bulletin (San Francisco, CA)*, May 13, 1873, 1.

67. "Visit to the State Almshouse, Tewksbury," *Providence (RI) Evening Press*, August 24, 1869, 3.

68. Tewksbury Almshouse, "Tewksbury Almshouse Intake Record: Watts, Alma," *Tewksbury Almshouse Intake Records [1854–1884]*, accessed August 25, 2022, https://tewksburyalms.omeka.net/items/show/38839.

69. "United States Census, 1870," database with images, *FamilySearch* (https://www.familysearch.org/ark:/61903/1:1:MD32-F1T: 29 May 2021), Anna Watts in entry for Louisa E. Small, 1870.

70. Tewksbury Almshouse, "Tewksbury Almshouse Intake Record: Watts, Alma," *Tewksbury Almshouse Intake Records [1854–1884]*, accessed August 25, 2022, https://tewksburyalms.omeka.net/items/show/38839.

71. "Massachusetts Marriages, 1695–1910, 1921–1924," database, *FamilySearch* (https://www.familysearch.org/ark:/61903/1:1:FCWQ-6JV: 28 July 2021), Frenchy A. Johnson, 1873.

72. "Negroes Taking Refuge at Fort Monroe," *Frank Leslie's Illustrated Newspaper*, June 8, 1861, 55, and illustrations, 56–57; Edward Lillie Pierce, "The Contrabands at Fortress Monroe," *Atlantic Monthly*, November 1861, 626–40.

73. "Massachusetts, Boston Tax Records, 1822–1918," database with images, *FamilySearch* (https://www.familysearch.org/ark:/61903/1:1:68BG-LWGG: 10 December 2021), Frenchy A. Johnson, 1873.

74. For a detailed discussion of Dickerson and the A.M.E. Church, see Dennis C. Dickerson, "William F. Dickerson: Northern Preacher/Southern Prelate," *Methodist History*, April 1985, 135–52; see also "The Colored Race," *Boston Globe*, December 27, 1873, 8.

75. Lincoln University, *Catalogue of the Officers and Students of Lincoln University, 1865–66* (Oxford, PA: Britton Press, 1866), 5–9.

26   *Edward H. Jones*

76. Dennis C. Dickerson, *The African Methodist Episcopal Church: A History* (Cambridge, UK: Cambridge University Press, 2020), 560.

77. Britannica, The Editors of Encyclopaedia. "African Methodist Episcopal Church." *Encyclopedia Britannica*, February 25, 2022. https://www.britannica.com/topic/African-Methodist-Episcopal-Church.

78. "United States Census, 1880," database with images, *FamilySearch* (https://www.familysearch.org/ark:/61903/1:1:MHXV-NXZ: 14 January 2022), Frenchy Johnson in household of Sarah Johnson, Boston, Suffolk, Massachusetts, United States; citing enumeration district, sheet, NARA microfilm publication T9 (Washington, DC: National Archives and Records Administration, n.d.), FHL microfilm.

79. "Boat Race," *Boston Journal*, October 13, 1875, 2.

80. See Lanouette, "Triumph of the Amateurs," 49.

81. "Boat Race," *Boston Journal*, October 13, 1875, 2.

82. Ibid.

83. "Inflation Calculator," U.S. Official Inflation Data," https://www.officialdata.org.

84. "Courtney at Home," *New York Herald*, February 22, 1879, 10.

85. "Courtney and Johnson," *Democrat and Chronicle (Rochester, NY)*, July 22, 1879, 4.

86. "Won Fame with Oars," *Inter Ocean (Chicago, IL)*, March 6, 1898, 40.

87. "Was Often a Victor: The Notable Rowing Career of George Hosmer," *Boston (Sunday) Herald*, March 27, 1898, 27.

88. "The International Races," *Brooklyn Daily Eagle*, September 15, 1870, 3.

89. "The Saratoga Regatta," *New York Tribune*, July 12, 1879, 1.

90. "The Pedestrian Contest," *Nebraska State Journal (Lincoln)*, May 20, 1887, 2. For a detailed look at the sport of competitive walking in the nineteenth century, see Matthew Algeo, *Pedestrianism: When People Watching People Walk Was America's Favorite Spectator Sport* (Chicago, IL: Chicago Review Press, 2014).

91. "Oar and Paddle," *Forest and Stream*, August 22, 1878, 49.

92. "Echoes," *Harvard Echo*, May 18, 1880, 4.

93. "Won Fame with Oars," *Inter Ocean (Chicago)*, March 6, 1898, 40.

94. "Hanlan Wins Handily—Will It Be Courtney's Turn Next?" *New York Herald*, June 21, 1878, 6.

95. "Frenchy A. Johnson," *Binghamton (NY) Daily Times*, October 18, 1877, 13.

96. "Courtney's Competitor," *New York Sun*, July 15, 1879, 2.

97. "Frenchy A. Johnson," *Binghamton (NY) Daily Times*, October 18, 1877, 13.

98. "Oar and Paddle," *Forest and Stream*, August 22, 1878, 49.

99. "Silver Lake Regatta," *New York Times*, August 16, 1878, 5.

100. "Oar and Paddle," *Forest and Stream*, August 22, 1878, 49.

101. "Muscular Movements," *Boston Globe*, January 29, 1879, 2. For a newspaper advertisement announcing the rowing machine exhibition, see "Grand Athletic Exhibition," *Boston Globe*, January 26, 1879, 3.

102. "The Pugilistic Record of Jake Kilrain," *Dayton (OH) Herald*, June 29, 1889, 6.

103. "Rowing on the Passaic," *New York Tribune*, August 9, 1883, 2.

104. "Fights of Other Days," *National Labor Tribune (Pittsburgh, PA)*, July 7, 1904, 2; "Jake Kilrain Was Star Oarsman in His Younger Days," Corbett's Corner, *Memphis (TN) Commercial Appeal*, April 17, 1919, 17.

105. William E. Harding, *Jake Kilrain's Life and Battles* (New York: Richard K. Fox, 1888), 5.

106. James J. Corbett, "Jake Kilrain Was Star Oarsman in His Younger Days," Corbett's Corner, *Memphis (TN) Commercial Appeal*, April 17, 1919, 17.

107. "Sully Is Winner," *Trenton (NJ) Evening Times*, July 9, 1889, 1.

108. "Sullivan!" *New York Herald*, July 9, 1889, 3.

109. "Sullivan Is Champion," *Daily Inter Ocean (Chicago)*, July 9, 1889, 2.

110. "Crime in This City," *Boston Daily Advertiser*, December 9, 1876, 4.

111. "Sound Sense from Chautauqua," *Daily Graphic*, October 20, 1879, 774, and illustration, 773.

112. "Hanlan and Courtney," *New York Herald*, August 10, 1879, 10.

113. "Inflation Calculator," U.S. Official Inflation Data, https://www.officialdata .org.

114. Fletcher E. Ward, *Chautauqua Lake's Great Race: The Courtney-Hanlan Fiasco* (Bemus Point, NY: self-pub, 2014), 67–104; "Sound Sense from Chautauqua," *Daily Graphic*, October 20, 1879, 724.

115. "Courtney-Hanlan," *Frank Leslie's Illustrated Newspaper*, November 1, 1879, 139, illustrations, 137.

116. "Lost by Fraud!: The Great Race at Chautauqua Lake," *Democrat and Chronicle (Rochester, NY)*, October 17, 1879, 4.

117. "The Hanlan-Courtney Sham," *Tionesta (PA) Forest Republican*, October 22, 1879, 3.

118. Ibid.

119. "The Great Race at Chautauqua Lake," *Democrat and Chronicle (Rochester, NY)*, October 17, 1879, 4.

120. "At Toronto," *Montreal (Quebec) Gazette*, October 4, 1878, 2; "In Contrast," *Montreal Gazette*, October 4, 1878, 2.

121. "Courtney's Cutter," *Daily Inter Ocean (Chicago)*, October 17, 1879, 2.

122. "The Chautauqua Fizzle," *Wheeling (WV) Register*, October 21, 1879, 1.

123. "The Hanlan-Courtney Fiasco," *Boston Journal*, October 17, 1879, 4.

124. "Sawed in Twain," *Evansville (IN) Courier and Press*, October 17, 1879, 1.

125. "Courtney's Cutter," *Daily Inter Ocean (Chicago)*, October 17, 1879, 2.

126. "Frenchy Johnson's Lies," *Daily Expositor (Brantford, Ontario)*, October 17, 1879, 1.

127. "Boating," *Turf, Field, and Farm*, December 5, 1879, 379.

128. "The Hanlan-Courtney Fiasco," *Boston Journal*, October 17, 1879, 4.

129. "Frenchy Johnson's Lies," *Daily Expositor (Brantford, Ontario)*, October 17, 1879, 1.

130. "An Interesting Talk with Frenchy Johnson," *Boston Daily Globe*, September 9, 1879, 3.

131. "The Sculling Race on Chautauqua Lake a Fizzle," *New York Herald*, October 17, 1879, 3.

132. "A Great Race Not Rowed," *Cincinnati (OH) Daily Gazette*, October 17, 1879, 2.

133. "The Sculling Race on Chautauqua Lake," *New York Herald*, October 17, 1879, 3; see also Lanouette, *The Amateurs.*

134. "No Race Today, A Dastardly Deed Will Prevent a Contest," *Boston Globe*, October 16, 1879, 1.

135. "Oarsmen of the Early '70's [*sic*]," *Boston Herald*, February 27, 1898, 40.

136. Walter Brown, Improvement in Seats for Row-Boats. U.S. Patent 107,439, issued September 20, 1870.

137. "The Champion Sculling Match," *Daily Eastern Argus (Portland, ME)*, September 14, 1868, 2.

138. Walter Brown, Improvement in Seats for Row-Boats. U.S. Patent 107,439, issued September 20, 1870.

139. "The English Universities' Boat Race," *New York Herald*, April 21, 1873, 6.

140. Lewis Sheldon Welch, and Walter Camp, *Yale, Her Campus, Class-Rooms, and Athletics*, (Boston: L.C. Page, 1899), 462–64.

141. Casper W. Whitney, "Walter Camp," *Harper's Weekly*, March 5, 1892, 226–27.

142. Hartford Powel Jr., *Walter Camp: The Father of American Football* (Boston: Little Brown, 1926), 52–55.

143. Walter Camp Diary Notes, 1876–80, Walter Chauncey Camp Papers, Series V, Manuscript Group 125, Box 66, Folder 2, Reel 47 (HM 137, Box 47U), Manuscripts and Archives, Yale University Library.

144. "Yale Log," *Yale Daily News*, February 25, 1878, 2.

145. "Yale Log," *Yale Daily News*, March 13, 1879, 2.

146. Lewis and Camp, *Yale, Her Campus*, 462–64.

147. Ibid.

148. "The Sliding Seat," *Dallas (TX) Morning News*, June 4, 1912, 6.

149. "Oaric Champions," *Boston Herald*, April 10, 1898, 32.

150. "The Pittsburg[h] Regatta," *New York Herald*, August 8, 1879, 6.

151. "Johnson and Ross," *Boston Globe*, June 2, 1880, 2; "Pompey Pummelled," *St. John (New Brunswick, Canada) Daily News*, June 4, 1880, 3; "Sporting Matters," *St. John (NB) Daily News*, June 7, 1880, 3.

152. "Johnson and Ross," *Boston Globe*, June 2, 1880, 2.

153. "Pugistlic Puller Pompey," *St. John (NB) Daily News*, June 8, 1880, 3.

154. "Thames Grove Regatta," *New York Herald*, July 30, 1880, 9.

155. "Frenchy Johnson," *Fall River (MA) Daily Herald*, August 18, 1881, 4.

156. *Fowler's Modern English Usage*, 3rd. ed. (1996), *s.v.*, "consumption."

157. "Glass Ball Shooting at Lynn," *Boston Globe*, July 21, 1880, 2.

158. Adam H. Bogardous, Improvement in Spherical Glass Targets. U.S. Patent 189,422, filed March 26, 1877, and issued April 10, 1877.

159. "Advertisement for Sure Break Glass Balls," *Forest and Stream*, May 23, 1878, 313.

160. "Advertisement for Paine's Feather-Filled Glass Balls," *Forest and Stream*, March 28, 1878, 152; Ira A. Paine, Improvement in Glass-Ball Targets. U.S. Patent 196,379, filed September 22, 1877, and issued October 23, 1877.

161. "Advertisement for Bogardus' Glass Ball Traps," *Forest and Stream*, March 28, 1878, 152; Adam H. Bogardus, Improvement in Ball-Throwers for Shooting Practice. U.S. Patent 188,334, filed February 22, 1877, and issued March 13, 1877.

162. See 20-BORE [pseud.], *Practical Hints on Shooting* (London: Paul Trench, 1887), 365.

163. See "Another Opinion on Trap Shooting," *Forest and Stream*, April 29, 1880, 253.

164. "Dips and Splashes," *Boston Globe*, September 22, 1878, 8.

165. "Stray Shots," *Boston Globe*, August 15, 1880, 5.

166. "Letter from Boston," *Sacramento Daily Union*, October 2, 1865, 1.

167. Captain Luis F. Emilio, *The Assault on Fort Wagner, July 18, 1863* (Boston: Rand Avery, 1887), 11.

168. *Glory*, directed by Edward Zwick (Culver City, CA: Columbia Tristar Home Video, 1989), DVD.

169. "The Shaw Guards," *Boston Globe*, August 10, 1876, 4.

170. "Stray Shots," *Boston Globe*, August 15, 1880, 5.

171. "Glass Ball Shooting in Florida," *Boston Globe*, January 5, 1880, 4; "Glass Balls at Walnut Hill," *Boston Globe*, July 9, 1880, 2; "The Raymond Sportsmen's Club," *Boston Globe*, July 9, 1882, 12.

172. "Persons and Things," *Detroit Evening News*, September 1, 1880, 3.

173. "On His Honor," *Boston Globe*, February 27, 1881, 5.

174. "Frenchy Johnson," *Fall River (MA) Daily Herald*, August 18, 1881, 4.

175. "Aquatic Department," *Turf, Field, and Farm*, December 22, 1882, 419.

176. "Minor Events Near Home," *Boston Herald*, December, 19, 1882, 5; "Death of Frenchy Johnson," *Boston Globe*, March 20, 1883, 5.

177. "Athletic and Aquatic," *Cincinnati Daily Gazette*, March 5, 1881, 8.

178. "Frenchy Johnson Dead," *New York Clipper*, March 24, 1883, 3.

179. "Stray Notes," *New York Globe*, April 7, 1883, 4.

180. "Death of Frenchy Johnson," *Boston Globe*, March 20, 1883, 5.

181. "The Champion in Danger," color lithograph, *Darktown Comics Series*, New York: Currier & Ives, 1882, from Library of Congress Prints and Photographs Division, https://www.loc.gov/resource/pga.06526/; "The Champion in Luck," color lithograph, *Darktown Comics Series*, New York: Currier & Ives, 1882, from Library of Congress Prints and Photographs Division, https://www.loc.gov/resource/pga.06527/.

182. "The Event of the Season," *Daily Union-Leader (Wilkes-Barre, PA)*, February 27, 1880, 4.

183. "Jeffries' Camp Orders Stanley Ketchel Put Off the Grounds, [He Had] Been Around That Nigger [Jack Johnson]," *Lewiston (ID) Tribune*, July 4, 1910, 1; "Welch Impeachment Rests to Cheer As 'Nigger' [Jack Johnson] Is Licked," *Tulsa (OK) World*, April 6, 1915, 6.

184. "Boating Gossip," *Boston Globe*, June 13, 1878, 4; "Celebrated Scullers," *Democrat and Chronicle (Rochester, NY)*, July, 10, 1879, 4; for an additional example of stereotypical racist dialect, see "Aquatics," *Daily Inter Ocean(Chicago)*, April 11, 1887, 7.

30   *Edward H. Jones*

185. *The Boy in Blue,* directed by Charles Jarrett (Beverly Hills, CA: Twentieth Century Fox, 2006), DVD.

186. "The Oarsmen of Boston," *Boston Herald*, June 5, 1881, 11.

187. "The Amateurs," *Democrat and Chronicle (Rochester, NY)*, July 17, 1879, 4.

188. E. H. Jones, from "Frenchy at the Oars" (author's unpublished poem, 2022).

BIBLIOGRAPHY

"A Great Race Not Rowed," *Cincinnati (OH) Daily Gazette*, October 17, 1879.

"Advertisement for Bogardus' Glass Ball Traps," *Forest and Stream*, March 28, 1878.

"Advertisement for Paine's Feather-Filled Glass Balls," *Forest and Stream*, March 28, 1878.

"Advertisement for Sure Break Glass Balls," *Forest and Stream*, May 23, 1878.

Algeo, Matthew. *Pedestrianism: When People Watching People Walk Was America's Favorite Spectator Sport.* Chicago: Chicago Review Press, 2014.

"An Interesting Talk with Frenchy Johnson," *Boston Daily Globe*, September 9, 1879.

"Another Opinion on Trap Shooting," *Forest and Stream*, April 29, 1880.

"Aquatic Department," *Turf, Field, and Farm*, December 22, 1882.

"Aquatics," *Daily Inter Ocean (Chicago)*, April 11, 1887.

"At Toronto," *Montreal (Quebec) Gazette*, October 4, 1878.

"Athletic and Aquatic," *Cincinnati Daily Gazette*, March 5, 1881.

Bagg, Lyman. *Yale College Annals: I. Boating, 1843–79.* New York: Henry Holt, 1879.

Barnes, Samuel. *Instruction and Hints on Rowing.* Galveston: S.W. Barnes, 1891.

"Boat Race at Centre-Harbor," *New Hampshire (Concord) Statesman*, August 7, 1852.

"Boat Race," *Boston Journal*, October 13, 1875.

"Boating Gossip," *Boston Globe*, June 13, 1878.

"Boating," *Turf, Field, and Farm*, December 5, 1879.

"Boston Music Hall, Grand Athletic Exhibition," *Boston Globe*, January 26, 1879.

"Celebrated Scullers," *Democrat and Chronicle (Rochester, NY)*, July 10, 1879.

"Champion Scull Race in Montreal," *Hawaiian Gazette (Honolulu, HI)*, November 13, 1878.

"Contraband Negroes," *Pine and Palm*, August 17, 1861.

Corbett, James J. "Jake Kilrain Was Star Oarsman in His Younger Days," Corbett's Corner, *Memphis (TN) Commercial Appeal*, April 17, 1919.

"Courtney and Johnson," *Democrat and Chronicle (Rochester, NY)*, July 22, 1879.

"Courtney at Home," *New York Herald*, February 22, 1879.

"Courtney-Hanlan," *Frank Leslie's Illustrated Newspaper*, November 1, 1879.

"Courtney's Competitor," *New York Sun*, July 15, 1879.

"Courtney's Cutter," *Daily Inter Ocean (Chicago)*, October 17, 1879.

"Crime in This City," *Boston Daily Advertiser*, December 9, 1876.

"Death of Col. Aaron Burr," *Alexandria Gazette*, September 17, 1836.

"Death of Frenchy Johnson," *Boston Globe*, March 20, 1883.

"Death of Mr. Madison," *Alexandria (VA) Gazette*, July 2, 1836.

Dickerson, Dennis. "William F. Dickerson: Northern Preacher/Southern Prelate." *Methodist History*, April 1985.

Dickerson, Dennis. *The African Methodist Episcopal Church: A History.* Cambridge: Cambridge University Press, 2020.

"Dips and Splashes," *Boston Globe*, September 22, 1878.

"Echoes," *Harvard Echo*, May 18, 1880.

Edward Lillie Pierce, "The Contrabands at Fortress Monroe," *Atlantic Monthly*, November 1861.

Emilio, Luis. *The Assault on Fort Wagner, July 18, 1863*. Boston: Rand Avery, 1887.

"Fights of Other Days," *National Labor Tribune (Pittsburgh, PA)*, July 7, 1904.

"Frenchy A. Johnson," *Binghamton (NY) Daily Times*, October 18, 1877.

"Frenchy Johnson Dead," *New York Clipper*, March 24, 1883.

"Frenchy Johnson," *Fall River (MA) Daily Herald*, August 18, 1881.

"Frenchy Johnson's Lies," *Daily Expositor (Brantford, Ontario)*, October 17, 1879.

"Glass Ball Shooting at Lynn," *Boston Globe*, July 21, 1880.

"Glass Ball Shooting in Florida," *Boston Globe*, January 5, 1880.

"Glass Balls at Walnut Hill," *Boston Globe*, July 9, 1880.

Glory. Directed by Edward Zwick. Culver City, CA: Columbia Tristar Home Video, 1989, DVD.

"Grand Athletic Exhibition," *Boston Globe*, January 26, 1879.

"Great Scullers' Race," *New York Herald*, September 27, 1877.

"Hanlan and Courtney," *New York Herald*, August 1, 1979.

"Hanlan Wins Handily—Will It Be Courtney's Turn Next?" *New York Herald*, June 21, 1878.

Harding, William. *Jake Kilrain's Life and Battles*. New York: Richard K. Fox, 1888.

"In Contrast," *Montreal Gazette*, October 4, 1878.

"Inclined to Be Funny," *St. Louis Globe-Democrat*, October 23, 1879.

"Jeffries' Camp Orders Stanley Ketchel Put Off the Grounds, [He Had] Been Around That Nigger [Jack Johnson]," *Lewiston (ID) Tribune*, July 4, 1910.

"Johnson and Ross," *Boston Globe*, June 2, 1880.

Kambourian, Elizabeth Cann. *The Freedmen's Bureau in Virginia: Names of Destitute Freedmen Dependent upon the Government in the Military Districts of Virginia*. Westminster: Heritage Books, 2009.

Lanouette, William. *The Triumph of the Amateurs: The Rise, Ruin, and Banishment of Professional Rowing in the Gilded Age.* Guilford: Lyon Press, 2021.

"Latest by Mail," *Daily Press and Dakotaian (Yankton, SD)*, October 21, 1879.

"Letter from Boston," *Sacramento Daily Union*, October 2, 1865.

Lincoln University. *Catalogue of the Officers and Students of Lincoln University, 1865–66.* Oxford: Britton Press, 1866.

"Lost by Fraud!: The Great Race at Chautauqua Lake," *Democrat and Chronicle (Rochester, NY)*, October 17, 1879.

"Minor Events Near Home," *Boston Herald*, December, 19 1882.

Mueller, Edward. *The Queen of Sea Routes: The Merchants and Miners Transportation Company*. Fleischmanns: Purple Mountain Press, 1999.

"Muscular Movements," *Boston Globe*, January 29, 1879.

Navarro, Yvonne. *First Name Reverse Dictionary: Given Names Listed by Meaning*. Jefferson, NC: McFarland, 1993.

"Negroes Taking Refuge at Fort Monroe," *Frank Leslie's Illustrated Newspaper*, June 8, 1861.

"New Rowing Club," *Galveston (TX) Tri-Weekly News*, September 26, 1873.

"No Race Today, A Dastardly Deed Will Prevent a Contest," *Boston Globe*, October 16, 1879.

"Oar and Paddle," *Forest and Stream*, August 22, 1878.

"Oaric Champions," *Boston Herald*, April 10, 1898.

"Oarsmen of the Early '70's [*sic*]," *Boston Herald*, February 27, 1898.

"Obituary of Elizabeth Claypoole," *Poulson's American Daily Advertiser (Philadelphia, PA)*, February 1, 1836.

"On His Honor," *Boston Globe*, February 27, 1881.

Peck, Elizabeth Hafkin. "Black Migration to Boston in the Late-Nineteenth Century." PhD Dissertation, Brandeis University, 2006.

"Persons and Things," *Detroit Evening News*, September 1, 1880.

Peverelly, Charles. *The Book of American Pastimes*. New York: Charles Peverelly, 1866.

"Pompey Pummelled," *St. John (New Brunswick, Canada) Daily News*, June 4, 1880.

Population of the United States in 1860; Compiled from the Original Returns of the Eighth Census, Joseph C. G. Kennedy, Supt. of Census. Washington, DC: Government Printing Office, 1864.

Powel, Hartford. *Walter Camp: The Father of American Football*. Boston: Little Brown, 1926.

"Pugistlic Puller Pompey," *St. John (NB) Daily News*, June 8, 1880.

Records of the Bureau of Refugees, Freedmen, and Abandoned Lands, 1861–1880, RG 105. Washington, D.C.: National Archives and Records Administration, n.d., roll 130; FHL microfilm.

"Regatta at St. Mary's Georgia," *New York Evening Star*, February 1, 1836.

"Regatta, at St. Mary's," *American Turf Register and Sporting Magazine*, March 1836.

"Regatta," *Daily Georgian (Savannah)*, April 23, 1849.

"Riley Scoops the 'Frenchman,'" *Cleveland Leader*, July 7, 1879.

"Rowing on the Passiac," *New York Tribune*, August 9, 1883.

"Rowing Regatta on the Charles," *Boston Globe*, July 4, 1878.

"Rowing Ripples," *Forest and Stream*, May 2, 1878.

"Sawed in Twain," *Evansville (IN) Courier and Press*, October 17, 1879.

"Silver Lake Regatta," *New York Times*, August 16, 1878.

"Single Sculls," *Cheyenne (WY) Daily Leader*, August 9, 1879.

"Sound Sense from Chautauqua," *Daily Graphic*, October 20, 1879.

"Sporting Matters," *St. John (NB) Daily News*, June 7, 1880.

"Sporting Notes," *Jersey (Jersey City) Journal*, September 25, 1879.

"Sporting Summary," *Sporting Chronicle (Lancashire, England)*, April 23, 1880.

"Stray Notes," *New York Globe*, April 7, 1883.

"Stray Shots," *Boston Globe*, August 15, 1880.

"Sullivan Is Champion," *Daily Inter Ocean (Chicago)*, July 9, 1889.

"Sullivan!" *New York Herald*, July 9, 1889.

"Sully Is Winner," *Trenton (NJ) Evening Times*, July 9, 1889.

Tewksbury Almshouse, "Tewksbury Almshouse Intake Record: Watts, Alma," *Tewksbury Almshouse Intake Records [1854–1884]*, accessed August 25, 2022, https://tewksburyalms.omeka.net/items/show/38839.

"Thames Grove Regatta," *New York Herald*, July 30, 1880.

"The Amateurs," *Democrat and Chronicle (Rochester, NY)*, July 17, 1879.

The Boy in Blue. Directed by Charles Jarrett. Beverly Hills, CA: Twentieth Century Fox, 2006, DVD.

"The Champion Oarsmen," *Ottawa (Ontario) Daily Citizen*, September 30, 1878.

"The Champion Sculling Match," *Daily Eastern Argus (Portland, ME)*, September 14, 1868.

"The Charleston Regatta," *Georgia (Macon) Citizen*, November 20, 1852.

"The Chautauqua Fizzle," *Wheeling (WV) Register*, October 21, 1879.

"The City Regatta," *Boston Globe*, July, 6, 1880.

"The Colored Race," *Boston Globe*, December 27, 1873.

"The Courtney-Riley Race To-Day," *New York Herald*, September 27, 1877.

"The English Universities' Boat Race," *New York Herald*, April 21, 1873.

"The Event of the Season," *Daily Union-Leader (Wilkes-Barre, PA)*, February 27, 1880.

"The Great Boat Race Today," *Montreal (Quebec) Daily Witness*, October 16, 1879.

"The Great Race at Chautauqua Lake," *Democrat and Chronicle (Rochester, NY)*, October 17, 1879.

"The Hanlan-Courtney Fiasco," *Boston Journal*, October 17, 1879.

"The Hanlan-Courtney Sham," *Tionesta (PA) Forest Republican*, October 22, 1879.

"The Harvest of Death," *Daily Evening Bulletin (San Francisco, CA)*, May 13, 1873.

"The International Races," *Brooklyn Daily Eagle*, September 15, 1870.

"The Oarsmen of Boston," *Boston Herald*, June 5, 1881.

"The Pedestrian Contest," *Nebraska State Journal (Lincoln)*, May 20, 1887.

"The Pittsburg[h] Regatta," *New York Herald*, August 8, 1879.

"The Pugilistic Record of Jake Kilrain," *Dayton (OH) Herald*, June 29, 1889.

"The Raymond Sportsmen's Club," *Boston Globe*, July 9, 1882.

"The Regatta at Lake Winnipiseogee," *Boston Semi-Weekly Atlas*, August 7, 1852.

"The Rowing Regatta," *Boston Evening Transcript*, July 5, 1878.

"The Saratoga Regatta," *New York Tribune*, July 12, 1879.

"The Savannah Regatta," *Charleston (SC) Courier*, May 13, 1839.

"The Sculling Race on Chautauqua Lake a Fizzle," *New York Herald*, October 17, 1879.

"The Shaw Guards," *Boston Globe*, August 10, 1876.

"The Single-Scull Race," *Boston Globe*, June 18, 1878.

"The Sliding Seat," *Dallas (TX) Morning News*, June 4, 1912.

Thomas, J. *A Comprehensive Medical Dictionary.* Philadelphia: J. B. Lippincott, 1875.

Tozer, Basil [20-BORE, pseud.]. *Practical Hints on Shooting.* London: Paul Trench, 1887.

"Two Thousand Contrabands at Fortress Monroe," *Pine and Palm*, August 10, 1861.

"Visit to the State Almshouse, Tewksbury," *Providence (RI) Evening Press*, August 24, 1869.

"Was Often a Victor: The Notable Rowing Career of George Hosmer," *Boston (Sunday) Herald*, March 27, 1898.

Walter Camp Diary Notes, 1876–80, Walter Chauncey Camp Papers, Series V, Manuscript Group 125, Box 66, Folder 2, Reel 47 (HM 137, Box 47U), Manuscripts and Archives, Yale University Library.

Ward, Fletcher. *Chautauqua Lake's Great Race: The Courtney-Hanlan Fiasco.* Bemus Point: Fletcher Ward, 2014.

Weinert, Richard, and Colonel Robert Arthur, *Defender of the Chesapeake: The Story of Fort Monroe*. Shippensburg: White Mane Publishing, 1989.

"Welch Impeachment Rests to Cheer As 'Nigger' [Jack Johnson] Is Licked," *Tulsa (OK) World*, April 6, 1915.

Welch. Louis, and Walter Camp. *Yale, Her Campus, Class-Rooms, and Athletics*, Boston: L.C. Page, 1899.

Whitney, Casper. "Walter Camp," *Harper's Weekly*, March 5, 1892.

"Won Fame with Oars," *Inter Ocean (Chicago, IL)*, March 6, 1898.

"Yale Log," *Yale Daily News*, February 25, 1878.

"Yale Log," *Yale Daily News*, March 13, 1879.

Chapter 2

Black Brahmin Birdies

Golf and the Life of George Franklin Grant (1846–1910)

Lane Demas

George Washington Forbes, age twenty-three, was a waiter working at Harvard University's Memorial Hall in November 1887, on hand to witness Harvard's 250th anniversary celebration. The distinguished guests attending included US president Grover Cleveland and Massachusetts governor Oliver Ames, part of a procession of dignitaries and faculty who marched past the young man. A "long line formed and got under way headed by the college president," he recalled, followed by the guests and faculty. Already "enchanted by the glamour of the spectacle," Forbes was soon struck by the "terra cotta face" of a "somewhat undersized doctor, with elastic dignified step, and richly robed in his red and purple gown." The sight of a Black professor marching in a sea of elite White people transfixed him. "There had been hardly a thought of seeing a colored man in line at all, to say nothing of one's being present as part of the governing board of the University! The whole thing appeared to be a dream then, and has remained indelibly in my mind by reason of the honor thus shown the colored race."[1]

The man Forbes saw was Dr. George Franklin Grant, the second African American to graduate from a dental school in the United States and the first to receive a faculty appointment in Harvard's history.[2] He is also among the earliest identifiable African American golfers, recognized since 1991 by the United States Golf Association (USGA) for inventing and patenting the modern golf tee. To call Grant a pioneer of the American game would be an understatement: he likely played golf before Massachusetts had any golf courses. A fascinating biography in the history of race and sport, George F. Grant's story helps illuminate the intersection of race, class, and a game traditionally synonymous with White privilege in Boston—and nationwide—during a critical era when America's cities underwent profound change, African American politics grew increasingly fraught, and sport and leisure impacted the struggle for citizenship and civil rights more than ever.

By no means elite, Grant's early life was nevertheless characterized by relative economic stability, robust interracial civic engagement, and an acceleration of freedom and opportunity. His father, Tudor E. Grant, born in 1800, escaped slavery in Maryland before settling in 1832 along the shores of Lake Ontario in Oswego, New York. There the elder Grant became a businessman, eventually operating multiple barbershops and marrying Phillis Pitt, a Black woman from Virginia.[3] By the time their son George—one of seven children—was born on September 15, 1846, the Grant family was in the vanguard of Black freedom and the growing fight against slavery. As a boy, George and his father frequented the new Oswego Public Library, a racially integrated center of progressive thought and action opened by famed abolitionist Gerrit Smith in 1857. George later spoke positively of his time in Oswego's public schools, which he considered academically strong and racially integrated.[4]

The period's turmoil and the destructive trauma of slavery and discrimination impacted daily life in Oswego, however. Young George learned this reality through his elders' accounts of the South, but also firsthand, as his family's home became a stop on the Underground Railroad. He later told his daughter stories of being awakened in the night as a boy by fugitive slaves seeking shelter and readying for the perilous journey to Canada.[5] Also evident in Grant's youth was an urge for independence—to get away from people and seek solitude—a desire that reappeared later in life, and perhaps helped draw him to golf. After arguing with his father over clothing, Grant left home at age fifteen and found work assisting Dr. Albert Smith, a White Oswego dentist who was "struck with the boy's earnestness." He apprenticed under Smith for five years, learning to construct dental prostheses in Smith's lab before venturing to Boston in 1867 in search of further training.[6]

Arriving at age twenty-one with just twelve dollars, Grant found himself in a city seeking to recover from the Civil War and undergoing rapid change.[7] Boston featured a long-standing Black community that had already grown dramatically, developed a reputation for fiercely confronting racial discrimination, and sported its own professional class. He was certainly not the city's first Black dentist. John S. Rock had trained at Philadelphia's American Medical College and moved to Boston in 1853, where he practiced as both a dentist and a doctor. Rock's clientele included a mix of fugitive slaves, free Black Bostonians, and White patients. As a leading voice in the community during and after the Civil War, Rock's public writings and speeches highlighted job discrimination and racism in the city, challenging Boston to live up to the lofty rhetoric of the abolitionist movement it headquartered. Black workers in a range of industries—from shipping to domestic service—struggled to secure employment and fair wages. Black professionals were not immune from economic challenges, either. Rock had difficulty making a living through his dental practice and transitioned to law, eventually becoming the first African American admitted to practice before the US Supreme Court.[8] Other leading professionals included Robert Morris, the first Black lawyer to win a jury trial in US history. Morris had helped Black families sue the city in 1847—when Grant was an infant—to desegregate the public school system. The landmark suit and subsequent battle featured many African American lawyers and professionals in Boston and faced a series of setbacks before culminating in 1855, when Massachusetts passed the nation's first law prohibiting school segregation, twelve years before Grant's arrival.[9]

Meanwhile, the modern game of golf had yet to emerge. Sporadic instances of golfers in the public parks of cities like Charleston, South Carolina, and Savannah, Georgia, in the late 1700s had long petered out by the time Grant was born in 1846.[10] But by 1850, Boston was already in the process of reshaping its natural world to fit the period's ideals of public leisure and recreation. Theories about race and ethnicity influenced the city's decisions regarding parks, including anti-Irish prejudice that prompted authorities to limit the creation of pastoral space for antebellum neighborhoods rapidly expanding with immigrants from Ireland. So, too, were African Americans denied access. Throughout the early 1800s, the city had customarily excluded Black residents from accessing Boston Common every day of the year except for "Negro Election Day."[11]

Grant initially boarded in the home of well-known Black abolitionist and politician John Jay Smith, who was elected to the Massachusetts House of Representatives in 1868, the year after his new tenant arrived. Grant evidently endeared himself to his landlord's family: his first wife was Smith's daughter Georgiana, who died in 1891 (Grant married a second wife, Frances B. Bailey, in 1895). He eventually fathered four daughters, two from each marriage.[12]

Grant was quickly accepted to Harvard University's new dental school, located close to his home in Beacon Hill, and graduated in 1870 with a class of twenty-two students. The following year, Harvard offered him a position as an assistant in the Department of Mechanical Dentistry. In 1874, he particularly impressed colleagues by designing a rubber device to treat a young woman with a severe cleft palate. That year he was promoted to "Demonstrator of Mechanical Dentistry," and obtained annual reappointment in the late 1870s and early 1880s.[13] In 1884, he was again promoted, this time to a three-year, full faculty position: instructor in treatment of cleft palate and cognate diseases. He was reappointed for an additional three years in 1887 before resigning from Harvard in 1889.[14]

Grant experienced positive interactions and enjoyed his professional experience at the elite institution. His groundbreaking faculty appointment was evidence of profound social change taking place on campus in the late nineteenth century. Grant served as a personal dentist to leading faculty and administrators, including Charles W. Eliot, Harvard's president from 1869 to 1909. Grant was a cofounder of the Harvard Odonatological Society, later served as president of the Harvard Dental Alumni Association, and continued to donate to the school for the rest of his life. His position gave him full access to the school's dental lab, where he invented an "oblate palate" prosthetic for treatment of misaligned palates. By the end of his time there, he was an international authority, traveling to Europe to demonstrate his device and treating patients from across the United States and other nations.[15]

Still, the more progressive Harvard of Grant's day did not fully accommodate Black faculty or students—nor, perhaps, the idea of a Black golfer. Grant's salary appears to have been meager, likely the primary reason he chose to resign in 1889 and devote himself fully to private practice.[16] Moreover, although he was close to Eliot—and the president wrote glowingly of Grant to at least one colleague—the political and racial ideas Eliot shared with certain Harvard faculty clashed with the opinions of some Black Bostonians.[17] In its landmark 2022 presidential committee report *The Legacy of Slavery at Harvard*, the institution called Eliot's racial legacy "paradoxical." The president had indeed championed Harvard's enrollment of more Black students and the hiring of Grant as its first Black faculty member. Nevertheless, Eliot also chose to award Booker T. Washington an honorary degree in 1896, giving Harvard's "imprimatur to a man who achieved fame by urging Blacks to accommodate rather than fight racial exclusion, discrimination, and segregation." Even more problematic, Eliot joined Harvard faculty who publicly espoused the virtues of studying biological racial difference, promoted racial eugenics, and "touted race science and the virtues of segregation."[18] This group (which also included history professor Albert Bushnell Hart, mentor to undergraduate W. E. B. Du Bois at the time) welcomed Booker T. Washington to Boston several times, while—in the words of one historian—the few Black students "lived a marginal existence at the school."[19] Even in the arena of sport, Eliot again proved willing to sacrifice ideals and progressive impulses in the face of public sentiment. The Boston Brahmin had initially championed the expansion of amateur, restrained, "gentlemanly" intercollegiate sport. Yet by the time Grant resigned, Eliot had caved to students and alumni who wanted to win at all costs.[20]

George Grant started playing golf at an unknown point early in his career at Harvard. His job in Cambridge, and perhaps desire for more space, prompted him to buy a house in Arlington Heights, about five miles from campus. Golf historian Calvin Sinnette wrote that Grant was playing in a meadow near this home by "the mid-1880s," although that date seems to come not firsthand but via his daughter Frances, who was born in 1895.[21] Regardless, Grant's engagement with the game by the early 1890s would still place him among the first in the nation to do so, especially in the Black community. If in fact he was tinkering in the mid-1880s, it would be contemporary with the opening of the nation's first dedicated "golf course" (Oakhurst Links, established in White Sulphur Springs, West Virginia, in 1884) and years before dedicated courses were open in Massachusetts. Even a later date in the 1890s would still mean his golfing predated, or was contemporary with, Boston's first private dedicated holes (the six holes constructed at the Brookline Country Club in 1893), the first mention of golfers in Boston's Franklin Park (1890), the opening of the nation's first public course at New York City's Van Courtlandt Park (1895), or Boston's first public course at Franklin Park (1896).[22]

Moreover, Grant was not alone as he experimented with the game in Arlington Heights. He eventually enlisted at least two of his daughters to play and caddie with him. Frances "hated" golf, but nevertheless went along "for the ride." Her sister Helene liked it more, and both girls "worshipped the masculinity and the dominance and the vibrant interest of our father."[23] Golf quickly became his favored elite leisure activity, although there were others: he reportedly enjoyed playing variations of bridge in the winter months or when weather prevented outdoor activities.[24] Grant also golfed with friends, including leading Black Bostonians such as Archibald Grimké, a former slave and graduate of Harvard Law School. Grimké was a nationally recognized civil rights advocate, early opponent of Booker T. Washington, and future American consul to the Dominican Republic. Grimké's legal partner, Butler Wilson, was also a Black graduate of Harvard Law and regularly joined the golfers. Grimké later became an early leader in the National Association for the Advancement of Colored People (NAACP) after its establishment the year before Grant's death in 1909, including serving as president of its Washington, DC, branch, while Butler would go on to join the NAACP's national board of directors. Howard Lee, a Black Boston restaurateur, also played golf with the men.[25] Without a dedicated course fully open to African Americans, they continued golfing in the meadows surrounding Grant's Arlington Heights home. While Grant and his associates would eventually be eligible to play Boston's public course at Franklin Park, it is unclear if they did. Moreover, the city would have allowed them only after White golfers had finished, or during off-peak hours.[26]

Grant's interests in innovative devices and invention spilled into his hobbies. By 1890, he had purchased another home in Beacon Hill, an impressive brownstone at 108 Charles Street. In the city he was closer to more patients, with whom he consulted in a large front room of the house that served as his office as well as his own dental lab. He held on to the Arlington Heights property, however, in part because of the space it allowed for golf and the tranquility outside the city.[27] Grant grew tired of continually stooping to create a natural "tee" for his golf balls, which early players accomplished by pinching mounds of earth together or mixing sand with water to create a substance with sufficient viscosity. In his lab at 108 Charles, he developed a reusable tee—an invention he considered important enough to patent in 1899. The tee featured a wooden peg at bottom but sported a flexible, latex tube at its crown. The resin, *gutta percha*, was the same Grant and fellow dentists used in their orthodontia labs.[28]

Grant's US patent was the first issued for a golf tee, and the contraption foreshadowed what became the standard wooden tee in the twentieth century.[29] However, he faced long odds of profiting from the invention, and perhaps did not intend to. Frances recalled that her father frequently handed out the tees, which he had manufactured in a small Arlington Heights shop, to his golfing friends "as he would a stick of candy."[30] But he otherwise made no attempt to market them or expand manufacturing. In some ways, the idea was too far ahead of its time: few Americans played golf in 1899, and though some players used various strategies for teeing the ball, most continued playing with earth or sand tees. On the other hand, Grant's tee—and his life in golf—paralleled his professional experience. Like dentistry and Harvard, golf was an institution undergoing profound expansion and change in the 1880s and 1890s. Perhaps Grant hit balls in his meadow before America had any golf courses, but by the time he patented the tee, Northeastern states, like New York and Massachusetts, had hundreds.[31]

While there was little money in golf tees, there was the credit of being a Black player and innovator recognized in a game traditionally associated with elite Whiteness. But here, interestingly, Grant's Harvard and dentistry exploits diverged from his contributions to golf, for he was immediately recognized and historically honored for the former but not the latter. White and Black Bostonians heralded him as a leading man of the city. Years after George Forbes was enthralled seeing the golfing dentist promenade with President Cleveland at Harvard, Forbes became the Boston Public Library's first African American librarian. Compiling eighteen biographies of historically important Black Bostonians, Forbes included Grant along with giant figures like Benjamin Banneker, Daniel Coker, Paul Cuffee, David Walker, and James Monroe Trotter.[32] White organizations and institutions also acknowledged his non-golfing contributions. The *Washington Post* lauded Grant's dental practice in 1897, while his death in 1910 drew an outpouring of support and acknowledgment. The American Academy of Dental Science provided an honorable letter of praise, while obituaries of Grant ran in a range of publications, from the nation's major dental journals to national Black newspapers like the *Baltimore Afro-American*. Closer to home, the *Boston Globe* called him an esteemed "lecturer, writer, inventor and international authority on mechanical dentistry."[33] A scholarly study of Black Boston shortly after his death called him the most "noteworthy" Black dentist in the city, while Forbes wrote that Grant's funeral at 108 Charles Street was "one of the largest and most representative gatherings of friends irrespective of race we have noted at a public funeral."[34]

Yet none of these accolades mentioned golf. Instead, history soon forgot Grant's contributions to the game, crediting instead a White dentist from New Jersey—William Lowell—with inventing the modern golf tee in 1924, twenty-five years after Grant's 1899 patent. Lowell, too, made little money from his tees, which he painted red and marketed as the "Reddy Tee." He gave $1,500 to US Open champion Walter Hagen and British Open champion Joe Kirkwood to promote the Reddy Tee in 1922, and he spent most of the profits suing copycat manufacturers for patent infringement. By the time golf tees became a hot commodity, the market was flooded; by 1940 there were over 150 registered patents for tees of every imaginable design and material. Still, golf's prominent institutions, including *Golf Digest* and the USGA, continued to credit Lowell with inventing the tee for decades. Not until 1991, in part due to the work of historian Wornie Reed, did the USGA recognize Dr. Grant instead of Dr. Lowell.[35] In light of his overall acceptance at Harvard and in dentistry, this prolonged snubbing of Grant's golfing testified to the power of golf exclusivity at the turn of the twentieth century, an elitism that centered racial exclusion more than class antagonism. After all, both Grant and Lowell were successful dentists living relatively elite lives in the Northeast. "We were not rich, but we lived comfortably," Frances recalled. "My father had burlap bags of golf tees, but he gave them away instead of selling them. He was an avid golf fan. . . . He loved challenges, but once he overcame them, he lost interest and moved on to something else."[36]

Golf enforced a class barrier in Boston during his lifetime, but that was a divide Grant overcame with apparent ease. Racism, meanwhile, was rampant in the early game, including criticism directed at specific Black golfers and plans for Black golf courses or resorts, along with racist images, items, and jokes that lampooned the mere idea of Black golf. Edward Kemble, best-known for illustrating Mark Twain's 1885 *Adventures of Huckleberry Finn*, featured racist caricatures of Black golfers in his drawings during the period. During the 1920s, James Robertson and Sons, a British manufacturer of jams and preserves, sent US customers a series of racist "golliwog" pins in a popular mail-away campaign, the first of which was the "Golly Golfer." But the most provocative commercial racist caricature, "Nigger Head" golf tees, replaced the memory of Grant's invention with a violent image a decade after his death: the tees came in a package depicting a Black man's head pierced by a tee.[37]

The fact that Grant's Boston was a city teeming with African American athletic renown, notably in sporting and recreational activities associated with middle- or upper-class Americans, made such racist caricatures even more antagonistic: they were visible precisely because Black middle-class leisure was, too. Boston by 1900 was home to celebrated Black boxers and baseball players (such as pugilists George Dixon and Sam Langford), but also a notable group of African Americans in more urbane activities. These included the greatest cyclist of the 1890s and 1900s, Marshall "Major" Taylor, and William Henry Lewis, the pioneering college football player who served as an assistant coach at Harvard from 1895 to 1906. Charles H. Jackson, a Black mechanic in the city, invented a deep-sea diving suit in 1919 that was used to set a new world's record the following year.[38] Porter Washington, who in 1928 won the most elite tournament for Black players at the time, the United Golfers Association (UGA) national championship, played golf for years while working as a chef in Boston.[39]

Clearly, the image of an elite Black golfer and Harvard dentist in such a context was socially and politically powerful. Less certain is how Grant himself chose to navigate the shifting landscape of Black social politics. By the 1890s, supporters of conservatism and progressivism struggled for the soul of Black Boston. Exemplified in the popularity of Booker T. Washington, conservatives tended to remain loyal to the national Republican Party and eschew the establishment of more strident Black civil rights organizations in the North. Meanwhile, progressives assailed Washington's vision and leadership, calling for Black voters to exercise political independence and establish national progressive organizations unafraid to speak against both the nation's major parties. Grant generally aligned his politics and social networks with the period's Black liberal elite, despite many professional African Americans in the city who did not, especially some associated with Harvard. William Lewis, the university's celebrated Black football player and coach, publicly feuded with anti-Washington and anti-Republican voices by the time he was nominated to the Massachusetts legislature in 1901 and appointed assistant U.S. attorney in Boston. Three months before Grant died in 1910, Lewis—a fellow Black Harvard man and athlete—received the highest federal appointment of any African American at that point in history (assistant US attorney general) and delivered the commencement address at Washington's Tuskegee Institute in Alabama.[40]

Grant at times associated himself with Boston liberal leaders such as Edwin Walker (the son of fiery abolitionist David Walker), William Monroe Trotter, and his golfing partner, Archibald Grimké. In 1903, close friends Trotter and Grimké led a group that publicly protested and confronted Booker

T. Washington in front of a crowd of two thousand when Washington visited the city for a meeting of the National Negro Business League. Police were called in to disperse what the press described as a "riot."[41] Seven years later, Grimké cofounded the city's NAACP chapter; Boston hosted the organization's second national conference in 1911, the year after Grant's death.[42] Grant and his family were clearly close to the Grimké and Trotter families. His second wife, Frances, worked with Trotter's wife to raise funds for Black women's charities, while Grant himself served with William Trotter on the board of a progressive Boston voting rights organization.[43] Archibald's daughter, Angelina Weld Grimké, was a poet and playwright whose work appeared in leading progressive publications, including the NAACP's *Crisis* and Urban League's *Opportunity*. She penned "Hushed by the Hands of Sleep," a short poem dedicated "to George F. Grant," presumably soon after his 1910 death. It was eventually published at the height of the Harlem Renaissance in a 1927 volume of poetry edited by Countee Cullen.[44] Intriguingly, Grimké's two verses centered on a key theme for both dentists and golfers: hands (Frances recalled how her father "was extremely deft with his hands"). Moreover, Grimké herself may have had interests in sport, having pursued a degree in physical education—although some scholars suggest she did so to hide her sexuality as "a closeted lesbian."[45] Regardless, the poem's eventual publication seventeen years after his death is further evidence of Grant's connection to Black Boston's most progressive circles, and it forever cements him in the literature of the Harlem Renaissance.

Nevertheless, Grant's social politics were complicated. Frances said her father possessed "a little bit of snootiness," explaining his reaction when she reported that her teacher was marching with a union of cigar makers out on strike. Dad was "something of a Tory," she remembered, "outraged by this lack of what he considered professional attitude." Nor did Grant have much of a relationship with the Black Christian Church, which remained the most powerful African American institution in the city: "he had a kind of contempt for the Negro ministry at the time." She also reported that her father, unlike some Black liberals in Boston, remained supportive of the Republican Party and the Theodore Roosevelt administration. While his golf companion, Archibald Grimké, was organizing fierce, public campaigns denouncing Booker T. Washington, Grant was quietly hosting William T. Williams—Washington's protégé and assistant at Tuskegee—at his Arlington Heights home.[46] Fiery conversations and intriguing political debate may well have been a part of those golfing escapades in the quiet meadows of Arlington Heights.

Seclusion and golf were both strategies Grant used to navigate the social politics of elite Boston, including his large network of diverse friends and acquaintances. Grant again proved a sporting innovator; for him, this new game simultaneously facilitated elite, urbane social and political interaction, or provided natural, individual solitude and a celebration of open outdoor space. Millions of subsequent Americans have since recognized this curious dichotomy in golf.

According to Frances, "harassment" from constant visitors soon "got on my father's nerves," and Grant sold the Arlington Heights property to purchase another some fifty miles farther from the city, this time in tiny Chester, New Hampshire. There, he died from liver cancer in 1910.[47] George Grant left Harvard and Boston behind, but his legacy of Black golf remained. Franklin Park, which the *Boston Globe* called one of best public courses in the nation soon after his death, eventually became a critical site for African American golf in New England. While crime and disrepair blighted the course by the 1970s, leaving only four holes playable, its majority Black players fought to keep it open, some even bringing their own lawn mowers to care for the site. Subsequently reinvigorated, it today hosts thirty-four thousand rounds per year and remains a predominantly African American golf course.[48] In 1938, Black golfers from Boston and Medford established the Bay State Golf Association—the organization that hosted the 1941 UGA national championship at Canton's Ponkapoag Golf Course. The organization continued to host annual tournaments and fundraisers for the remainder of the century.[49]

Still, Grant's status as an elite Black man in golf remained uncommon for the twentieth century, and even to this day. Prominent Black Bostonians had long maintained a presence at resort locales near the city, such as Oak Bluffs on Martha's Vineyard, where African American vacationers included Harvard footballer William H. Lewis.[50] Nevertheless, public courses in the region were generally able to resist integration far longer than other businesses. Some continued to engage in blatant discrimination and make deceptive claims of privatization even after World War II. In 1947—thirty-seven years after Grant's death—a Black accountant from Chicago lost his case when he sued a public course on Martha's Vineyard for turning him away while on vacation. In the 1960s, the Kennedy family faced criticism for frequenting all-White private courses on Cape Cod; "I heard the Kennedys wouldn't allow any colored at their country club," wrote one civil rights supporter in a 1964 letter to Martin Luther King Jr.[51] During the 1963 US Women's Amateur at Williamstown's Taconic Golf Club, a fellow competitor confused Ann Gregory—the top Black female player in the country—for a maid. By 1971, the Boston NAACP was protesting the PGA Tour's Massachusetts Classic over South African golfers Gary Player and Harold Henning and their support of apartheid.[52]

Grant's legacy of Black innovation in golf—and of using the game both to build community and personally confront discrimination in Boston—continues. So, too, did he leave an elite legacy of service that family descendants in the city subsequently channeled. Grant's granddaughter, Georgine Russell Hill, became a prominent civil rights activist in both Boston and Bermuda before her death at age ninety-five in 2014 (her husband served in Bermuda's parliament). Jay Butler, currently a law professor at the University of Virginia, received a bachelor's degree in history from Harvard University in 2006 and conducted his undergraduate research on Grant, his great-great-grandfather.[53] Through generations of one family, and over a century of Boston history, the indelible counternarrative of George F. Grant tinkering with clubs, balls, and tees in his meadow—in *his* Boston—before most White Americans even knew the word "golf" remains a powerful testament to the city's role in shaping African American history and continues to uproot our understanding of the game of privilege.

NOTES

1. George W. Forbes, "Biographical Sketch of George F. Grant" (unpublished typescript manuscript, c. 1910), 5, George Washington Forbes Papers, Boston Public Library Archives and Special Collections.

2. "Dr. George Franklin Grant: Pioneering Dentist, Teacher, Inventor," Biographical brochure, Harvard University School of Dental Medicine, accessed September 9, 2023, hsdm.harvard.edu/files/dental/files/george_grant_bio_brochure_0.pdf.

3. "Interview with Frances O. Grant" (typescript manuscript, October 1977), 1, Black Women Oral History Project Interviews, 1976–1981, Arthur and Elizabeth Schlesinger Library, Radcliffe Institute for Advanced Study, Harvard University; "Tudor Grant Came Out of Slavery and into History," and "Son Invented Wooden Tee for Golfing," *Syracuse Post-Standard*, February 17, 2003, B1; "Dr. George Franklin Grant: Pioneering Dentist."

4. Forbes, "Biographical Sketch of George F. Grant," 2; "Blacks Used Library," *Syracuse Post-Standard*, February 26, 2004, B1; "Oswego Public Library," *Syracuse Post-Standard*, February 10, 2011, 4.

5. "Interview with Frances O. Grant," 1; Calvin H. Sinnette, *Forbidden Fairways: African Americans and the Game of Golf* (Chelsea, MI: Sleeping Bear Press, 1998), 10; Guilford Jones, "Historically Speaking: Dr. George F. Grant," *Black Sports*, July 1973, 12–13.

6. Forbes, "Biographical Sketch of George F. Grant," 2–3; "Memorial to Dr. George Franklin Grant," *Journal of the Allied Dental Societies* 5, no. 1 (March 1910): 374.

7. Forbes, "Biographical Sketch of George F. Grant," 3.

8. Jacqueline Jones, *No Right to an Honest Living: The Struggles of Boston's Black Workers in the Civil War Era* (New York: Basic Books, 2023), 2–3, 136–37.

9. Stephen Kendrick and Paul Kendrick, *Sarah's Long Walk: The Free Blacks of Boston and How Their Struggle for Equality Changed America* (Boston, MA: Beacon Press, 2004).

10. George Kirsch, *Golf in America* (Urbana: University of Illinois Press, 2009), 2–3; Sinnette, *Forbidden Fairways*, 5; Charles Price and George C. Rogers, *Carolina Lowcountry: Birthplace of American Golf, 1786* (Charleston, SC: Sea Pines Co., 1980); "The Birthplace of American Golf," *Charleston Post and Courier*, August 5, 2012; Lane Demas, *Game of Privilege: An African American History of Golf* (Chapel Hill: University of North Carolina Press, 2017), 2–3.

11. Michael Rawson, *Eden on the Charles: The Making of Boston* (Cambridge, MA: Harvard University Press, 2010), 157–58, 299.

12. "Georgine Hill, 95, Civil Rights Activist, Arts Supporter," *Bay State Banner*, February 6, 2014, 15; *Hearing Before the Subcommittee on Parks, Recreation, and Renewable Resources*, US Senate, August 25, 1980 (Washington, DC: US Government Printing Office, 1980), 35; Forbes, "Biographical Sketch of George F. Grant," 7.

13. *Harvard University Bulletin* 2, no. 7 (October 1881): 224 and no. 10 (October 1882): 365. Grant's title in 1882 was noted as "Demonstrator of Operative Dentistry"; Forbes, "Biographical Sketch of George F. Grant," 3–4; "Dr. George Franklin Grant: Pioneering Dentist."

14. *Harvard University Bulletin* 5, no. 1 (October 1887): 3 and no. 7 (October 1889): 423.

15. "Interview with Frances O. Grant," 5; Harvard Dental School donation checks and acknowledgment letters, Box 6, Folder 129, James Weldon Johnson Collection in the Yale Collection of American Literature, Beinecke Rare Book and Manuscript Library [hereafter Johnson Collection]; Forbes, "Biographical Sketch of George F. Grant," 6; "Dr. George Franklin Grant: Pioneering Dentist"; "Son Invented Wooden Tee," B1; Robert Bruce Slater, "The First Black Faculty Members at the Nation's Highest-Ranked Universities," Journal of Blacks in Higher Education 22 (Winter 1998): 97.

16. Forbes, "Biographical Sketch of George F. Grant," 5.

17. Letter from Charles W. Eliot to "Mr. Lewis," Box 6, Folder 129, Johnson Collection.

18. Presidential Committee on Harvard and the Legacy of Slavery, *The Legacy of Slavery at Harvard: Report and Recommendations of the Presidential Committee* (Boston: Harvard University Press, 2022), 80–83, 213, n. 147.

19. Mark R. Schneider, *Boston Confronts Jim Crow, 1890–1920* (Boston: Northeastern University Press, 1997), 77; W. E. B. Du Bois, "A Negro Student at Harvard at the End of the 19th Century," *Massachusetts Review* 1, no. 3 (Spring 1960): 440, 450.

20. Ronald A. Smith, "The Lost Battle for Gentlemanly Sport, 1869–1909," in *The Rock, the Curse, and the Hub: A Random History of Boston Sports*, ed. Randy Roberts (Cambridge: Harvard University Press, 2005), 160–77.

21. Sinnette, *Forbidden Fairways*, 10; "Interview with Frances O. Grant," 1.

22. John Williamson, *Born on the Links: A Concise History of Golf* (Lanham, MD: Rowman and Littlefield, 2018), 35; Kirsch, *Golf in America* 71, 75.

23. "Interview with Frances O. Grant," 8.

24. Wornie L. Reed, "Sports Notes," *Trotter Review* 5, no. 3 (Fall 1991): 21.

25. Sinnette, *Forbidden Fairways*, 10.

26. Danny McDonald, "'It's City Golf: In Historic Franklin Park, a Diverse and Thriving Course," *Boston Globe*, November 7, 2020.

27. Robert Taylor, "Little Things That Capture Old Boston," *Boston Globe*, June 8, 1982, 1; "Interview with Frances O. Grant," 9–10; Sinnette, *Forbidden Fairways*, 10.

28. "Dr. George Franklin Grant: Pioneering Dentist."

29. Erv Dyer, "George F. Grant Gave the World a Tee," *Crisis*, September/October 2007, 24.

30. Quoted in Sinnette, *Forbidden Fairways*, 11; "Dr. George Franklin Grant: Pioneering Dentist."

31. Demas, *Game of Privilege*, 72.

32. George Washinton Forbes Papers, Boston Public Library.

33. Dr. Grant's Funeral," *Boston Daily Globe*, August 23, 1910, 10; "Famous Dentist Dies," *Afro-American*, September 3, 1910, 7; "Colored American Notes," *Washington Post*, February 21, 1897, 7; Letter from the American Academy of Dental Science, November 5, 1910, Box 6, Folder 130, Johnson Collection; *Journal of the Allied Dental Societies* 5, no. 1 (March 1910): 374–75; *Dental Items of Interest* 33, no. 1 (January 1911): 73–74; *Dental Brief* 26, no. 1 (January 1911): 56–57; *The Dental Cosmos* 53, no. 1 (January 1911): 125–26; *Dental Review* 25, no. 1 (January 1911): 113–14.

34. Forbes, "Biographical Sketch of George F. Grant," 6; John Daniels, *In Freedom's Birthplace: A Study of the Boston Negroes* (New York: Houghton Mifflin, 1914), 360.

35. Reed, "Sports Notes," 21; Demas, *Game of Privilege*, 5–6.

36. Jones, "Historically Speaking," 13.

37. Edward Kemble, *The Blackberries and Their Adventures* (New York: R. H. Russell, 1897), 43; Robert M. MacGregor, "The Golliwog: Innocent Doll to Symbol of Racism," in *Advertising and Popular Culture*, ed. Sammy R. Danna (Bowling Green, OH: Bowling Green State University Press, 1992), 127; Janette Faulkner, *Ethnic Notions: Black Images in the White Mind* (Berkeley, CA: Berkeley Art Center, 1982), 69; Demas, *Game of Privilege*, 30–31.

38. Robert C. Hayden, *African Americans in Boston: More Than Three Hundred Fifty Years* (Boston Public Library, 1992), 153.

39. Demas, *Game of Privilege*, 111–12.

40. "Closing Exercises Held at Tuskegee," *Birmingham Age-Herald*, May 27, 1910, 6; Millington W. Bergeson-Lockwood, *Race over Party: Black Politics and Partisanship in Late Nineteenth-Century Boston* (Chapel Hill, NC: University of North Carolina Press, 2018), 155–56, 183; Zebulon Vance Miletsky, *Before Busing: A History of Boston's Long Black Freedom Struggle* (Chapel Hill, NC: University of North Carolina Press, 2022), 3, 43–50.

41. Bergeson-Lockwood, *Race over Party*, 183.

42. Miletsky, *Before Busing*, 57.

43. "In Aid of St. Monica's Home," *Boston Daily Globe*, November 24, 1904, 5; "Centenary of Garrison's Birth," *Boston Daily Globe*, October 18, 1905, 3.

44. Countee Cullen, ed., *Caroling Dusk: An Anthology of Verse by Negro Poets* (New York: Harper and Brothers, 1927), 36; Carolina Herron, ed., *Selected Works of Angelina Weld Grimké* (New York: Oxford University Press, 1991), 5–8, 41.

45. Herron, *Selected Works of Angelina Weld Grimké*, 7; "Interview with Frances O. Grant," 9.

46. "Interview with Frances O. Grant," 1–3, 4, 10.

47. "Interview with Frances O. Grant," 4–5.

48. Blake Gumprecht, *North to Boston: Life Histories from the Black Great Migration in New England* (New York: Oxford University Press, 2023), 54; McDonald, "'It's City Golf.'"

49. Hayden, *African Americans in Boston*, 155.

50. Adelaide M. Cromwell, "The History of Oak Bluffs as a Popular Resort for Blacks," in *African Americans on Martha's Vineyard*, ed. A. Bowdoin Van Riper (Edgartown, MA: Martha's Vineyard Museum, 2017), 66.

51. Katharine Knap to Martin Luther King, April 17, 1964, folder 14, box 11, series 1, part 1, Records of the Southern Christian Leadership Conference, King Library and Archive, Martin Luther King Jr. Center for Nonviolent Social Change, Atlanta, Georgia; Demas, *Game of Privilege*, 160.

52. Demas, *Game of Privilege*, 218, 226.

53. "Georgine Russell a Bride," *Guardian* (Boston), November 30, 1940, 1; "Georgine Hill," 15; "Harvard Senior is Bermuda's Rhodes Scholar," *Harvard Gazette*, February 2, 2006; Author email correspondence with Jay Butler, September 2023.

BIBLIOGRAPHY

"Blacks Used Library," *Syracuse Post-Standard*, February 26, 2004.

Bergeson-Lockwood, Millington. *Race over Party: Black Politics and Partisanship in Late Nineteenth-Century Boston*. Chapel Hill: University of North Carolina Press, 2018.

"Centenary of Garrison's Birth," *Boston Daily Globe*, October 18, 1905.

"Closing Exercises Held at Tuskegee," *Birmingham Age-Herald*, May 27, 1910.

"Colored American Notes," *Washington Post*, February 21, 1897.

Cromwell, Adelaide. "The History of Oak Bluffs as a Popular Resort for Blacks," in *African Americans on Martha's Vineyard*, ed. A. Bowdoin Van Riper. Edgartown: Martha's Vineyard Museum, 2017.

Cullen, Countee, ed., *Caroling Dusk: An Anthology of Verse by Negro Poets.* New York: Harper and Brothers, 1927.

Daniels, John. *In Freedom's Birthplace: A Study of the Boston Negroes*. New York: Houghton Mifflin, 1914.

Demas, Lane. *Game of Privilege: An African American History of Golf*. Chapel Hill: University of North Carolina Press, 2017.

"Dr. George Franklin Grant: Pioneering Dentist, Teacher, Inventor," Biographical Brochure, Harvard University School of Dental Medicine, accessed September 9, 2023, hsdm.harvard.edu/files/dental/files/george_grant_bio_brochure_0.pdf.

"Dr. Grant's Funeral," *Boston Daily Globe*, August 23, 1910.

Dyer, Erv. "George F. Grant Gave the World a Tee," *Crisis*, September/October 2007.

Faulkner, Janette. *Ethnic Notions: Black Images in the White Mind.* Berkeley: Berkeley Art Center, 1982.

"Famous Dentist Dies," *Afro-American*, September 3, 1910.

Forbes, George. "Biographical Sketch of George F. Grant" (unpublished typescript manuscript, c. 1910) George Washington Forbes Papers, Boston Public Library Archives and Special Collections.

"Georgine Hill, 95, Civil Rights Activist, Arts Supporter," *Bay State Banner*, February 6, 2014.

"Georgine Russell a Bride," *Guardian* (Boston), November 30, 1940.

Gumprecht, Blake. *North to Boston: Life Histories from the Black Great Migration in New England.* New York: Oxford University Press, 2023.

"Harvard Senior Is Bermuda's Rhodes Scholar," *Harvard Gazette*, February 2, 2006.

Harvard University Bulletin 2, no. 7 (October 1881).

Harvard University Bulletin 5, no. 1 (October 1887).

Hayden, Robert. *African Americans in Boston: More Than Three Hundred Fifty Years.* Boston Public Library, 1992.

Hearing Before the Subcommittee on Parks, Recreation, and Renewable Resources, US Senate, August 25, 1980. Washington, DC: US Government Printing Office, 1980.

Herron, Carolina ed., *Selected Works of Angelina Weld Grimké*. New York: Oxford University Press, 1991.

"In Aid of St. Monica's Home," *Boston Daily Globe*, November 24, 1904.

"Interview with Frances O. Grant," 5; Harvard Dental School donation checks and acknowledgment letters, Box 6, Folder 129, James Weldon Johnson Collection in the Yale Collection of American Literature, Beinecke Rare Book and Manuscript Library.

"Interview with Frances O. Grant" (typescript manuscript, October 1977), 1, Black Women Oral History Project Interviews, 1976–1981, Arthur and Elizabeth Schlesinger Library, Radcliffe Institute for Advanced Study, Harvard University.

Jones, Guilford. "Historically Speaking: Dr. George F. Grant," *Black Sports*, July 1973.

Jones, Jacqueline. *No Right to an Honest Living: The Struggles of Boston's Black Workers in the Civil War Era.* New York: Basic Books, 2023.

Kemble, Edward. *The Blackberries and Their Adventures.* New York: R. H. Russell, 1897.

Kendrick, Stephen, and Paul Kendrick. *Sarah's Long Walk: The Free Blacks of Boston and How Their Struggle for Equality Changed America.* Boston: Beacon Press, 2004.

Kirsch, George. Kirsch, *Golf in America.* Urbana: University of Illinois Press, 2009.

Letter from the American Academy of Dental Science, November 5, 1910, Box 6, Folder 130, Johnson Collection. *Journal of the Allied Dental Societies* 5, no. 1 (March 1910).

MacGregor, Robert. "The Golliwog: Innocent Doll to Symbol of Racism," in *Advertising and Popular Culture*, ed. Sammy R. Danna. Bowling Green: Bowling Green State University Press, 1992.

McDonald, Danny. "It's City Golf: In Historic Franklin Park, a Diverse and Thriving Course," *Boston Globe*, November 7, 2020.

"Memorial to Dr. George Franklin Grant," *Journal of the Allied Dental Societies* 5, no. 1 (March 1910).

Miletsky, Zebulon Vance. *Before Busing: A History of Boston's Long Black Freedom Struggle.* Chapel Hill: University of North Carolina Press, 2022.

"Oswego Public Library," *Syracuse Post-Standard*, February 10, 2011.

Presidential Committee on Harvard and the Legacy of Slavery, *The Legacy of Slavery at Harvard: Report and Recommendations of the Presidential Committee.* Boston: Harvard University Press, 2022.

Price, Charles, and George C. Rogers. *The Carolina Lowcountry: Birthplace of American Golf, 1786.* Charleston: Sea Pines Co., 1980.

Rawson, Michael. *Eden on the Charles: The Making of Boston*. Cambridge, Harvard University Press, 2010.

Reed, Wornie. "Sports Notes," *Trotter Review* 5, no. 3 (Fall 1991).

Schneider, Mark. *Boston Confronts Jim Crow, 1890–1920*. Boston: Northeastern University Press, 1997.

Sinnette, Calvin. *Forbidden Fairways: African Americans and the Game of Golf.* Chelsea: Sleeping Bear Press, 1998.

Slater, Robert Bruce. "The First Black Faculty Members at the Nation's Highest-Ranked Universities," Journal of Blacks in Higher Education 22 (Winter 1998): 97.

"Son Invented Wooden Tee for Golfing," *Syracuse Post-Standard*, February 17, 2003.

Smith, Ronald. "The Lost Battle for Gentlemanly Sport, 1869–1909," in *The Rock, the Curse, and the Hub: A Random History of Boston Sports*, ed. Randy Roberts. Cambridge: Harvard University Press, 2005.

Taylor, Robert. "Little Things That Capture Old Boston," *Boston Globe*, June 8, 1982.

"The Birthplace of American Golf," *Charleston Post and Courier*, August 5, 2012.

"Tudor Grant Came Out of Slavery and into History," *Syracuse Post-Standard*, February 17, 2003.

W. E. B. Du Bois, "A Negro Student at Harvard at the End of the 19th Century," *Massachusetts Review* 1, no. 3 (Spring 1960).

Williamson, John. *Born on the Links: A Concise History of Golf.* Lanham: Rowman and Littlefield, 2018.

Chapter 3

Kittie Knox, Boston Cyclist in the 1890s

The War between Exclusion and Inclusion

Lorenz J. Finison

"The Murky Goddess of Beanville"

From the *Southern Cycler*, 1895

Kittie Knox. They tried to slow her down and keep her in a long skirt and on a "ladies'" bike, and they tried to kick her out of the League of American Wheelmen (LAW), but it did not stop her. A "scorcher" and one-hundred-mile (century) cyclist of 1890s Boston, she defied both racial restrictions and norms about what proper women should look like and do on a bike. This is the story of her resistance, persistence, and embrace of opportunities, and of her communities, supporters, and opponents.[1]

BEGINNINGS

Kittie Knox (also known as Katherine, Kitty, or Katie) was first noticed in print as a cyclist by the faraway Black newspaper *Indianapolis Freeman* in 1893. They saw her bicycling around Martha's Vineyard, Massachusetts, an island vacation spot, and home of working and sojourning African Americans. "Miss Katie Knox and Miss Viola Wheaton," the *Freeman* reported, "two of Boston's fair ones, are active members" of the Riverside Cycle Club (RCC),

Figure 3.1. Katherine "Kittie" Knox became became a member of the League of American Wheelmen in the early 1890s. By 1894 the League had passed a color bar, but she defied it.. Credit: Image originally printed in *Bearing* and is held by Smithsonian Libraries and Archives, Washington DC.

a Black club of West End Boston and Cambridge. The young women "are graceful riders."[2] Boston cycling officials like Charles Percival remembered her presence, too, at the state League of American Wheelmen (LAW) annual meets at Cottage City on Martha's Vineyard.[3]

As the *Freeman* may have hinted, Kittie came from a racially mixed family. Her father, John H. Knox (born around 1838), a tailor originally from Philadelphia, was noted in the 1880 Census as "Mulatto," while her mother, Katherine (Towle, born about 1838), was a White woman from rural Maine.

Both Kittie and her brother, Ernest, were labeled "Mulatto" by the census taker.[4] Kittie's race and skin tone made her the object of much controversy, and some opportunity. Her capacity to negotiate multiple worlds was likely due to the nature of her family and polyglot neighborhood. She was no "tragic mulatta"—a stereotypical figure in melodramatic books and stage plays popular in Kittie's time. Such a character discovers she has a "drop" of "black blood," a revelation with tragic emotional consequences. Kittie knew who she was. Yet she, too, was doubtless affected by what, in 1897, W. E. B. Du Bois, a Black Fisk and Harvard graduate born and raised in Great Barrington, Massachusetts, called a "double consciousness," a "two-ness—an American, a Negro; two souls, two thoughts, two unreconciled strivings; two warring ideals in one dark body."[5]

THE BOSTON CONTEXT

Boston had a special history that may have attracted African Americans like John Knox. Massachusetts abolished slavery in 1780, prohibited segregation on public transit in 1842, legalized interracial marriage in 1843, and required public school desegregation in 1855. The city was a hotbed of abolitionism from the 1830s through the 1860s, a movement led by people like William Lloyd Garrison, Wendell Phillips, and Frederick Douglass. In the 1850s, Black men petitioned to drop the word *White* from the state militia law and support an all-Black "Massasoit Guard" (a John H. Knox—perhaps Kittie's father—signed one such petition).[6] Although the Governor's Council rejected the petition, it provided an inspiration for the Massachusetts Fifty-Fourth and Fifty-Fifth Regiments in the Civil War, all-Black units with White officers. Boston's abolitionists and their opponents struggled repeatedly. In the 1850s, they fought off "slave catchers" who came to Boston to reclaim runaways, intensifying after the passage of the federal Fugitive Slave Act of 1850. Anti-draft riots broke out in 1863 (although at nowhere near the scale of the New York riots of that year), when Irish immigrants began receiving draft notices. Bostonians cheered its returning Black troops "quite enthusiastically as they marched through the streets."[7] A Boston Common monument in their honor, and one commemorating their fallen White commander Robert Gould Shaw, joined another recent monument honoring Crispus Attucks of the Boston Massacre.[8]

Kittie's parents were married in New Bedford in 1871. John Knox was listed as Black and Katherine Towle as White. John had been in Boston at least as early as 1865, and perhaps he arrived as a teenager a decade before that, with some possible stays in New Bedford.[9] In 1853, New Bedford had the largest percentage of Black population among Northern cities (8.8 percent).

Frederick Douglass had escaped enslavement to arrive in 1838. Black politicians, along with Quaker abolitionist families, banished from Boston many years before by the religiously intolerant Puritans, were pre–Civil War leaders. The Quakers came to dominate the whaling industry, which had an ethnically diverse workforce. New Bedford public schools were integrated well before Massachusetts prohibited school segregation.[10] New Bedford also sent "unattached" units of Black troops to fight in the Civil War.

Kittie's mother grew up in rural East Parsonsfield, Maine, and she was a mill worker in Biddeford in 1860. Perhaps she was drawn to New Bedford when a new cotton mill—Potomska—opened there in 1871, promising housing to attract new workers from declining farms and villages in rural northern New England and Canada.[11] It is not known where John and Katherine (Kate) met or how they came to be in New Bedford at the time of their marriage, but their stay was short. John and Kate moved to Somerville and then to locations in East Cambridge. Kittie was born in 1874, two years after her older brother, Ernest. John bought a house at Sixth and Munroe on filled tidal-marsh land near the sewage-filled Broad Canal—a marginal location typical for Black and low-income immigrant residents. The canal sickened residents at low tide. By 1880, the family moved away from the canal to live at Sixth and Charles. Their neighbors were Scottish and German, along with Canadian and Irish first- and second-generation families farther along the street. The census taker in 1880 noted that the Knox family was "the only colored family" in the census district. A few years later, Kittie's parents separated, and John died in Boston in 1883. Kate crossed the West Boston Bridge to work as a seamstress and doubtless passed her skills to Kittie. In 1885, Kittie was noted in the Cambridge newspapers for her singing ("Stand Up for Jesus") and recitation of a Bible verse ("Christ is risen") at the Broadway Baptist Church Sabbath School, and in 1889 for her graduation from Allston School, next to the church. Both were mostly White institutions, unlike what she would soon experience in Boston.

By the early 1890s, Kate, Katie, and Ernest had moved a short distance across the Charles River to the corner of Irving and Cambridge streets in the West End of Boston—and to a very different racial environment. This was a micro-segregated neighborhood. Individual housing units and adjacent buildings might be segregated, but not a whole neighborhood—unlike the vast tracts of segregated housing of the twentieth century. Kittie's side of Irving Street was racially mixed ("American" or British-Canadian), and her cross-street neighbors were mostly Black.[12] Her own building, a storefront with lodging above and behind, included Black and Black-Canadian barber/hairdressers and a Russian-Jewish shoemaker. They were side by side with a liquor store/bar tended by an Irish immigrant bartender and his son.

The West End was the center of Boston's Black population and activism. It had a thin "elite" group, who were proprietors or professionals, what the famed Black intellectual W. E. B. Du Bois would call the "Talented Tenth."[13] Many of these residents held themselves aloof from others: a slightly larger class of skilled workers—including tailors, seamstresses, cooks, coachmen, and a few bicycle repairers—and a great mass of laborers, porters, laundresses, and servants.[14] They were forced into daily labor at low wages, shut out of most government and factory jobs, and unable to save money to buy homes. Most of these individuals lived in poverty in tenements or in poorly lit and ventilated alleyways and "courts."

Despite this, Black Bostonians had a high opinion of Boston's racial/political atmosphere, compared to other cities.[15] One formerly enslaved woman, a nurse for the troops in the Civil War who had come to Boston, wrote years later, "I have been in many States and cities, and in each I have looked for liberty and justice, equal for the black as for the White, but it was not until I was within the borders of New England, and reached old Massachusetts, that I found it."[16] Boston Blacks had continuous representation in the State legislature from 1867 to 1901, and between 1876 and 1895, the Black community sent a representative to the Boston City Council. In 1877, Boston produced the highest rate of Black "out-marriage" ever recorded: 38 percent. Most of these were residents in Kittie's West End.[17] The neighborhood was also home to many immigrants. Thus, Kittie had access to a wide variety of people and likely maintained some contact with her mother's Towle family in rural Maine as well.[18]

DANCING AND CYCLING

Kittie became a seamstress and dressmaker, perhaps due to the example of her tailoring father and seamstress mother, and showed off some stylish outfits. She attended Black social dances and gatherings, such as an 1892 dance at the "A.S.C.," a club of young men of the West End,[19] and the Benevolent Fraternity of Coachmen's ball.[20] She also danced at a ball given by members of Company L, Sixth Massachusetts Volunteer Militia.[21] This unit was the military descendant of the Massachusetts Fifty-Fourth and Fifty-Fifth Regiments, and the first such unit in the nation to have Black officers. Company L had its own bicycling unit composed of many members of the RCC.[22] Thus, Kittie was well acquainted with the Black community, and with these Black cyclists.

Kittie was actively involved with White cyclists as well. Reporters noticed her at Chestnut Hill Reservoir in 1893 and 1894 as large crowds of cyclists—racers and recreationalists—gathered there during the "cycling craze."

Traditionalist women rode sedately in long skirts on drop-frame "women's" bicycles. Kittie wore knickerbockers, or bloomers, and rode a diamond frame "man's bike"—and she scorched.

THE LAW AND THE COLOR BAR

Kittie joined the League of American Wheelmen (LAW) around 1893, but her membership was soon threatened. By 1890, Reconstruction was over, and White Northerners gradually withdrew support for Black civil rights. Many restrictive laws were passed in Southern states, and more were to come. As early as 1891, a movement began within the LAW, led by the Louisville, Kentucky, club, to deny Black membership. For several years a constitutional amendment was defeated, but then it passed in 1894 by a two-thirds vote. The Massachusetts delegates voted "no," as did several other Northern delegations. The bar on Black membership in the LAW set off a furious protest among the Black cyclists of the RCC. Robert Teamoh, a racing judge for the club and an honorary member, *Boston Globe* reporter, and state representative from Kittie's West End neighborhood, introduced a bill into the Massachusetts state legislature condemning the color bar: "Resolved that the general court deprecates the action of [the League of American Wheelmen] as regards the enforcement of discriminations of their character as a revival of baseless and obsolete prejudices."[23] The legislature agreed.[24] The RCC went further, demanding answers from the Union [Black] Cycle Club of Louisville as to why its president had supported the color bar. The RCC suspected bribery. There were also "many words of condemnation at the supposed actions of some of the States in trading their votes and opinions for selfish reasons."[25] The Massachusetts delegation was also suspected, despite its "no" vote, of offering to cease resistance to the color bar in return for getting the 1895 LAW Annual Meet to come to Boston. The Meet went to Asbury Park, New Jersey, instead.

It became apparent that reversing the color bar would be difficult, but the RCC persevered. In 1895, a large group met at the Chalres Street AME (African Methodist Episcopal) Church in the West End. The Riversiders reported that they had support from George Perkins, a lawyer, former state representative, member of the Press Cycling Club, Good Roads commissioner, and vice president of the LAW. RCC wanted to lodge a protest at the LAW's winter meeting in New York.[26] Boston's chief counsel, Sterling Elliott, encouraged the protesters and said he would arrange for the RCC to have a hearing at the meeting.[27] Teamoh volunteered to represent RCC cyclists in New York but didn't show up, and the motion to rescind the color bar never came to a vote. That, together with a scandalous incident in which

Teamoh visited the governor of Virginia and was too accommodationist and subservient, doomed his chances for reelection in the West End.

The Charles Street AME Church in the West End had a long protest tradition. Frederick Douglass, Sojourner Truth, and William Lloyd Garrison all rallied with the congregation before the Civil War.[28] In the 1890s, Black residents had plenty to protest: the collapse of Reconstruction, failure to pass a Federal Elections bill to protect Southern Black male voting rights, an epidemic of lynching, and the failure of federal anti-lynching bills. Rights were threatened further as the *Plessy v. Ferguson* decision eviscerated federal public accommodations law.[29] In addition, residents met at nearby St. Augustine's Church and protested under-policing of the area, especially around the street-corner saloons, and requested more officers to patrol from six to eleven every evening.[30] The Colored National League met at Charles Street, and Josephine St. Pierre Ruffin's New Era Club and the National Conference of Colored Women of America (founded in Boston 1895) debated the place of Black women in the larger context of Black and women's rights.[31]

Despite efforts to repeal the LAW's color bar, it remained in place. Efforts to start up an alternative national Black cycling organization modeled on the LAW also fizzled.[32] But the color bar did not stop Kittie. She traded her cycling outfits for ball dresses and was described as "handsomely gowned in blue satin, with gauze bodice of old rose and white, with a green satin ribbon" at a March 1895 dance of the Consolidated Cycling Clubs of Boston (CCC), an umbrella organization of predominately White clubs, attended by the leadership of Boston cycling.[33]

THE CONTENTIOUS CYCLING SEASON OF 1895

With the dancing and politicking of the winter behind them, cyclists looked forward to warmer weather, and a chance to get out of the crowded, polluted, and smelly city and bike free into the countryside. Members of the RCC set off on long journeys into the suburbs, the seacoast, the Lakes District of the Charles River, and rural areas. They were occasionally noted by the press for their participation in Company L, and their connection to Kittie Knox (although she was never claimed as a member, being a woman, she likely participated in their Ladies' Days).

Traditionalist men and women strongly opposed women's racing. *Bearings*, the cycling trade magazine, reported on results from women's races at Buffalo, provoking a storm of opposition from letter writers and from *Bearings*: "We do not see how any self-respecting woman can so far forget herself as to appear before an audience to race. The spectacle of half-a-dozen females straining every muscle, perspiring at every pore, and bent over their handle-bars in a weak imitation of their brothers, is enough to disgust the most enthusiastic of wheelmen."[34]

The opposition continued through the 1890s. As more and more women like Kittie wanted to ride long and ride fast, the LAW admonished that "Any attempt to have women bicycle races recognized by the L.A.W. will be bitterly fought."[35] Further, the LAW "threatens to suspend any male riders who compete on a track where there are female riders."[36]

Given that opposition, on July 4, 1895, the Waltham Cycle Park advertised men-only amateur races for trophies and professional races for a one-thousand-dollar cash prize. Also, they hosted the first-ever women's cycling costume contest. Kittie designed her own outfit—bloomers, sack coat, ordinary bicycle cap, and gaiters—and took her lap around the track. Her style was part of a revolution in women's thinking and action, called colloquially "the New Woman" or "the Coming Woman."[37] She beat four White women but was hissed by traditionalists in the grandstand. Apparently, they hissed all the bloomer- and knickerbocker-wearing women—but one of the judges, Charles Percival, later reported that he thought it was because of her race. Her victory was publicized by newspapers all over the nation, and she became a mini celebrity.

Just a few days later, her arrival at the annual national LAW Meet at the new socially and racially segregated resort of Asbury Park, New Jersey, was anticipated with great interest, and some opposition. She wore her Waltham-winning outfit, and a New Jersey newspaper described her as "handsome and very graceful" and a "light mulatto."[38] The newspapers covered Kittie Knox far more frequently than any other part of the Meet; the controversy surrounding her appearance guaranteed attention. When she came into the registration area with her League credentials, she was refused a Meet badge by host club officials. According to some reports, she "walked out defiantly with her wheel," but according to others, she "very quietly went her way." The *New York Times* reported: "Miss Knox did a few fancy cuts in front of the clubhouse and was requested to desist."

Her opponents hailed from various regions and pointed, either passively or overtly, to the larger national implications of her admittance. The Louisville paper endorsed her dismissal, writing that the "officials acted properly."[39] The *New York Times* noted regretfully that this would "temporarily reopen the color line question."[40] The *Southern Cycler* was outraged that Kittie was admitted, calling her "a saddle-colored damsel from Boston," "the murky goddess of Beanville," and "several checks shy of the complexion requirement."[41] The local "kickers" threatened to appeal to the LAW's secretary, Abbot Bassett, upon his arrival from Boston.[42]

Kittie Knox's supporters countered with strength and a resolve for equality. Massachusetts LAW officials argued that since she was a member before the color bar was passed, she deserved to get her badge and stay. An official with Boston's Press Cycle Club interceded and got Kittie her badge. George Perkins, a Bostonian and a member of the LAW Executive Committee, said she was a member and could stay a member if she liked; he threatened reprisals for anyone who tried to keep her out.[43] Bassett, LAW's secretary, was a Kittie Knox supporter, thus muting the "kickers" threat to seek a higher authority on the matter. A Chicago paper noted: "She was a member of the League before the by-law excluding colored people was adopted and has not allowed her membership to lapse. She came from the city of beans without an escort, and was refused admittance at several hotels, but finally obtained accommodation [at a private house], and her league credentials as well. She took part in all the runs."[44] Another Bostonian, cycle inventor, manufacturer, publisher, and Massachusetts LAW chief consul Sterling Elliott, praised the many newspapers that defended Kittie's rights.[45] Perkins went further and threatened League lawsuits against the hotels and restaurants that denied Kittie entrance.[46]

With a strong contingent of supporters in her corner and an internal resolve, Kittie Knox continued her quest to be treated with equality. Arthur Zimmerman (a world-famous racer and friend of Major Taylor, an up-and-coming Black racing champion) asked Kittie to join in a run to Zimmerman's nearby home for one of LAW's tours. She "got her revenge" and rode "right up with the best."[47] At the evening League Ball, she and a young White Bostonian were first on the dance floor. She never lacked a partner. Some observers said that her partners just wanted to prove a point—to show that LAW "makes no distinction against colored persons and believes in equal rights."[48] Several of the women cyclists left the dance and threatened to leave LAW if she was allowed to stay, but she danced the whole night through. The cycling press crowded around, drawn by the sensation, and headlined Kittie in hundreds of newspapers across the United States and Canada.

The influence of Kittie Knox's embodied protests expanded beyond her race to that of her gender. Despite the long-skirt dress code the traditionalist lady cyclists asserted, at Asbury Park their hold slipped. Of the fifty-seven women in the ladies' division of the LAW parade, reporters counted thirty-three bloomers, ten short skirts, and the remainder in the "conventional habit." Kittie Knox and her young modern cyclists—the Coming Women— won the battle.[49]

THE RETURN TO BOSTON: SUCCESSES AND BARRIERS

After the Meet, Kittie returned to Boston with new opportunities to ride fast and long at her level. In August 1895, the Massachusetts Division of LAW appears to have thumbed its collective nose at the national color bar, and at the long-skirt tradition too. They selected Kittie, along with Ida Halstat, a young White Dorchester rider, to be pacesetters for the state League's ride from Boston to their summer meet campground at Lake Quinsigamond, near Worcester. The *Worcester Spy* wrote that Kittie was a "most enthusiastic young wheelwoman," and did not seem to mind the long trip a bit, unlike half of the cyclists who took the train from South Framingham on account of a heavy wind. The *Spy* noted that she was a "mulatto of striking and attractive feature" and that she dined amiably with the cyclists at their resting place in Westborough. The *Spy* sketched her coasting down a Worcester hill along with a vivid description: "neat suit of bloomers, of a gray material, while on her head of black wavy hair a blue bicycle cap was jauntily perched."[50] Early in September, on a century ride from Boston to Providence, seventy riders were caught in a rainstorm on the way home, and many boarded a train back to Boston. The *Boston Journal* noted that Kittie was the only woman in the second division to finish, among a dozen survivors. She was "muddy but not at all played out."[51] Persistence.

Her success came with trouble instigated by some White riders. A new club, the Boston Wheelmen, planned a century ride to Newburyport. Kittie and a dozen Black men, likely from the RCC, registered in advance. Word spread, and the Wheelmen voted to exclude the Black riders. A Black cyclist and Boston City Councilman Charles Hall brought a lawsuit against the Boston Wheelmen,[52] likely based on the Massachusetts public accommodations law. Three Boston clubs supported the suit, but the LAW opposed it. Ultimately, the suit failed, perhaps only because a bike ride, unlike a barbershop or roller-skating rink, did not qualify as a public accommodation under Massachusetts law.

No Kittie Knox supporter, Boston Wheelmen Club captain William Handy claimed defensively to the press, "I was thoroughly overwhelmed by the members who wanted to exclude the colored fellows." He claimed that he had many friends among "colored men" and did not want them to think "that I was out against them."[53] But on a club ride, apparently, not too many of them! According to the *Boston Globe* account, Kittie had made plans to ride tandem with a "young [White] physician." When he learned that the Boston Wheelmen had refused to admit "one of the best woman cycle riders in New England, solely because she was colored, [he] grew indignant and did not participate in the ride."[54] Another Boston club, the Roxbury Wheelmen, joined the battle, promoting their own ride to Newburyport with a color bar, headlined in the *Boston Daily Standard*: "Roxbury Wheelmen Bar Negroes from Their Century Run."[55]

The Massachusetts chapter of the Century Road Club of America (CRCofA) advertised a century ride *without* a "color line" soon after the Roxbury Wheelman staged their protest ride. CRCofA stated that their decision was made "at the earnest solicitation of many clubs." Cyclists were told to send registrations to state centurion Charles Percival (a Kittie Knox supporter and judge at her Waltham victory).[56] The rained-out ride finally happened on November 17. Notably, CRCofA's need to explicitly state their position demonstrates the issue's importance and centrality in the fall of 1895.

Mercifully, perhaps, that ended the 1895 cycling season, a scene of exclusion and inclusion, and of wind and rain. But that did not end the argument. Percival revealed that several other states had roundly criticized the Massachusetts CRCofA chapter for not using a color bar, and the national executive committee inserted one into their rules. Percival lamented: "So it seems by this latter-day action of the Century Road Club, America's second largest cycling organization, that there is very little or no place in the different fields of American sports for the negro, and that his White brethren have no desire or use for him except at election time."[57] Kittie Knox's fight for equality continued.

PROMINENCE

Despite the color bar, Kittie Knox achieved acclaim among Boston cyclists. She returned to a CCC dance in April 1896 in a "batiste and blue silk" costume with "dresden trimmings."[58] The following month, the *Boston Post* headlined her a "Champion Woman Scorcher," and their reporter praised her cycling and attitude:

> Of all Boston's feminine scorchers, the most famous is the popular Kitty Knox. . . . She is known everywhere and there is not a track in the country which she would not be welcome were it not for the L.A.W.'s edict [banning women's racing]. Miss Knox is a member of the L.A.W. and is proud of it. Their orders, however, have not stopped her scorching, and every Sunday she may be seen whirling along on her flying wheel to the great admiration and envy of her sister riders. Before the [anti-racing] edict of the L.A.W. came out, she won many races at different tracks in the state. Last year she won several prizes for wearing the best costume.

The writer went on to admire her "staying powers," and that she was a "century rider of note."[59] *The Post* also noted that she was out and about with prominent racers like Nat Butler and Burns Pierce,[60] who would soon (1897) team with Marshall "Major" Taylor in the famous Boston Pursuit team to defeat a Philadelphia team at the Charles River Track.[61]

The desire to write about Kittie Knox spread. Even a small coastal port city newspaper like the *Salem Gazette* mentioned her, describing her as "the finest feminine wheelwoman in Boston." On her visit, a Black bike shop owner, Richard Washington, showed her "points of historic interest" while riding "a Hunter tandem, for which Washington is agent."[62] The big news of 1896 was the huge Labor Day *Boston Herald* Bicycle Parade. Thousands of cyclists wheeled down Commonwealth Avenue, and thousands more watched. RCC members were riding as the Bicycle Unit of Company L of the Sixth Massachusetts Volunteer Militia. Among the many military units parading on bikes, Company L received a special prize for "good appearance" and presented themselves, unlike many, parading with an American flag.[63] In November 1896, the *Boston Journal* reported in a column, "Wheeling Whispers," that: "Miss Kitty Knox, well-known to many Boston cyclists, has returned home from a pleasant visit to Paris, where she delighted in many spins on her wheel."[64] What was she doing in Paris? One theory is that she had found a new opportunity to express her dancing and cycling skills by becoming a member of a traveling vaudeville troupe—like Isham's Octoroons.

ISHAM'S OCTOROONS AND ORIENTAL AMERICA

John Isham was a light-skinned man, enough to pass for White when he needed to. Central to his vaudeville troupes' concept was the exploitation of America's skin color fascination, and its often serious and dangerous implications for Black persons. During the slavery era, light skin appeared in the offspring of many White Southern masters and enslaved Black women—like those of Thomas Jefferson and Sally Hemings. In his autobiography, DuBois describes the prevalence of this practice, stating in detail his own ancestry (African, Haitian, Dutch, and French-Huguenot) and the varieties of skin color among his relatives—some passing for White and others light Mulatto, yellow, and dark Black.[65] Mixed-race children born to slave mothers were sometimes given privileges, such as working in the masters' houses rather than the fields. Some even received a modicum of education while remaining enslaved. Often their Black brethren resented this privileged treatment, leaving the mixed-race children subjected to isolation and othering from their own communities while still facing threats of harm from White society.

White fascination with dark skin evolved into some social opportunities for the African Americans in the late 1800s. Boston newspaper commentators were most approving of light-skinned Black public figures. West Ender Josephine St. Pierre Ruffin ran for the Boston School Committee in 1896, and a newspaper columnist described her as "a fine and stately lady at whom the casual observer would look several times before discovering any traces of negro blood." In contrast, the columnist described RCC cycling judge and state representative Teamoh as a "full blooded negro."[66] Octoroon troupes of the 1890s represented a transformation in entertainment: instead of casts of White actors in blackface putting on shows about plantation life, African Americans played this role. Isham's Oriental America troupe went a step further, showing sophisticated Black life.

Kittie explored these newfound opportunities by leaning into her interests even further. In August 1897, the *Indianapolis Freeman* reported that Kittie performed with Isham's Octoroons at Minot's Eighth Avenue Theatre in New York.[67] The *Boston Post* noted that she was "taking lessons in trick riding with the intention of going on the vaudeville stage."[68] In October, at Boston's Old Howard Theatre, she rode as "Kittie T. Knox of Boston, a wheelwoman," and as part of a bicycle race onstage with three other women.[69] Isham promoted several octoroon troupes and at least one of them performed in Europe. Was she in Paris to perform as part of Isham's Octoroons? Or another troupe? Or was this an error by the reporter? No passenger list survives that would verify her sailing to or from Europe, so this episode in her life is still a mystery.

A newspaper reporter noted her in an audience, along with Nat Butler, Fred St. Onge, and other leaders, including William Handy, at the mid-winter 1897 roller-racing competitions.[70] In the warming spring, despite the CRCofA's new color bar, she joined their ride from Boston to Newburyport and back, lunching and resting at Wolfe Tavern, and arriving back in Copley Square just moments behind the leaders.[71]

DECLINE AND DEATH

As the cycling craze collapsed—its White gentlemen founders deserted it for the new country clubs, fast automobiles, and motorcycles—cyclists quit the sport, and newspapers devoted to it fewer columnists and inches of type. From a high point in the *Boston Globe* and *Boston Herald* references to "bicycle" in 1895–1896, attention rapidly fell. Baseball eclipsed cycling in 1900–1901, and football, too, in 1905.[72]

Anti-Black propaganda spread further in American culture, generating an increasingly hostile and exclusionary environment. Black-faced minstrel shows became popular as wintertime entertainment among cycling

64   *Lorenz J. Finison*

clubs. Musicians circulated anti-Black sheet music, as in "All Coons Look Alike to Me," which a band played at a match race billed as "Black vs. White"[73] between Major Taylor and Eddie McDuffee at the Charles River Cycle Park in 1898.[74] Referring to Reconstruction and Reaction, DuBois lamented, "The freedman has not yet found in freedom his promised land . . . " and " . . . the shadow of a deep disappointment rests upon the Negro people."[75] Kittie Knox cycled and continued dancing, within and across racial lines, during the post–Reconstruction Era and offered courageous resistance to it. In February 1898, she danced at Boston's Paul Revere Hall in the Grand United Order of [Black] Odd Fellows ball.[76] She persevered in cycling with large groups, doing century rides in August and September 1899 from Boston to Newburyport, notably marking the Boston newspaper's last mention of her.[77]

On October 11, 1900, at the age of twenty-six, Kittie Knox died of kidney disease at Massachusetts General Hospital, just a few blocks from her West End home. She was buried at Mount Auburn Cemetery in Cambridge, a favored resting place for middle-class and elite Bostonians, especially among abolitionists and their families.[78] RCC leader Joseph Gardner Holmes is also buried there, as is the activist Josephine St. Pierre Ruffin and William Handy, Kittie Knox's nemesis from the Boston Wheelmen fracas of 1895. Her West End Black community declined, as many African American West Enders moved to the South End to join Southern Black migrants who had recently moved there, and then moved again to Roxbury or other small enclaves in the close-in Boston suburbs.[79]

LEGACY

Kittie Knox lay forgotten until 1972. Historian Robert Smith's *Social History of the Bicycle* gives her one sentence.[80] Andrew Ritchie gave her more in his 2004 book, *Ethnicity, Sports, Identity: Struggles for Status.*[81] Neither of them had access to significant digitized newspaper archives or to the digitized genealogical assets now available. Knowledge of her struggles has become larger still, as in my recent *Boston's Cycling Craze: 1880–1900: A Story of Race, Sport, and Society.*

In 2013, Kittie Knox's story and that of the RCC began anew. A stone, designed by David Sullivan, was installed by Mount Auburn Cemetery. The cambridge vice mayor spoke in her honor amidst her Maine relatives, including her second cousin, Nancy Towle Millett; Major Taylor's great-granddaughter, Jan Brown; Joseph Gardner Holmes's grandniece, Lynda Lee Rollins; and this author. In the past decade, cycling magazines and national cycling organizations have been publishing articles about her. The League of American

Bicyclists grants an annual Kittie Knox award for champions of equity, diversity, and inclusivity in the bicycling movement.[82] The City of Cambridge named a bike path in her honor. Both Boston and Cambridge mayors slated Kittie Knox Days on the city's official calendars. A commuter bike facility featuring a Kittie Knox mural recently opened at Cambridge Crossing. The University of Massachusetts, Boston archives, recently started a Kittie Knox Legacy Collection. Mass-Bike, a statewide advocacy organization, organizes an annual Kittie Knox ride in partnership with the New England Cycling Coalition for Diversity. Mass-Bike and Plays-in-Place raise funds for a series of Kittie Knox plays to be performed by high school, college, and community theater groups all across the country. Jazz Dottin's YouTube film chronicles Kittie Knox's historical sites. Farther away, the Major Knox Adventures organization, combining Major Taylor and Kittie Knox legacies, sponsors rides in the Washington, DC, area. Portland and Seattle generate Kittie Knox initiatives. In Oakland, California, a young woman operates a mobile bike repair clinic called Hard Knox. Transportation organizations such as the American Association of State Highway and Transportation Officials and the National Association of City Transportation Officials also honor her. The Black press, like Harlem's *Amsterdam News,* recognizes her as well.

CONCLUSION

Kittie Knox represented the very present conflicts alive in her historical time and place, many of which continue to this day, perhaps unconsciously or in a different language. Americans seldom refer to mixed-race peoples as mulatto or octoroon, and yet consciousness of skin tone gradations and racial ancestry is never far from the surface of public and family life. Assimilation and contrast tendencies, as theorized by Muzafer Sherif and Car Hovland, are at work here.[83] People perceive others close to them to be even more similar (assimilation), and those who are further away racially or culturally as even more different (contrast). Many of Kittie Knox's Boston contemporaries tried to assimilate her, by placing her as a pacesetter for cycling events, for example. Others tried to contrast (distance) her, as in denying her admission to a century ride where she registered along with a dozen Black men. They were perceived as more distant, because of a different combination of race, gender, skin color, and their number, and they may have been seen as more threatening to the social mores as a result.

Kittie straddled the color line. She was involved in many mostly White cycling events—but not in their clubs. She was never a member of the two major women's cycling clubs of the time, the Woodbridge club of North Cambridge or the Bostonian club of the South End. She maintained ties with

Black cyclists and middle-class Black cultural institutions and participated in the wintertime dances in Boston and in Cambridgeport. Kittie was possibly accepted in predominantly White spaces as a singular (and light-skinned) individual, without the accompaniment of significant numbers of Black men. They apparently had little trouble amateur racing in the Boston area—RCC cyclists were an unremarked part of these events. Major Taylor also rode his first amateur races in the Boston area unimpeded, unlike what he faced in his home state, Indiana. As he accelerated his professional standing, Taylor was both a teammate with White cyclists and at times at odds with them. He could not compete on Southern tracks to gain national championship points—a circumstance that drove him to Europe and Australia to make a living at racing.

Recreational events carried an intimate sociable expectation, such as dining and camping together on equal-status terms. Sterling Elliott, 1896 elected president of the LAW, echoed this when explaining his reversal on the color bar. In an interview published by *Zion's Herald*, a Methodist publication, he reported how he first fought against the race prejudice of the LAW color bar: "It seemed narrow and mean." But over the next few years, his view on membership changed: "while in mere business relations I can treat the Negro as any other man, socially I don't want him with me. There are banquets, meets, theatre parties, chapter rooms, and countless other social functions in which the White and colored people cannot come together on a plane of equality. . . . He cannot socially become a member with us." And finally, "such is the law of the League of American Wheelmen, and such the unwritten but inexorable law of social Boston."[84]

Support for Kittie Knox seems to have risen out of the "old" leadership of cycling both in Boston and nationally. This includes leaders like Frank Weston, Percival, Bassett, and Elliott, too, before he changed views following a term of national leadership. They represented the Abolitionist/Reconstruction generation—Elliott perhaps less so due to his Midwestern roots. Her opponents in Boston (e.g., the Boston Wheelmen and the Roxbury Wheelmen) seem to have been among more youthful cyclists. This foretells the waning of support for Black rights among White Bostonians, as Mark Schneider chronicled in *Boston Confronts Jim Crow: 1890–1920*. Support became complicated among Black Bostonians as well. Civil rights leaders like Ruffin and DuBois fought against both Black and White adherents of Booker T. Washington's accommodationist politics and industrial training focus, which he applied at the Tuskegee Institute.[85]

The frequent support for Kittie Knox among cyclists and the non-Southern newspapers highlights a further issue. This contrasts with the White-only constitutional amendment, passed just a year earlier. Perhaps this is a testament to the power of a well-organized and passionate minority (Southern LAW delegates). They had leverage, promising growth in Southern membership, and therefore greater support for the Good Roads movement if the White-only provision was passed (against a less passionate and less single-issue Northern majority, although the promised growth never happened).

Kittie Knox's life and community is a fertile ground for exploring interactions of race, skin color, gender, and politics in the late nineteenth century. She, along with Major Taylor, has become a twenty-first-century rallying point for cyclists committed to diversity, equity, and inclusion. Kittie Knox's epitaph might be summarized in the first line of an 1896 song entitled "The Coming Woman," which released on sheet music featuring a cover photograph of a young light-skinned woman:

"Oh, the coming woman of our land, With courage true as steel;

Is the pretty maid who is not afraid to ride upon a wheel."[86]

NOTES

1. Recent scholarship on women cyclists that offer a deeper historical context on gender and cycling include Christine Bachman-Sanders, "Harmless Pleasure: Feminist Liberation and Whitenormative Conquest for the New Woman Cyclist of the 1890s (Ph.D. Dissertation: University of Minnesota, 2020).

2. "The Summer Girl," *Indianapolis Freeman*, June 17, 1893; the *Freeman* noted another Boston friend, Benzina Reese, on their jaunts later in the summer. "The Summer Girl," *Indianapolis Freeman*, August 5, 1893. Black newspapers had a nationwide network of local "correspondents" eager to share their observations. Cottage City is now Oak Bluffs, Martha's Vineyard.

3. "May Be Racing Today," *New York Times*, July 10, 1895. Percival also remembered her at Springfield and Waltham.

4. The 1880 U.S. Census Mulatto category included "quadroons, octoroons, and all persons having any perceptible trace of African blood." The instructions for 1890 were to: "Be particularly careful to distinguish between blacks [three-fourths or more black blood], mulattoes [three-eighths to five eighths black blood], quadroons [one fourth black blood], and octoroons [one-eighth or any trace of black blood]." Unlike today, the census taker was tasked with the choice, not the resident.

5. W. E. B. Du Bois, "Strivings of the Negro People," *Atlantic Monthly* 80.2 (August 1897): 194–98.

6. Massasoit was a famous Wampanoag chief, present as the Pilgrims landed in 1620.

7. "Summary of News," *Boston Investigator*, September 13, 1865.

8. Augustus Saint-Gaudens designed the monument. It was unveiled in 1897. Boston Massacre Crispus Attucks was also honored with a monument shared with other victims of the massacre on Boston Common in 1889.

9. During the mid-1860s, he is listed as John Knox or John H. Knox and living in the West End or in Chelsea and working in Boston as a tailor or clothing cleaner. His death listing at Boston City Hospital shows him as born in Philadelphia.

10. Van Gosse, *The First Reconstruction: Black Politics in American from the Revolution to the Civil War* (Chapel Hill: University of North Carolina Press, 2021).

11. Jeremy Wolin, "Potomska Mills Housing," *Rhode Tour*, accessed February 16, 2023, https://rhodetour.org/items/show/79; Joshua L. Rosenbloom, "The Challenges of Economic Maturity: New England, 1880–1940," in Peter Temin (Ed.), *Engines of Enterprise: An Economic History of New England* (Cambridge: Harvard University Press, 2000), 174.

12. Elizabeth Pleck notes that on one index, Boston was more segregated than other Northern cities of the time. But none of these cities was anywhere near the macro-segregation of our present time where square miles of residences are almost completely segregated. Pleck, Elizabeth. *Boston, 1865–1900: Black Migration and Poverty.* (New York: Academic Press, 1977).

13. W. E. B. Du Bois, "The Talented Tenth," in Booker T. Washington (Ed.), *The Negro Problem* (New York: James Pott & Company, 1903): 33–75.

14. Pleck, *Boston, 1865–1900: Black Migration and Poverty*; Jacqueline Jones, *No Right to an Honest Living: The Struggles of Boston's Black Workers in the Civil War Era* (New York: Basic Books, 2023); Stephan Thernstrom, *The Other Bostonians: Poverty and Progress in the American Metropolis, 1880–1970* (Cambridge: Harvard University Press, 1973). Thernstrom classifies coachmen as unskilled, but a careful accounting of the job duties suggests a high degree of skill in handling horses compared with a "groom."

15. Mark R. Schneider, *Boston Confronts Jim Crow: 1890–1920* (Boston: Northeastern University Press, 1997).

16. Susie King Taylor, *Reminiscences of My Life in Camp with the 33rd United States Colored Troops, Late 1st S.C. Volunteers* (Boston, 1902).

17. Pleck, *Boston, 1865–1900: Black Migration and Poverty*. Most out-marriages were between Black men and White women largely due to occupational patterns, migration and immigration, and differential death rates.

18. Two pictures of "Katie" Knox have been found in Towle family scrapbooks.

19. "'Twas a Pretty Occasion: Seventh Anniversary of the A.S.C. Club of the West End," *Boston Globe*, March 11, 1892. Held at Social Hall of the G.U.O.O. F. Building, North Russell Street, near the center of the Black community in the West End.

20. "In Odd Fellows Hall: Benevolent Fraternity of Coachmen's Fifth Annual Ball," *Boston Globe*, January 4, 1893.

21. "They Marched in Style: Members of Company L, Sith, Were Out in Full Dress," *Boston Globe*, February 16, 1893. Cotillion Hall was in the huge Mechanics Building at the corner of Huntington and West Newton streets.

22. Other RCC members included Joseph Gardner Holmes, Horace Wheaton, Nathan Saunders, and Oliver Dobson. Many other New England militias had cycling units for that moment in time. The U.S. Army didn't like them, apparently, and they were never used in the Spanish-American War.

23. *Massachusetts House Journal*, February 21, 1894, 335.

Kittie Knox, Boston Cyclist in the 1890s 69

24. The first African American state legislator was elected in 1866. Briefly there were two running as Republicans. Eventually gerrymandering and demographic shifts and splits in the African American community reduced the possibilities, and from 1902 to 1947, there were no Black legislators.

25. "Riverside Cycle Club," *Boston Post*, March 4, 1894.

26. "Riverside Cycle Club," *Boston Herald*, February 10, 1895. The RCC also reached out for support from "colored" cycling clubs in New York, Brooklyn, and Philadelphia.

27. "Riverside Cycle Club," *Boston Globe*, February 10, 1895.

28. During the 1890s, Boston's African American community began to move from Beacon Hill to the South End and Roxbury sections of the city. The migration was spurred by the arrival of new immigrant groups that were favored over the African Americans for jobs and housing.

29. Massachusetts had its own state-level public accommodations law, passed in 1866.

30. "Cambridge St. Protests," *Boston Globe*, May 22, 1895.

31. Ruffin protested the suffragette's decision to bar Black women from a national conference and to "sell" White Americans on suffrage on the basis that this would dilute the power of Black men's votes.

32. "Rivals of the L.A.W.: Colored Cyclists to Have Their Own Organization," *Repository* [Canton, OH] August 2, 1896. The Hannibal Athletic Club of Washington, DC, had elaborate plans for annual meets, parades, racing, and a national publication. But the plan never came to fruition.

33. "Their First: Consolidated Cyclists a Grand Success Bicycle Belles Out," *Boston Post*, March 20, 1895. Other major newspapers of the time, the *Boston Globe* and the *Boston Herald*, also covered the dance and Kittie's attire.

34. "Women Race at Buffalo," *Bearings* 11.26 (July 25, 1895); "The Women Again," *Bearings*, 11.26 (July 25, 1895). Women did sometimes race as professionals, but these were "spectacles": "English Trade Notes," *Bearings*, 7.25 (January 16, 1896); "'Jack' Boston," *Bicycle World and L.A.W. Bulletin*, May 10, 1889, 34; Women professionals like the famed Louise Armaindo did "spectacle racing," which was not controlled by the LAW. See Lorenz J. Finison, *Bicycling Inclusion and Equity* (Needham, MA: Lorenz J. Finison, 2023).

35. "L.A.W.'s Big Meeting," *Worcester Daily Spy*, February 7, 1897.

36. "For Women Cyclists," *Washington Evening Star*, March 13, 1897.

37. Henry T. Bray, composer, and A.M. Hall, lyricist, "The Coming Woman," Chelsea, MA, Ryder Music Pub. Co., 1896. https://www.loc.gov/resource/mussuffrage.mussuffrage-100067/?sp=1.

38. "LAW," *Warren* [NJ] *Evening News*, July 22, 1895.

39. "Good Things," *Louisville Courier-Journal*, July 14, 1895.

40. "Invaded by Bicyclists," *New York Times*, July 9, 1895.

41. "The Knox Incident," *Southern Cycler*, August 1895. The *Southern Cycler* repeatedly voiced concerns about the "color line," including a report in 1896: "A colored man served in an official capacity at a recent race meet in Philadelphia, and

now the colored women are going to wear bloomers in Louisville. Where are we 'at' anyway?" *Southern Cycler*, 1896 (no month).

42. "Invaded by Bicyclists," *New York Times*, July 9, 1895.

43. "At Asbury Park," *Wheel and Cycling Trade Journal* 15.21 (July 12, 1895): 25–26.

44. "A Mulatto Girl Attracts Attention," Daily Inter-Ocean [Chicago], July 14, 1895.

45. "In the Cycling World," *New York Tribune*, July 20, 1895.

46. "Crack-r-Jacks Preparing at Asbury Park Cycle Track," *Buffalo Morning Express*, July 11, 1895.

47. "Can't Lose Her," *Boston Globe*, July 11, 1895.

48. "Fine Racing by Cyclists, *New York Times*, July 12, 1895.

49. "Color Line Drawn," *San Francisco Call*, July 10, 1895. The traditionalists were supported by the *Wheelwoman*, published by Mary Sargent Hopkins in Boston—1895–1897.

50. "Midsummer Meet," *Worcester Daily Spy*, August 9, 1895. The group's resting place was the Whitney House in Westborough.

51. "A Quick Run," *Boston Journal*, September 10, 1895.

52. A Black lawyer, Edgar Benjamin, represented the rejected cyclists.

53. "Kittie Knox Refused," *Boston Daily Standard*, September 16, 1895.

54. "Drew the Color Line: Writs Issued Against Boston Wheelmen for Discriminating Against Miss Knox and Others," *Boston Globe*, November 6, 1895.

55. "Roxbury Wheelmen Bar Negroes from Their Century Run," *Boston Daily Standard*, October 1, 1895; "Color Line Drawn," *Boston Daily Journal*, October 1, 1895.

56. "Another Century," *Boston Herald*, October 27, 1895.

57. Charles Percival, "Colored Man and Wheel," *Boston Post*, December 1, 1895.

58. "Dance of the Cyclers," *Boston Globe*, April 7, 1896.

59. "Women Scorchers: They Can Hold Their Own with the Men on the Road," *Boston Post*, May 17, 1896. A contemporary Irving Street neighbor describe Kittie: "On holidays . . . sometimes as many as eighty miles had to be accomplished in one day. Oftentimes Kate Know would ride . . . everyone a male member except herself. . . . She would wear . . . a navy-blue uniform—bloomers and long stockings, and a middy blouse, and she rode a man's bicycle. . . . Many wanted to marry her, but she turned a deaf ear. . . . The beauteous lady lived fifty years ahead of the times, having the courage to live her own life. . . . I doubt if Boston will ever produce another Kate Knox." Walter Stevens, *Chip on My Shoulder: Autobiography* (Boston, Meador Publishing Company: 1946): 35-36

60. "Thousands Out," *Boston Post*, May 18, 1896.

61. "Boston Won," *Boston Journal*, July 22, 1897.

62. *Salem Gazette*, May 22, 1897. The Hunter tandem bicycle was manufactured by the Hunter Arms Company in Fulton, New York.

63. "Parade Prize Winners," *Boston Herald*, August 30, 1896.

64. "Wheeling Whispers," *Boston Journal*, November 17, 1896.

65. W. E. B. Du Bois, *Autobiography of W. E. B. Du Bois: A Soliloquy on My Life from the Last Decade of Its First Century* (New York: International Publishers, 1968).

66. "Negroes for Office: Political Tidal Wave in Boston for Colored People," *Repository* (Canton OH), December 15, 1896. Ruffin was running on a "silver Democrat ticket." African American leaders like Frederick Douglass were light-skinned as well.

67. "The Stage," *Indianapolis Freeman*, August 28, 1897; "A Hot Time at the Old Howard," *Boston Herald*, October 24, 1897.

68. "Bicycle News," *Boston Post*, August 27, 1897.

69. Six months later, the Octoroons returned to the Old Howard, but Kittie's role was taken by another cyclist: Jeanine Robinson. "Warm Babies at the Old Howard," *Boston Herald,* March 27, 1898.

70. "Bob Urquhart's Medal," *Boston Post*, February 14, 1897. Roller-racing at the West Newton Street rink.

71. "Under 12 Hours," *Boston Post*, June 28, 1897; "Century under Road Club Auspices," *Boston Globe*, June 28, 1897.

72. Based on yearly counts of word bicycle, baseball, and football from 1883–1915. Source: Genealogy Bank (*Boston Herald*) and newspaper archives (*Boston Globe*).

73. Finison. . . . The song was written by a Black songwriter Ernest Hogan, who regretted it later in life.

74. Ibid.

75. W. E. B. Du Bois, "Strivings of the Negro People," *Atlantic Monthly* 80.2 (August 1897): 194–98.

76. The Grand Order was the segregated Black version of the International Order of Odd Fellows, a fraternal organization founded in 1843.

77. "Double Century," *Boston Globe*, August 21, 1899; "Rode 100 Miles," *Boston Post*, September 25, 1899.

78. Her cause of death was chronic parenchymatous nephritis and heart failure. The cause of her disease is unknown, although there were many related environmental and occupational exposures in that era. Her individual gravesite was purchased the day after her death by William Goddard, an 1865 Harvard College graduate, a gentleman of leisure, heir to a shipping merchant's declining fortune, and a "pioneering" resident of Back Bay (291 Marlborough Street). He lived with his widowed mother and two Irish servants. He died in 1907 and was buried in the Goddard family plot. His relationship to Kittie Knox is unknown. He had no known connection to the bicycling world. It is possible that the seamstress mother and daughter or the tailor father (John) might have had some business or other relationship to the Goddard family. (Sources: Mount Auburn Cemetery records, Harvard College Class Secretary alumni publications, and obituaries).

79. Cambridgeport, West Newton, Wes Medford, and Malden.

80. Robert A. Smith, *A Social History of the Bicycle: Its Early Life and Times in America* (New York: American Heritage Press, 1972).

81. Andrew Ritchie, "Major Taylor and the 'Color Question' in the United States," in J.A. Mangan and Andrew Ritchie, eds., *Ethnicity, Sports, Identity: Struggles for Status* (London: Frank Cass, 2004).

82. Katherine T. (Kittie) Knox Award of the League of American Bicyclists. Presenting our 2020 Award winners | League of American Bicyclists (bikeleague.org).

83. Muzafer Sherif and Carl Hovland, *Social judgment: assimilation and contrast effects in communication and attitude change* (New Haven: Yale University Press, 1961).

84. "The Negro in Boston," *Zion's Herald* 74.29 (July 15, 1896): 454–55.

85. Schneider, *Boston Confronts Jim Crow: 1890–1920*. W. E. B. Du Bois was an opponent of Booker T. Washington, and he championed a classical college education for the "Talented Tenth" future Black leaders of America. The term *Talented Tenth* was invented by a White man, Henry Lyman Morehouse, for whom the great Morehouse College was named, in *Independent* magazine in 1896, seven years before Du Bois popularized it in 1903. W. E. B. Du Bois, "The Talented Tenth," in Booker T. Washington (Ed.) *The Negro Problem* (New York: James Pott & Company, 1903): 33–75.

86. *The Coming Woman* by A.M. Hall and H.T. Bray. It was published in nearby Chelsea by Clement Ryder, a blind music teacher, pianist, and composer. Henry T. Bray, a blind musician/music teacher from Central Massachusetts, was the composer, and A.M. Hall was the lyricist. The figure photo on the front cover of the sheet music was taken against the same studio backdrop as one of Kittie Knox's family photos, and the figure is clearly what the newspapers referred to a "light mulatto." The photo is possibly one of Kittie Knox. The juxtaposition of her feature story of 1896 in the *Boston Post*, and the publication date of the music, 1896, makes this very likely.

BIBLIOGRAPHY

"A Hot Time at the Old Howard," *Boston Herald*, October 24, 1897.

"A Mulatto Girl Attracts Attention," Daily Inter-Ocean [Chicago], July 14, 1895.

"A Quick Run," *Boston Journal*, September 10, 1895.

"Another Century," *Boston Herald*, October 27, 1895.

"At Asbury Park," *Wheel and Cycling Trade Journal* 15.21 (July 12, 1895).

Bachman-Sanders, Christine. "Harmless Pleasure: Feminist Liberation and Whitenormative Conquest for the New Woman Cyclist of the 1890s (Ph.D. Dissertation: University of Minnesota, 2020).

"Bicycle News," *Boston Post*, August 27, 1897.

"Bob Urquhart's Medal," *Boston Post*, February 14, 1897.

"Boston Won," *Boston Journal*, July 22, 1897.

"Cambridge St. Protests," *Boston Globe*, May 22, 1895.

"Can't Lose Her," *Boston Globe*, July 11, 1895.

"Century under Road Club Auspices," *Boston Globe*, June 28, 1897.

"Color Line Drawn," *Boston Daily Journal*, October 1, 1895.

"Color Line Drawn," *San Francisco Call*, July 10, 1895.

"Crack-r-Jacks Preparing at Asbury Park Cycle Track," *Buffalo Morning Express*, July 11, 1895.

"Dance of the Cyclers," *Boston Globe*, April 7, 1896.

"Double Century," *Boston Globe*, August 21, 1899.

"Drew the Color Line: Writs Issued Against Boston Wheelmen for Discriminating Against Miss Knox and Others," *Boston Globe*, November 6, 1895.

Du Bois, W. E. B. *Autobiography of W. E. B. Du Bois: A Soliloquy on My Life from the Last Decade of Its First Century*. New York: International Publishers, 1968.

Du Bois, W. E. B. "Strivings of the Negro People," *Atlantic Monthly* 80.2 (August 1897).

Du Bois, W. E. B. "The Talented Tenth," in Washington, Booker T., ed. *The Negro Problem*. New York: James Pott & Company, 1903.

"English Trade Notes," *Bearings*, 7.25 (January 16, 1896).

"Fine Racing by Cyclists, *New York Times*, July 12, 1895.

Finison, Lorenz. *Bicycling Inclusion and Equity*. Needham, MA: Lorenz J. Finison, 2023.

"For Women Cyclists," *Washington Evening Star*, March 13, 1897.

"Good Things," *Louisville Courier-Journal,* July 14, 1895.

Gosse, Van. *The First Reconstruction: Black Politics in American from the Revolution to the Civil War.* Chapel Hill: University of North Carolina Press, 2021.

"In Odd Fellows Hall: Benevolent Fraternity of Coachmen's Fifth Annual Ball, *Boston Globe*, January 4, 1893.

"In the Cycling World," *New York Tribune*, July 20, 1895.

"Invaded by Bicyclists," *New York Times*, July 9, 1895.

"Jack Boston," *Bicycle World and L.A.W. Bulletin*, May 10, 1889.

Jones, Jacqueline. *No Right to an Honest Living: The Struggles of Boston's Black Workers in the Civil War Era*. New York: Basic Books, 2023.

"Kittie Knox Refused," *Boston Daily Standard*, September 16, 1895.

"L.A.W.'s Big Meeting," *Worcester Daily Spy*, February 7, 1897.

"LAW," *Warren* [NJ] *Evening News*, July 22, 1895.

Massachusetts House Journal, February 21, 1894.

"May Be Racing Today," *New York Times*, July 10, 1895.

"Midsummer Meet," *Worcester Daily Spy*, August 9, 1895.

"Negroes for Office: Political Tidal Wave in Boston for Colored People," *Repository* (Canton OH), December 15, 1896.

"Parade Prize Winners," *Boston Herald*, August 30, 1896.

Percival, Charles. "Colored Man and Wheel," *Boston Post*, December 1, 1895.

Pleck, Elizabeth. *Boston, 1865–1900: Black Migration and Poverty.* New York: Academic Press, 1977.

Ritchie, Andrew "Major Taylor and the 'Color Question' in the United States," in J.A. Mangan and Andrew Ritchie, eds., *Ethnicity, Sports, Identity: Struggles for Status*. London: Frank Cass, 2004.

"Rivals of the L.A.W.: Colored Cyclists to Have Their Own Organization," *Repository* [Canton, OH] August 2, 1896.

"Riverside Cycle Club," *Boston Globe*, February 10, 1895.

"Riverside Cycle Club," *Boston Herald*, February 10, 1895.

"Riverside Cycle Club," *Boston Post*, March 4, 1894.

"Rode 100 Miles." *Boston Post*, September 25, 1899.

Rosenbloom, Joshua. "The Challenges of Economic Maturity: New England, 1880–1940," in Temin, Peter ed., *Engines of Enterprise: An Economic History of New England.* Cambridge: Harvard University Press, 2000.

"Roxbury Wheelmen Bar Negroes from Their Century Run," *Boston Daily Standard*, October 1, 1895.

Schneider, Mark. *Boston Confronts Jim Crow: 1890–1920.* Boston: Northeastern University Press, 1997.

Sherif, Muzafer, and Carl Hovland, *Social Judgment: Assimilation and Contrast Effects in communication and attitude change*. New Haven: Yale University Press, 1961.

Smith, Robert. *A Social History of the Bicycle: Its Early Life and Times in America.* New York: American Heritage Press, 1972.

"Summary of News," *Boston Investigator*, September 13, 1865.

Taylor, Susie King. *Reminiscences of My Life in Camp with the 33rd United States Colored Troops, Late 1st S.C. Volunteers*. Boston: Taylor, 1902.

"The Knox Incident," *Southern Cycler*, August 1895.

"The Negro in Boston," *Zion's Herald* 74.29 (July 15, 1896).

"The Stage," *Indianapolis Freeman*, August 28, 1897.

"The Summer Girl," *Indianapolis Freeman*, August 5, 1893.

"The Summer Girl," *Indianapolis Freeman*, June 17, 1893.

"The Women Again," *Bearings*, 11.26 (July 25, 1895).

"Their First: Consolidated Cyclists a Grand Success Bicycle Belles Out," *Boston Post*, March 20, 1895.

Thernstrom, Stephen. *The Other Bostonians: Poverty and Progress in the American Metropolis, 1880–1970*. Cambridge: Harvard University Press, 1973.

"They Marched in Style: Members of Company L, Sith, Were Out in Full Dress," *Boston Globe*, February 16, 1893.

"Thousands Out," *Boston Post*, May 18, 1896.

"'Twas a Pretty Occasion: Seventh Anniversary of the A.S.C. Club of the West End," *Boston Globe*, March 11, 1892.

"Under 12 Hours," *Boston Post*, June 28, 1897.

"Warm Babies at the Old Howard," *Boston Herald*, March 27, 1898.

"Wheeling Whispers," *Boston Journal*, November 17, 1896.

"Women Race at Buffalo," *Bearings* 11.26 (July 25, 1895).

Wolin, Jeremy. "Potomska Mills Housing," *Rhode Tour*, accessed February 16, 2023, https://rhodetour.org/items/show/79.

"Women Scorchers: They Can Hold Their Own with the Men on the Road," *Boston Post*, May 17, 1896.

Chapter 4

"Under Wraps"

The Life and Legacy of Sam Langford

Andrew Smith

The best lens to view the complexity of Sam Langford, one of the greatest Black heavyweights in prizefighting history, is arguably through his worst performance: a short, disappointing exhibition with White middleweight Stanley Ketchel. In early 1910, both Langford, the "Colored Heavyweight Champion," as well as British Heavyweight Champion and reigning World Middleweight Champion Ketchel, were regarded as top contenders for Jack Johnson's World Heavyweight Championship. When they agreed to meet in the ring, some considered this an elimination bout, with the victor earning the next shot at Johnson. If the fight game had been an organized and regulated sport, it might have been that simple. But in the chaos of professional boxing during the early twentieth century, there was a lot more to manage behind the scenes than was represented between the ropes.

Langford versus Ketchel was a six-round affair in which two of the hardest hitters in their respective weight classes failed to score a knockdown and rarely threw, let alone connected, on any meaningful blows. It ended in a draw, with fans and reporters alike chiding the two combatants for a blatant fraud. Yet Langford and Ketchel both came out as winners. The reality is that they needed to meet quickly before Johnson scheduled his next title defense. Because Langford weighed somewhere between 170 and 180 pounds at this point in his career, and Ketchel's Middleweight Championship stipulated a maximum of 160 pounds, the two agreed to a catch-weight exhibition match at 165. An exhibition, however, would not legitimize a claim to challenge Johnson, so they would have to meet later, with a 160-pound limit, to compete for Ketchel's title. Therefore, a close, if not contested exhibition early

75

Figure 4.1. Sam Langford was a professional boxer that earned the nickname "Boston Bonecrusher." During his 24-year career, he competed in multiple weight classes and fought over 300 recorded matches. White champions, including Jack Dempsey, refused to fight him, and thus denied Langford a world title in the United States. He held the World Colored Heavyweight Championship five times during his prime years from 1910–1918. Credit: Haeckel/Getty Images

in 1910 would allow them to build interest for a middleweight championship fight shortly afterward.

While an exhibition typically took place in an "athletic club" with limited capacity for a relatively low purse, if they generated excitement, their real fight could fill an arena or even a stadium and almost certainly generate a five-figure payout for each combatant. The right to meet Johnson afterward, and potentially take his title, was a million-dollar proposition. Langford was bigger, stronger, and more experienced, and for him, winning outright might have been easier than "carrying" Ketchel. It was not the first, and it certainly would not be the last, time Langford fought "under wraps"—actively trying *not* to win, or at least not to win too quickly—because he stood to gain more from the optics of a closer battle than a decisive victory. As was usually the case, Langford achieved his goal in the ring. Yet in this instance, like so many others across Langford's three-decade-long career, events outside the ring derailed him. Before he and Langford could execute their plan, Ketchel was murdered by the jealous husband of his current girlfriend. Langford lost the big purse, suffered another setback in his quest to get a World Heavyweight

"Sam was invincible," the boxing historian and founder of the *Ring* magazine, Nat Fleischer, once wrote, at least "when his hands weren't tied." But Langford was born, raised, and competed in an environment that was hardly a meritocracy. His hands were almost always tied one way or another. Stuck between countries, cultures, socioeconomic classes, and weight classes, Langford had to be more than a great athlete or trained pugilist to succeed. He was clever, resourceful, adaptable, and a strategic investor in his own resources. Those traits launched him from the tiny inlet of Weymouth Falls, Nova Scotia, to the pinnacle of prizefighting, allowing him to travel the globe on the strength of his popularity, and engender enough goodwill that a generation past his retirement—long after his fighting days were done—the boxing community still subsidized his basic needs.

The fulfillment of needs was about all that could be expected for most Black Canadians born in Weymouth Falls, Nova Scotia, during the 1880s. The town was one of several in the Canadian Maritimes where formerly enslaved people from the American colonies were invited to settle in exchange for serving in the British Military during the American Revolution. But those "Loyalist" settlements in Canada could become just as racialized and under-resourced as the spaces apportioned and restricted to African American, Indigenous, or specific ethnic groups in the United States.

A clear composite of his charming, five-foot-tall mother and hardened, six-foot-tall father, young Sam Langford could win a crowd just as quickly as he won a fight, even from his earliest days. Growing up with six siblings in a small bungalow he once described as "no bigger than a doghouse," Langford saw few opportunities to change his fortunes there.[1]

The Langford family's experience—his mother died young, his father worked hard in manual labor positions and drank hard afterward—was not unique in places such as Weymouth Falls during the late 1800s. But Sam was not ready to accept his fate. By the turn of the twentieth century, he left his childhood home and was living and working wherever he could between the Canadian Maritimes and the American Northeast. The young teenager eventually made it all the way to Boston and found work cleaning up at the Lenox Athletic Club—a popular venue for quasi-legal boxing matches in Beantown. Joe Woodman ran the club, as well as a nearby drugstore, and he not only paid but also housed and fed Langford for a time. Recognizing, or perhaps succumbing to, Langford's growing interest in the fight game, Woodman allowed him to spar with some of the talent scheduled to compete at upcoming Lenox bouts. But because he was so young, and barely one hundred pounds, Woodman did not let Langford fight in his club; if he wanted experience, Woodman pointed him to the amateur boxing tournaments at the

Roanoke Athletic Club instead. When Langford succeeded—perhaps winning as many as twenty amateur bouts within his first year—Woodman became his manager, making Langford a professional who was fighting for prize money in Boston by 1902.[2]

Woodman might have been hesitant to enter Langford into the prize ring, but once committed, they went full steam ahead. He had Langford engaged in rings all around Boston, including Lenox, two or three times every month. By December 1903, Langford's impressive record and growing reputation earned him a match with "the Old Master," Joe Gans—a veteran of ten years and more than one hundred recorded victories. The still-growing teen-aged Langford came in heavier than the natural lightweight Gans. Although annual record books pegged Langford at about 135 pounds, he walked around heavier than that and likely had to cut between five and ten pounds in the days before their bout just to make the agreed-upon weight limit. Regardless of their size differential, the Old Master taught the young pupil several tricks in the first few rounds. Langford learned quickly, catching up to Gans as the fight wore on and winning the decision after fifteen rounds. Beating such a well-known boxer as Gans was significant for Langford in more ways than one. It certainly gave him credibility in Boston, where Gans was a favorite, and beyond New England as well—leading Langford to his first fight outside of the region, when he took on Jack Blackburn in Philadelphia the next year. But preparing for that bout made Langford realize that "reducing" to make weight for matches with lighter opponents was not physically or financially fulfilling; no one earned fame or fortune with a nickname like the "Boston Tar Baby." So Langford stopped cutting, kept growing, and committed himself to fighting bigger boxers for larger purses—more like the "Boston Bonecrusher."[3]

The following September, Langford earned a shot at the welterweight title held by another international transplant to the Boston boxing scene, the "Barbados Demon," Joe Walcott. Again, Langford stepped in the ring with a notable veteran, and again he enjoyed a size advantage, but this time he could only muster a draw. Walcott was the aggressor early on, though Langford once more learned from his experienced opponent and took control of the action later in the fight. By the fifteenth round, when Langford extended his arm, as was customary before the final stanza, Walcott refused to touch gloves and instead started throwing haymakers. The fight ended wildly, but even though Langford had drawn blood and scored a knockdown earlier, the referee called it a draw, and Walcott retained his title. Fleischer reported that the crowd was "displeased by the decision"; nonetheless, it bolstered Langford's reputation. Even writers from outside the Hub, like New York's Arthur Lumley, started to take notice. Lumley wrote, prophetically, that Langford could win the welterweight title or even the next class up, middleweight, "though he may outgrow both divisions before he reaches his peak!"[4]

In 1904, Langford married Martha Burrell, a dressmaker in Boston.[5] Originally from Philadelphia, Burrell moved to Boston, plying her trade in a bigger city. Langford, after reaching a measure of financial independence, became known as a fashionable and fastidious dresser in Beantown, so it is not surprising that the two would have found each other. Ironically, it was not until after he set down roots with his wife that Langford engaged in a tour outside the New England area, taking on well-known welterweights like Blackburn and Young Peter Jackson in Pennsylvania and Maryland. But he and Woodman set their sights even higher. Though he tipped the scales at just over 160 pounds at the time, Langford wanted to compete in the sport's premiere division—he saw himself as a legitimate heavyweight.

On Christmas Day 1905, Langford fought his first real heavyweight in Joe Jeanette, who was about five inches taller and probably thirty pounds heavier when they stepped in the ring. As expected, at least by the growing fan base who watched and read about Langford's boxing skill and surprising power in the ring, Sam put up a good fight. But he still took a beating from the bigger Jeanette, who was older than Langford, although not as experienced. Langford's corner threw in the sponge after eight rounds of action, signaling to the referee that they were stopping the fight before Sam incurred any more damage.[6] Unlike Gans or Walcott, however, this was not a one-and-done meeting between Langford and Jeanette. The two would go on to fight more than a dozen times over their respective careers, and the margin of difference was reduced to null as Langford grew into his aspirations and became a leading heavyweight contender in professional boxing.

After his game performance against Jeanette, the reigning Colored Heavyweight Champion, Jack Johnson, agreed to face off against Langford. Johnson was, according to many boxing aficionados, already the best prizefighter in the world, but due to the "color line," which protected White heavyweight champions from defending their titles—and potentially losing them—to a Black challenger, Johnson could only claim a stake in the "colored" iteration during the spring of 1906, when he toed the scratch against Langford. In this match, Langford was a full six inches shorter than his opponent and as much as fifty pounds lighter. But he rose to the challenge, going the full distance with Johnson. He even scored a debatable knockdown, though Johnson was awarded the decision with no arguments, following their fifteen entertaining rounds. The two boxers fought again just a couple of days later in an exhibition fundraiser to benefit victims of the recent earthquake in San Francisco. Langford approached that fight with the same energy, even though Johnson's title was not up for grabs in this setting. He desperately wanted a real rematch with Johnson, and even more so a few years later, when

Johnson finally convinced a White champion, Tommy Burns, to defend the title against him—promptly became the first Black heavyweight champion in the gloved prizefighting era.[7]

Woodman acknowledged many years later that he intentionally exaggerated Langford's knockdown of Johnson, which most ringside observers agreed was just a slip, to generate interest in Langford, get him more fights overall, and hopefully convince Johnson to give him another title shot.[8] It didn't work. Not only did Johnson avoid a rematch with Langford, but many others refused to meet him as well. A middleweight boxer with heavyweight abilities was not an attractive opponent to aspiring pugilists, and many of them gave the "Boston Bonecrusher" a wide berth. Like his childhood in Weymouth Falls, Langford would not accept his fate as a hamstrung prizefighter in the United States. He split with Woodman and sought out assistance from a journalist to explore fighting overseas.

Although there is debate over which journalist Langford contacted to broker the deal—New York's Sam Austin or Boston's "Doc" Almy—in the spring of 1907, Langford was booked for two matches in London. Accompanied by bantamweight Al Delmont and his manager, J. McQuillan, but no journalists (it is likely whoever did broker the matches did so discreetly so as not to step on Woodman's toes), Langford set sail in March and began training for his contests at London's National Sporting Club (NSC), including one against the NSC middleweight champion, James "Tiger" Smith. Langford knocked Smith out in the fourth round, and six weeks later, he KO'd Geoff Thorne at the same location before the end of the first. Between bouts, Langford agreed to do shows and demonstrations at London music halls. All told, he racked up roughly five thousand dollars during his first international visit—building a fan base in England that he would tap in to later.[9]

Langford had good reason to return stateside, even if he was earning more money across the Atlantic: Martha was pregnant, and in July 1908, she gave birth to Charlotte, named after Langford's mother.[10] He reunited with Woodman and focused on a singular goal: now that boxing's "color line" had been crossed, and Jack Johnson reigned as the undisputed heavyweight champion of the world, Langford wanted his shot to take the crown. Woodman and Langford arranged fewer matches in Boston in pursuit of opportunities to travel around the country, take on more prestigious opponents, and justify Langford's claim as the number-one heavyweight contender.

Langford went coast to coast, racking up victories from New York to San Francisco, often by knockout, and usually against heavier opponents. At the same time, Woodman amped up his campaign against Johnson through the ballyhoo he wrote about their previous match. He also produced a letter of intent held by the NSC and signed by Johnson, promising to meet Langford—though Woodman downplayed details like the fact that the letter

"Under Wraps" 81

was sent before Johnson became champion and came from a manager who no longer represented him.[11] But it was clear that Johnson had no more interest in defending his title against Langford, or any other Black challenger, than his White predecessors. Langford and Woodman pursued other titles that may not have had the cachet of the world championship yet could still buttress his argument for a rematch with Johnson.

The first, and most lucrative, was to revisit Covent Garden and vie for the British Heavyweight Championship against William "Iron" Hague. Not only did it promise a new title, but the interest he generated in his first trip to London prompted a $7,500 purse, which marked a career high for Langford as well. In training camp at "Jolly Jumbo's" near Stonebridge Park, the mood was fittingly upbeat, despite the mounting pressure on Langford. Hague was only a couple of inches taller, and their reach probably did not differ by much, but "Iron" was more than two hundred pounds of solid Yorkshireman and came by his nickname honestly. Coupled with the fierce hometown crowd, this shaped up to be Langford's toughest test.[12]

The stakes were raised, quite literally, just hours before the fight, when someone in Langford's camp placed the traditional side bet but did so in the wrong currency. Intending to wager ten thousand dollars, the bet instead was made for ten thousand *pounds,* at a time when British currency was valued roughly five times higher than the US dollar. Losing to Hague would bankrupt Langford and make it much harder for him to earn in the future, since his championship aspirations would go down with him. Unsurprisingly, when the bell sounded, Langford came out more cautiously than normal, which suited Hague better. In the fourth round, the hometown favorite connected with a right hand that knocked Langford down, to a patrician chorus of "hear, hear!" Langford got up, however, and charged back with renewed vigor, knocking Hague down and out before the end of the round while replying to the crowd with a nasal "there, there!"[13]

This time, Langford did not stick around London to earn any ancillary income—the purse and side bet payout was plenty, and Woodman had another title in his sights. Having claimed the British Heavyweight Championship, Langford's next fight had to be against a viable Black heavyweight. Since Johnson had refused Black challengers after taking the world championship, Woodman and Langford argued that he "vacated" the Colored Heavyweight Championship, and they wanted to claim that title as well. Less than two months after beating Hague in London, Langford won a six-round decision in Pittsburgh against the six-foot-tall Klondike Haynes, aka "Black Hercules," and immediately proclaimed himself the new Colored Heavyweight Champion.

Ironically, the next move in their attempt to overcome the interracial color barrier was prompted by the man who established a color line for the heavyweight championship in the first place: John L. Sullivan. Frustrated—as were many fight fans—by Johnson's substandard challengers early in his title reign, Sullivan opined that middleweight champion Stanley Ketchel or Langford would be able to beat Johnson if he would agree to their challenge. Ketchel and Langford hastily agreed to an exhibition bout at a catch weight of 165 pounds, with the understanding that if the matchup looked fair, they would schedule a bona-fide title match for the 160-pound Middleweight Championship. Although the first suitor for this exhibition, New York's prestigious Fairmont Athletic Club, became the focus of renewed debate over the legality of prizefighting in New York and had to cancel the event, Philadelphia's National Athletic Club quickly agreed to host. Regardless of where it came off, the six rounds of lackluster pugilism could have been deemed a crime. Yet despite the negative reaction, there was still an appetite in the sporting public to see the real version of Langford versus Ketchel later in 1910 and anoint Johnson's next opponent.[14]

When Ketchel was murdered, Langford felt a shot as well. His path to what would almost certainly have been the biggest purse of his career, and quite likely earn him another world title in a different weight class, disappeared in an instant. So, too, did the opportunity to ratchet pressure on Johnson to defend his championship against Langford. Just as before, Langford left the country to find more money and better conditions while he and Woodman plotted another tack for 1911. He took care of Bill Lang in London, and then made his first landing on the Continent, where he engaged in another first: his inaugural meeting with another Black heavyweight of the era, Sam McVea, in Paris. The two Sams battled regularly over the next decade, in the United States and abroad, yet this first encounter ended in a draw, foreshadowing many of their bouts. McVea was bigger, tipping the scales at over two hundred pounds, but Langford was in his mid-twenties and still growing. He had surpassed the official heavyweight range of 175 pounds. Fleischer suggested he could walk around at "196 pounds, in trained condition, every inch of him hard flesh," even though he never hit the five-foot-eight mark. They were both terrific physical specimens, as well as talented boxers, which made their engagements highly entertaining to watch. Langford's performances in England and his tilt with McVea in France attracted a mix of high and low society, which engendered a lot of foreign and domestic press. Though some came to believe Johnson would never defend his title against another Black heavyweight, and John L. Sullivan had sharply changed his tune about Johnson, noting that it would take someone much bigger than Langford to cut him down, rumors swirled that the champ might change his mind.[15]

A dearth of White hopes limited Johnson's earning potential, so Black hopefuls like McVea and Langford stayed ready for their chance. Hugh D. "Huge Deal" McIntosh, the same promoter who had bankrolled Johnson's winning title bout against Canadian Tommy Burns, was similarly opportunistic. He felt just as strongly about the intraracial appeal of Johnson against Langford and McVea as he did about the interracial title fight between Johnson and Burns in 1908. McIntosh was reportedly willing to put up more than fifty thousand dollars for those matches, to be held in Australia. Langford and McVea raced "Down Under" before the end of 1911. But once again, forces outside of Langford's control disrupted his plans. In 1912, Johnson was arrested under spurious charges of violating the Mann Act, which prohibited transporting women across state lines for immoral purposes, and he subsequently went into an exile that inhibited his ability to defend the title. Without a clear next step, Langford stayed in Australia, fighting for money that it turned out he and Woodman were losing faster than they could earn by betting on anything with odds on it—and usually guessing wrong. But staying out of the sporting world's gaze, fighting only rematches with old foes or non-events with no-names, also made longer odds on their championship aspirations.[16]

It took two years and at least ten fights before Langford and Woodman were able to leave Australia. When they returned to the United States, there was no longer any doubt that Langford was a heavyweight. Listed in record books at 175, he more often weighed in at 190 pounds and had no intention of fighting down any time soon. He maintained the Colored Heavyweight Championship in the United States, and the International Boxing Union headquartered in Paris announced that Johnson had vacated the World Championship by failing to meet qualified challengers like Langford, so when Langford won a narrow decision against Joe Jeanette in Paris, the French authorities proclaimed him their World Champion. But there were no crowds watching Langford's versions of the title—British, French, "Colored," or otherwise. In 1915, the same year Johnson lost his World Heavyweight Championship to Jess Willard in Cuba, Langford had another close decision with Jeanette, but he came out on the wrong end and lost his Colored Heavyweight Championship; the French and British had already "stripped" him of their titles, officially for not defending against their contenders, but more likely because he was not fighting in their countries. For the first time, Woodman suggested to the press that Langford might be ready to hang up his gloves and plow his career earnings into a farm he'd purchased with Martha near Milford, Massachusetts. The fight game was a dirty business, too, but at least after a day on the farm, Langford would be able to wash the muck off.[17]

That announcement never came from Langford, however. He kept fighting, often against familiar foes, in what became known as the "Langford League," which included Joe Jeanette, Sam McVea, and Harry Wills. That group passed around the Colored Heavyweight Championship while the World Heavyweight Championship was sequestered behind a renewed "color line" as Willard and his successor, Jack Dempsey, took on exclusively White challengers—a trend that lasted two more decades. Langford lost the Colored Heavyweight Championship to Wills for the last time in 1918. After sixteen years and approximately two hundred recorded bouts, even one of Langford's loudest supporters, Nat Fleischer, acknowledged that "by degrees he began to put on fat, which slowed him up considerably," and his eyesight was also declining, which made it significantly harder to see the punches he couldn't avoid. Yet still he pressed on, using all the tricks of his years in the trade to cushion the blows, land his shots, and outlast opponents to earn a living.[18]

At their fourteenth meeting, in August 1920, Langford beat McVea one final time; before the end of the year, McVea died of pneumonia. Jeanette called it quits shortly after, in 1922, and used his nest egg to become a land-lord in Harlem. Wills was younger and did not have as many bouts under his belt, so he left the "Langford League" behind to pick up a national chase for a title shot with Dempsey, especially in the new "Mecca of Boxing" anchored by Tex Rickard's rebuilt and relocated Madison Square Garden. Langford, by contrast, headed farther south. He spent most of the 1920s fighting below the border, laying claim to one final title as the "Champion of Mexico." Over forty years old, and mostly blind, Langford won more than sixty of the nearly one hundred bouts recorded between 1920 and 1926. One newspaper suggested that the Prohibition Act helped sustain his career, since "he no longer can get his gin when he wants it," though it is doubtful he experienced any trouble purchasing alcohol in Mexico, and he probably could have found purveyors in the United States as well. In between bouts, he reportedly ran a boxing and wrestling club in Los Angeles, though it likely yielded little if any profit. By mid-decade, boxing writers described him as "feeling his man out rather than seeing him" in Mexico and noted that he "groped his way to his corner feeling along the rope." But even if he was using a fistic version of the Braille system toward the end of his career, most of Langford's wins still did not need a referee's decision. As he frequently boasted, he brought his own "referees" in the two-fisted power punches he could throw from either side and any angle—even as he declined.[19]

After seeing the other side of a short fight hundreds of times, Langford suffered a first-round stoppage in 1926, and he finally conceded defeat to age and ocular degeneration. Though he was bankrupt, divorced, and blind, his decades of great fights engendered much goodwill, and he was offered a *pro bono* surgical remedy for his eyes. Immediately he claimed his vision was restored, yet like so many of Langford's victories over the years, this success was to be short-lived. His eyesight diminished again. More friends set up a tribute in his honor to raise some funds, and they even persuaded local officials to give him a symbolic security position to earn some money, but Langford slowly faded into the background of the Great Depression and World War II in Black urban America.[20]

During the mid-1940s, a reporter "rediscovered" Langford, living in squalid conditions in New York City, and a new generation of boxing aficionados joined in another tribute and fundraiser for him. This time, they used the money raised to set up a trust from which Langford was given a fixed income and housing back in the Boston area. Although he argued to get a bigger portion of the money earlier, he never wavered from his refrain that his basic needs were met, and his memories of fame and fortune sustained him. Shortly after he passed away in 1956, the Boxing Hall of Fame announced its inaugural class, including Langford as one of the honorees in its "Old Timers" category. The honors and accolades in boxing were juxtaposed by the unmarked grave in Cambridge where he was laid to rest.[21]

The "Langford Legacy" was bolstered not only by the documented and verified results in the ring over his long and successful career, but also by the stories—true, invented, apocryphal, or a mix of all three—that traveled with him. Multiple writers cited more than one instance in which Langford identified a spot on the canvas before the fight, showed his opponent, and later knocked him out on that very spot. In one story, Langford extended his arm at the start of a round in the middle of a fight, prompting the other fighter to respond, "This isn't the last round," to which Langford allegedly replied, "It is for you!" before ending the fight promptly. The story was told repeatedly with only the name of the opponent changing regularly.

Another often-repeated narrative of Langford exercising complete control over the outcome of a fight suggested that, during a particularly cold snap in a northern location, someone told Langford there was an early train coming through, and Sam insisted they book it. Then he tore out after the opening bell, KO'd the challenger quickly, and headed straight for the station. Perhaps the most likely, and telling, story of Langford's general wit and boxing expertise has been told from the perspective of a young up-and-comer asking why Langford kept going to the body so much, or by a veteran who threw a wild haymaker only to have Langford slip it and deliver a punch straight to his posterior. Asked, in less polite terms, why he would do that, Langford was said to have replied. "Because the head has eyes." He was always thinking, maneuvering, and striking, not only in the ring, but as an aspiring professional determined to overcome obstacles—height, weight, social class, and skin tone—to emerge victorious and become a champion.

Sam Langford fought his way out of rural poverty and up into the heaviest division in prizefighting, if not the highest echelon of professional sports, in the early twentieth century. His success was due to more than just athleticism or skill; he understood the context of the fight game in this era, especially for a Black boxer. Langford demonstrated great prowess, not only in winning, but in knowing how to win—even if it meant holding back, carrying opponents, or staying "under wraps" until he was free to let loose. The "Boston

Bonecrusher" plotted a trajectory to capture the most prestigious title in the entire sporting world at that time, despite possessing too much melanin in his skin cells and not enough weight on the scales. That he was never able to capture the World Heavyweight Championship—and the fact that he was both a great friend to many and an awful gambler, leading him to bankruptcy from the time he retired to the end of his life—are not really indicators of his abilities in the business of boxing. Langford entered the fight game with few assets, and not only built a record, but a following—a brand—that outlasted his career.[22]

NOTES

1. Clay Moyle, *Sam Langford: Boxing's Greatest Uncrowned Champion* (Seattle: Bennett and Hastings, 2008), 23; "Supermen of the Ring," *All America Sports*, in Joyce Sports Research Collection, University of Notre Dame [JSRC].

2. Moyle, 26–33; Nat Fleischer, *Black Dynamite vol. 4: "Fighting Furies": Story of the Golden Era of Jack Johnson, Sam Langford, and their Contemporaries* (New York: C.J. O'Brien, 1939), 126–28; "Tham Langford the Tar Baby" in JSRC.

3. *World's Annual Sporting Records, 1906*, in JSRC; Nat Fleischer, *Black Dynamite vol. 3: "The Three Colored Aces": George Dixon, Joe Gans, Joe Walcott, and Several Contemporaries* (New York: C.J. O'Brien, 1938), 164–65; Fleischer, *Black Dynamite vol. 4*, 129; Moyle, 44.

4. *Lowell Sun*, September 6, 1904; Fleischer, *Black Dynamite, vol. 3*, 257–58; Lumley quoted in Moyle, 52.

5. Moyle, 54.

6. Fleischer, *Black Dynamite, vol. 4*, 137; Moyle, 57–59.

7. Moyle, 63–70; Fleischer, *Black Dynamite, vol. 4*, 58.

8. Fleisher, *Black Dynamite, vol. 4*, 55–56; and Fleischer, "The Langford Legend," *Ring*, April 1956, 38–39.

9. Moyle, 76–82; *Black Dynamite, vol. 4*, 145–46; "The Life and Battles of Sam Langford," *Health and Strength* (London), 1909; *Boston Globe*, March 6, 1907.

10. Moyle, 88.

11. *Black Dynamite, vol. 4*, 154; Moyle, 92–93.

12. "The Life and Battles of Sam Langford."

13. Moyle, 106–08.

14. Moyle, 115 and 139; Fleischer, "Sam Langford, One of Ring's Marvels," *Ring*, August 1923, 38; Frank Coultry, "Shadows of the Past—Sam Langford," *Ring*, November 1923, 11.

15. Fleischer, *Black Dynamite, vol. 4*, 160–61; "English Lady Sees Fight; Is Enthusiast" and "M'Vey and Sam Langford Draw," both in JSRC.

16. Moyle, 210, 251–52, and 261–62; "Sam Langford's Plight," *Ring*, June 1924, 22.

17. *T.S. Andrews' Worlds Sporting Annual Record Book, 1912*, in JSRC; Moyle, 295–99.

18. H.M. Beany Walker, "Come Out Fighting Was Langford's Idea," *Los Angeles Examiner*, December 18, 1936; Fleischer, *Black Dynamite, vol. 4*, 169.

19. "Prohibition Is a Good Thing for Langford"; "Says Bob Edgren"; "Sam Langford Turns from Fistic to Wrestling Game"; and "Sam Langford, Almost Blind, Fight Winner"—all in JSRC.

20. "Sam Langford Can Now See After Treatment to Eye"; "The Ups and Downs of Sam Langford"—both in JSRC.

21. "Langford, Conqueror of Champions, Dies"; "Langford Grave Unmarked Site"—both in JSRC; Daniel M. Daniel, "Hall of Fame Dedicated," *Ring*, January 1956, 26–27.

22. These stories are told and retold in a variety of sources, but an unpublished manuscript by Nat Fleischer—"Sam Langford's Humor," in JSRC—collects many of them, and the repetition of some is identified clearly in Moyle, 18 and 123.

BIBLIOGRAPHY

Coultry, Frank. "Shadows of the Past—Sam Langford," *Ring*, November 1923.

Daniel, Daniel M. "Hall of Fame Dedicated," *Ring*, January 1956.

Fleischer Nat. *Black Dynamite Volume 3: "The Three Colored Aces": George Dixon, Joe Gans, Joe Walcott, and Several Contemporaries.* New York: C.J. O'Brien, 1938.

Fleischer, Nat. "Sam Langford, One of Ring's Marvels," *Ring*, August 1923.

Fleischer, Nat. *Black Dynamite Volume 4: "Fighting Furies": Story of the Golden Era of Jack Johnson, Sam Langford, and their Contemporaries.* New York: C.J. O'Brien, 1939.

Lowell Sun, September 6, 1904.

Moyle, Clay. *Sam Langford: Boxing's Greatest Uncrowned Champion.* Seattle: Bennett and Hastings, 2008.

"Sam Langford's Plight," *Ring*, June 1924.

"Supermen of the Ring," *All America Sports*, in Joyce Sports Research Collection, University of Notre Dame.

"The Langford Legend," *Ring*, April 1956.

"The Life and Battles of Sam Langford," *Health and Strength* (London), 1909.

Walker, H.M. Beany. "Come Out Fighting Was Langford's Idea," *Los Angeles Examiner*, December 18, 1936.

Chapter 5

Marshall "Major" Taylor

The Worcester Whirlwind

Lorenz J. Finison and Lynne Tolman

In the fall of 1895, teenaged Black cyclist Marshall "Major" Taylor moved to Massachusetts from his birthplace in Indianapolis, Indiana. He went with his employer, mentor, and coach, Louis "Birdie" Munger, a White former bike racer who was establishing a new bicycle factory in Worcester, forty-seven miles west of Boston. Taylor had raced in Indianapolis, but his career suffered under Jim Crow segregation. He and Munger figured that his best bet for a future in cycling lay elsewhere. From 1895 to 1900, Taylor developed his racing talents in North America, facing off against White racers and occasionally teaming up with them. He also became a dominant international racer, traveling to Europe, Australia, and New Zealand through the next decade for professional challenges and opportunities. Retiring in 1910, he returned home to declining fortunes before moving to Chicago, where he died in 1932. Major Taylor's experiences during his early Massachusetts-based career helped shape a legacy that is evolving to this day. While Munger's hopes for a welcoming racial climate were realized to some extent in the Northeast, Taylor continued to encounter closed doors and open hostility, but he triumphed many times over these obstacles.

Born in 1878, Taylor first raced at age eleven in 1890, coming under the mentorship of Munger, who saw in Taylor the potential of a great champion and vowed to help him reach the pinnacle of the sport. Black clubs and Black races in the Midwest gave Taylor his early opportunities to shine.[1] But it soon became apparent that racial segregation in cycling would put an unbreakable ceiling on his progress.

Several factors likely attracted Munger and Taylor to Massachusetts, especially its liberalism and its strong manufacturing traditions. Massachusetts

Figure 5.1. Marshall Walter "Major" Taylor held several world and national bicycle championships earning him the reputation as "The Fastest Bicycle Rider in the World." Taylor confronted and overcame racial discrimination to dominate the cycling world at the turn of the twentieth century. His achievements brought him a level of fame and financial success experienced by few African American athletes during his era. Image provided by Harvard University.

had a long history of abolitionism, going back well before the Civil War, exemplified by the writings and orations of such figures as William Lloyd Garrison and Frederick Douglass. The state supported the all-Black (but led by White officers) Massachusetts 54th and 55th regiments in the Civil War.

In 1875, at the urging of Massachusetts senator Charles Sumner, Congress passed a Civil Rights Act that banned racial discrimination in public accommodations. But in 1883, the Supreme Court struck down that law, finding that discrimination by individuals or private businesses was constitutional. By the end of that year, Massachusetts passed a state-level law banning discrimination in public accommodations, and other New England states followed suit. But they did not have the last word on segregation. In 1890, Louisiana passed a law requiring "equal but separate" railway coaches for Black and White passengers. A light-skinned, multiracial man named Homer Plessy challenged that law in 1892. His case, *Plessy v. Ferguson*, went all the way to the Supreme Court, which upheld the Separate Car Act in 1896.[2] In the ensuing years, segregation became more firmly entrenched, especially in the Midwest and South.

Thirty years after the Civil War and closer to the cycling world, a Southern faction of the League of American Wheelmen (LAW), led by Louisville, Kentucky, member William W. Watts, pushed a "Whites-only" membership rule for the League's recreational side. The amendment passed in 1894, though it was opposed by many Northerners, including the Massachusetts delegation. Shortly thereafter, Riverside Cycle Club member and *Boston Globe* reporter Robert Teamoh, the sole Black member of the Massachusetts Legislature, persuaded his fellow legislators to pass a resolution condemning the League's color bar.

The Riverside club protested the LAW's action, too. And its members publicly demanded that their fellow White cyclists take up their cause, which they did, at least briefly. In July 1895, Kittie Knox, a young biracial cyclist, won a cycling costume contest near Boston, then went on to the LAW national meet in Asbury Park, New Jersey. There she was met by acts of both exclusion (her credentials were challenged, and she was kept out of hotels and restaurants) and inclusion (Massachusetts cycling officials in attendance defended her right to participate). Knox's experience at Asbury Park was reported in newspapers across the country and was debated in the cycling press. The story no doubt was known to Munger and Taylor. Less well-publicized was the exclusion of Kittie Knox and a group of Black men from a local century ride promoted by a Boston cycling club in August 1895—which led to an unsuccessful lawsuit by those men against the club under Massachusetts' own public accommodations law.[3]

Worcester looked to be an ideal location for Munger to establish a bicycle factory. It had easy access to two great centers of bicycling: New York had the largest number of cyclists in the country, and Boston had the highest density of cyclists. Massachusetts also had a long history of metal machining, with a talented labor pool gaining experience in early cycle production in Boston (Pope Manufacturing Co., which also had operations in Hartford, Connecticut), Waltham (Charles Metz's Waltham Manufacturing Company, maker of Orient cycles), Springfield (Hendee Manufacturing Co.), and Fitchburg (Iver Johnson Arms and Cycle Works). Worcester itself was a center for related industries that could supply components such as steel sprockets and leather saddles.

Worcester also had a small but energetic Black population of about one thousand, out of about one hundred thousand residents in all, a critical mass that could support an active Black bicycling club. The Albion Cycle

Club formed in the spring of 1895, before Taylor's arrival that fall. The club focused on road racing and wholeheartedly welcomed Taylor, given news of his cycling prowess in Indianapolis. Taylor went from winning a five-mile fairgrounds match race presented by the all-Black See-Saw Club of Indianapolis on Labor Day[4] to logging the fastest time in the Albion Club's ten-mile race in Worcester in late October.[5] Taylor started from the scratch position (i.e., he was given no time or distance advantage) in the handicapped race, and he succeeded in passing all but two of the sixteen riders. Taylor was more than two minutes faster than the first rider to cross the finish line, who had a five-minute head start.[6]

Decades later, Taylor recalled Worcester offering him a "cordial welcome," especially because he was allowed to join the YMCA. As a child, he had been stung when the YMCA in Indianapolis drew the color line. In Worcester, the YMCA director was willing to work with Taylor, developing strength workouts that became a key component of his athletic training.

Taylor found lodging in Worcester with an older friend from the Albion Club, a carpet layer and upholstery installer named Ben Walker. Walker and his wife and children lived on Parker Street in a tiny, mostly Black neighborhood consisting of about twenty households of renters near Beaver Brook Park.[7] By 1900, the Walkers had moved around the corner to Mason Court, and the census showed most of their neighbors were born in Massachusetts or neighboring states, as were their parents. Unlike those in Indianapolis, few were from the South. One neighbor family consisted of two White grandparents, a White daughter, and two Black grandchildren. Taylor likely had daily interaction with Black, White, and mixed-race residents.

Taylor was well-known enough that in January 1896, his presence was noted in press coverage of a cycling trade show at Madison Square Garden in New York City, along with fellow Munger employee Oscar Hedstrom (who would later team with George Hendee to establish a pioneering bicycle and motorcycle company). Both Taylor and Hedstrom were listed at the trade show as being from Middletown, Connecticut, where Munger had another bicycle factory.[8]

On Patriots' Day in April 1896, Taylor and Hedstrom traveled to the Dedham Cycle Club's annual ten-mile handicapped race from Dedham to Needham, Massachusetts. Taylor got a handicap of a minute and a half, and Hedstrom got fifty seconds. Two other riders who would figure in Taylor's future, Nat Butler and Burns Pierce, were in the scratch position. Another racer, Nat's brother Frank, had a handicap of 1:50.[9] Taylor finished seventeenth in the race, of over 150 riders entered, but had the sixth-fastest time.

On May 9 that year, local teams competed in a ten-mile road race in Worcester. The Albions pinned great hopes on Taylor, "colored champion road-rider-of-the-world," but he came in sixth of twenty-six riders, behind

Worcester-area riders from clubs such as Vernon, Worcester, Viking, and Boyd (named after Munger's business partner).[10] The race was a model of integration in the riders, the race officials, and the spectators. It appeared Munger and Taylor had made a good choice.

On May 16, the Albions staged their second ten-mile road race, and the Worcester press dubbed Taylor the "famous local colored flyer." Riding from scratch position, Taylor won in twenty-nine minutes, seven seconds, shaving eight seconds off his previous time.[11] He won a silver cup and a gold watch, the non-cash prizes identifying him as an amateur in an amateur race.

As Taylor's reputation spread, he ventured farther from his base in Massachusetts. He was one of four scratch riders at Lindenhurst, New Jersey, on May 23, winning the time prize against a field of thirty-five that included some of the New York area's best riders.[12]

The following week, Taylor returned to New Jersey for the famed Irvington-Milburn race, a twenty-five-miler.[13] Listed again as a Middletown rider, he finished twenty-third with a handicap of 1:40, but was well up on time: 1:10:07, tied for fifth place. Of the 153 who started the race, only seventy-four finished. The rest dropped out, many of them injured. Half a mile from the finish, someone threw a bucket of ice water in Taylor's face. Taylor shrugged it off, calling it an "accident," but given how often White riders later objected to Taylor's participation in races, it may well have been an intentional move to keep him from winning.[14]

On December 1, 1895, Taylor showed his climbing strength as he summited a legendary Middletown hill at Crystal Lake Park, known as a "terror to cyclists." He went up the hill on a Munger bicycle with a sixty-eight-inch gear.[15] The following June, he did it again.[16] Taylor was well-trained for such an event, having summitted George Street, a steep, narrow street in downtown Worcester. He also won an open one-mile race in New Haven, Connecticut.[17] And he placed second in a July 4th half-mile race in Meriden, Connecticut.[18] With these successes, he returned briefly to the Midwest.

Back in Indianapolis, in July 1896, Taylor set his first world record, unofficially, and shattered the record for the new Capital City Track. But the feat offended White sensibilities and he was banned from the track. It was clear that his opportunities lay in the East. He returned in November to New York City to prepare for more racing, now sponsored by the Stearns bicycle company.[19]

On Thanksgiving Day, Taylor competed in Jamaica, Long Island, New York, in a twenty-five-mile handicapped road race. Taylor's record was strong enough that he was given scratch position. The race was spoiled a bit by fans who "almost mobbed" a couple of farmers who attempted to drive their farm vehicles over the road in the face of the racing cyclists, as well as by a "strike" by a few riders angry at the "poor prize list." Taylor was listed with the Calumet Cycle Club of New York City.[20] The cycling press reported that he and the other two scratch men, F.A. Richt and F.A. Munz, "worked poorly together and were never in it." Still, Taylor had the second-fastest time, Munz the third, and Richt the fourth.[21]

It was time for Taylor to turn professional. While he had been unable to join the League of American Wheelmen because of the color bar, on his eighteenth birthday, November 26, 1896, he registered as a professional with the LAW Racing Board. Then came an opportunity: the Six-Day Race at Madison Square Garden. Safely inside and away from the brutal weather, Taylor made his professional debut in a curtain-raiser the night before the big endurance race began. He won the half-mile exhibition race. Aided by a twenty-five-yard handicap, he beat the reigning national champion, Eddie Bald, who would become a great rival.[22] Taylor sat up a lap too soon but quickly realized his mistake and still won by twenty yards. This victory vaulted him onto the national stage. The coverage in the *Brooklyn Daily Eagle*, showing the biases of the era, introduced Taylor as "mascot of the South Brooklyn Wheelmen," the club with whom he had been training, and pointed out, in case "mascot" was not explicit enough for its readers: "He is a colored man." The newspaper story described Bald as "straining every nerve to catch the runaway African" while "the darkey held his own." The report continued: "The South Brooklyn contingent went wild over their 'dark secret from Gowanus,' as they called him."[23]

In the main event, the contestants, all White except Taylor, cycled nonstop for six days except to eat or briefly sleep. Taylor came in eighth, logging 1,732 miles. The sixth-place finisher was Burns Pierce, whom Taylor would meet many times in his career.[24]

By the close of 1896, Taylor established himself as the "colored champion" of America, and as a leading racer overall. He had ridden all the cycle racing modes: short and medium distances on tracks, medium and longer distances on the road, handicapped and match races, and the grueling six-day. He was now a professional looking for new challenges. Following the Six-Day Race, Taylor did exhibitions on stationary "home trainers" and prepared for the 1897 racing season. At a January 1897 indoor meet in Brooklyn described as a "red hot board floor affair," Taylor finished third behind Teddy Goodman and Sam Brock.[25] In Indianapolis, Taylor had road-raced, but his main strength was as a sprinter on the track, not a distance rider, and that pattern continued in his early years in the East. In the 1897 season, at Harrisburg, Pennsylvania, he set a one-mile track record in the Pennsylvania Colored Wheelmen's Association race, all the while calling out to his pacemakers to speed up.[26] Taylor solidified his commitment to track racing at Philadelphia; Portland, Maine; Providence, Rhode Island; Newark, New Jersey; Manhattan

Beach, New York; Detroit; Worcester, Springfield, Cambridge and Waltham, in Massachusetts, and he raced against the best the nation had to offer.

While his Massachusetts-based competitors accepted his right to race, they nevertheless did everything they could to defeat him. They formed combinations against him, boxed him in, blocked him into a "pocket," elbowed him, and otherwise used tactics on the borderline or crossing the line of legality. A reporter for the *Boston Post* in June 1897 wrote: "at Charles River Park he has not had the best of treatment," but "because he is an American citizen, born of colored parents, [there] is no valid reason why he should receive any different treatment at the hands of the racing men, spectators, or officials."[27] In his autobiography, Taylor reflected: "I found that the color prejudice was not confined to the South entirely, in fact it had asserted itself against me even in and around Boston. . . . A deliberate foul on me at Waltham on Memorial Day when I was pushed off the track, and another foul committed against me at the Charles River track were the beginning of my racing difficulties."

But he teamed up with White racers who had been his rivals before and whom he would compete against in the future, including Nat and Frank Butler and Burns Pierce. All three were immigrants from Nova Scotia who had Northern Irish heritage. In the economic hard times of the early 1890s, they took the boat to Boston in search of employment. They found jobs, and bike racing, and, eventually, Major Taylor. Eddie McDuffee, Taylor, and the three Canadian immigrants made up a five-man pursuit team formed for one race, Boston versus Philadelphia, in July 1897 under the lights (and with the added attractions of music and fireworks) at the Charles River Park.[28] This was one of the earliest racially integrated teams in professional sports. The Boston team won the race. Within weeks, the onetime teammates were racing against each other at Manhattan Beach on Long Island, at the Crescent Park track in Providence, and at Wilkes-Barre, Pennsylvania. Taylor's teammates were hard competitors when he raced against them, but they never questioned his right to be on the track.

On September 10, Taylor went to the Waverly, New Jersey, fairgrounds track for a national circuit race, facing off against Nat Butler and Taylor's nemesis, a Californian named Floyd McFarland. A reporter noted that all the riders worked together in pairs, except for Taylor, who had no ally. Still, Taylor maneuvered into position for the final sprint, "winning in a most sensational manner." McFarland came in third.[29] Throughout his career, Taylor avoided alliances on the track, lest his victories carry an asterisk indicating that the Black rider did not or could not win by his own ability.

Taylor's threat as a competitor angered some of the White riders, who resented his winning prestige and prize money, and this led to increasing attempts to isolate him on the track and within professional racing. After Taylor was crowded into the fence and crashed in a Worcester race on August

96   *Lorenz J. Finison and Lynne Tolman*

31, he told reporters that he had "a dread of injury every time I start in a race with the men who have been on the circuit this year. They have threatened to injure me, and I expect that before the season is finished, they will do so."[30]

On September 23, Taylor raced at a Taunton, Massachusetts, track, losing to Tom Butler. He was the younger brother of Nat and Frank, who had been his mates on the Boston pursuit team. Taylor edged out William Becker, a Minnesota rider, for second place. Angered by this, Becker came up behind Taylor, choked him, and left him unconscious. Spectators, indignant at the treatment of the local hero, threatened to attack Becker, but police intervened. After a few days, the LAW fined Becker fifty dollars, and other White riders stepped in to pay the paltry penalty. Before the punishment was meted out, Taylor was notably silent on the incident. Aware that he already had sympathy from the press, and possibly wary of giving the officials any reason to turn against him, Taylor did not explicitly mention the choking in letters home to Walker from his next racing engagement, in Cleveland, Ohio, where he won one-mile and two-mile events.[31] But thirty years later, in his autobiography, Taylor complained bitterly about the Taunton assault, offering it as another example of racism in the Boston area.[32]

The season did not end well. On a southern extension to the national circuit, pressure mounted to exclude Taylor, so he could not accrue enough points to contend for the national championship. In town after town, either promoters refused his entry, or White riders refused to race if Taylor was allowed in the competition. The southern extension itself was abandoned in Atlanta because of a yellow fever plague.[33] Eddie Bald took the top national honor on points, repeating his 1896 win.

Such incidents and rejections notwithstanding, a level of acceptance in New England and New York helped Taylor flourish as an amateur racer and during his first year as a pro, in 1897. But ultimately, he was stymied at the national level and vowed to go to France. However, his religious objection to racing on Sundays stopped him from doing so until 1901, when he was a big enough star to get a no-Sunday-racing clause in his contract.

The 1898 season did not start well for Taylor. His White competitors went to Florida to train, and Taylor's new trainer, Willis Troy, inquired about joining them in February. He was told that the White riders would object. An alternative was to go alone to Savannah, Georgia, which had a good track. But in Savannah, Taylor suffered a variety of indignities and harassment, including a written death threat, after an encounter with some local riders who did not care to ride with him—and who did not like it when he passed them on the road and left them behind. The note said: "Mr. Taylor, if you don't leave here before 48 hours, you will be sorry. We mean business. Clear out if you value your life." It was signed "White Riders," with a crude sketch of a skull-and-crossbones.[34] So, it was back to New York and cold training runs in Brooklyn, in Long Island, and on the Coney Island bike path.

The racers and their fans wanted more and more speed, and pacers became a big (and increasingly expensive) part of a racer's entourage. It started with tandems: two men, themselves good riders, staying out in front of the star on one bike with double the horsepower. They blocked the wind, allowing the star to go faster than he could alone. That soon led to triplets, quadruplets, and even quintuplets. Then, faster tandems took to the track, paced by quintuplets and septuplets. Even that was not enough, and motorized pacing machines came into use, although their reliability was not secured until well into the twentieth century. Many of Taylor's speed records were paced and then motor-paced.

A significant track race in 1898 pitted Taylor against a rival who had been his Boston pursuit teammate and exemplified promoters' use of racial identity to build an audience. Souvenir pinback buttons handed out to spectators advertised the race as "Black vs. White / Taylor vs. McDuffee," and showed headshots of the two racers. Taylor excelled at short distances, while McDuffee specialized in middle distances, like the thirty miles in question. The purse was $1,500. Thirteen thousand fans saw Taylor enter the track to the tune of "The Warmest Baby in the Bunch," written by George M. Cohan and later used in the movie *Yankee Doodle Dandy*. McDuffee rolled out to "All Coons Look Alike to Me," written by a Black performer, Ernest Hogan, a ragtime pioneer who later regretted his contribution to the racist "coon song" craze. The two racers got bouquets at the start, then shook hands and were off, Taylor behind a pacing quad and McDuffee behind a pacing quint. McDuffee won by a lap, and for various distances during the race, he set world records.

In 1898, Taylor focused on speed records, which he could do solo, rather than deal with the White racers who ganged up against him on the track and the bureaucratic maneuvers that threatened his eligibility. At the end of the year, he held seven world records, including the coveted one mile. When Taylor competed individually and relied on his own cycling ability, his performance was unmatched.

Southern organizers tried again to block him from racing in the late-fall search for warmer weather. But Albert Mott, chairman of the LAW Racing Board, told the St. Louis promoters that he would not grant them a national circuit racing date if they did not accept an entry from Taylor. Taylor entered but could not get hotel accommodations or meals, and when the Saturday race was rained out and postponed to the next day, Taylor refused to start because of his religious stance against Sunday racing. In the end, he was forced to abandon the tour for the second year in a row, losing any opportunity to get enough points for the national championship. Tom Butler was declared the national champion.

During the years 1897 through 1900, a battle played out between the LAW Racing Board, riders, and promoters who desired independence and formed their own associations. One key issue was the refusal of the LAW to sanction races where Taylor was excluded. In turn, part of their motivation to create another league was to isolate Taylor and his allies. In 1899, the LAW and the rival National Cycling Association ran separate national championship circuits. While Taylor led the LAW series in points at the end of the season, the existence of the parallel NCA championship races, which featured many of the other top riders, left him without a clear claim to the title of top rider in America. Taylor also captured the world one-mile championship in 1899 in Montreal, but he would not have an undisputed U.S. championship until 1900, after the two leagues made peace. That did not stop *The Freeman*, a Black newspaper in Indianapolis, from trumpeting Taylor's successes in 1899, in a list of his victories headlined "'Major' Taylor, the Champion." The paper claimed him as the "Indianapolis Wonder."

Fresh off his world championship in Montreal, Taylor used a straw purchaser to buy a newly built house on Hobson Avenue in an all-White neighborhood in Worcester. Worcester's reaction was ambivalent. Immediately, neighbors put up money to buy the house from Taylor for $2,000 more than the $2,850 he had paid. He refused, and the residents grew to accept their distinguished neighbor. The press seemed amused at the neighbors' reaction, and in some cases condemned their small-mindedness. Massachusetts had strong public accommodations laws, at least on paper, but these would not protect the potential purchaser of a house. Later, restrictive covenants became more explicit in keeping Black and Jewish buyers out. Taylor lived in that house for twenty-five years, first as a bachelor with his younger sister, and then with his wife and their daughter.

The house purchase in January 1900 came at the height of Taylor's American career. He raced as a celebrity in his adopted hometown that summer, riding a paced exhibition mile at the opening of Worcester's new velodrome, the Coliseum, to set the time to beat for that track: 1:37.2. He also won a half-mile race at that meet in a "hot finish."[35]

A year later, after winning the 1900 national championship but despairing of getting a fair shake in American bicycle racing, Taylor went on his first European tour, from March through June 1901. After that, most of his racing was overseas, where his Blackness was often perceived as more of a curiosity than a threat, and he was treated as an international superstar. He never again competed for the U.S. points championship. However, after racist American rivals followed him to Australia in 1904 and thwarted him at every turn, Taylor was soured on the sport and hung up his wheels for three years.

Table 5.1. Taylor's 1899 League of American Wheelmen Race Record

May 30	Two-mile handicap, $500 sweepstakes, from scratch	Boston	First
June 10	One-mile match race, versus Tom Butler	Westboro, Mass.	Lost
June 16	One-third-mile open	Boston	First
June 16	Twenty-five-mile paced race, versus Eddie McDuffee		Won
July 1	One-mile match race, versus Tom Butler		Won
July 6	One-mile championship	St. Louis	First
July 8	One-mile championship	Chicago	First
July 8	Two-mile handicap	Chicago	Third
July 12	One-mile championship	Janesville, Wis.	Second
July 12	One-mile open	Janesville, Wis.	First
July 12	Five-mile handicap, from scratch	Janesville, Wis.	First
July 26	Two-mile championship	Ottumwa, Ia.	Second
July 26	One-mile open	Ottumwa, Ia.	First
July 27	One-mile championship	Ottumwa, Ia.	First
July 29	One-mile championship	Chicago	First
Aug. 12	One-half-mile open	Montreal	Second
Aug. 12	One-mile world's championship	Montreal	First
Aug. 12	Two-mile open	Montreal	First
Aug. 16	One-third-mile championship	Boston	Second
Aug. 18	One-half-mile championship	Boston	First
Aug. 28	One-mile championship	Brockton, Mass.	First
Sept. 8	One-half-mile open	Worcester, Mass.	First
Sept. 8	Five-mile pursuit	Worcester, Mass.	First
Sept. 20	One-mile open	Taunton, Mass.	Second
Oct. 12	One-mile invitation	Peoria	First
Oct. 12	Two-mile open	Peoria	First
Oct. 12	Five-mile open	Peoria	First

Source: "'Major' Taylor, the Champion," *Indianapolis Freeman*, December 30, 1899.

In 1907, he came back from "retirement" and raced three more seasons in Europe. His first race on U.S. soil in five years was a winter training race in Boston in 1908, as he struggled to regain form for another season in Europe.

Taylor's years after his final retirement from cycling were marked by a series of automobile-related business failures, but also by two signal accomplishments: winning an old-timers' race at the Newark velodrome in 1917 and writing his 431-page autobiography, based on hundreds of news clippings saved in his voluminous scrapbooks. Copyrighted in 1928 and self-published in 1929, the book was titled *The Fastest Bicycle Rider in the World: The Story of a Colored Boy's Indomitable Courage and Success Against All Odds* and was dedicated to Munger.

In the foreword, Taylor insisted that he was not just bragging, but seeking to "perpetuate my achievements on the bicycle tracks of the world for the benefit of all youths aspiring to an athletic career, and especially boys of my own group as they strive for fame and glory in the athletic world." It was a plea for fair treatment, unlike what he had experienced. He insisted, "We ask no special favor or advantage over other groups in the great game of life; we ask only for an even break." Taylor wrote "in a spirit calculated to solicit simple justice, equal rights, and a square deal for the posterity of my down-trodden but brave people, not only in athletic games, but in every honorable game of human endeavor." It is fair to ask: How much did the world pay attention to his purposes? Initially, they would not pay much. Sales of the book were meager, and he ended up selling copies out of the back of his car wherever he could. For example, he was welcomed at a 1929 motorcycle rally in Worcester by the rally organizer, his old friend Fred "Kid" St. Onge, an ex-racer, pacer, bicycle trick rider, and vaudevillian comic on two wheels.

In 1930, separated from his wife and daughter, with his fortune depleted, Taylor moved from Worcester to Chicago, where he lived in a Black branch of the YMCA. He died in poverty in 1932. He was buried in an unmarked grave in a historically Black cemetery, seemingly forgotten except for an obituary in the Black newspaper *Chicago Defender.* Briefer versions of the obit were picked up in other newspapers. But the example of his career of struggle and success was not forgotten by everyone.

In 1948, racers from his era calling themselves the Bicycle Racing Stars of the Nineteenth Century, with money from Frank Schwinn, had Taylor reburied with a headstone and a bronze plaque with the following epitaph:

> *World's champion bicycle racer* who
> *Came up the hard way without hatred in his heart,*
> *An honest, courageous, and God-fearing,*
> *clean-living, gentlemanly athlete.*
> *A credit to his race who always gave out his* best.
> *Gone but not forgotten.*

At the ceremony, Black track-and-field athlete Ralph Metcalfe, an Olympic medalist in 1932 and 1936, talked about Taylor's place in history.

Worcester cyclists never forgot Taylor either, putting his name on bike races for decades. In 1937, the Worcester Cycle Club, headed by Walter Greenquist, an old friend of Taylor's, awarded a Major Taylor Memorial Cup to the winner of a five-mile race for the New England stars at the Sturbridge Fairgrounds.[36] After a hiatus in racing during World War II, Joe Cote, a racer since the 1930s, placed sixth in a 1948 race in Worcester and was awarded the Major Taylor trophy as the first Worcester rider to cross the finish line.[37]

A race flyer from 1965 announced the "23rd Annual 'Major' Taylor Memorial 50," a hilly fifty-mile race starting and finishing at Lake

Quinsigamond State Park.[38] In 1980 and 1981, the Worcester Whirlwind criterium was codirected by former US national cycling team member and coach Bill Humphreys and Jerry Dunn, executive director of the Worcester Crisis Center, as a fundraiser for the center.

Elsewhere, Taylor's story and American interest in the sport of cycling itself receded. Then, in the 1970s, several forces intervened. The environmental movement, celebrated by Earth Day 1970, kicked into high gear and started a resurgence in bicycling interest. That was further fueled by the 1973 oil crisis, which sent gasoline prices soaring. The decade also saw a rise in Black consciousness and in efforts to document Black contributions to American life.

Newspapers began publishing historical articles about Taylor. George Reasons, a progressive White *Los Angeles Times* columnist, included Taylor in an early 1970s series called "They Had a Dream," chronicling the contributions of Black Americans. Picked up by a wire service, the Major Taylor column ran in over one hundred newspapers across the country.[39] In 1971, Black sportswriter Wendell Smith, who got his journalistic start working for the Black newspaper *Pittsburgh Courier*, wrote a series for the *Chicago Sun-Times* titled "Black Heroes in Sports History." One column was on Major Taylor.[40] This, too, was distributed by wire service.

In 1972, the Stephen Greene Press in Brattleboro, Vermont, published an abridged version of Taylor's autobiography.[41] Robert Anderson, who had raced for the Major Taylor prize, was encouraged by Cote to write an introduction to reacquaint readers with bicycle racing terms.[42] At least one nationally distributed Black newspaper, the *Baltimore Afro-American*, published a book review.[43] But readers wanted a bicycle racing how-to, not a history book. Sales were poor, and the book did not go beyond the first printing. The top ten cyclists in the Putney (Vermont) Bicycle Club's Tour of the Valley bicycle races in May 1972 received copies as a prize. So, by 1972, Major Taylor was becoming known again—but slowly.

In the late 1960s, Black Los Angeles cyclists gathered to discuss Taylor's autobiography and legacy, and to ride and race. In 1970, they honored both Taylor and their ideal of fast riding by naming their club Major Motion. The club affiliated with the United States Cycling Federation in 1972.[44] It was the first contemporary club known to be inspired by Taylor. Major Motion specifically mentioned the importance of bringing Black youth into the sport and the clean-living lifestyle Taylor exemplified. The club's constitution stated a commitment to "promote bicycling for recreation, health, transportation, and sport."[45] In a program overview, likely from the early 1980s, the group described themselves as a "group of young men from the Los Angeles inner city" who "saw that there was a drastic lack of knowledge in the inner city about the advantages of cycling." Goals included coaching youth, bike safety programs in schools, a bike path task force, scholarships for collegiate cyclists, cycle touring, clinics, coaching for competition, developing neighborhood cycling clubs to increase awareness, participation in national and international cycling events, a motocross program, and cycling film production.[46] These objectives were built on the aspirations that Major Taylor had spelled out in the foreword to his autobiography.

In 1978, cyclists in Columbus, Ohio, established the Major Taylor Cycling Club—the first to explicitly use the champion's name. Like Major Motion, the Columbus club emphasized physical fitness, and even included the position of nutritionist in its charter. An early member recalls that they admonished one another to practice healthy lifestyles. The club credo added to its Ten Health Commandments: "Thou shalt uphold the Major Taylor club name in the true spirit of the 'Major' so that bicycling will be recognized and enjoyed as a miracle of transportation for health and the well-being of future generations."[47] Since then, dozens of Major Taylor cycling clubs have sprouted up across the country, and a few have been established overseas. Many of the clubs consist predominantly of people of color, but in the spirit of inclusion that Major Taylor embodied, none are exclusively Black.

In 1982, the Major Taylor Velodrome opened in Indianapolis. Also in the 1980s, tennis great Arthur Ashe included Taylor in his three-volume compendium of Black athletes, *Hard Road to Glory.* The occasional newspaper or magazine story revived Taylor's name, and in 1988, a Major Taylor biography by Andrew Ritchie told the fuller story. Since then, at least four other full-length biographies have been published, as well as children's books. A two-part television miniseries, *Tracks of Glory*, was first broadcast in 1992.[48]

In Worcester, as the centennial of Major Taylor's world championship approached, the nonprofit Major Taylor Association was formed in 1998 with the goal of erecting a permanent memorial in the city where Taylor made his home. The Major Taylor statue outside the Worcester Public Library was dedicated in 2008, with three-time Tour de France winner Greg LeMond as keynote speaker. Major Taylor's grandson, great-grandchildren, and great-great-grandchildren attended.

The Major Taylor Association continues as an educational resource. Its signature fundraiser since 2002 is the George Street Bike Challenge for Major Taylor, an uphill time trial, retracing Taylor's ascents. Also in Worcester, a permanent exhibit called the Major Taylor Museum was opened in 2021 in a former courthouse redeveloped into an apartment building. The Friends of the Bicycling History Collections at the University of Massachusetts—Boston have established a special interest group to collect materials about Major Taylor's legacy.

Bike shops and museums have taken interest in displaying bicycles that Taylor rode or might have used. One of Taylor's racing bikes, a

1903 single-speed Peugeot with a steel frame and wooden rims, came into the hands of Joe Cote, who donated it to the U.S. Bicycling Hall of Fame in Davis, California.

Tributes have multiplied. Murals and sculptures depicting the 1899 world champion have been installed in several cities, including Indianapolis; Denver; Chicago; Oakland, California; and Richmond, Virginia. Taylor also has been memorialized in music: "Never on Sunday" in 2004 by blues musician Otis Taylor, no relation, and "The Cyclist" in 2017 by jazz saxophonist Bobby Watson, as well as advertising: Hennessy cognac's "Never stop. Never settle" commercial in 2018 was an ironic tribute given that Major Taylor was a teetotaler.

Beyond the tributes, which serve to introduce Major Taylor's name and image outside the cycling world, are invocations of Taylor's example that are more specifically geared to demonstrate or achieve the values of belonging, striving, diversity, and fairness. At the statue dedication in Worcester, Olympic hurdler Edwin Moses, honorary national chairman of the Major Taylor Association, said Taylor's name belongs in the pantheon of athletes who have broken racial barriers, such as Arthur Ashe, Tommie Smith, Muhammad Ali, Hank Aaron, Jack Johnson, Jesse Owens, Fritz Pollard, Kenny Washington, and Jackie Robinson.

Who else followed Major Taylor through the doors that he helped open? In bike racing, competitors of color remain a small minority. Ned Chandler in the 1910s and '20s was known as "the second Major Taylor." Black sprinters Herb Francis and Hall-of-Famer Oliver "Butch" Martin joined Unione Sportiva Italiana in New York City, raced around Central Park, and made the US Olympic team: Francis in 1960 and Martin in 1964 and 1968.[48] Nelson Vails, a silver medalist in track cycling at the 1984 Olympics in Los Angeles, was the first African American cyclist since Major Taylor to triumph on the world stage. Track cyclist Giddeon Massie was the most recent Black cyclist from the United States to compete in the Olympics, in 2004 and 2008.

At the national level, Black riders who have emerged from the pack include Rahsaan Bahati, US pro men's national criterium champion in 2008, and Justin Williams, eleven-time US national champion in track and road cycling since 2006. Bahati was a mentor to Williams, who in turn runs a team called L39ion of Los Angeles (the creative spelling of *Legion* incorporates Williams's family history in the 39th Street neighborhood of South LA), which mentors young African American and Hispanic riders with the explicit goal of increasing diversity and inclusion in cycling. "I started off my career on a Major Taylor–affiliated cycling club [Major Motion]," Williams said at the dedication of a Major Taylor mural in Indianapolis in 2021. "He was my standard; I wore his silhouette every time I went to the line."[49]

Collegiate bike racing is part of the pipeline, too. Indiana University had an all-Black squad named Team Major Taylor for a few years in its vaunted Little 500 race, the competition made famous by the movie *Breaking Away*. In 2021, St. Augustine University in Raleigh, North Carolina, became the first historically Black college or university to form a cycling team, and the riders pay homage to Taylor with a quotation from his autobiography on their jerseys: "In a word, I was a pioneer and therefore had to blaze my own trail."

Taylor's legacy is accelerating in three areas outside of racing: recreational cycling, youth development, and bike advocacy. A growing number of Major Taylor cycling clubs are leaders, by example, in the push for diversity, equity, and inclusion as well as in biking. To help diversify high-profile recreational events, the Major Taylor Cycling Club of Kansas City negotiated for spots in the Unbound Gravel ride, and an alliance of Major Taylor clubs entered athletes in several triathlons in 2020 and 2021 under an Ironman Foundation initiative called Race for Change. Major Taylor is also the inspiration and namesake for youth programs—in Philadelphia; Seattle; Reno, Nevada; and Macon, Georgia, to name a few—that use bike repair classes and bike riding itself to help bring out kids' character strengths. Addressing racial disparities in health is an explicit goal of several programs that use Major Taylor's name and story to motivate people to bike for physical fitness and mental health benefits.

With his career shaped by both obstacles and victories during the thirty-five years he lived in Massachusetts, Taylor stood up for equal rights, equal opportunity, and respect, making gains for himself and future generations. The 1896 Telegram race in Worcester, with the Albion Club's Black members accepted as both racers and race marshals, was an example of Black people securing legitimacy in cycling. Major Taylor's making the cut for the 1897 Boston versus Philadelphia pursuit race was an example of earning access. When Taylor was threatened and injured by opponents' dirty tactics in race after race in 1897, the *Boston Post* recognized his right to dignity, urging "prompt action on the part of the Racing Board."[50]

A century ago, Taylor had his eyes on the prize of equity, of leveling the playing field. Taylor called it "a square deal," a common slogan in the late nineteenth century and a favorite phrase of Teddy Roosevelt's, who said: "When I say that I am for the square deal, I mean not merely that I stand for fair play under the present rules of the game, but that I stand for having those rules changed so as to work for a more substantial equality of opportunity and of reward for equally good service."[51] Roosevelt titled his 1904 book *A Square Deal for Every Man*. He was known to admire Taylor as an athlete, and Taylor displayed portraits of Roosevelt and Booker T. Washington in his home. Taylor used the term *square deal* nineteen times in his autobiography, particularly in the rhyming verses that precede each chapter and aptly summarize the equality he envisioned.

NOTES

1. Marshall W. "Major" Taylor, *The Fastest Bicycle Rider in the World: The Story of a Colored Boy's Indomitable Courage and Success Against All Odds* (Worcester: Wormley Publishing Company, 1928).

2. Steve Luxenberg, *Separate* (New York: W.W. Norton, 2019).

3. Lorenz J. Finison, *Boston's Cycling Craze, 1880–1900: A Story of Race, Sport, and Society* (Amherst and Boston: University of Massachusetts Press, 2014).

4. "Taylor's Great Race," *Freeman* (Indianapolis), September 7, 1895.

5. "Sixteen Men in a Hurry," *Worcester Sunday Telegram*, October 20, 1895.

6. "Couldn't Break It," *Worcester Daily Spy*, October 20, 1895.

7. U.S. Census, 1900, Worcester City, Ward 7, District 1773.

8. "Crowds at the Garden," *New York Tribune*, January 22, 1896.

9. Dedham Cycle Club race program, Patriots' Day 1896, Original at Dedham Historical Society.

10. "Casey the Winner," *Worcester Daily Spy*, May 10, 1896.

11. "Albion's Road Race," *Worcester Daily Spy*, May 17, 1896.

12. "Glory for Maj. Taylor," *Worcester Daily Spy*, May 23, 1896.

13. "The Cyclers' Derby," *Jersey City News*, May 29, 1896; "Cyclists Bite the Dust," *New York Daily Tribune*, May 31, 1896; "Memorial Day Races," *Referee and Cycle Trade Journal* (volume 17, number 54), June 4, 1896.

14. Andrew Ritchie, *Major Taylor: The Extraordinary Career of a Champion Bicycle Rider* (Baltimore, MD: The Johns Hopkins University Press, 1996), 90. Original edition (San Francisco, CA: Bicycle Books, 1988).

15. "Middletown," *Hartford Courant*, June 9, 1896.

16. "An Impossible Feat," *Referee and Cycle Trade Journal* (volume 16, number 7), December 12, 1895.

17. "Track Record Lowered," *Boston Herald*, June 21, 1896.

18. "Bald's Record Still Stands," *Referee and Cycle Trade Journal* (volume 17, number 10), July 9, 1896, 70; "Returned to the Fold," *Wheel and Cycle Trade Journal* (volume 17, number 21), July 10, 1896, 68.

19. "City Happenings," *Freeman*, November 21, 1896.

20. "Jamaica Long Road Race," *New York Tribune*, November 27, 1896.

21. "The Tatham Road Race," *Referee* (volume 18, number 5), December 3, 1896.

22. "Weinig's Good Race," *Buffalo Sunday Morning News*, December 6, 1896.

23. "Henshaw Wins a Handicap," *Brooklyn Daily Eagle*, December 6, 1896.

24. "He Broke All Records," *Salt Lake Herald*, December 13, 1896.

25. "Eaton Fell and Goodman Won," *Referee and Cycle Trade Journal* (volume 18, number 12), January 21, 1897, 54.

26. *Harrisburg Telegraph*, July 28, 1897.

27. "Among the Wheelmen," *Boston Post*, June 6, 1897.

28. "The Great Inter-City Team Race," *Boston Herald*, July 18, 1897.

29. "Wins in Spite of All," *Boston Globe*, September 11, 1897.

30. "Taylor Says It Is So," *Worcester Telegram*, September 20, 1897.

31. Lynne Tolman and Andrew Ritchie, "Marshall 'Major' Taylor—Letters from 1897," *Boneshaker* (volume 22, number 219), Summer 2022, 4–9.

32. Taylor, *The Fastest Bicycle Rider in the World.*

33. Ritchie, *Major Taylor*, 81.

34. Ritchie, *Major Taylor*, 90.

35. *Worcester Telegram*, August 18, 1900.

36. "Expect Many Noted Names in Entries," *Evening Gazette* (Worcester, MA), June 18, 1937. Greenquist entered the half-mile old-timers race.

37. "Providence Cyclist Wins 25-Mile Race," *Worcester Telegram*, August 2, 1948.

38. Worcester Cycle Club, race flyer for September 19, 1965, Bob and Becky Anderson Collection, Bicycling History Collections, University of Massachusetts-Boston Archives.

39. George Reasons's wife, Mona, did much of the research for the "They Had a Dream" columns, and George did the writing, according to their daughter, Rebecca Edwards. Personal communication with Lorenz Finison, August 7, 2022.

40. Wendell Smith, "Major Taylor: Record Breaker on a Bike," *Evening Star*, Washington, DC, August 29, 1971.

41. The editor, Wesley S. Griswold, summarized chapters 13, 21–26, 30–32, 34, 43, 50–56, 61–63, 66–69, and 71–89.

42. Stephanie Greene, personal communication with Lorenz Finison, August 9, 2022; Bevan Quinn, personal communication with Finison, August 9, 2022; Robert Anderson, personal communication with Finison, August 15, 2022.

43. Joseph H. Jenkins, "World's Fastest Bike Rider," *Baltimore Afro-American*, June 6, 1972.

44. Chuck Johnson inspired them at the start, and the first Major Motion president was Charles Erwin, followed by James Choice. Mike Bunton, personal communication, August 13, 2022; Mfuniso Usafi, personal communication with Lorenz Finison, August 23, 2022.

45. Constitution and By-Laws of Major Motion Cycling Club, n.d., Bicycling History Collections, University of Massachusetts-Boston Archives.

46. Program Overview, n.d., Bicycling History Collections, University of Massachusetts-Boston Archives.

47. "The Major Taylor Club Credo," adapted from the "Ten Health Commandments" by Paul and Patricia Bragg. https://michelleberrybliss.com/2013/05/08/10-health-commandments-by-paul-and-patricia-bragg/.

48. Oliver Martin was the biracial son of a member of the all-Black 92nd Infantry Division (Buffalo Soldiers) fighting in Italy during World War II, where he met and married an Italian woman. Oliver Martin, personal communication with Lorenz Finison, September 5, 2022; Peter Nye, *Hears of Lions: The History of American Bicycle Racing* (New York: W.W. Norton, 1988).

49. "A Mural of Legendary Cyclist Major Taylor Is Unveiled in Indianapolis," *Bicycling*, accessed August 17, 2022, www.bicycling.com/news/a37545933/major -taylor-mural-indianapolis.

50. Taylor, *The Fastest Bicycle Rider in the World*, 20, quoting a *Boston Post* clipping (no date given) from his scrapbooks.

51. Richard D. Heffner and Alexander B. Heffner, *A Documentary History of the United States, Updated & Expanded*, 10th edition (New York: Penguin, 2013), 146. Roosevelt championed Black troops in the Spanish-American War: In a 1903 speech in Springfield, Illinois, he stated, "It was my own good fortune at Santiago to serve beside colored troops. A man who is good enough to shed his blood for his country is good enough to be given a square deal afterwards." "Last Speeches on President's List," *New York Times*, August 22, 1899.

BIBLIOGRAPHY

"A Mural of Legendary Cyclist Major Taylor Is Unveiled in Indianapolis," *Bicycling*, accessed August 17, 2022, www.bicycling.com/news/a37545933/major-taylor -mural-indianapolis.

"Albion's Road Race," *Worcester Daily Spy*, May 17, 1896.

"Among the Wheelmen," *Boston Post*, June 6, 1897.

"An Impossible Feat," *Referee and Cycle Trade Journal* (Volume 16, Number 7), December 12, 1895.

"Bald's Record Still Stands," *Referee and Cycle Trade Journal* (Volume 17, Number 10), July 9, 1896.

"Casey the Winner," *Worcester Daily Spy*, May 10, 1896.

"City Happenings," *Freeman*, November 21, 1896.

"Couldn't Break It," *Worcester Daily Spy*, October 20, 1895.

"Crowds at the Garden," *New York Tribune*, January 22, 1896.

"Cyclists Bite the Dust," *New York Daily Tribune*, May 31, 1896.

"Eaton Fell and Goodman Won," *Referee and Cycle Trade Journal* (Volume 18, Number 12), January 21, 1897.

"Expect Many Noted Names in Entries," *Evening Gazette* (Worcester, MA), June 18, 1937.

Finison, Lorenz. *Boston's Cycling Craze, 1880–1900: A Story of Race, Sport, and Society.* Amherst: University of Massachusetts Press, 2014.

"Glory for Maj. Taylor," *Worcester Daily Spy*, May 23, 1896.

"He Broke All Records," *Salt Lake Herald*, December 13, 1896.

Heffner, Richard, and Alexander Heffner. *A Documentary History of the United States, Updated & Expanded*, 10th Edition. New York: Penguin, 2013.

"Henshaw Wins a Handicap," *Brooklyn Daily Eagle*, December 6, 1896.

"Jamaica Long Road Race," *New York Tribune*, November 27, 1896.

Jenkens, Joseph. "World's Fastest Bike Rider," *Baltimore Afro-American*, June 6, 1972.

"Last Speeches on President's List," *New York Times*, August 22, 1899.

Luxenberg, Steve. *Separate*. New York: W.W. Norton, 2019.

"Memorial Day Races," *Referee and Cycle Trade Journal* (Volume 17, Number 54), June 4, 1896.

"Middletown," *Hartford Courant*, June 9, 1896.

Nye, Peter. *Hears of Lions: The History of American Bicycle Racing*. New York: W.W. Norton, 1988.

"Providence Cyclist Wins 25-Mile Race," *Worcester Telegram*, August 2, 1948.

"Returned to the Fold," *Wheel and Cycle Trade Journal* (Volume 17 Number 21), July 10, 1896.

Ritchie, Andrew. *Major Taylor: The Extraordinary Career of a Champion Bicycle Rider.* Baltimore: The Johns Hopkins University Press, 1996.

"Sixteen Men in a Hurry," *Worcester Sunday Telegram*, October 20, 1895.

Smith, Wendell. "Major Taylor: Record Breaker on a Bike," *Evening Star*, Washington, DC, August 29, 1971.

Taylor, Marshall. *The Fastest Bicycle Rider in the World: The Story of a Colored Boy's Indomitable Courage and Success Against All Odds.* Worcester: Wormley Publishing Company, 1928.

"Taylor Says It Is So," *Worcester Telegram*, September 20, 1897.

"Taylor's Great Race," *Freeman* (Indianapolis), September 7, 1895.

"The Cyclers' Derby," *Jersey City News*, May 29, 1896.

"The Great Inter-City Team Race," *Boston Herald*, July 18, 1897.

"The Tatham Road Race," *Referee* (Volume 18, Number 5), December 3, 1896.

Tolman, Lynne, and Andrew Ritchie, "Marshall 'Major' Taylor—Letters from 1897," *Boneshaker* (Volume 22, Number 219), Summer 2022.

"Track Record Lowered," *Boston Herald*, June 21, 1896.

U.S. Census. 1900. Worcester City, Ward 7, District 1773.

"Weinig's Good Race," *Buffalo Sunday Morning News*, December 6, 1896.

"Wins in Spite of All," *Boston Globe*, September 11, 1897.

Chapter 6

Louise Mae Stokes Fraser

An Overlooked Legend

Leslie Heaphy

Although she qualified to compete in track and field at the 1932 and 1936 Olympic Games, Louise Stokes was replaced by White runners and did not race in either event. The only reason given by the American Olympic Committee for the switch was that the team needed to choose its best runners for the competition, and Stokes did not rise to the top. This choice seems odd given Stokes's preliminary heats and trials times where she had beaten several White runners chosen to compete in her place. Although she could not compete, Stokes's selection for the 1932 Olympics was historic, making her one of the first two Black women chosen for an American Olympic team. Although Stokes's name is not as easily recognized, it should be. Famed female African American track and field Olympians Wilma Rudolph, Jackie Joyner-Kersee, Florence Griffith Joiner, Alice Coachman, and Sha'Carri Richardson became household names after breaking records at the Games. In the 1930s, Stokes and her teammate Tidye Pickett dominated the track, regularly breaking records despite facing a multitude of race-related challenges. Based on her accomplishments in the sport, Stokes deserves serious mention alongside Rudolph and her notable counterparts. During a time when America and the world did not easily accept Black people, Stokes became a trailblazer who, in qualifying for the Olympics in 1932 and 1936, cleared the way for all who followed in her footsteps.

Stokes's life began humbly and her running career early. Born in Malden, Massachusetts, on October 27, 1913, Stokes was the oldest of six children. Her sister Alice died in a fire at the age of four. Her mother, Mary, was a domestic, and her father, William, was a gardener who also worked as a furnace stoker in the winter. The family struggled to make ends meet, often clothing their children in hand-me-downs received from the families for whom Mary worked. Stokes began competition running at Malden's Beebe Junior High School. She also liked playing basketball. Due to her quickness on the court, teammates encouraged her to join the Onteora Track Club, operated by local postal worker and park commissioner William H. Quaine.

Despite her initial reservations to run for Quaine, Stokes's talent flourished under his tutelage. Quaine had been a star athlete in the 1890s, excelling in football, golf, tennis, and track, who actually dissuaded Stokes from joining his team. Stokes needed convincing to show him her ability because she was shy and did not believe she had any real talent. She worried that a star like Quaine would not select her. Stokes initially struggled, and then, under his tutelage, learned how to race. She started consistently winning sprints, high jump contests, and standing broad jump competitions. Her Malden neighbors remembered seeing her often running around the city on her own and with her fellow runners. While others in the club recognized Stokes's talent, they saw her as just another member of the team.[1]

As her running career accelerated, Stokes set numerous records, winning races throughout New England and beyond. Quaines helped her learn to overcome her tendency to jump the starting gun, which then put her in contention for the victory every time she stepped onto the track. As a high school junior, Stokes set a New England record in the one-hundred-meter distance while tying the world record of eight feet, five and three-quarter inches in the standing broad jump, beating a previous record set by Katherine Mearls. Stokes logged one of her early running losses against Mearls—a loss that almost drove Stokes to stop running. Instead, she persevered. In 1930, Stokes won the 220-yard dash, finishing twenty-nine seconds ahead of Pansy Madeira of the Boston Swimming Association. At seventeen, she won the fifty-yard dash in six and one-third seconds over the highly favored Olive Hasenfus. By 1931, she was a local star. She was awarded the 1931 James Michael Curley Cup as the outstanding female track performer of the year. Mary Carew of Medford claimed the runner-up slot and found herself competing regularly against Stokes throughout their careers.[2]

From there, Stokes's success multiplied. She held the New England Amateur Athletic Union (NEAAU) and national broad jump titles in 1931, tying the world record of eight feet, five and one-half inches in December 1931 and again in April 1932. She claimed the New England one-hundred-yard title in 1931 and retained it in 1932, beating out Carew to solidify her position as the "Malden Meteor." At the Annual Boston Field Days at Norumbega Park in June 1932, Stokes triumphed in both the fifty- and one-hundred-yard dash. In both events, she beat Carew, the local favorite. Stokes's long strides and speed overcame a staggered start, and she brought home the victory. Those who saw Stokes run regularly knew they were witnessing something truly special. When she competed, the audience and attention grew. Local papers had nicknamed her the "Malden Meteor," and regional papers called her "the sensational daughter of Mercury."[3] Eventually, she began believing she could achieve her dream of competing in the Olympics.

Stokes earned her place on the 1932 American Olympic team after a fourth-place finish in the hundred-meters in Evanston, Illinois. At the Olympic trials, all the runners except the favorite, Ethel Harrington, took part in seven races, competing in over one-hundred-degree temperatures. Harrington missed the finish line in her first heat due to the extreme heat, but the Olympic committee let her run in the final. She finished first, knocking everyone else down a slot. From a field of more than three hundred runners, Stokes was one of the select few chosen to be part of the four-hundred-meter relay team. It seemed that her dream was about to come true.[4]

As members of the four-hundred-meter relay team, Stokes and her friend Tidye Pickett became the first two Black women selected to an American Olympic squad, and they faced prejudice, even from their own teammates. Consumed by a mix of excitement and concern, the two high schoolers did not realize they were making history. On a competition trip to Los Angeles, Stokes and Pickett's teammates ostracized them. Their team put them in a sleeping bunk by the service area, they were not included in a Denver Radio interview with the other runners, and they were not invited to attend the team banquet, instead left to eat in their room alone. According to some accounts, Babe Didrikson, a White woman and the biggest name on the US team, added to their mistreatment by throwing water at them one night. Even with all the difficulties they encountered, Stokes was excited about the trip since she had never traveled that far before. She promised her mother she would remember everything and tell her family all about it when she returned home. However, the discriminatory treatment she and Pickett endured continued after their arrival in Los Angeles, where both runners found themselves separated from their teammates for both housing and meals. Of the nearly two thousand athletes taking part in the games, only fifteen were people of color, and of that number, Stokes and Pickett were the only women.

The two women endured the snubs because all they wanted was to run. Unfortunately, after watching the individual events, they were both replaced on the relay team by two White runners chosen by coach George Vreeland. The only explanation Vreeland offered them was that he'd picked the runners with the best skill at the baton handoff. Stokes and Pickett had to sit and watch their team win the race and set a world record without being part of the relay. This snub was not totally unexpected, given the racial tensions in America in the 1930s. Sadly, it would not be the last time Stokes endured such an insult. In fact, her not being selected to run the event she had justly qualified for was the beginning of her erasure from the pantheon of women's track and field.[5]

Stokes came home from Los Angeles with a desire to compete in the 1936 Berlin Olympics. She decided that the Olympics would be her ticket to making something of her life. Her running career dominated her life, so consuming her time and attention that she ended up failing her senior classes and not graduating from high school.

To prepare for the 1936 Olympic Games, she entered every race she could. The Roxbury American Legion Post hosted a star-studded event in late July 1933 that attracted not only Stokes, who was there to defend her titles, but also national champions Alice Arden and Olive Hasenfus. Stokes and Hasenfus found themselves racing for the titles together in two events—the fifty- and one-hundred-meter dashes. Large crowds came out to see all the national champions compete. Stokes easily defended her fifty-meter national title and won the one-hundred-yard scratch race handily as well. The newspapers reported that Stokes was so far ahead she could have walked across the finish line. Because she was competing in multiple running events, she did not defend her 1932 national high jump title. She did compete regularly in the high jump, often against her closest rival, Helen Phillips, who always seemed to hold one of the top-three spots alongside Stokes at every meet.

While she continued to compete in the high jump and the standing broad jump, Stokes's true focus was on the sprints.[6] At the ninth Annual Women's Indoor Track and Field Championships in 1934, held in Brooklyn, New York, Stokes (the outdoor champion) finished third in the fifty-meter sprint behind Olympian teammate Stella Walsh and Canadian Olympian Mildred Fizzell. That August, Stokes took part in two major meets in Maine and Massachusetts as she worked toward a return to the Olympics. She lost for the first time in two years at Rangeley, Maine, but reclaimed her titles a week later in the fifty- and one-hundred-meters at Norumbega Park. Stokes won a hotly contested one-hundred-meter race in September 1934 at the forty-fifth Annual Associated Clans picnic. Starting from a handicap, Stokes came from behind to defeat Hasenfus by over a meter. Stokes defended her fifty-meter title in September 1935 on a day that belonged to the new phenom Helen Stephens, who set a world record in the hundred-meters. Stokes went undefeated in the fifty-meter race for two straight years before losing in August 1935. She regained her title in the fifty-meter (6.9 seconds) while also winning the high jump and broad jump. Stokes also won the twenty-five-yard race at the same Boston championship meet, while her younger sister Julia, a junior high runner, won titles in the novice twenty-five-yard dash and a Class B twenty-five-yard dash. That September, Stokes also showed her versatility when she beat Hasenfus for the New England Senior title in the two-hundred-meter race.[7]

Continuing her preparation for another run at the Olympics, Stokes found herself competing with her younger sister Julia in March 1936 at the NEAAU Indoor championships. Julia won two junior novice races while her older sister won the broad jump, high jump, and twenty-five-yard dash. Five titles came home to the Stokes house after that meet. Louise was ready for the Olympic trials.[8]

When the 1936 Olympic trials were held at Brown University, Stokes once again qualified. She joined the four-hundred-meter relay team after finishing a disappointing fourth in the one-hundred-meter finals. Olympic favorite Stella Walsh considered Stokes a formidable adversary in the one-hundred-meter dash. Receiving word that she would again be part of the team, Stokes needed help from her hometown to raise money to travel with the team to Berlin. Her hometown rose to the occasion. They raised $680—$11,172 in today's dollars and plenty of money to send her to the Olympics in Germany.

Stokes arrived in Berlin to cheer on her teammates and prepare to run the relay. She had a front-row seat to watch Jesse Owens's historic race as she dreamed of making some history of her own. Sadly, the games turned into a repeat of 1932, when Stokes was replaced by a White runner for the four-hundred-meter relay. Again, no explanation was given, though most assumed it was related to Hitler's racial prejudice. Once again, Stokes sat in the stands and watched her team win the gold medal without her. That was her last chance to compete in the Olympics; the 1940 and 1944 games were cancelled due to World War II.[9]

Despite her disappointment, Stokes received a hero's welcome when she returned home, and she soon began to prepare for the 1940 Olympics. She continued to race in the fifty- and one-hundred-meter distances, but she also paid more attention to the standing broad jump, in which she had held records for seven years. She hoped that might be her event in 1940. Sadly, the war derailed her dream. Running had brought her great joy but also some of the biggest disappointments in her life. It was time to move on.

With her Olympic dreams destroyed, Stokes ended her running career, but she was not done with sports. She became a professional bowler, helping to establish the Colored Women's Bowling League. She won many awards over the next three decades, competing at nearly every bowling alley in New England. Stokes was part of the Cordettes, a team that competed in Harrisburg, Pennsylvania, in 1963 and drew more than three hundred female bowlers. Stokes was also part of a larger effort to provide opportunities for Black bowlers through the Negro National Bowlers Association (NNBA). In its first three years, the NNBA signed up over 1,800 Black bowlers, male and female. Stokes did not stop being a competitor just because her career on the track did not work out as she had hoped. Instead, she became a pioneer in a second sport, opening doors for others who deserved a chance to compete.[10]

Stokes's personal life flourished after her competing days ended. In 1944, she married Wilfred R. Fraser Sr. Together they had a son, Wilfred Jr., as they raised his daughter, Ann Shirley, together. For nearly twenty years, Stokes worked as a clerk for the Massachusetts Department of Corporations and Taxation, retiring in 1975. Stokes passed away in Boston on March 25, 1978. She is buried in Mount Hope Cemetery in Boston.[11]

After her death, her community and her fans did not forget what she'd achieved. Several honors came her way, but only one tribute came while she was still alive. In 1974, the New England Amateur Athletic Union set aside a day in her honor, awarding Louise Stokes trophies to winners in the forty- and fifty-meter races, as well as the four-hundred-meter relay. In 1980, the Roosevelt Park fieldhouse was renamed in her honor, and in 1987, her hometown recognized Stokes with a statue outside Malden High School as part of the Louise Stokes Fraser Memorial Plaza. The statue, which depicts her crouching in the starting blocks, bears an inscription that acknowledges her selection to the 1932 and 1936 Olympic teams even though she was deselected for the actual competition.

Though the acts of others prevented her from achieving her Olympic dreams, Stokes has been recognized by her hometown of Malden and the state of Massachusetts as one of the best track-and-field athletes in America. Bridgewater State College inducted Stokes Fraser into their Hall of Black Achievement in 1999, honoring her long career in track and bowling. In 2020, a new 3.2-mile river loop was unveiled along the Malden River to celebrate her accomplishments. The plaque reads, "Dedicated to Louise Stokes, Malden High, Track Star and First African American Woman U.S. Olympian 1936." Even in this honor, her story is not correctly told, since she made the Olympics in 1932 as well. Continuing to tell her story helps to preserve a legacy that should never be forgotten.[12]

NOTES

1. Louise Stokes Fraser, Massachusetts Hall of Black Achievement, https://vc .bridgew.edu/hoba/30/, accessed January 2, 2023; Ann Chandler Powell, *In the Blocks: An Olympian's Story*, 1996, Chandler/White Pub. Co.; Bob Duffy, "Trailblazer Went Nowhere Fast," *Boston Sunday Globe*, September 10, 2000, E1, E10.

2. Chris Caesar, "Black History Month: Louise Stokes Fraser," February 14, 2012, https://patch.com/massachusetts/malden/black-history-month-louise-stokes-fraser; Howell, *In the Blocks*, 14015.

3. "Trailblazer Went Nowhere Fast," 1931, E10; "Women's Track Meet April 16," *Boston Globe*, April 8, 1932, 27; "Olive Hasenfus Loses," *Boston Globe*, June 27, 1931, 10; Jerry Nason, "Fine Sports Program Carded at Roxbury," *Boston Globe*, July

27, 1931, 16; "Malden Girl Sets Broad Jump Record," *Boston Globe*, December 31, 1931, 9; "Louise Stokes Nips Mary Carew Twice," *Boston Globe*, June 27, 1932, 8; "N. E. A. A. A. U Dash Title," *Boston Globe*, July 5, 1930, 9.

4. Doris Pieroth, *Their Day in the Sun: Women of the 1932 Olympics*, 1996, University of Washington Press.

5. Louise Mae Stokes Fraser, https://www.findagrave.com/memorial/216266511/louise-mae-fraser, accessed December 21, 2022; Howell, *In the Blocks*, 66–67.

6. "Women Stars in Norumbega Meet," *Boston Globe*, July 29, 1933, 6; "Louise Stokes Retains Title," *Boston Globe*, July 31, 1933, 6.

7. "Stella Walsh Sets World Dash Mark," *Brooklyn Times Union*, April 15, 1934, 16; "Stella Walsh, Olympic Stars, Headlines Meet of Women Track Aces," *Green Bay Press-Gazette*, April 14, 1934, 14; "Louise Stokes Takes Exciting Clans Dash," *Boston Globe*, September 4, 1934, 20; "Louise Stokes in Norumbega Meet," *Boston Globe*, August 23, 1935, 17; "Helen Stephens Wins Two Events in Women's Track," *Hartford Courant*, September 15, 1935, 48; "Louise Stokes in Norumbega Meet," *Boston Globe*, August 23, 1935, 17; "Louise Retains One N. E. Title, Adds Another," *Boston Globe*, March 20, 1936, 30; "Stella Walsh, Olympic Star, Headlines of Women Track Aces," *Green Bay Press-Gazette*, April 14, 1934, 14; "Phillips vs. Stokes Again," *Boston Globe*, February 15, 1934, 21.

8. "Louise Retains One N. E. Title, Adds Another, *Boston Globe*, March 20, 1936, 30.

9. "German Girls Picked to Win," *Arizona Republic*, February 11, 1936, 12.

10. "Teams in Bell Meet Saturday," *Sunday News* (Lancaster, PA), April 14, 1963, 33; Patricia Dooley, "Jim Crow Strikes Again: The African American Press Campaign against Segregation in Bowling during World War II," *Journal of African American History*, Vol. 97, No. 3 (Summer 2012), 270–90; "Louise Stokes Obituary," *Boston Globe*, March 29, 1978, 59.

11. Ann S. Brown Obituary, *Athol Daily News*, February 10, 2011, 2.

12. Bob Duffy, "Stokes: Nowhere, Fast," *Boston Globe*, September 10, 2000, 65, 74; "Louise Stokes Fraser, Won Olympic Medals in Los Angeles, Berlin," *Boston Globe*, March 29, 1978, 59; and "Hall of Black Achievement Heritage Celebration," *Boston Globe*, January 28, 1999, 112; Heather Mayer Irvine, "Race of a Lifetime," https://www.tracksmith.com/journal/article/race-of-a-lifetime.

BIBLIOGRAPHY

"Ann S. Brown Obituary," *Athol Daily News*, February 10, 2011.

Dooley, Patricia. "Jim Crow Strikes again: The African American Press Campaign against Segregation in Bowling during World War II," *Journal of African American History*, Vol. 97, No. 3 (Summer 2012).

Duffy, Bob. "Trailblazer went Nowhere Fast," *Boston Sunday Globe*, September 10, 2000.

"German Girls Picked to Win," *Arizona Republic*, February 11, 1936.

"Hall of Black Achievement Heritage Celebration," *Boston Globe*, January 28, 1999.

"Helen Stephens Wins Two Events in Women's Track," *Hartford Courant*, September 15, 1935.

Irvine, Heather Mayer. "Race of a Lifetime," https://www.tracksmith.com/journal/article/race-of-a-lifetime.

"Louise Mae Stokes Fraser," https://www.findagrave.com/memorial/216266511/louise-mae-fraser, accessed December 21, 2022.

"Louise Retains One N. E. Title, Adds Another," *Boston Globe*, March 20, 1936.

"Louise Stokes Fraser, Massachusetts Hall of Black Achievement," https://vc.bridgew.edu/hoba/30/, accessed January 2, 2023.

"Louise Stokes Fraser, Won Olympic Medals in Los Angeles, Berlin," *Boston Globe*, March 29, 1978.

"Louise Stokes in Norumbega Meet," *Boston Globe*, August 23, 1935.

"Louise Stokes Nips Mary Carew Twice," *Boston Globe*, June 27, 1932.

"Louise Stokes Obituary," *Boston Globe*, March 29, 1978.

"Louise Stokes Retains Title," *Boston Globe*, July 31, 1933.

"Louise Stokes Takes Exciting Clans Dash," *Boston Globe*, September 4, 1934.

"Malden Girl Sets Broad Jump Record," *Boston Globe*, December 31, 1931.

Nason, Jerry. "Fine Sports Program Carded at Roxbury," *Boston Globe*, July 27, 1931.

"N. E. A. A. A. U Dash Title," *Boston Globe*, July 5, 1930.

"Olive Hasenfus Loses," *Boston Globe*, June 27, 1931.

"Phillips vs. Stokes Again," *Boston Globe*, February 15, 1934.

Pieroth, Doris. *Their Day in the Sun: Women of the 1932 Olympics*. Seattle: University of Washington Press, 1996.

Powell, Ann Chandler. *In the Blocks: An Olympian's Story*. Philadelphia: Chandler/White Publishing Company, 1996.

"Stella Walsh, Olympic Star, Headlines of Women Track Aces," *Green Bay Press-Gazette*, April 14, 1934.

"Stella Walsh Sets World Dash Mark," *Brooklyn Times Union*, April 15, 1934.

"Teams in Bell Meet Saturday," *Sunday News* (Lancaster, PA), April 14, 1963.

"Women Stars in Norumbega Meet," *Boston Globe*, July 29, 1933.

"Women's Track Meet April 16," *Boston Globe*, April 8, 1932.

Chapter 7

Lou Montgomery

Tackling Jim Crow

Susan A. Michalczyk

Born in Brockton, Massachusetts, in 1920, Lou Montgomery and his two brothers grew up on Snow Street, in a house owned by their mother, Roberta, and their grandmother, Bertie. As one of the few Black families living in Brockton at that time, the Montgomery family found connection and respect within their supportive neighborhood, church, and public-school communities. They were dedicated members of the Lincoln Congregational Church and regularly attended athletic events at Brockton High School. Whether at Eldon Keith Field, or on Snow Street, Roberta Montgomery played a central role, guiding and supporting Lou, his friends, and his teammates.

Acknowledged as an outstanding athlete throughout high school and college, Lou excelled in baseball, basketball, and football. At Brockton High School, Lou was a member of the school's varsity team, the Red and the Black, and was recognized by sports journalists as "the highest scorer and one of the finest running backs of his day."[1] He was also admired by his teammates for his leadership and mentoring skills and was chosen as their team captain.

Without question, Montgomery was an all-star athlete whose winning statistics place him among the best, most notable, and most acclaimed athletes in the sport of football. As longtime New England news reporter and journalist Clark Booth noted: "Montgomery remains a great story, but too little known. He was arguably the first great black college sports star from our region, one of the mainstays of the Frank Leahy pre-war B.C (Boston College) powerhouse."[2] Montgomery won every game he played, and he consistently led his high school and college football teams to victory and fame, yet he was denied fair and equal treatment, denied the honor and respect he himself gave to his

Figure 7.1. Lou Montgomery integrated Boston College's athletic programs as a star running-back in 1937. The prevalence of Jim Crow segregation in the South prevented him from playing in the 1940 Cotton Bowl and 1941 Sugar Bowl. Without Montgomery, Boston College lost both games. After graduation, the Brockton born Montgomery established a semi-professional football team in New England called the Black Eagles. Credit: Boston College Athletics.

Lou Montgomery 119

teammates and the game he loved, and targeted both by the racism of the Jim Crow era, and the greed of a college football system that placed money and fame above justice and human dignity.

In the early decades of the twentieth century, Brockton, Massachusetts, was the largest city in Plymouth County. Located about twenty miles from Boston, Brockton was primarily a city of first-generation Irish and Italian immigrants, living in clearly defined ethnic communities that included churches, schools, and shops. The one unifying aspect of Brockton from the turn of the century through the 1930s was its shoe industry, which relied upon the city's immigrant population to fill the factories with inexpensive labor.

Church records document a significant increase in the immigrant population, which rose from 4,032 in 1885 to 17,709 in 1915 as new immigrants arrived from Ireland, Sweden, England, Canada, Italy, and Russia. During the years Lou Montgomery and his family lived in Brockton, the city's Black population comprised only 10 to 15 percent of the whole and remained low as the decades passed. When he attended Brockton High School, from 1933 to 1937, Lou was the only Black student. A few decades later, when the Great Migration extended farther outward from large East Coast cities like Boston, Brockton became a destination for southern Blacks.

With his outstanding athletic achievements, Montgomery was recognized by sports writers along the East Coast. Establishing a strong foundation for his hometown and its high school sports teams, he helped Brockton to become known as the City of Champions. "The Great Migration pushed many African American families north from southern states to find jobs, education, housing, and better overall opportunities. The ultimate population jump that took place helped Brockton, Massachusetts become The City of Champions."[3]

By the time Lou entered Brockton High School in 1933, he had grown accustomed to being the only Black student in his class. Although Brockton's neighborhoods and churches reflected their ethnic roots as families and extended families settled in various sections of the city, Brockton High represented a larger and more diverse community for both students and faculty. While in high school, Lou was consistently recognized by teammates, coaches, and local sports writers as a natural athlete and leader for his exceptional sportsmanship. His oldest daughter, Joanne, recalled that her father got along incredibly well with everyone he met, describing him as a gentle man with inner strength, a kind heart, and a charismatic personality.[4]

As a young Black man living in a predominantly White community, Lou retained his sense of balance and integrity, largely thanks to his mother's influence and guidance, and to an unexpected connection with another classmate and teammate from Brockton, Frank Saba. As a son of Syrian immigrants, Frank was not considered part of the White majority in the city or at the high school. As a result, both young men were linked together on the football field, calling themselves brothers. It was a bond they shared as close friends and as teammates at Brockton High, and later as rivals in college, with Lou playing for Boston College and Frank playing for the College of the Holy Cross.[5]

Known as "schoolboy football's highest scorer and one of the finest backs seen in his day," Montgomery was the unanimous choice of Boston Sports writers for the 1937 all-scholastic team. He was nicknamed "Hula" Lou for his swiveling hip agility, and the "Brockton Express" for his unmatched speed on both offense and defense. As a running back standing about five-foot-seven and weighing around 150 pounds, he was also called Lightning Lou, leading and inspiring his teammates to victory in all but a handful of games during his four-year high school career. The *Brockton Enterprise* recorded all of team captain Lou Montgomery's high school achievements, calling him "the Brockton High ace, tough to stop, swinging down the field on a jaunt that covered forty-seven yards. . . . A regular toe dancer as he moves through the scrimmage line, Montgomery becomes a streak when really under way."[6]

Playing at Eldon Keith Field, under the leadership of coach E. Marion Roberts and captain Louis Montgomery, sportswriters reported that "the Red and Black group clicked well as a team, while Montgomery and Saba were doing the heavy ground-gaining on running plays, and a Montgomery dash netted a first down at Brockton's twenty-nine-yard line as the third quarter ended with Brockton in the lead, 26–0."[7] For their extraordinary achievements on the football field, both men were acknowledged in the Brockton High School Athletic Hall of Fame: Montgomery in 1937, and Saba in 1938.[8]

As the 1935 football season was coming to an end, Montgomery and Saba were injured during one of the games, with team captain Lou briefly hospitalized for treatment. An early insight into Lou's approach to life: creating stability and purpose, no matter the instability around him, emerges in his clever and mature response to the unexpected injuries and schedule changes. In high school, Lou had already demonstrated a strong sense of self-awareness, along with an equally powerful awareness of the contemporary social structure. As a young Black man growing up in Jim Crow America, Montgomery understood he had no control over the circumstances around him, and he focused instead on controlling his response, in order to restore balance and meaning in his own life. His ability to overcome unexpected challenges by shifting the focus from the pain of isolation and disappointment to the hope of possibility and connection, defines an inner strength of character equal to his athletic attributes. Although Lou was not released from the hospital until after the scheduled practice and was fully aware that his coach and teammates were concerned about the upcoming game, Lou showed adaptability, humor, and resilience. "Just to prove he is in tip-top condition and ready for action Saturday afternoon, Capt. Montgomery favored his teammates to a tricky tap dance and wound up with an eccentric dance. Yes! He's in perfect shape, ready for lively action."[9]

Throughout his high school years, Lou excelled academically while playing four sports and winning letters in football, baseball, basketball, and track. Brockton High, along with a few other large public high schools in Massachusetts, was well-known among national recruiters for college football.

> E.M. Roberts, athletic director of Brockton schools, once said that he had never seen Lou's successor or equal on any athletic field. On his graduation, Lightnin' was voted the outstanding athlete of his class and sports-writers of the state gave him the highest honor that can be paid to a schoolboy, that of the out-standing performer in the state for the year.[10]

Respected and trusted by his teammates from Brockton High, and his colleagues from the Massachusetts All-Star Scholastic football team, Lou lived an experience uncommon to most Black Americans of this time. Certainly not as secure as the privileged majority, and yet, in his day-to-day life with his teammates and coaches in football, baseball, and basketball, Lou preserved his integrity and sense of self by making his sports world the anchor for all other aspects of his life. The account of his final high school game, published in the *Brockton Enterprise*, affirms his popularity among teammates and fans:

> Captain Lou Montgomery led his Brockton High eleven to a 16 to 0 victory over the previously unbeaten Waltham team, at Waltham, yesterday, before 12,000. He finished his brilliant career by scoring two touchdowns, the first on a 68-yard run, and the second on a 90-yard dash, and adding one of the extra points by rushing. His teammates carried him off the field on their shoulders, in the midst of a throng of Brockton fans, who rushed to the field to congratulate the star.[11]

Throughout his life, fully aware of the inequalities of racism and prejudice in a country that claimed liberty and justice for all, yet openly preached hate and self-righteousness, Lou never shied away from the endless pressures and unfair burden he shouldered: in his childhood as "the first" Black athlete in Brockton's public schools, and through young adulthood, as "the first and only" Black athlete at Boston College in the late 1930s and early 1940s. His mother, as well, made a commitment to her son, his friends, and his team, and she was given a special seat at every football game. In return, Roberta Montgomery made her home a place of welcome for Lou's friends and teammates, and she was fondly remembered by all who knew her.[12] The city of Brockton, and the many people whose lives had been touched by Lou and his family, showed the depth of their friendship and respect that had deepened over the years by creating a scholarship fund for Lou that supplemented his Boston College football scholarship, making it possible for him to attend college.[13]

As a senior at Brockton High School, where he excelled academically and athletically, Lou, his family, and teammates all understood that with college would come the hope of a professional career in football or baseball. The running back star of Brockton was ready to look beyond his hometown, buoyed by the strong support of Massachusetts' sports writers and of his All-Scholastic teammates. The offers to play college football arrived from Columbia, UCLA, Ohio State, and Boston College, bringing feelings of immense pride across the city and, most especially, within the Montgomery household.

The decision to attend college brings with it opportunities to fulfill the basic truths promised to all American citizens: "Life, Liberty, and the pursuit of Happiness"—a life-changing experience for a better future, not a negation of potential and promise. All the good moments of his childhood, and his experiences as a young teen in Brockton that had countered the racism and prejudice beyond the provincial limits, could no longer push back against the racial hatred that seeped through so much of America in the early and mid-twentieth century, as Lou and his family grappled with the painful reality of leaving home and driving through parts of the country that still worshiped the inequalities of the Confederacy. Remarkable that in 1937, the entire All-Scholastic high school team, all students from eastern Massachusetts, chose to attend Boston College. They established what would be known as "the Team of Destiny," all of whom would go on to play professional football, with the exception of two members of the team: George Kerr, who chose to enter the priesthood, and Lou Montgomery, who chose to sacrifice his own career for the love of his school, for his team, for his family, and for the game.[14]

Sports historian and journalist Glenn Stout clearly presents the cruel reality of racism in America, which significantly limited the freedom of choice for Montgomery and his family, very much aware of the inequalities of power and privilege, even for the most accomplished Black college athletes. The decision to accept an offer to become a team player on one of these major college sports campuses came with sometimes subtle, and sometimes nuanced, racial prejudice. Lou Montgomery, as did so many other young Black athletes of his day, understood, faced, and overcame the irony of playing in solidarity with a team, and playing in isolation, as the "first" or "only" Black member on the field during the game:

> In the late 1930s, there were just a handful of black athletes playing major college sports in the United States. I mean, you had Jackie Robinson and

Kenny Washington out at UCLA and a smattering of players elsewhere. But on hardly any team in the country, there were no more than one or two players of African-American heritage playing major college sports in a major sport like football or basketball or something like that.[15]

Reflecting upon his decision, in an interview with Glenn Stout, forty years later, Lou acknowledged the complicated decision-making process that led to his attending Boston College and not UCLA:

My guys had told me that you know they would intercede for me out here in UCLA, if I wanted to, but at that time California. . . . I was scared to go past the Mississippi, scared to go south, because every time I went there, I damn near got annihilated and I was just scared to go to any far distance. So, I just told them, "No, we go to BC" and the guys made a pact. It was an informal pact, but still to me it was a pact, and we all went to the same school. When I arrived, I realized that I was the only black on the team. I did not know there had not been any of ahead of me, but I soon found out.

Richard Johnson, the curator of the Sports Museum of New England, believed that Lou Montgomery's decision to stay local, rather than risk traveling to the West Coast for college, was the only real option at the time:

Because he knew a lot of the young players that were being recruited to come play for the Eagles and they were going to have a great team. So here was an opportunity for him. There were not many black players playing for even Eastern and Northern schools at the time; an isolated player here and there, oftentimes this would be one of the two or three best players on a given team.[16]

Framing it not only within the larger historical context of America's racist social structure, but also within the very personal experience of a seventeen-year-old high school senior looking for a few familiar faces to ease the transition to college, Johnson offers insights into Lou's reasoning. His assessment of the times and the players recognizes the individual loss to Lou, for his personal and professional career, as well as the greater damage done to college athletics throughout the country, due to the pervasive and persuasive nature of racial segregation of the Jim Crow laws:

And so, the star of Brockton High School turns down a chance to go to UCLA where he would have been a teammate of Jackie Robinson's and Kenny Washington's. They would have overlapped for two years. Instead, he chose to remain at home, and so we have Boston College opening its arms to this great local star. And other local stars at the same time; Charlie O'Rourke was in the same class. They brought in players who they knew would help them reach greatness.[17]

The supportive experience of growing up within a community rooted in acceptance, not segregation, increased Lou's confidence that he would enjoy an equally positive experience at Boston College. The city of Brockton provided stability, acceptance, and opportunity for Lou Montgomery throughout his childhood, and as the outstanding athlete in the graduating class of 1937. Lou's mother, Roberta, always his strongest ally, placed her son's future welfare above her own comfort and security, choosing to sell her home in Brockton and move to Roxbury, to lessen the strain on Lou's daily commute to campus.[18] Still, Lou, the only Black athlete, and one of only three Black students at Boston College at the time, faced discrimination and humiliation once he passed through the college gates. The reality of living in the Black community of Roxbury and traveling to the all-White world of Chestnut Hill required careful planning. Lou chose to commute very early in the morning and later in the evening, when fewer White Bostonians would be on the buses and trains. In this way, he was able to avoid being spat on, threatened, and harassed by hostile Bostonians.[19]

Lou Montgomery understood the significance of his role, in much the same way as another young Black college athlete, Jackie Robinson, had while playing for UCLA's sports teams at about the same time: not only as an outstanding athlete, but also as a representative for all members of the Black community, in a society too ready and willing to judge the other as inferior and unworthy. Fortunately, both the local White press and the national Black press consistently acknowledged Lou Montgomery's achievements, highlighting his team spirit, goodwill, and strength of character, which no doubt provided some security and encouragement.[20] Given the reality of Jim Crow laws, which violated standards of justice and perpetuated a racist America in the North, as well as the South, the courageous few helped forge a path and offer a glimpse of hope for other young Black athletes.

And yet Lou never mentioned the racism, hatred, and struggles to his teammates; rather, he was always seen as a leader. In protecting his team, he sacrificed a part of himself, and his dedication and commitment reflect his extraordinary tolerance, even as intolerance and exploitation dominated his college sports career. In later years, the Montgomery family acknowledged that their father and grandfather endured painful moments due to the racist attitudes of other teams and the university's failure to act against such injustice. Joanne Montgomery recalled that her father's teammates provided connection and friendship:

> With his college teammates, Lou found acceptance and support: I do think he, really truly, loved his colleagues, and they loved him. And they protected him as much as they could, knowing what the situation was back there in those days.[21]

George Kerr's younger brother, Peter, recalled the friendship between Lou and his brother, on and off the field:

> Montgomery, who came from Brockton, Massachusetts, never realized his vast potential as a college football player at BC. Some, including Peter Kerr, have theorized that his considerable talents could have been better utilized. . . . While he attended BC, Montgomery was a regular at the Kerr home. "My brother often brought Lou home for dinner," said Peter. "He liked my mother's simple Irish cooking."[22]

Leaving the familiarity of Brockton, where local Massachusetts high school football teams focused on the love of the game, for Chestnut Hill, where college teams from north and south focused on fame and fortune, radically altered Lou's expectations, as racial prejudice and inequality crushed his hopes to continue to excel as a college athlete. As a freshman, Lou caught the attention of coach Gil Dobie, as well as his classmates, for his unique playing style, chronicled in the school's newspaper, the *Heights*:

> Among the new freshman players are several well-known stars of last year's high school and prep school football teams. In the backfield there is Charlie O'Rourke who was an all-scholastic forward passing expert at Malden high, and Lou Montgomery the colored flash from Brockton High School. Montgomery was the unanimous choice of the Boston sports writers last year for the all-scholastic team.[23]

The new head coach, Frank Leahy, also recognized Lou's outstanding athletic abilities as a running back. Always looking for a way to highlight his own coaching success, Leahy saw an opportunity to capitalize on the exceptional skill of his players: "Frank Leahy had one foot out the door for all those years. He wanted bigger and better things and his route to glory at Notre Dame meant Boston College was a waystation."[24] Similarly, in their search to become bigger and better, Southern colleges created new bowl games, extending the season and expanding northward. What began as a financially lucrative investment soon evolved into racial confrontation: "The 1940 Cotton Bowl and the 1941 Sugar Bowl revealed the fierce determination of white southerners to maintain the color line in college football and the willingness of ambitious northern universities to abandon their black players in pursuit of athletic success and financial rewards."[25]

Leahy's personal ambition, coupled with Boston College's ambition to establish itself as a first-class football school, meant sacrificing principles and integrity, and violating the ethics of humanism and religion. As the football season progressed, both coach and college looked past Lou's humanity, reducing him to an object to be used for Leahy's personal gain,

126   *Susan A. Michalczyk*

and the university's financial profit: a perfect storm, with the addition of the "Gentlemen's Agreement" coming out of the Jim Crow South.

Adding Southern college teams to build a stronger schedule eventually led to moral and ethical confrontations along the geographical boundaries of racism. Most Northern teams, including Boston College, were willing to bench their Black players when meeting their opponents in Southern states, while insisting that on Northern ground, on their home fields, Black athletes were entitled to fair and equal treatment. "Still, there were schools who stood their ground and said, you know, 'he plays and we play; he doesn't play, we don't play.' BC would not have been the first to do this. There was precedent."[26] In striking contrast to the lack of support shown by the university and most of the White Boston newspapers, the school's student newspaper, as well as members of the Black press, including the National Negro All-American Association of Sports Editors, continued to stand with Lou, recognizing his value and acknowledging his achievements on the football field:

> Perhaps the most spectacular player of Frank Leahy's squad is "Hula" Lou Montgomery, the swivel-hipped Junior from Brockton . . . in his scamperings to date he has far surpassed all predictions made for him by the leading sports-writers. Lou attended Brockton High School and for three years he was a sensation because of his gridiron gallopings.[27]
>
> This year the going has been better for Monty and many people have been in the stands just to see Lou start "jiving" through the line of the opposing team. . . . The captain of the Lebanon Valley team perhaps best described Lou when, after the game he commented, "Boy, that guy has got music in his feet." Captain, you're right. And watch him tap out "For Boston" on next Saturday.[28]

Along with Montgomery, Leahy's Team of Destiny included Charlie O'Rourke, Mike Holovak, and Gene Goodreault. Thanks to these outstanding football players "in 1939, BC racked up 216 points, which was a tune-up for 1940 when BC exploded for 320 points while limiting the opposition to fifty-two."[29] Leahy added Montgomery as a running back at the start of Lou's junior year, and "Lou averaged just under ten yards a carry, which might have led the country. But he was held out of certain games because he was not allowed to play in those games."[30]

> The hard-working athlete who is also a hard-working student is a real B.C. man. There's no doubt about it, but 20-year-old Lou Montgomery who had the distinct honor of being co-captain last Saturday, is having his best year at Boston College. The former Brockton flash, who was really a flash, is everybody's favorite. Popular Lou has played in three games thus far and in each one of

them, has delighted the fans with his inimitable display of speed, dodging and elusiveness. . . . Take a bow, Lou Montgomery.[31]

As the goal shifted to increasing visibility for a winning program, Lou lost playing time, beginning with game three of the 1939 season against the University of Florida. Officials from the University of Florida, citing the Gentlemen's Agreement, threatened to cancel if Boston College allowed Lou to travel to Florida and play with the team. This would not be the last time university officials failed to stand up against racism.

> Under Leahy, Boston College started having a lot more success at becoming a big-time football school. It was very lucrative, and they were determined not to let anything stand in their way. And essentially, they allowed money to override the morality of the issue.[32]

Lou was assured that things would work out, and that he would be able to play in future games, yet sadly, that was never the case. Southern teams became more emboldened, implementing the racist terms of Jim Crow at home games as well. More time was put into preserving the image of the game and its teams than was ever given to preserving Lou's dignity or the dignity of the game.

> If you look at the arc of his career at Boston College, he makes the starting lineup in 1939. He's one of the stars of the team. Then that Florida game comes and he can't play. And then Boston College starts looking ahead and realizing that they might be going to a bowl game and they might be facing the same situation where they have to play a team from the South. And his playing time starts to go down. And then in 1940, knowing this situation exists, his playing time is diminished from the start. He has a lesser role in 1940 than he did in 1939, although by any measure he was one of the most talented backs on the team. But Frank Leahy, knowing that he might not have one of his most talented players for the most important games of the season—the bowl game at the end of the season—as a coach, he has to look for alternatives. So, he stops playing Lou.

As win followed win, Coach Leahy focused on the best ways to utilize his players for ever greater glory. What could have become a watershed moment for racial equality never materialized, as Boston College chose to accept terms offered by Southern universities, steeped in segregationist tradition.

> In preliminary discussions, Cotton Bowl officials made it clear that southern custom precluded Montgomery's participation. Although coach Frank Leahy publicly grumbled about the exclusion, BC nonetheless quickly accepted the invitation. In reality, benching Montgomery presented no great moral dilemma for the Jesuit-run institution, since the school had already done so twice during

the 1939 regular season for home games against Auburn and the University of Florida.[33]

A key contributor to the 1939 winning season, Montgomery was left on the sidelines, a casualty of racism and greed, as the team prepared for victory in Dallas at the 1940 Cotton Bowl. Since Boston College had already allowed Southern schools to dictate racist policy earlier in the season—without encountering strong criticism from the press—they were caught off-guard by the condemnation of journalists from the Black and White press, along with fans and some of Lou's teammates.

> "The black and white press denounced the 'cruel snub.'" The Pittsburgh *Courier* criticized Boston College for abandoning its democratic and Christian ideals. Jack Miley of the New York *Daily News* scored BC for one of the most "spineless, mealy-mouthed, weak-kneed, craven bits of business in the whole history of college football." . . . "Even Hitler, to give the bum his due, didn't treat Jesse Owens the way the Cotton Bowl folk are treating Lou Montgomery—with the consent of the young Negro's alma mater. . . . For Adolf, at least, let Owens run, and . . . he had the good grace not to try to bar Jesse before the games got under way." Miley's sentiments were shared by many eastern sports fans.[34]

The university's public relations department protected those in positions of power, placing full responsibility for Montgomery's sidelining on their young student-athlete's shoulders, by fabricating a response from Lou that shielded the coach and the university from blame:

> I think that letter came from me, but it didn't come in terms of a letter. It came in terms of an interview of what I would like to say to the public. Anyhow, I think the idea was that I wanted to say something, but I didn't want to write letters to friends and people, because everyone was asking me, you know, the same question. So, I think the idea was that if we got a letter published, then everybody would see it. Yeah so, we talked about things, and the letter came from that talk, but it wasn't anything that I sat down and wrote out myself. I don't think I would've done anything like that.[35]

The complicity of the university in upholding the racist policies of the South ended in defeat at the Cotton Bowl. "I think we'd have won the game if you'd been playing for us,"[36] Coach Leahy told his benched star player.

Encouraged by his teammates, his fans, and his love of the game, Lou kept his focus on playing football during his senior year at Boston College, even as the Eagles chose to look beyond Lou, frequently replacing him with White teammates on the field at Fenway Park as they kept their focus on another

Bowl game and the Gentlemen's Agreements made among these Northern and Southern college teams.

> At times, they basically said they did not want to take the field unless he was on the sidelines with them with an opportunity to play. So, part of his magnanimity and part of his greatness as a teammate was that he appreciated their sentiments but he knew the forces at work against them all and did not want those being brought to bear on his teammates and friends. I mean, a total class act.[37]

Lou's daughter remembered her father's talking about the racism he lived through during his college football career, with both sadness and insight: "I do think he, really truly, loved his colleagues, and they loved him. And they protected him as much as they could, knowing what the situation was back there in those days, He encouraged them, he did, encouraged them to play."[38]

Realistically, there was not much eighteen- and nineteen-year-old college students could do in response to their university's decision to tolerate the racism that was hurting their teammate and tainting the game they all loved. Yet there were many others in positions of leadership who placed the burden on this young team, forcing Lou to become the anchor and the voice of reason to protect not only his teammates, but also the racist rules of the game, for both the 1940 Cotton Bowl and the 1941 Sugar Bowl. Along with Montgomery's unforgettable statistics and athletic accomplishments, feelings of regret have become part of this story of injustice, a reminder that by failing to take a stand, the bystander cannot be innocent: "We played by their rules."[39]

While none of Montgomery's teammates spoke out at the time, in later years some former team members expressed regret that they had not done enough to support Montgomery. The reflections of two teammates, Mike Holovak and Charlie O'Rourke, could stand as testimony of the response and sentiments of too many generations. Mike Holovak later condemned the fact that Montgomery "couldn't play [solely] because he was a Negro. This was in 1941. January 1. A whole world was going to war. And we quit on a big battle. We—as players—should have refused to play" in the Sugar Bowl.[40] Richard Johnson recounted a discussion with Chuckin Charlie O'Rourke:

> Charlie revealed to me that he and a number of the players on the team were really broken up and very, very dismayed at how Lou was treated and that it was really hurtful. He said: "I wish we could have done more," and his first emotion was feeling sadness that, they all worked and played together, they were a real team—they were a great team—but the greatness was diminished by the fact that this injustice was done and they witnessed it.[41]

Lou had not been allowed to join his team in Dallas for the 1940 Cotton Bowl. For the 1941 Sugar Bowl, he did accompany the team to New Orleans to play in an All-Black College All-Star game. Repeating the pattern from the previous year, the university chose to appease their racist opponents, agreeing to exclude Lou from the field for Sugar Bowl practices and the game. Since there was not as much outcry in the lead-up to the 1941 bowl game, it was a simpler process for "school administrators, who ignored criticism from a few sportswriters and students, and cravenly agreed to withhold Montgomery from postseason play."[42] Unable to be with his teammates, Montgomery stayed with Ralph Metcalfe, a silver medalist at the 1936 Nazi Olympics, where Jesse Owens had won the gold.

Prevented from fulfilling his own dream of playing in a bowl game, Montgomery remained a team player. Although it was a tremendous loss for him, personally and professionally, he survived the hatred and disrespect directed at him with resilience, intelligence, and an ability to adapt no matter how demeaning the circumstances. His strength of character and charismatic personality come through in the words of his teammate's younger brother:

> Montgomery, known for his slight build and blinding speed, traveled with the team to New Orleans, but did not dress for the game. The Sugar Bowl might have slighted him, but he had the last laugh: while the Sugar Bowl rivals played for pride, he was paid in cold, hard cash—as much as $1,000, according to Peter Kerr, to play in the Black College All-Star game.
>
> On the way home to Boston, Montgomery was the only player with a wallet filled with bills and change in his pocket. "On the train on the way home, Lou was the only one who had any money," recalled Peter, who traveled with the BC team to the game. "He was a generous guy. I remember him smiling and buying drinks for everyone."[43]

An education major, Montgomery moved to Hartford, Connecticut, following his graduation, where he established the Black Eagles, a semipro Black football team in New England, and worked in the insurance industry. In the 1950s, he moved to Fairmont, West Virginia, with his family, where he taught high school math for several years. In addition to his teaching, Lou coached the high school football team. On one occasion, he was able to bring his team of fifteen students—a team that under Lou's direction, had never lost a game—to Massachusetts to play a game at his alma mater, Brockton High School. For Montgomery, it was an unforgettable experience. He later recalled his excitement about coaching a near-win—as well as the important conversation he had with his students about race. Acknowledging the discomfort and fear his young team felt playing for the first time against a team of White students in a stadium filled with White fans, Lou spoke from personal experience, reminding "his guys" that they could play their game without fear, because he had brought them to his home, to his place.[44]

Lou Montgomery 131

Eventually, almost thirty years after deciding against moving to the West Coast to play football for UCLA, Montgomery settled in Oakland, California. Although they continued to visit family and friends in New England, he and his wife, Marie, called California home for the rest of their lives. Montgomery spent several years working with Western Airlines, while he and his wife raised their three children. In retirement, he remained dedicated to his family and to playing sports, helping on the field during school games with his children and grandchildren and adding yet another sport, golf, to his athletic accomplishments.[45]

Much has changed since Lou Montgomery played high school sports in Brockton. His hometown still has a strong athletics program, and a winning football team, although today the team and the city are much more ethnically diverse. Unlike the small number of Black families who called Brockton home during the Montgomery family's years there, the number of Black residents has risen to 44 percent, comprising the majority of the city's population. At Boston College and other colleges and universities across the country, Black athletes are no longer in the minority in team sports.

Certainly, Lou Montgomery made major contributions in breaking barriers, as the first Black athlete and one of the first Black students at Boston College, and he deserves to be remembered and honored. Yet that remembrance must include an awareness of his sacrifices and the sacrifices of many other young Black athletes, in Boston and across America, who lost much in the fight for racial equality.

> Lou Montgomery paid the price his entire life. Everybody wants to make it a happy ending. Well, it wasn't a happy ending. He didn't get to pursue his chosen profession, because of racial prejudice. That's something that shouldn't be forgotten. He paid a price for the rest of his life.[46]

In the early history of Boston College football, amid the celebratory atmosphere surrounding their status as "National Champions," few questioned the absence of Lou Montgomery, with many choosing instead to accept an agreement that offered fame, while preserving prejudice.

Montgomery, who died in 1993 at the age of seventy-two, accomplished much in his life. He is remembered as an honorable man who, as a student-athlete, made sacrifices out of love for his school, his team, his family, and the game. His granddaughter, Tracey Riley, reflected upon his quiet strength in not succumbing to the indignities he faced while in college: "The love of the game superseded the hatred of the people, which I think really speaks volumes about what my grandfather was like as a person."[47]

The achievements of this young Black athlete from Brockton, Massachusetts, cannot be diminished. Classmates described him as "a popular man whom classmates will never forget, and a man who never played a losing game of football for BC."[48] His contributions to the game of football, his determination to help others, and his commitment to racial justice, though at times overshadowed by racism and greed, endure. As a young man, in high school and in college, Lou demonstrated more understanding, compassion, and decency in all aspects of his life, on the field and off, than all the powerful men, institutions, and laws that governed the early decades of the twentieth century. Throughout his life, and in the range of careers he pursued, Lou Montgomery taught by example, with humility and inner strength, accepting the moments of recognition without judgment or bitterness, no doubt aware of the bitter ironies in his life. He was chosen as guest speaker at the New England's Unsung Football Heroes dinner, on December 5, 1940, only a few weeks before the 1941 Sugar Bowl. In 1950, in New York City, Lou received the James J. Hoey Award for the promotion of interracial justice. As president of the Catholic Interracial Council of Hartford, Connecticut, Lou worked with religious and lay Catholics from New York and Connecticut to improve racial equality and understanding.

Shortly after his death, Lou was named to the Boston College Hall of Fame, and almost twenty years later, his alma mater paid tribute to him by retiring his jersey. In 2021, Montgomery became the first recipient of the ACC UNITE Award, created to honor individuals affiliated with the league who have made an impact in the areas of racial and social justice.[49] Montgomery's legacy is inextricably linked to his love of football, his friends, and his family, as poignantly recalled by his daughter, Joanne:

> Well, daddy loved football. He loved to play. He loved each and every one of his colleagues. He loved the game itself. And he would do anything, I think, to play the game. Even when they told him that it was a possibility that he couldn't play, because of the color of his skin, he loved the game so well, and loved his team so well, that he himself, chose not to play.[50]

Yet, as he later came to realize, his choices were limited. His decision to act honorably, and his willingness to educate and encourage others to follow his lead, speaks to his achievements on and off the field. Lou's own words reflect his lifelong belief in, and commitment to, working for social justice and eradicating racism: "The brotherhood of man is not based on color, nationality, or race, and if this doctrine were spread throughout the world, and lived up to, our interracial problems would disappear."[51]

NOTES

1. "Aces in Holiday Duel," *Brockton Enterprise*, November 1936.

2. Clark Booth retired New England journalist and sportscaster, correspondence, August 24, 2012.

3. Maureen Boyle, *The Great Migration to Brockton* project, accessed May 8, 2022, http://brocktonsgreatmigration.blogspot.com/p/a-different-kind-of-housing-crisis.html.

4. Joanne Montgomery interviews (Sept. 2012/April 2015) for *Lou Montgomery: A Legacy Restored* documentary (2016).

5. Paul F. Saba interviews (February 2016) for *Lou Montgomery: A Legacy Restored* documentary (2016).

6. "He's Off—And Tough to Stop," *Brockton Enterprise*, Fall 1936.

7. "Medford Loses to Red and Black," *Brockton Enterprise*, Fall 1936.

8. Brockton High School Athletics Hall of Fame documents, accessed May 8, 2022, https://www.bpsma.org/uploaded/Athletics/Hall_of_Fame/Hall_of_Fame_Members.pdf.

9. "Montgomery and Saba in Shape" *Brockton Enterprise*, November 1935.

10. "Eagles Have Best Record Since Golden Year 1928 Leahymen Have Won Eight, Lost One Heartbreaker to Inferior 'Gators,'" *Heights*, December 1, 1939, Vol. XIX, No. 38, accessed May 8, 2022, https://newspapers.bc.edu/?a=d&d=bcheights19391201.2.8&e=-------en-20--1--txt-txIN-------.

11. "Brockton Beats Waltham 16–0," *Brockton Enterprise*, Fall 1936.

12. Joanne Montgomery interviews (Sept. 2012/April 2015) for *Lou Montgomery: A Legacy Restored* documentary (2016).

13. Willie A. Wilson Jr., Brockton resident, professor, and curator of the Brockton Historical Society, interviewed October 30, 2022, for *Lou Montgomery: His Story Is Our Story* (documentary by Susan and John Michalczyk).

14. *Lou Montgomery: A Legacy Restored.* Michalczyk documentary (2016).

15. Glenn Stout interview, August 8, 2015, for *Lou Montgomery: A Legacy Restored* documentary (2016).

16. Richard Johnson interview, April 25, 2015, for *Lou Montgomery: A Legacy Restored* documentary (2016).

17. Ibid.

18. Joanne Montgomery interview, April 2015: "My grandmother sold her house in Brockton so that my dad would be able to commute from Boston to Boston College a lot easier than it was to get from Brockton to Boston. And she did that, it was a wonderful sacrifice."

19. Dan Bunch interview, May 6, 2015, for *Lou Montgomery: A Legacy Restored* documentary (2016).

20. Glenn Stout interview, August 8, 2015: "Everybody's in the stands cheering. In the African American community, yes, they knew what was going on. But they had no voice in Boston at the time. They had no power, they were segregated in a few small neighborhoods and a few small newspapers."

21. Joanne Montgomery interview, April 2015, for *Lou Montgomery: A Legacy Restored* documentary (2016).

22. Wally Carew Jr., *A Farewell to Glory: The Rise and Fall of an Epic Football Rivalry, Boston College vs. Holy Cross* (Worcester, MA: Ambassador Books, 2003), p. 87.

23. "Kansas State Invades Alumni Field," *Heights* (Boston College student newspaper), October 1, 1937, Vol. XVIII, No. 1, accessed May 8, 2022, https://newspapers.bc.edu/?a=d&d=bcheights19371001.2.11&e=-------en-20--1--txt-txIN-------.

24. Richard Johnson interview, April 25, 2015, for *Lou Montgomery: A Legacy Restored* documentary (2016).

25. Charles H. Martin, *Benching Jim Crow: The Rise and Fall of the Color Line in Southern College Sports, 1890–1980* (Champaign, IL: University of Illinois Press, 2010), p. 373.

26. Mark Dullea, loumontgomerylegacy.com: 1929: *In 1929, Georgia Tech was invited to play in the Rose Bowl against the University of California. California was not inclined to pull its lone black player in deference to Southern white sensitivities. As a result, Georgia Tech agreed to play the game on California's terms.*

1916: *Harvard University chose to cancel a dual track meet at the U.S. Naval Academy in Annapolis, Maryland because Navy officials refused to allow Harvard's star long jumper—an African American—to participate.*

27. "Eagles Have Best Record Since Golden Year 1928 Leahymen Have Won Eight, Lost One Heartbreaker to Inferior 'Gators,'" *Heights*, December 1, 1939.

28. Ibid.

29. Wally Carew Jr., *A Farewell to Glory: The Rise and Fall of an Epic Football Rivalry, Boston College vs. Holy Cross*, p. 271.

30. Mark Dullea interview, April 25, 2015, for *Lou Montgomery: A Legacy Restored* documentary (2016).

31. *Heights*, Oct. 25, 1940.

32. Glenn Stout interview, August 8, 2015, for *Lou Montgomery: A Legacy Restored* documentary (2016).

33. Charles H. Martin, *Benching Jim Crow: The Rise and Fall of the Color Line in Southern College Sports, 1890–1980.* Champaign: University of Illinois Press, 2010, p. 374.

34. Thomas G. Smith, "Outside the Pale: The Exclusion of Blacks from the National Football League, 1934–1946." Journal of Sport History, Vol 15, No. 3, Special Issue: The Black Athlete in American Sport (Winter 1988), p. 270.

35. Glenn Stout, audio interview with Lou Montgomery.

36. Richard Johnson interview, April 25, 2015, for *Lou Montgomery: A Legacy Restored* documentary (2016).

37. Ibid.

38. Joanne Montgomery interview, April 2015, *Lou Montgomery: A Legacy Restored* documentary (2016).

39. *Lou Montgomery: A Legacy Restored* (Michalczyk documentary).

40. Murray Sperber, *Onward to Victory: The Crises That Shaped Modern College Sports* (NY: Henry Holt & Co., 1998), p. 72.

Lou Montgomery

41. Richard Johnson interview, April 25, 2015.

42. Charles H. Martin, *Benching Jim Crow: The Rise and Fall of the Color Line in Southern College Sports, 1890–1980.* Champaign: University of Illinois Press, 2010, p. 374.

43. Wally Carew Jr., *A Farewell to Glory: The Rise and Fall of an Epic Football Rivalry, Boston College vs. Holy Cross*, p. 87.

44. Glenn Stout, audio interview with Lou Montgomery.

45. Jim Fenton, "Brockton's Montgomery finally earns his football due at Boston College," *Enterprise*, August 31, 2012, accessed April 2015, https://www .enterprisenews.com/story/sports/pro/2012/08/31/brockton-s-montgomery-finally -earns/40040859007/.

46. Glenn Stout interview, August 8, 2015, for *Lou Montgomery: A Legacy Restored* documentary (2016).

47. Tracey Riley interview, September 2012.

48. *Sub Turri* BC yearbook 1941, p. 219.

49. ACC UNITE Awards 2021, accessed June 26, 2022, https://theacc.com/news /2021/9/23/general-acc-announces-inaugural-unite-award-recipients.aspx.

50. Joanne Montgomery interview, April 2015, for *Lou Montgomery: A Legacy Restored* documentary (2016).

51. "Donahue Presents 1950 Hoey Awards; Annual Presentation of Interracial Justice Awards, *New York Times*, October 30, 1950, p. 14.

BIBLIOGRAPHY

"ACC UNITE Awards 2021." https://theacc.com/news/2021/9/23/general-acc -announces-inaugural-unite-award-recipients.aspx.

"Aces in Holiday Duel," *Brockton Enterprise*, November 1936.

"Brockton Beats Waltham 16–0," *Brockton Enterprise*, Fall 1936.

"Brockton High School Athletics Hall of Fame Documents," accessed May 8, 2022, https://www.bpsma.org/uploaded/Athletics/Hall_of_Fame/Hall_of_Fame _Members.pdfMontgomery.

Carew, Wally. *A Farewell to Glory: The Rise and Fall of an Epic Football Rivalry, Boston College vs. Holy Cross.* Worcester: Ambassador Books, 2003.

"Donahue Presents 1950 Hoey Awards; Annual Presentation of Interracial Justice Awards," *New York Times*, October 30, 1950.

"Eagles Have Best Record Since Golden Year 1928 Leahymen Have Won Eight, Lost One Heartbreaker to Inferior 'Gators,'" *Heights*, Volume XIX, Number 38 (December 1, 1939).

"Eagles Have Best Record Since Golden Year 1928 Leahymen Have Won Eight, Lost One Heartbreaker to Inferior Gators," *Heights*, December 1, 1939.

Fenton, Jim. "Brockton's Montgomery Finally Earns his Football Due at Boston College," *Enterprise*, August 31, 2012.

"He's Off—And Tough to Stop," *Brockton Enterprise*, Fall 1936.

"Kansas State Invades Alumni Field," *Heights,* Volume XVIII, Number 1, October 1, 1937.

Martin, Charles. *Benching Jim Crow: The Rise and Fall of the Color Line in Southern College Sports, 1890–1980.* Champaign: University of Illinois Press, 2010.

"Medford Loses to Red and Black," *Brockton Enterprise*, Fall 1936.

"Saba in Shape" *Brockton Enterprise*, November 1935.

Smith, Thomas. "Outside the Pale: The Exclusion of Blacks from the National Football League, 1934–1946." *Journal of Sport History*, Volume 15, Number 3 (Winter 1988).

Sperber, Murray. *Onward to Victory: The Crises that Shaped Modern College Sports* (New York: Henry Holt & Co., 1998).

Chapter 8

Constructing Legends

Pumpsie Green, Race, and the Boston Red Sox[1]

Robert E. Weir

In 2009, the Boston Red Sox held a Jackie Robinson Day celebration to honor African American and Latino players. Three years later, the Red Sox held a one-hundredth birthday party for its iconic stadium, Fenway Park. Elijah "Pumpsie" Green played key roles in each event. In 1959, Green became the first African American to wear a Red Sox uniform. In so doing, he also took down Major League Baseball's final segregation barrier and became an important symbol of racial reconciliation for the city of baseball. Or so the story goes.

Folklorist Richard Dorson once observed, "The legends of a given period in American history reflect the main concerns and values, tensions and anxieties, goals and drives of that period."[2] Dorson's remark should be amended to add that legends are reconfigured over time to reflect changing social mores. Sometimes they also embody historical amnesia and myopia.

I found myself thinking of legends during the summer of 2012, as I was preparing a public talk on Elijah "Pumpsie" Green, the man who broke the color barrier for the last Major League Baseball (MLB) team to integrate, the Boston Red Sox, in 1959. This chapter's central theme is that Pumpsie Green was an unlikely legend, and he only became one because of the part he played—sometimes unwittingly, sometimes against his will, and sometimes willingly—within Boston's greater racial drama. But it wasn't Green who led me to muse upon legends; it was a White player, Johnny Pesky, who died as I was working on this chapter.

Figure 8.1. Elijah "Pumpsie" Green tested the Boston Red Sox's legacy of racism when he became the team's first African American player in 1959. Green was the last Black player to integrate into a major league baseball team. Jackie Robinson shattered the color line with the Brooklyn Dodgers twelve years earlier in 1947. Green found comfort and support in the friendship of Celtic Bill Russell during his playing days. Russell helped Green navigate the difficulties posed by racist fans in the city they represented. Credit: National Baseball Hall of Fame and Museum.

Constructing Legends 139

"Legend" is, in popular parlance, among the most imprecise and cavalierly misused labels in the English language.[3] For this chapter, I adopt the scholarly understanding of legends: they are repeated, secular folktales with human beings at their center. They are regarded by many as "true," but they often contain exaggerated or invented dimensions, projections, and beliefs that do not pass evidential muster. Folklorist Jan Brunvand calls them forms of "folk history" that are "soon distorted by oral transmission."[4] That is to say, legends are generally *not* true in their entirety. In many cases, Brunvand observes, this becomes less the case as time passes and stories are repeated. The very act of narrative repetition leads to embellishment; the story, if you will, gets "better" over time.

Few American cultural pursuits have spawned as many legends as baseball, a sport often used as a metaphor for the nation itself.[5] To illustrate the embellishment process, let us consider Johnny Pesky (1919–2012), whose narrative intersected with Pumpsie Green's. When Pesky died at the age of ninety-two on August 13, 2012, his eulogies were a frothy mix of biography and embellished legend. Of his baseball prowess there is little doubt; Pesky is a Hall of Fame inductee with a lifetime batting average of .307. He played for the Red Sox eight seasons during 1942 to 1952, his tenure interrupted by three years of military service during World War II. In 1952, the Red Sox traded Pesky, Walt Dropo, and three others to Detroit for a past-his-prime George Kell, aging pitcher Dizzy Trout, and two obscure players.[6] Pesky made his way back to Boston as a manager in 1963, just as Pumpsie Green was leaving Boston, but his teams had a winning percentage of just .451, and he was fired with two games left in the 1964 season. From 1969 through 1974, Pesky served as a Red Sox broadcaster, and for the next thirty-seven years, he was a permanent fixture with the team as a coach (1975–1984) and as a respected assistant and special instructor (1985–2012).

Then there is Pesky the legend. The fair/foul demarcation of Fenway Park's short right field is dubbed "Pesky's Pole," where legend holds that the diminutive second baseman poked cheap home runs into the seats. This simply isn't true. The five-foot-nine-inch Pesky was known more for getting on base than driving in runs. He had just 404 RBIs in 5,515 MLB plate appearances and hit only seventeen home runs in his ten-year career. Of his homers, just six came at Fenway Park. Pesky's Pole was the colorful invention of broadcaster Mel Parnell—one he repeated during 1965 and 1966, when the Red Sox were woeful, Fenway Park was generally two-thirds empty, and keeping radio listeners interested was a challenge.

Over time, Parnell's small joke became received truth—a classic hallmark of how legends migrate and mutate. It also reminds scholars to seek motives when encountering counterfactual history.[7] Sportswriters, broadcasters, and front-office executives often contribute to baseball legend for reasons ranging from joke telling and hyperbole to attempts to whitewash history. We can see legend at work by telling Pumpsie Green's story backward, from the end to the beginning. On April 17, 2009, Green threw out the ceremonial first pitch at Fenway Park's Jackie Robinson Day celebration, just two months shy of the fiftieth anniversary of Green's debut with the Red Sox. He lobbed the ball to David Ortiz, a popular Dominican player who has played for the Red Sox since 2003. At that event, Red Sox CEO Larry Lucchino noted: "The legacy of players like Pumpsie Green and Jackie Robinson is evidenced by the diversity of players like Jim Rice, Mo Baughan, Dave Roberts, and David Ortiz as part of the Red Sox's more recent history. . . . [W]e owe both Pumpsie Green and Jackie Robinson a debt of gratitude for their courageous contributions to the game and to society."[8]

Lucchino's remarks may be true, but only if one emphasizes the word *recent*. His celebratory tone conveniently ignored decades of pre– and post–Pumpsie Green racism within both the Red Sox organization and the city of Boston. Moreover, Lucchino's analogy to Jackie Robinson is one Green never made. Green knew and admired Robinson, but he never considered himself in Robinson's class. He remarked, "He [Robinson] did something I think only he could have done."[9] Indeed, Lucchino parsed his comments carefully because, as we shall see, his organization's racial history is a rather depressing one.

Three years later, on April 13, 2012, Green took part in the one-hundredth birthday bash for Fenway Park. Writing for the *Boston Globe*, Dan Shaughnessy—a key architect of baseball's "Curse of the Bambino" legend—waxed hyperbolic.[10] He noted that Pumpsie Green was there "with the other gods of our youth—Carl Yastrzemski . . . Jim Rice, Dwight Evans."[11] Green was a gentleman, and one should not belittle the challenges of being the first Black player for a team and a city that mostly didn't want him. He was never, however, among baseball's "gods."[12]

CONSTRUCTING A COUNTERFACTUAL LEGEND

Stories abound of baseball's Negro Leagues greats who would have been stars in MLB if given the chance—Josh Gibson, Oscar Charleston, Buck Leonard, Willie Wells, Satchel Paige—but such is not Pumpsie Green's story. Green was a utility infielder with a limited skill set. He was a superb base runner with occasional power as a hitter, but he compiled a substandard .246 career batting average and was prone to erratic fielding. He was out of MLB in 1964 at the age of twenty-nine because of a poor fielding and a weak throwing arm that was exposed whenever he didn't play second base. The harsh reality of Major League Baseball is that bench players—Black or

White—who lack flexibility have, simply, little utility. Had Green not been the *first* African American to play for the Boston Red Sox, he would have been mentioned in the same breath as lesser mortals of a team memory, such as Chuck Schilling, Carroll Hardy, and Don Buddin, infielder teammates during Green's years in Boston.

Green's exceedingly modest baseball statistics make him a problematic legend and taint recent Red Sox ceremonies with an acrid odor of tokenism. That is precisely the charge leveled by Howard Bryant, an African American sports reporter with ESPN. He witheringly denounced Fenway Park's Jackie Robinson Day celebration as mythologizing the past: "In today's world of political correctness, marketing polish, and media savvy, baseball has become expert at selling memories, and the game seems untroubled if those memories don't exactly align with history." Green arrived in Boston a year after Ozzie Virgil Sr. integrated the Detroit Tigers, the next-to-last team to integrate, and three years after Jackie Robinson *retired*. Even hockey's Boston Bruins integrated before the Red Sox. "What is to be celebrated?" Bryant asked. "That the Red Sox put off integrating as long as possible? To celebrate that occasion is to do something corporations—and do not forget that baseball *is* a corporation—do very well. They are experts at scrubbing history, at massaging a negative into a positive."[13]

There is a considerable merit to Bryant's blast, though he underestimates Green's personal off-the-diamond drama. Green and others like him played roles (even when small) in helping dismantle the *de jure* Jim Crow and set the stage for ongoing battles against *de facto* discrimination. Historians have long recognized the importance of sports in presaging more sweeping progress in the civil rights struggles of African Americans. During the 1930s and 1940s, for example, boxer Joe Louis and track star Jesse Owens foreshadowed reconsiderations of race embodied in the 1941 creation of the Committee on Fair Employment Practice and the "Double V" campaign of African American soldiers during World War II.[14] Jackie Robinson's 1947 MLB debut with the Brooklyn Dodgers took place a full seven years before the US Supreme Court ordered public school desegregation pursuant to its ruling in *Brown v. the Board of Education of Topeka, Kansas.*

Both Pumpsie Green and outfielder Sam Jethroe—who played for the Boston Braves in 1950, nearly a decade before Green played for the Red Sox in 1959—factored into the city of Boston's struggles with institutional racism, though the slowly developing arc of that struggle was such that a moment of silence might have been more appropriate than self-congratulatory ceremonies. It took five decades before Pumpsie Green morphed into a baseball legend, and even today it's hard to escape the feeling that he and recent players of color are conveniently and counterfactually used as symbols of Boston's redemption from an unfortunate racist past.

Pumpsie Green fits the profile of what mythologist Joseph Campbell called the "reluctant" hero, a humble individual with little desire to be special.[15] It was a fluke that Green was the first Black Red Sox player. His debut came on July 21, 1959, just one week in advance of the debut of talented right-handed pitcher Earl Wilson (1934–2005). Had Wilson not served two years in the US Marines in 1957 and 1958, he would have surely been Boston's first Black player.[16]

Pumpsie Green never dreamt of integrating a major league team, much less the Boston Red Sox. In his words, "I never thought of playing pro ball. To me, baseball was just a game to . . . have fun with. That was all."[17] His aspiration was to ease into an ongoing integration effort, not to break new ground like Jackie Robinson. A local team, the Oakland Oaks, of the Pacific Coast League (PCL), stirred the California-born Green's racial pride. The Oaks integrated in 1948, eleven years before the Red Sox, and sported professional baseball's first interracial roommates, Black shortstop Artie Wilson and White second baseman Billy Martin. Green wanted to play for the Oaks, an AAA minor league team, but one that lacked affiliation with an MLB parent club and managed its affairs independently. This gave it and other PCL teams an ambiguous status somewhere between AAA and MLB ball, with some baseball scholars asserting that some of its teams were on par with MLB franchises.[18]

Pumpsie Green came close to attaining his more modest dream. He played his first minor league baseball for the Wenatchee Chiefs of the Western International League in 1953 and was with the Stockton Ports in 1955, both lower-level feeder clubs for the Oaks. He was scheduled to play for Oakland in 1955, but the case-strapped Oaks relocated to Vancouver, British Columbia. As a way of increasing team value, Green's contract was sold to the Red Sox. Overnight, the racial equation changed for Pumpsie Green. It was the difference between easy integration and becoming a racial pioneer for an organization with a reputation of being the most racist in all of professional sports.

As Howard Bryant noted in his incisive work, *Shut Out: A Story of Race and Baseball in Boston*, "Pumpsie Green was not by nature a trailblazer."[19] That is correct, despite the fact that Green balked in 1955 when the Red Sox sought to assign him to the Montgomery Rebels, the team's A-level minor league affiliate. Green asked, "Do you know what's going on in Montgomery? I don't think there was a black man in America who wanted to go to Montgomery, Alabama, in 1955."[20] That Red Sox management would even contemplate such a posting is troubling. At best, the Red Sox were clueless; at worst, they wanted Green to fail, and his signing was mere symbolism meant to placate critics. Green avoided Montgomery; instead, he played for Stockton, California; Albany, New York; San Francisco, California; and

Oklahoma City, Oklahoma, from 1955 through 1957 before advancing to the AAA Minneapolis Millers during 1958 and 1959.

The higher Green rose, the more he bore the burdens of others' public dreams. The National Association for the Advancement of Colored People (NAACP), Boston's small-but-growing African American community, White liberals, and beleaguered Red Sox fans fed up with years of mediocre teams, all seized upon Green as a symbol of both unfairness and Red Sox futility. As Green languished in the minor leagues, these groups charged that Green was the latest of a long line of talented players of color turned away by a racist-to-the-core organization.

Upon making the Red Sox in June 1959, Green became a symbol of hope for Boston's African American community, a role he neither sought nor wished for. In his words, "I'm no martyr. No flag carrier. I'm just trying to make the ball club, that's all. I'm not trying to prove anything but that. I'm not interested in being the first Negro to make the Red Sox."[21] The NAACP sought out Green, and he was photographed with leaders on several occasions, but he was unnerved by the media attention and resented groups that wanted him to be their public spokesperson. As Green recalled his Red Sox debut: "It was something to write about, to holler about, to scream about. . . . [T]he NAACP people called me, asked me a lot of questions. Everybody called, and after everybody called, more people called. I wouldn't take their calls because I didn't have anything to say."[22]

Green, by choice, sought to reject the symbolism behind his Red Sox debut. "I didn't really spend a lot of time thinking about it," he said. "I spent most of my time thinking about stuff like how to hit a curveball."[23] His greatest awareness was of his own limitations. In his words, "I was a good ballplayer, but I knew I wasn't a great one."[24]

THE RED SOX UNDER TOM YAWKEY

Green sought to avoid the limelight, but there was too much bad racial blood within both the team and the city of Boston to allow him to be just another player in the clubhouse. The man who did not wish to walk in Jackie Robinson's footprints would soon be tossed into a city whose racial tensions were more analogous to those of Montgomery, Alabama, than to his native Oakland.

Mabray "Doc" Kountze, the editor of the *Boston Guardian*, a Black newspaper, remarked in 1993 that he was "heartbroken" that the Red Sox was the last team to integrate because he had hoped they'd be the first.[25] He should not have been surprised. Social history and cultural geography reveal that Boston was, simply, a tough town in which to be Black, and the Red Sox embodied those challenges.

The term *plantation mentality* is often used to describe the Red Sox clubhouse and the management style of team owner, Tom Yawkey. His adoptive father and uncle, Bill Yawkey (1875–1919), was heir to a Michigan lumber fortune, but he spent most of his later years on a twenty-five-thousand-acre former rice plantation in South Carolina in the heart of the Jim Crow South and within an easy drive of Ty Cobb's home near Augusta, Georgia. The latter fact matters; Bill Yawkey owned the Detroit Tigers from 1903 to 1919, a time in which Ty Cobb was the Tigers' star player and was so close to the Yawkeys that he was viewed as a family member. Cobb was also a vicious racist who imparted his views to the Yawkeys. Bill Yawkey found it easy to tolerate Cobb's racism because, like many White Americans, he accepted the Jim Crow presumptions of his day as the natural order of things. Bill Yawkey also befriended Cap Anson, a nineteenth-century player often said to have spearheaded MLB's color ban in the 1880s.[26]

Bill Yawkey died during the 1919 influenza epidemic, but his legacy lived on both in Detroit and in the attitudes of his heir, Thomas. It was no coincidence that the Tigers were the next-to-last MLB team to integrate, or that the Red Sox, purchased by Tom Yawkey in 1933, was the last team to do so. As Bryant notes, the younger Yawkey (1903–1976) grew up in Michigan, went to school in Tarrytown, New York, and lived for a time in New York City after his father's death, but much of his time was spent in South Carolina, where he absorbed the racism of mentors such as Cobb and Anson, and that of future employees such as Eddie Collins, Mike "Pinky" Higgins, and Joe Cronin. The latter three were also drinking cronies.

Akin to Bill Yawkey's style with the Tigers, Tom was often an absentee owner of the Red Sox, preferring to spend time in South Carolina while others ran the team and he rubber-stamped their decisions. His *laissez-faire* management style served to deflect Yawkey from direct involvement in racist decision-making, but in Howard Bryant's words, "The Red Sox were a decidedly southern team."[27] As we shall see, some individuals defended Yawkey, but the only evidence-based open question is whether he was a blatant or passive racist. Although Doc Kountze might have dreamt of an integrated Red Sox, fellow African American sportswriter Sam Lacy was under no such illusions; he declared emphatically that a first-class Black Red Sox player was unlikely "as long as Yawkey is the owner."[28]

BOSTON: SOUTH CAROLINA COMES
TO MASSACHUSETTS

Among the more troubling aspects of Red Sox lore is the transformation of Tom Yawkey into a legend enshrined in the National Baseball Hall of Fame, and whose name adorns the two-block street on which Fenway Park is located. There was little to applaud during Yawkey's tenure as Red Sox owner, and racist practices were the norm during the fifty-nine years in which he and his wife/widow, Jean, owned the team (1933–1992). Still, one must ask how it was possible for the Yawkeys to maintain a plantation mentality so far north of the Mason-Dixon Line. Why did the city of Boston countenance racist patterns that both embarrassed the city and prevented the Red Sox from excelling on the field?

The urban history analog to the Pesky's Pole legend is that Boston has ever been a beacon of racial tolerance. At best, its record was mixed; by the early twentieth century, there wasn't much in Boston that would have troubled a die-hard South Carolina segregationist. Much of the city's greatest racial progress had occurred in the pre-Revolutionary and antebellum periods. Boston then was, occasionally, a city of firsts for African Americans—the first Black landowner ("Ken" in 1656), the first published African American woman poet (Phyllis Wheatley, 1772), the first order of Black Freemasons (Prince Hall, 1787), and (perhaps) the home of the first Black abolitionist group (the Massachusetts General Colored Association, 1826). Massachusetts abolished slavery in 1780 and integrated its schools in 1855. By the 1850s, supporters hailed and Southerners assailed Boston as a center of abolitionist fervor. Boston was home base for White antislavery advocates such as Theodore Weld, the Tappan brothers (Arthur and Lewis), Wendell Phillips, and William Lloyd Garrison, and articulate Black voices such as David Walker, Sarah Roberts, Lewis Hayden, Frederick Douglass, and Ellen and William Craft.

Strident abolitionism and the city's resistance to the Fugitive Slave Act made Boston seem far more enlightened than it actually was. Anti-abolitionist Whites, for instance, allegedly poisoned Black antislavery activist David Walker in 1830, African Americans were banned from Boston Common until 1836, it took a lawsuit to integrate the city's schools, and a White mob broke up an abolitionist meeting headed by Frederick Douglass as late as 1860. Still, there were other surface gains throughout the nineteenth century: the first Black Harvard grad (Richard Greener, 1870), the city's first Black councilman (John J. Smith, 1878), and the Commonwealth's first Black judge (George Ruffin, 1886). Between 1866 and 1897, twelve Black

146 *Robert E. Weir*

Bostonians served as state representatives, and ten were elected to the Boston City Council. (Tellingly, there were none of either from 1897 to 1946.)

The salient demographic fact about Boston, though, is that until the late 1950s, there simply weren't that *many* African Americans in the city. In 1820, for instance there were 1,690 Black residents in a city of 43,298; by 1850, the Black population had fallen by half, though the city population had more than tripled. In 1880, there were 5,873 African Americans in Boston, but the city's overall population had again tripled to nearly 363,000.[29] Northern cities such as New York, Brooklyn, and Philadelphia had Black populations ranging from 9 percent to over 12 percent; Boston's nineteenth-century high-water mark was closer to 4 percent.

For most of the nineteenth century, the city's small Black population was confined to the western slope of Beacon Hill, a section unflatteringly dubbed "Nigger Hill" by White Bostonians. Moreover, as Zebulon Miletsky observed, most of the gains made by Black Bostonians in the nineteenth century quickly came undone in the early twentieth. Miscegenation battles, the discriminatory practices of White labor unions, and de facto patterns of housing discrimination were such that by 1920, in Miletsky's words, Boston "was no longer the city of Garrison. . . . Boston was . . . becoming the city of Jim Crow."[30]

Boston remained an overwhelmingly White city for much of the twentieth century. When former Negro Leagues star Sam Jethroe donned a Boston Braves uniform in 1950, over 801,000 people lived within the city limits. The city's Black population nearly doubled between 1940 and 1950, but it was still less than forty-six thousand, which left Boston nearly 95 percent White. This was about to change.

Social tension and rapid social change often go hand in glove. Pumpsie Green took the field just nine years after Jethroe, but by then important demographic shifts were under way. Boston's non-White population had been steadily and inexorably migrating southward: from Beacon Hill to the South End to Roxbury and North Dorchester. It was also growing and stood at roughly sixty-three thousand. Unlike the past, this made the city more than 9 percent Black, as growth coincided with the first wave of White flight. In 1960, roughly 90 percent of all African Americans lived in or near Dorchester, once Jewish and Irish neighborhoods. Resentment toward incomers was magnified by "blockbusting," a pernicious practice in which Realtors hoodwinked White homeowners into selling their homes at below-market prices through lurid tales of how a coming flood of minority residents would further suppress property values. Blockbusting was where self-fulfilling prophecy intersected with predatory capitalism. Realtors and rental agencies gained cut-rate housing stock, which they rented or sold at marked-up prices to people of color, who, by custom, could not live elsewhere.

The infamous Boston school-busing crisis occurred a dozen years after Pumpsie Green left Boston, but its seeds germinated as he played there. Between the years in which Jethroe played for the Boston Braves (1950–1952) and Green for the Red Sox (1959–1962), the population of the city declined by more than 14 percent. All told, 31 percent of Whites left Boston between 1950 and 1970, most of them fleeing to the suburbs. Those who remained within the city hunkered down in enclaves that historian Ronald Formisano graphically described as "defended neighborhoods" in his study *Boston Against Busing: Race, Class, and Ethnicity in the 1960s and 1970s.*[31]

In the late nineteenth century, Boston was often compared favorably with (allegedly) racially enlightened Southern cities such as Atlanta; by the latter third of the twentieth, it drew a less-flattering comparison to Belfast, Northern Ireland, with various ethnic groups claiming "their" neighborhoods as the "real" Boston—the North End for Italian Americans; South Boston, Brighton, and Charlestown for Irish Americans; Chinatown for Asians; East Boston and the Fenway for mixed groups of Whites; Dorchester, Mattapan, and North Roxbury for African Americans; and the suburbs for affluent Whites. The constant, in Monica McDermott's words, was that "being white was equated with power and privilege, if not necessarily affluence."[32]

De-facto housing segregation meant the city's neighborhood schools were becoming monochromatic even as Pumpsie Green and Earl Wilson added a splash of color to Fenway Park. By 1962, 60 percent of all Black students attended just thirty-five schools; eight years later, 81 percent of all Black students would have needed to be bused to attain court-ordered racial balance in city schools.[33] Even more ominously, the city's Blackest schools in Dorchester stood adjacent to its Whitest, those in South Boston.

The defended communities of Boston's school crisis were first made manifest in cultural terms. As Barry Bluestone and Mary Huff Stevenson observed, "The region may have a fascination with sports, music, and fine art, but one is apt to encounter a sea of white faces at a Red Sox or Celtics game, a Boston Symphony event, or an opening at the Museum of Fine Arts."[34] Sam Jethroe, though complimentary to Braves fans, recalled that in the early 1950s, he seldom strayed far from his hotel room in Kenmore Square during off days and did not go to the movies, where his presence might have raised notice. He spent most of his nights out in South End jazz clubs along Massachusetts Avenue that allowed Black patrons, especially the Hi-Hat Club on the corner of Columbus Avenue.[35]

As a California native, Green was insulated from some of Boston's racial dynamics. "I was aware of some of it," he recalls. "I had seen some things on TV."[36] He was about to get a baptism of fire. When Pumpsie Green arrived in 1959, Black Celtics' stars Bill Russell and K.C. Jones instructed him on where he would be welcome and places he should avoid. Topping the latter list was South Boston, the home, in Russell's words, of "brick-throwing racists."[37] Jethroe, Green, Russell, and Jones followed the path of Malcolm Little/X, who lived in Boston between 1940 and 1943; each only felt truly comfortable in Roxbury or Dorchester.

An optimistic reading of Boston's first professional Black athletes would locate them within the sociological phenomenon known as *marginal adaptation*, a term referencing fissures in society through which out-groups gain entrance into mainstream society. (Think, for instance, of the ways in which Black vaudevillians, musicians, and actors displayed their talents before White audiences.) Historical evidence does not allow such a reading for Boston. Although Bill Russell seethed with anger at his outsider status, at least he had supportive team management and cheering fans behind him; the same cannot be said for its first Black baseball players. Nationally, baseball historians note rising attendance levels when the first African Americans took the field.[38] That assertion is open for debate, but it's clear that Black players had little impact on baseball attendance in Boston.

Nor was there a niche into which Black baseball players fit. Boston never fielded a team in the official Negro Leagues, making it one of the few northern cities of consequence that never did so.[39] A handful of semipro teams had home bases in Boston, Cambridge, and West Newton, but each barnstormed rather than rely upon local attendance to meet costs. The Braves were the fifth major league team to integrate when Sam Jethroe signed in 1950, but his presence did not salvage the Braves' sinking box receipts. In the three years before his signing (1947–1949), the Braves averaged 14,681 fans per home contest.[40] The Braves saw soaring attendance from 1946 through 1949, but these were artificial highs aided by the increased demand for baseball once the Great Depression and World War II ended, and by a pennant-winning season in 1948.

The Braves, however, had long been Boston's "secondary" baseball team, due partly to the team's mediocre record on the field. In the eleven years before the outbreak of World War II—the 1931 to 1941 seasons—the Braves never finished higher than fourth in the eight-team National League, averaged just 4,487 fans per game, and were routinely at or near the bottom of the NL in attendance. In the three years in which Jethroe played in Boston, home attendance averaged 7,416 per game.[41] Although this represented an increase over the Depression years, Sam Jethroe's presence was not enough to keep the Braves from moving to Milwaukee in time for the 1953 season. In fact, Braves' ticket sales actually declined from 14,049 per game in 1949 to 12,648 in 1950, Jethroe's first year as a Brave, one in which he won Rookie of the Year honors. And if one takes away his rookie year, in which attendance was boosted as much by memories of the 1946 pennant as by Jethroe's exploits, the Braves averaged a woeful 4,992 patrons per game—roughly its Depression-era attendance. This contrasts dramatically with Cleveland, where Larry Doby's presence on an already-strong team led to surges at the box office.[42]

The Braves were admittedly mediocre—they finished fourth in each of Jethroe's Boston years—but the same can be said of the Red Sox. The Red Sox won the pennant exactly one time (1946) between 1933, when Tom Yawkey bought the team, and 1959, the year Pumpsie Green debuted with Boston. In fact, after the 1949 season, the Red Sox never finished above third until 1967. Nor did the Red Sox burn out the turnstiles. From 1933 through 1966, the Red Sox routinely ranked third to fifth (of eight) in attendance and just twice (1942 and 1956) ranked as high as second. In the three years before Pumpsie Green arrived, the Fenway not-so-faithful averaged 14,681 fans per game, and there were perpetual rumors that Yawkey planned to move the team. The team's less-than-robust attendance and its less-than-stellar play fueled those who linked the team's sagging fortunes to its refusal to put Black players in uniform.

Once again, the question must be raised: Whose decision was it to keep the Red Sox lily-White? *Boston Globe* sportswriter Will McDonough (1935–2003) insisted to his death that Tom Yawkey was not a racist and that the Red Sox simply couldn't find qualified Black players. More recently, Yawkey's personal secretary, Mary Trask, insisted, "I personally do not think he was (racist). I never saw that in him." She also claims she never heard him utter a racial epithet or say, "Don't get that guy because he's Black."[43] Alas, the historical record is at odds with McDonough and Trask.

McDonough's claim that the Red Sox could not find qualified Black players is absurd. When Doc Kountze remarked he had hoped that the Red Sox would be the *first* MLB team to integrate, he had in mind an infamous 1945 incident in which the Red Sox held a "tryout" for three Negro Leagues players: Sam Jethroe, outfielder Marvin Williams, and Jackie Robinson. The entire event was a sham designed to relieve pressure from the Black press, including Kountze, Sam Lacy of the *Chicago Defender*, and Wendell Smith of the *Pittsburgh Courier*; and to placate Jewish city councilor Israel Muchneck, who threatened to repeal exceptions to Massachusetts blue laws allowing the Sox to play Sunday games unless the team sought to integrate. Red Sox manager Joe Cronin didn't even bother to attend. Clif Keane of the *Boston Globe* reported that after a short period, someone in the stands shouted, "Get those niggers off the field.[44]

The remark might have been apocryphal, random, or issued from one of the two major suspects, general manager Eddie Collins or Yawkey. It was probably considered by both, if not actually verbalized, as neither had the slightest intention of signing a Black player. The 1945 sham tryout was merely the first of several less-than-sincere reconsiderations of race. In 1949, Red Sox scout Larry Woodall was dispatched to Birmingham, Alabama, to observe a promising Negro Leagues player. He arrived on a rainy day and stayed in his hotel room with the tart explanation, "I'm not going to waste my time waiting on a bunch of niggers." He simply filed a report asserting that the player in question was not one in which the Red Sox would be interested. That player was Willie Mays, one of the greatest players in MLB history.

No one reprimanded Larry Woodall. Then someone in the organization made the decision in 1950 to cut Piper Davis, the first Black player the Red Sox actually signed, after just eight months rather than ante up money due if his contract was renewed.[45] Someone looked the other way when Pinky Higgins, who managed the Red Sox between 1955 and 1960, remarked, "There'll be no niggers on this ball club as long as I have anything to say about it."[46] Two other Black players deemed "unqualified" for a Red Sox uniform were Hank Aaron and Billy Williams, both Hall-of-Famers. Clark Booth of the *Dorchester Reporter* summed up Yawkey's duplicity in the racism that swirled around his club: "As for Yawkey, he said not a bloody word."[47]

It was even worse than Booth noted. When Pumpsie Green came to the Red Sox in 1959, he was the franchise's first Black employee in *any* capacity. If ever a case could be made for removing an inductee from the Hall of Fame, Tom Yawkey would be an ideal candidate, even if he did have his finger on the pulse of community sentiment. Whether he was an overt racist like Higgins or a passive one is beside the point; Yawkey could not forever pretend that Jackie Robinson hadn't leveled MLB's color barrier. Nor could the city of Boston act as if the civil rights movement was happening far from Fenway Park. Changing demographic and social tides were about to storm Tom Yawkey's plantation.

PUMPSIE GREEN ENTERS AND EXITS
BOSTON'S RACIAL DRAMA

Boston's racial prehistory undoubtedly led reformers to heap unrealistic expectations upon Pumpsie Green. The final days of the Red Sox "plantation" were contentious and nasty. The 1950s is often miscast as a time of conformity, a shallow stereotype that (at best) applied to some suburban middle-class Whites and conveniently overlooks things such as the civil rights movement, teen rebellion, rising drug use, changing sexual mores, and cultural challenges posed by the Beats, rock and roll, and the "Folk Revival."[48] Some within the press also asked hard questions about the makeup of American society. The term *new journalism* did not gain currency until 1965, but in the 1950s, investigative reporters such as Edward R. Murrow, Marguerite Higgins, Mike Wallace, and I.F. Stone took it as their mission

Constructing Legends 151

to unearth stories, not wait for them to develop. The same ethos showed up among post–World War II sportswriters and frayed the chummy relations once the norm among writers, players, and management.

Although Pumpsie Green was unaware of most of it, as he was rising through the minors, Yawkey and the Red Sox found themselves under attack. Sportswriters such as Mabray Kountze, Larry Claflin, Peter Gammons, and Bud Collins complained loudly of Red Sox racism. For his trouble, Collins, then a thirty-year-old reporter for the *Boston Herald*, had Pinky Higgins smash a bowl of beef Stroganoff into his face. Higgins also spat tobacco juice on Claflin (just twenty-three) and called him a "nigger lover." Higgins's boorish behavior served only to increase the pressure on the Red Sox; gone were the days when team officials could display such arrogance and expect the press to suppress it. The status quo was shaken further by the presence of fans holding signs outside Fenway linking the team's on-the-field mediocrity and management's behind-the-scenes refusal to recruit Black talent. As sportswriter Howard Bryant put it, by 1959, the "Red Sox had grown to be an embarrassment, even to the most conservative baseball organizations."[49]

As pressure mounted, Pumpsie Green performed well enough in the minors to be drawn into Boston's racial drama. In mid-1958, Gene Mauch, his manager at Minneapolis, noted that Green "still has some things to learn about hitting . . . [but he] fields better than anyone up there."[50] During spring training in 1959, Green "was thumping the ball at a merry clip," registering a .444 batting average, more than 150 points higher than his shortstop competitor Don Buddin (.290).[51] Nonetheless, the Red Sox sent Green back to the minors, using the excuse that he had only hit .253 in the minors the previous year. Predictably, charges of racism flew fast and furious. The NAACP protested by blocking a parking lot plan near Fenway, while the Massachusetts Commission Against Discrimination launched an investigation into *why* the Red Sox had no Black employees.

As noted, the percentage of Black Bostonians nearly doubled during the 1950s, a demographic shift that led to hard questions about the city's racist past in general and Red Sox personnel decisions in particular. It did not sit well when sportswriters revealed that Green was not allowed to stay on the grounds of the Red Sox's spring training facility in Scottsdale, Arizona, because the city and the park were segregated. The *Boston Globe* informed readers that Green could not eat with the team, could not go to movies with other players, and often didn't even ride on the same bus.[52] Yawkey was visibly troubled by the press scrutiny. When the *Globe* speculated whether Tom Yawkey might simply "blow his top" at the backlash and "quit Boston," he angrily snapped his fingers and announced, "I could do it like that!"[53] His critics were unmoved by such bluster. The *Pittsburgh Courier*'s Wendell Smith angrily asked, "Whom do the Boston Red Sox think they are kidding . . .

?" Smith testily laid out the details of the team's sham tryout for Jackie Robinson and found it "strange" that "only Boston" found it impossible to find a "capable Negro player."[54]

Globe sportswriter Harold Kaese did what would have been unthinkable in the cozy press/management collusion of Yawkey's first two decades of team ownership: he revealed divisions within the Red Sox organization. In particular, Kaese signaled the negative impact that management racism placed on Don Buddin, "a young man already carrying a heavy enough burden." Buddin's modest talents, Kaese noted, were so overhyped that he was widely regarded as manager Mike Higgins's pet, a role he neither sought nor relished. Kaese intimated that Higgins saw Buddin as the White hope that would keep Green off the team, a vain hope as it turned out. Buddin was a light hitter, and a fielder so weak that he was nicknamed "E6."[55] With Green hitting .320 at Minneapolis and Buddin just .241 in Boston, management ran out of excuses for keeping Green in the minors. On July 3, the Red Sox abruptly fired Higgins and hired Billy Jurges to manage the team. In the eighth inning of a game in Chicago on July 22, 1959, baseball's last Jim Crow barrier fell when Pumpsie Green entered the game as a pinch runner. Green graciously made things easier for the team by telling the *Globe* he hadn't been ready for MLB in April.[56]

The next day, Green made his first start and failed to record a hit in three trips to the plate. Few thought much of this, as most players fared poorly against the opposing White Sox pitcher, future Hall-of-Famer Early Wynn. It was enough, though, to make him an afterthought on the lineup card. Press interest in Green was high. His Fenway Park debut occurred on August 4. An atypically large crowd of twenty-one thousand fans gave him a standing ovation, and Green promptly lined a triple off the left-field wall. Green recalls it as his single-greatest baseball thrill.[57] Green went on to appear in fifty games and log 172 at bats. Soon, though, local papers settled into noting Green's progress as they would any other player, for the simple reason that, after his Fenway debut, there weren't that many highlights. Green had just ten extra-base hits and a subpar slugging average of .320; he stole four bases; and he hit just .233. Green's test year was expected to be 1960, not 1959.

Except that it wasn't. After another torrid spring training and speculation that he would be the starting second baseman, Green slumped, and the Red Sox acquired thirty-six-year-old Bobby Thompson,[58] put him at first base, and pushed incumbent Pete Runnels to second. The *Globe* noted, "This will make a benchwarmer of Pumpsie Green."[59] And so it did, as his inconsistent hitting and fielding made him unable to dislodge Buddin at short. Green played in 133 games, mostly as a pinch hitter and a late-inning replacement. In sixty-one games at second base, he fielded .982, the league standard, but in forty-one games at short, he was significantly below average, with a

Constructing Legends 153

.951 fielding average. Buddin wasn't much better, with a .956 fielding average, but he hit .263, eighteen points higher than Green. Green also got on the wrong side of manager Billy Jurges by failing to execute a routine double-play ball. Jurges told reporters, "Some players have to be pushed a bit to play good ball. This is true of Pumpsie . . . he wasn't hustling enough." Green played sporadically until Buddin was injured in September.[60]

Green's 1960 fate was sealed in June when Jurges was fired and the Sox rehired Pinky Higgins. Higgins avoided the overt racial comments he'd made in the past, but Green recalls, "You'd just get a feeling [about Higgins]. He'd make his conversation as short as possible." Teammate Earl Wilson was less circumspect: "It's not very hard to tell if a guy likes you or dislikes you."[61] As noted, Green was mainly a late-game insert; he got just 260 at bats in 1960, just eighty-eight more than in 1959, when he appeared in just fifty games. Green blamed long stints on the bench for his poor fielding, but what little hope remained for him to secure more action was sabotaged when the press reported a heated conversation between Higgins and general manager Bucky Harris over the decision to have Green on the roster in the first place.[62]

With Higgins at the helm, Green's prospects looked grim for 1961. They did not improve when the Red Sox announced a "shortstop sweepstakes" in spring training between Green, Buddin, Runnels, and slick-fielding rookie Chuck Schilling, who won the contest. Schilling wasn't a great hitter (.253), but in 158 games at short, he made just eight errors, half as many as Green made in only fifty-seven games at short. Higgins opined that Green "doesn't have . . . the arm for shortstop," and that appears to have been a sound baseball evaluation rather than a racial judgment.[63] Green got just 219 at bats in 1961, a year of disappointment made worse by an appendectomy in May. He hit reasonably well as a pinch hitter, but at season's end, the Red Sox probably would have parted ways with Pumpsie Green had he not been the only Black player on the roster. (The team had shipped Earl Wilson back to the minor leagues.)[64]

Instead, the Red Sox traded Don Buddin to Houston for Eddie Bressoud, another light-hitting, heavy-handed infielder.[65] When Wilson came back to the Sox, tossed a no-hitter, and proved more capable with the bat than Green, the latter seldom left the bench. Green's only 1962 headline was of the wrong kind. On July 27, 1962, White pitcher Gene Conley grew agitated when the team bus sat motionless in heavy traffic near New York City's George Washington Bridge, and he persuaded Green to abandon the bus with him, grab a taxi, and supposedly embark on a spur-of-the-moment trip to Israel. Green repented of his impulsiveness before he boarded the plane, but Higgins was through with him, especially after the *Boston Globe* questioned whether Higgins was also "missing the bus in managing" the Red Sox.[66]

Red Sox management decided it was time for both men to go. In the off-season, Green was traded to the New York Mets with virtually no fanfare, and Johnny Pesky replaced Higgins as team manager. Neither Green nor Pesky thrived in their new posts. Green made six errors on just fifty-six chances in seventeen games for the 1963 Mets before being sent down to the minors, where he spent the last two and a half years of his baseball career. Nor was Pesky the answer to the Red Sox's managerial prayers.

Green enjoyed a brief resurgence in the minors at Buffalo, where he hit .308, but his hitting and fielding trailed off in 1964, the latter after a disastrous attempt to convert him to a third baseman. He played ten games as a first baseman in 1965, before quitting baseball at the age of thirty-one. As Green put it, "I went back to being a regular workingman." Until his retirement, Green worked with the Berkeley, California, school district, taught math, and did some coaching.[67] Said Green, "I never relaxed in Boston. Every game to me was like Opening Day. I felt pressure all the time."[68] In a similar vein, he remarked that though it was "special" to be the first Black player for Boston, "it made my blood pressure go up, too. I can't fail. I can't make a mistake. That was how I felt."[69]

As the years passed, Green grew more comfortable with having integrated the Red Sox. But when the *San Francisco Chronicle* asked him in 2009 if he was "proud" to have been a pioneer, he gave a refreshingly honest answer: "Now I am. Back then I learned to put it out of my mind, ignore race issues."[70] In 2006, he regaled writer Harvey Frommer with some of the trials of being the first Black player on the Red Sox: "I had no roommate . . . since I was the only Black on the team. It wasn't a law. But it was unwritten that Blacks did not room with whites. . . . I roomed with no one until Earl Wilson came along." He spoke mainly of day-to-day battles to function: "Some of the pressure and nervousness I put on myself. I know people expected a lot, especially the black community. . . . There were overtones of racial things . . . [that] could be heard not only at Fenway but any other ballpark. Sometimes terrible things would be yelled out, racial epithets."

Ever the self-effacing man, Green also noted, "For my contemporaries, what I did was a big deal." He admitted feeling a thrill when kids learned about his Red Sox days, but he insisted, "There's really nothing interesting about me. I am just an everyday person happy with what I did. . . . I would like to be remembered in Red Sox history as just another ballplayer."[71]

Except, of course, that is impossible. *Someone* had to be the first Black player for the Boston Red Sox, and Pumpsie Green was that person. His reluctance and his prosaic skills notwithstanding, Pumpsie Green is as much a part of Boston lore as Pesky's Pole. When I spoke with Green in September 2012, he had settled more deeply into his iconic role. "I'm proud of what little I did," he noted. "I'm relaxed about it, and I don't worry about what others

Constructing Legends 155

say." Memories of pressure have faded, and he now asserts, "If I had it all to do over, I'd do it the same way, at the same time, with the same team."[72]

HOW ARE YOU GOING TO KEEP
THEM ON THE PLANTATION?

Integration narratives too often end with path breakers, as if somehow their arrival opened doors and hastened the dismantling of all racial barriers. The *Oxford English Dictionary* credits a 1962 *New York Times* magazine story for the first recorded use of the term *tokenism* to describe the minimal rather than substantive presence of minorities within an organization.[73] That such a term would emerge while Green was still in a Red Sox uniform is eerily appropriate; it describes well Green's place on the roster and the Red Sox management's view of Black players for the next several decades. It's certainly the lens through which African American baseball fans viewed the Red Sox. Although Pumpsie Green's contributions to the Red Sox "legacy" would eventually be appreciated with the "gratitude" of which Red Sox CEO Larry Lucchino had spoken, such appreciations lay far in the future. In the short term, Green was part of a worsening racial climate within Boston and across the Commonwealth. Green's presence did little to attract patrons of Fenway Park. Fenway attendance actually dipped by an average of 2,597 patrons per game during the four years in which Green played to just 12,084. That figure would be even lower were it not for an average of 14,674 during the 1960 season; the Red Sox averaged just 9,164 during Green's last year in a Red Sox uniform, levels comparable to anemic franchises in Washington and Kansas City that would be moved in 1968 and 1971, respectively. While overall MLB attendance dropped in the early 1960s, Boston's attendance for 1962 was considerably below the American League average of 14,954 per game.[74] As Mel Parnell's colorful radio commentary had suggested, part of the problem was that the Red Sox were a mediocre team for which enthusiasm was hard to generate, but it was consistently so—there were no real "highs" or "lows" in team performance during Green's time in Boston.

Red Sox fortunes revived dramatically in 1967, when the team won the American League pennant for the first time since 1946. Alas, success on the field did little to break up the club's plantation mentality or ease racial tensions within the region. Green's departure after the 1962 season left just two Black players on the Red Sox roster, Earl Wilson and the seldom-used Al Smith. It would not be until 1966—the first year in which Dick O'Connell was general manager—that the Red Sox had more than two; that year, the roster contained eight Black players, of whom three were starters: Wilson, first baseman George Scott, and outfielder Reggie Smith. That team finished ninth (of ten), but the "Impossible Dream" season of 1967 saw the team go to the World Series, where the Red Sox lost a thrilling seven-game series to the St. Louis Cardinals. This was the turnaround year for the Red Sox as a business. More than 1.7 million fans poured into Fenway that year, the beginning of a run in which the park was often near capacity.

The 1967 Red Sox had five Black players. Noticeably absent was Earl Wilson, who was traded to Detroit in June 1966, after he complained of having been called a "nigger" at a bar near Winter Haven, Florida, where the Red Sox held their spring training camp. The *Boston Globe*'s Larry Claflin caught wind of the story, but Wilson begged him to suppress it so he could resolve the problem with team officials. Wilson dutifully reported the incident to manager Billy Herman, who told him, "Forget it. . . . It never happened." Wilson seethed for weeks before telling Claflin to run the story. Herman promptly labeled Wilson a troublemaker, and the pitcher was traded to Detroit for outfielder Don Demeter.[75] The untold story of 1967 might well be whether the Red Sox would have won the World Series with Wilson on their staff. He was 22–11 for the Tigers in 1967, a number of victories that matched Red Sox ace Jim Lonborg, and was ten games more than the next-best pitchers on their staff. Those two twelve-game winners, José Santiago and Gary Bell, lost three of the four games the Red Sox dropped in the World Series.

Earl Wilson was the first of several highly talented Black and Latino players to exit Boston bitterly and excel in new surroundings. He won fifty-six games and lost fifty-eight in seven years with the Red Sox, but he was 64–45 in just five seasons with Detroit. The Tigers were, with the exception of 1967, a superior team to the Red Sox, but three salient facts stand out. First, Wilson's earned run average (ERA) was nearly a full run lower in Detroit (3.18 to 4.10).[76] Second, Wilson excelled for the Tigers between the ages of thirty-one and thirty-five—that is, beyond the peak-age statistical norms for pitchers. Third, it is highly plausible that Wilson was traded because he had the temerity to complain about racism to an organization with explicitly racist views. He was a superior player in nearly every aspect of the game to the man for whom he was traded. (He was even a better power hitter. Wilson hit seventeen home runs with the Tigers; Demeter hit just ten with the Red Sox.) Wilson noted that with Boston, it wasn't unusual to "walk into a room and hear coaches saying, 'Nigger this, nigger that.'"[77]

In the period from 1967 to 1986, Boston fielded numerous talented Black and Latino players, including Reggie Smith, George Scott, Jim Rice, Luis Tiant, Dennis Boyd, Tony Armas, Ellis Burks, and Dave Henderson.[78] They also briefly signed aging former stars such as Luis Aparicio, Orlando Cepeda, Ferguson Jenkins, Juan Marichal, and Tony Perez. Only a few felt comfortable in Boston. Howard Bryant documented their struggles against racism in his book *Shut Out: A Story of Race and Baseball in Boston* (2002), and the

Constructing Legends 157

problem looks even worse when one highlights two dimensions to which Bryant paid less attention: the quickness with which Red Sox management gave up on highly regarded Black and Latino prospects, and the successful careers many of them experienced in other uniforms.

During the same 1967 to 1986 period, the Boston Red Sox fielded an average of 4.3 Black or Latino players per season. That's approximately 10.7 percent of the team's forty-man roster at a time when the league average was around 17 percent, and some teams surpassed the 40 percent mark.[79] More telling is that just seven players of color played as many as five consecutive years with the Red Sox.[80] Reggie Smith, who played for Boston from 1966 to 1973, had the potential to be the city's first Black superstar, but, like Wilson, he refused to play a compliant role. "I don't believe Boston was ready to accept an outspoken black. . . . We were stereotyped," Smith recalled. He regarded his 1974 trade to St. Louis as a form of liberation. Smith left Boston at the sabermetrician's peak age of twenty-eight, and for the next nine years, he was regarded as one of the most dangerous hitters in the National League.[81]

Post-Boston numbers are also higher for several other players, most notably Cecil Cooper, Juan Beniquez, and Ben Oglivie. George Scott came close to duplicating his nine-year production with the Red Sox in just five (and 1,400 fewer at bats) with Milwaukee, when he was traded there in time for the 1977 season. Scott also recalled that, in 1970, he sought an apartment in a Dedham complex where he knew there were vacancies. He was told, "They are all filled." Scott recorded that the Celtics' Bill Russell "told me this is basically a racist city. . . . He was right. It's just that kind of town."[82] New York Yankees' second baseman Willie Randolph (from 1976 to 1988) remarked that he got special joy out of beating the Red Sox because the team and the city were so racist.[83]

Scott and Randolph were correct—Boston was a profoundly racist city. In 1977, all of America became aware of Boston's racial tensions, courtesy of a Pulitzer Prize–winning photograph snapped by Stanley Forman in which Joseph Rakes, a White antibusing activist, attacked a Black pedestrian, Ted Landsmark, outside Boston City Hall. Forman's shocking photograph captured Rakes's attempt to strike Landsmark with the pointed staff of an American flag.[84] Alas, the assault on Landsmark was not an isolated incident. As we have seen, Boston's changing demographic face led to court-ordered busing programs to address the racial imbalance within city schools. Boston was convulsed by antibusing protests tinged with racial animus from 1974 through 1988. Busing ended in 1988, but this was because of White flight and the enrollment of White children in private schools, not because racial harmony had been achieved. By 1988, just fifty-seven thousand children were enrolled in Boston schools, down from over one hundred thousand in 1974; by the twenty-first century, 76 percent of Boston's public-school children were Black, though nearly 55 percent of residents within the city limits were non-Latino Whites.

It would be fair to say that the most profound social change in Boston from the time of Bill Russell and Pumpsie Green to the late 1980s was that people of color, such as Smith, Scott, and Randolph, had grown more assertive in calling attention to the everyday indignities that Russell had internalized, Green had suppressed, and Wilson had sought to mediate. Even Jim Rice, often called the Red Sox's first Black superstar, was uncomfortable throughout his sixteen years in Boston (1974–1989), though he did not publicly admit this until 2002. Rice was a hero on the field, but he was keenly aware that Bostonians cheered White outfielders Dwight Evans and Fred Lynn with greater fervency. Privately, Rice told rising star Ellis Burks to "get your six years and get the hell out of Boston," which is precisely what Burks did when he was eligible for free agency.[85] Burks was twenty-eight years old, peak performance age, when he left for the White Sox after the 1992 season.

Red Sox fans enjoy a reputation for fervency, but fandom parses differently by race. Few people of color cheered when the Red Sox captured the American League pennant in 1975. Howard Bryant, who grew up in Dorchester, recalls his seven-year-old self being taken to task by his grandfather for rooting for the Red Sox against the Cincinnati Reds during the World Series. Among Whites, that contest is remembered as another heartbreaking seven-game thriller (like that of 1967) in which an elusive championship slipped away; however, many Black baseball fans often recall it as the triumph of Joe Morgan, Tony Perez, Ken Griffey Sr., and George Foster over the racist Red Sox.[86]

The 1975 season was also the year that opened the door for baseball free agency. (Free agency allows a player to bargain with whomever he wishes at the end of his contract, if he has played six years in the Major Leagues.) Conventional wisdom holds that it altered baseball's racial equation and brought to reality Jackie Robinson's caustic observation that "Money is America's God, and businesspeople can dig black power if it coincides with green power."[87] Not quite. In theory, Boston was free to bid for the services of talented players of color, but Black talent often ignored the lure of Red Sox green and refused to sign there. That list included talented players such as Mel Hall, Tim Raines, Ken Griffey Jr., Marquis Grissom, David Justice, and Kirby Puckett.[88] The promise of riches was insufficient to erase the openly discussed perception among Black players that they would not be welcome in Boston. Such perceptions were reinforced by the exodus of talented Black and Latino free agents from Boston, including Beniquez, Oglivie, Cooper, Burks, Boyd, Bob Watson, Chico Walker, and Tony Armas.

Eleven years later, the Red Sox returned to the World Series, fandom remained divided by race, and Boston's racially charged social and sports

Constructing Legends 159

tensions spilled onto the campus of the University of Massachusetts, Amherst (UMass), ninety-four miles west of the city. Sociologist Monica McDermott trenchantly observed of Boston that civil relations between Blacks and Whites "can change in an instant—a rude exchange at a supermarket or a misunderstood exclamation can set the stage for an exuberant display of anti-black . . . sentiment."[89] Her remarks summarize what occurred in Amherst in the wee hours of October 27–28, 1986.

On October 25, 1986, the Red Sox were on the cusp of winning their first World Series since 1918, only to see the New York Mets score the tying run on a wild pitch, and the winning run on a grounder that slipped between first baseman Bill Buckner's legs for an error. Two nights later, the Mets won the World Series. A small group of Mets fans gathered outside the Southwest Residential Area of UMass to celebrate. Southwest houses 5,500 students in sixteen dorms, including five twenty-two-story towers built in the mid-1960s, when the university's student body had doubled. Part of the thinking behind the high-rises—an idea consonant with architectural design and theory of the day—was that the tall structures would be more inviting for students from metropolitan areas. Whether by design or unplanned circumstance, a large number of suburban White Bostonians and Black urbanites ended up in Southwest. The mix proved volatile.

The Southwest celebration devolved into heckling and fisticuffs between White Red Sox and Black Mets fans, the small gathering swelled to over 1,200, and the situation spiraled out of control. Before police had contained the riot shortly after midnight, bottles were hurled, fireworks had exploded, a sofa was thrown from a dormitory window, dumpsters were overturned, several dozen windows were smashed, and ten students were injured in fights. One, Yancey Robinson, an African American, was left in a neck brace.

The university's initial response was lackluster. Director of public safety Peter O'Neil acknowledged that Black and White students had clashed, but he insisted that the incident was not racial in nature, though both eyewitness reports (Black and White) and a subsequent fifty-two-page report issued by Frederick Hurst of the Massachusetts Commission Against Discrimination disagreed. The Hurst Report stated in no uncertain terms that minority students viewed the Mets as a "Black" team and the Red Sox as a "White" franchise.[90]

The UMass riot led to important (and ongoing) changes on the Amherst campus, but among the things pertinent to this study is that the Red Sox remained identified as a "White" team a full twenty-seven years after Pumpsie Green's debut. This was the case, despite the fact that the 1986 Red Sox fielded five African Americans and three Latinos, and the Mets six and three, respectively. Hadn't the Red Sox clearly turned the corner, with 20 percent of a forty-man roster consisting of players of color, a percentage in

160   *Robert E. Weir*

keeping with the overall representation of African Americans and Latinos in American society? Were UMass students acting upon outdated stereotypes?

It would seem not. Three months before the World Series, the Equal Employment Opportunities Commission ruled that the Boston Red Sox had discriminated against Black coach Tommy Harper when it fired him in 1985. In a case eerily reminiscent of Earl Wilson's, Harper had publicly complained of racism when he learned that the team had bought player memberships in a Winter Haven, Florida, Elks club that refused service to African Americans. Nor were things calm in Amherst. The UMass clash—originally called a "fight" in the local *Daily Hampshire Gazette*, but christened a "riot" in the Hurst report—was cited as a contributing factor in racial incidents on the campuses of nearby Smith and Mount Holyoke colleges, and as a factor in the beating of two Black UMass students by five Whites several months after the World Series ended. Those beatings were the final straw that led minority students to occupy the university's New Africa House in February 1987.

The Red Sox did not make a substantial dent in the team's plantation legacy until the late 1990s—nearly three decades after Pumpsie Green's departure and despite several decades' worth of intense scrutiny from sportswriters such as Larry Whiteside, Mike Barnicle, Steve Fainaru, and Gordon Edes.[91] Although the *Boston Globe*'s Will McDonough remained an embarrassing apologist for the Yawkey family, the team was stung by numerous racial discrimination lawsuits from former employees.[92] Jean Yawkey's death in 1992 opened the door for change, and by the late 1990s, players Pedro Martinez and Mo Vaughan, a Dominican and an African American respectively, were the faces of the franchise. Vaughan also groused about the team's treatment of minorities, but his free-agency departure in 1999 was more financially than socially motivated.[93]

PATHBREAKERS AND UNBROKEN PATHS

In 1944, just three years before Jackie Robinson reintegrated Major League Baseball, Swedish economist Gunnar Myrdal published *An American Dilemma: The Negro Problem in American Democracy*. Myrdal analyzed both pernicious and promising dimensions of American racial tensions, especially the gulf between White views of superiority on one hand, and the "American Creed" of fairness and equality on the other. Of all the problems Myrdal probed, none has proven more intractable than institutional racism— those discrimination mechanisms that are too deeply embedded in American society to be addressed on a case-by-case basis. Myrdal placed great faith in the power of democracy and of liberal social policies to transform both attitudes and institutions.

It would be facile to deny that great changes have occurred in racial relations since 1944; it would be equally facile to say that the "American dilemma" has gone away, or to deny that the pace of change is often glacial. For better or worse, positive steps to alleviate the American dilemma often remain case-by-case actions. Although it does not get the attention it deserves, sports has been and remains an arena in which social problems are highlighted and redress is sought. Figures such as Joe Louis and Jackie Robinson deserve to be mentioned in the same breath as post–World War II civil rights activists such as A. Philip Randolph, Dr. Martin Luther King Jr., and Rosa Parks, but what of individuals such as Elijah "Pumpsie" Green?

In 1947, African American sportswriter Wendell Smith cautioned readers of the *Pittsburgh Courier*, a Black newspaper, not to harbor unrealistic expectations. He wrote, "Remember, all our boys can't be a Robinson."[94] Smith meant that some Black players would fail athletically, but his words resonate more deeply. As we have seen, Pumpsie Green neither saw himself in Robinson's class, nor aspired to it. He was not gifted with Robinson's skill, nor did he wish to be seen as any sort of pioneer. "I knew that all the Major League teams had been integrated except for the Red Sox. People made me aware. They wouldn't let me forget it," said Green. But he added, "I got tired of it all."[95]

Where is it written that pathbreakers must be outspoken? Green's reluctance to play an outspoken role in America's civil rights drama in no way diminishes his accomplishment. Call him an accidental pioneer, but it nonetheless took tremendous inner reserve and strength of character to endure the isolation, frustrated ambitions, and acts of everyday indignity that marked Green's time in Boston. Green was aware he played for a manager and an organization that didn't want him. He was quickly made aware that Boston wasn't Oakland, and that for every person of color who wanted him to succeed, there were dozens of Whites who wanted him to fail. Pumpsie Green played a role in the Bay State's version of the American dilemma, but the reconsideration of race of which he was a part hasn't been easy, fast, or entirely transformative.

Green has never been assertive, but he is more so today than he was when he played. Back then, he measured his words carefully, even when riding the bench for Pinky Higgins. In 1997, thirty-two years after he left Boston, Green admitted that Higgins was racist. When asked why he remained silent at the time, Green responded, "I'm a diplomat. In other words, [saying nothing] was the best thing to say at that particular time."[96] In 1996, Green expressed disappointment that the Red Sox had not invited him to return for any official events, including an Opening Day ceremony honoring Jackie Robinson. That omission prompted the *Boston Globe*'s tart remark, "With the Red Sox, it seems some things never change."[97]

162   *Robert E. Weir*

The very next year, a Black former sales manager, Thomas Sneed, filed a racial discrimination suit against the Red Sox. Sneed was laid off after seven years, an action Sneed alleged was due to his engagement to a White woman. Reporter Joan Vennochi could hardly contain her skepticism when the team also announced it was hiring more minorities.[98] Nor did it escape attention that as late as 2003, the Red Sox had but three African Americans on their forty-man roster, none of whom was expected to make the twenty-five-man permanent roster.[99] And what does it say when Green was not part of the Red Sox's first official Jackie Robinson Day celebration in 2004, or that the team didn't invite him to take part in MLB's annual Jackie Robinson Day until 2009? Small wonder the latter event invited Howard Bryant's withering scorn.

Green remained collected as controversy swirled around the Red Sox. He even claimed to root for the Red Sox and the Giants, though he told me in 2012 that he seldom watched or followed baseball after his retirement and "finds it kind of boring to watch." By then, though, Green had been invited back to Fenway several times. Who could begrudge him for basking in delayed glory, or uttering the sanitized remark that he'd happily relive his experience in the same time, same place, and same way?[100] But one should also note remarks he made thirty years earlier that are preserved in the archives of the National Baseball Hall of Fame: "I knew [baseball] was a short life when I got into it. I got a chance to play in the major leagues. . . . I enjoyed it. That's all."[101]

Except that it can't be all. As sociologists Lawrence Baldassaro and Richard Johnson note in *The American Game: Baseball and Ethnicity* (2002), as much as MLB would like to use Pumpsie Green's generation of players and its annual Jackie Robinson Day celebrations as examples of how the national pastime "truly became the game that represented all of America . . . [it], more than most American social institutions, has mirrored the gradual and often difficult process of assimilation experienced by a succession of ethnic and racial groups."[102] Far more than the unfortunate 1986 UMass World Series incident lies between Green's departure from the Red Sox and Fenway Park's one-hundredth anniversary bash.

A small sampling of ongoing racial incidents at the national level includes Curt Flood's 1969 challenge to baseball's reserve clause; allegations of racism at the Dodgers' Vero Beach, Florida, complex in 1971; Hank Aaron's 1979 charge that prejudice toward African Americans remained a baseball staple; the 1987 firing of Dodgers' general manager Al Campanis after remarks suggesting that African Americans lacked the mental capacity to be managers and executives; Cincinnati owner Marge Schott's 1992 references to the "million dollar niggers" in her club; a 1992 study showing that attendance went down when Black pitchers started; and racist, homophobic, and nativist remarks made by Atlanta pitcher John Rocker in 2000.[103]

Constructing Legends 163

What have these incidents to do with Greater Boston? As NPR reporter Juan Williams documented in 2002, Boston hadn't moved beyond its legacy of racism.[104] It still hasn't. In 2009, the liberal bastion of Cambridge was sullied by an ugly incident in which a White police officer engaged in a racially tinged confrontation with Henry Louis Gates Jr., a Black Harvard professor who has devoted his career to racial justice. In 2012, two distressing incidents occurred that left no doubt that regional problems remained. On April 25, 2012, Joel Ward, a Black hockey player for the Washington Capitals, ended the Boston Bruins' playoff run with a seventh-game overtime goal. Twitter was filled with racist bile from crestfallen Bruins' fans.[105] In July, raw wounds opened in Manchester, New Hampshire, when Red Sox outfielder Carl Crawford—in the minors on an injury rehabilitation assignment—was racially slurred while signing autographs. The offender, an off-duty police officer, was fired, but it didn't escape notice that Crawford was traded to the Dodgers on August 25, 2012, as was Mexican American first baseman Adrian Gonzalez.[106] In scenarios eerily reminiscent of minority players from the time of Earl Wilson on, Crawford and Gonzalez seem to have revitalized their careers away from Boston: as of June 2013, Crawford was hitting .301—some forty-six points better than he did at Boston—and Gonzalez was hitting a robust .326.

The legacy of racism lives on in the reluctance of African American fans to attend games at Fenway Park, in plays such as the 2006 musical *Johnny Baseball* documenting the team's racist past, and in the Black and Latino neighborhoods of Chelsea, Dorchester, and Lawrence, where locals root for the Yankees in the midst of what is allegedly "Red Sox Nation."[107]

Americans should celebrate what individuals such as Pumpsie Green endured to make professional sports and society more inclusive. But they should not confuse those efforts with an unenlightened past as prelude to a racially healed present. Pumpsie Green, a humble man of modest dreams and talents, has been more gracious than team officials could have expected or deserve. But, like Pesky's Pole, Green's accomplishments are imbued with legend whose symbolism is greater than historical fact supports.

One should applaud Green's courage—even celebrate his modest career; after all, by most reckonings, fewer than 6 percent of all minor league players make it to the MLB level. But these achievements must be tempered by the reality that what we today celebrate is not necessarily what should have been. Ceremony, glitz, and slick public relations should not blind us to past struggles or anesthetize us to those that remain. Howard Bryant got it right when he wrote of Green's baseball debut: "This is the real truth about July 21, 1959. . . . When your organization is less interested in Willie Mays than a spell of bad weather, you get Pumpsie Green. When you have the jump on Billy Williams and he gets away, you get Pumpsie Green. When your top baseball man patronizes Jackie Robinson, you get Pumpsie Green. When you're one of the richest teams in the game and fail to capitalize for more than a decade on a pool of the most talented and economically desirable ballplayers in the history of the game, you get Pumpsie Green. When the state's corporate watchdog sues your organization . . . twice . . . for discriminatory hiring practices, you get Pumpsie Green. In short, you get trivia over what could have been triumph.[108]

Recent reconciliation efforts are a step in the right direction, though they might easily be viewed as little more than self-congratulatory pageantry in a region whose recent past has been marred by defended neighborhoods, campus riots, Black Harvard professors in dustups with White cops, battles over redistricting Boston's minority wards, and unpalatable brews of fandom and racism. These things are the antithesis of what many people hoped Pumpsie Green would represent. The Red Sox acknowledged Yawkey's racism by changing the street Yawkey Way back to Jersey Avenue. Perhaps Pumpsie Green Way would be more appropriate still.

Table 8.1. Minority Players in the Yawkey Family Era (1933–1992)
(* Designates player late in career)

Year	Player	Ethnicity	T # of Minorities	Fate of Player
1933–1959	None		0	
1959–	Pumpsie Green	African Am	3	Traded to NY Mets, 1963
	Earl Wilson	African Am		Traded to Detroit, 1966
	Bobby Avila*	Mexican		Released after twenty-two games
1960	Green	African Am	3	Taken by Washington in expansion draft
	Wilson			
	Willie Tasby			
1961	Green		1	
1962	Green, Wilson		2	
1963	Wilson	Mexican	3	Released, 1964
	Roman Mejias*	Puerto Rican		Traded to Houston, 4/66
	Felix Mantilla			
1964	Wilson, Mejias, Mantilla		4	Released after twenty-nine games
	Al Smith*			
1965	Wilson, Mantilla		2	

Year	Player	Ethnicity	T # of Minorities	Fate of Player
1966	Wilson	African Am		Traded to Milwaukee,
	George Scott	African Am		10/71; reacquired,
	Reggie Smith	Puerto Rican		12/76
	Jose Santiago	Cuban		Traded to Kansas
	Jose Tartabull	African Am		City, 6/79
	John Wyatt	African Am		Released after
	Joe Foy	Virgin Islands		injury, 1970
	Joe Christopher	African Am		Sold to Oakland, 5/69
	George Smith			Sold to NY Yankees, 5/68
				Went to Kansas City in
				draft, 10/68
				Released after twelve
				games
				Released, end of
				1966 season
1967	Scott, R. Smith,	African Am	7	Retired, 1968
	Santiago,			
	Tartabull,			
	Wyatt, Foy			
	Elston Howard*			
1968	Scott,	Puerto Rican	10	Traded to Cleveland, 4/69
	R. Smith, Santiago,	Puerto Rican		Traded to Chicago White
	Tartabull, Wyatt,	African Am		Sox, 12/70
	Foy, Howard			Released, 10/68
	Juan Pizarro			
	Luis Alvarado			
	Floyd Robinson			
1969	Scott, R. Smith,	African Am	7	Traded to White
	Santiago,	Mexican		Sox, 3/71
	Pizarro, Alvarado	Puerto Rican		nine games; traded to
	Vincente Romo			California, 6/69
	Joe Azcue			
1970	Scott, R. Smith,	Puerto Rican	6	Traded to Atlanta, 12/76
	Santiago,			
	Alvarado, Romo			
	Roger Moret			
1971	Scott, R. Smith,	Venezuelan		Retired, after
	Moret	African Am		1973 season
	Luis Aparicio*	Panamanian		Traded to Milwaukee,
	Cecil Cooper	Puerto Rican		12/76
	Ben Oglivie	Cuban		Traded to Detroit, 10/73
	Juan Beniquez			Traded to Texas, 11/75
	Luis Tiant			Left as free agent, 10/78

Year	Player	Ethnicity	T # of Minorities	Fate of Player
1972	R. Smith, Moret, Aparicio, Beniquez, Cooper, Oglivie, Tiant Tommy Harper Bob Veale* Lynn McGlothen	African Am African Am African Am	10	Traded to California, 12/74 Released, 10/74 Traded to St. Louis, 12/73
1973	R. Smith, Moret, Aparicio, Beniquez, Cooper, Oglivie, Tiant, Harper, Veale, McGlothen, Orlando Cepeda*	Puerto Rican	11	Released, 3/74
1974	Beniquez, Cooper, Tiant, Harper, Moret Jim Rice Diego Segui Juan Marichal*	African Am Puerto Rican Dominican	8	Played 15 seasons; retired as Red Sox Released, 4/76 Released, 10/74
1975	Beniquez, Cooper, Tiant, Moret, Rice		5	
1976	Cooper, Tiant, Rice Ferguson Jenkins* Bobby Darwin	Afro Canadian African Am		Traded to Texas, 12/77 Traded to Chicago Cubs, 5/77
1977	Rice, Jenkins, Darwin George Scott* Ramon Aviles Ramon Hernandez*	African Am Puerto Rican Puerto Rican	6	Second stint with Red Sox one game; sold to Philadelphia, 4/77 twelve innings; released, 8/77
1978	Scott, Rice, Tiant		3	
1979	Scott, Rice Bob Watson	African Am	3	Left as free agent, 11/79
1980	Rice Tony Perez Chico Walker Julio Valdez	Cuban African Am Dominican	5	Released, 11/82 Left as free agent, 10/84 Marginal player; released, 1983
1980	Luis Aponte	Venezuelan		Traded to Cleveland, 3/84
1981 (strike year)	Rice, Perez, Walker, Valdez, Aponte		5	
1982	Rice, Perez, Walker, Valdez, Aponte Dennis Boyd	African Am	6	Left as free agent, 11/89

Year	Player	Ethnicity	T # of Minorities	Fate of Player
1983	Rice, Perez, Walker, Valdez, Aponte, Boyd Tony Armas	Venezuelan	7	Left as free agent, 11/86
1984	Rice, Perez, Walker, Boyd, Armas, Mike Easler Jackie Gutierrez	African Am Colombian	7	Traded to NY Yankees, 3/86 Traded to Baltimore, 12/85
1985	Rice, Boyd, Armas, Easker, Gutierrez		5	
1986	Rice, Boyd, Armas Rey Quinones Don Baylor* Ed Romero LaSchelle Tarver Dave Henderson	Puerto Rican African Am Puerto Rican African Am African Am	8	Traded to Seattle, 8/86 Traded to Minnesota, 9/87 Released, 8/89 Released at end of season Traded to San Francisco, 9/87
1987	Rice, Boyd, Baylor, Romero, Henderson Ellis Burks Sam Horn	African Am African Am	7	Left as free agent, 12/92 Released, 12/89
1988	Rice, Boyd, Burks, Horn, Romero Lee Smith Carlos Quintana	African Am Venezuelan	7	Traded to St. Louis, 5/90 Spent career with Red Sox; retired, 1993
1989	Rice, Boyd, Burks, Horn, Romero, Quintana, L. Smith Luis Rivera	Puerto Rican	8	Left as free agent, 10/93
1990	Burks, Quintana, L. Smith, Rivera Tony Pena	Dominican	5	Left as free agent, 10/93
1991	Burks, Quintana, Rivera, Pena Mo Vaughan Josiah Manzanillo	African Am	6	Left as free agent, 10/98 Left as free agent, 3/92; returned, 2005
1992	Burks, Pena, Vaughan, Rivera Billy Hatcher	African Am	5	Left as free agent, 11/92

168 *Robert E. Weir*

NOTES

1. This chapter was originally published in 2014 as the following article: Robert E. Weir, "Constructing Legends: Pumpsie Green, Race, and the Boston Red Sox" *Historical Journal of Massachusetts* Volume 42, No. 2 (Summer 2014).

2. Richard Dorson, *America in Legend: Folklore from the Colonial Period to the Present* (New York: Pantheon, 1971): xiv.

3. In popular culture, the term *legend* is often attached to the entertainment figures who achieve commercial success, and the adjective *legendary* is applied to impressive or memorable people and events. See www.urbandictionary.com/define.php?term =legendary, accessed May 24, 2013.

4. Jan Brunvand, *The Study of American Folklore* (New York: W. W. Norton, 1978): 106.

5. Allen Guttman, *From Ritual to Record: The Nature of Modern Sports* (New York: Columbia University, 2012); Tristram Coffin, *The Old Ball Game: Baseball in Fiction and Folklore* (New York: Herder & Herder, 1971).

6. The Red Sox also traded Fred Hatfield, Don Lenhardt, and Bill Wright to Detroit and received Hoot Evers and Johnny Lipon in return.

7. Parnell was the victim of his own mythmaking. As he told the story, Pesky hit a walk-off homer to win a game Parnell was pitching in 1948. In truth, Pesky homered just one time when Parnell was pitching—in the first inning of a game in 1950.

8. Mike Petraglia, "Pumpsie Green Throws Out First Pitch," MLB.com, April 17, 2009. Retrieved August 10, 2012. Dave Roberts's inclusion in this list is also puzzling. His stolen base in a key 2004 postseason matchup with the New York Yankees notwithstanding, Roberts was a late-season acquisition who played just forty-five games with the Red Sox and was traded to the San Diego Padres in the offseason. Roberts's feat has been magnified in Red Sox legend. Roberts stole on catcher Jorge Posada, who threw out just 27 percent of runners in 2004, well below the league average of 32 percent.

9. "Red Sox Home Opener," *Boston Globe*, April 17, 1998.

10. Dan Shaughnessy, *The Curse of the Bambino* (London: Penguin Books, 1991). Shaughnessy collected numerous stories to explain why the Red Sox, until 2004, had not won a World Series since 1920, the year they sold Babe Ruth to the New York Yankees. It is not always clear when Shaughnessy is serious and when he's being ironic, but he does repeat some inaccuracies. The Sox last won a World Series in 1916, years *before* the sale. He also reports a story that Red Sox owner Harry Frazee sold Ruth to finance a failed Broadway show. This is untrue; Frazee was solvent. Moreover, the show in question was *No, No, Nanette*, anything but a failed show! It is noteworthy that Johnny Pesky played a role in the "curse." In game seven of the 1946 World Series against St. Louis, Pesky hesitated throwing the ball to home plate, allowing a run to score. St. Louis won the deciding game 4–3.

11. Dan Shaughnessy, "An Olde Towne Toast," *Boston Globe*, April 21, 2012.

12. Note: Shaughnessy was born in 1953 and grew up in Groton, an elite Boston suburb that is less than 1 percent Black. He graduated from Holy Cross College in 1975, when there were just twenty-nine Black students on campus. His first sports

Constructing Legends 169

beat job was in Baltimore in 1977, before coming to the *Globe* in 1981, eighteen years after Green was traded to the New York Mets. He would have been just six when Green debuted with the Red Sox. These biographical details suggest that it's unlikely that Pumpsie Green was a "god" of Dan Shaughnessy's youth. Source: Information on the number of Black students was provided by Mark Savolis, head of Archives and Special Collections at College of the Holy Cross University, in an email exchange of October 19, 2012.

13. Howard Bryant, "No Honor in Red Sox Anniversary," ESPN.com, July 21, 2009. Retrieved August 10, 2012. Note: That the Boston Bruins integrated before the Red Sox is highly significant. Until 1958, when Willie O'Ree got into two Bruins' games, the National Hockey League was 100 percent White. However, O'Ree was sent back to hockey's minor leagues and did not make it back to the NHL until 1961. He was again sent back down to the minors, and the NHL remained all White until 1974.

14. The double-V campaign, symbolized by forming a V shape with the second and third fingers on each hand, signaled the resolve of Black soldiers during World War II to secure a double "victory" over fascism abroad and racism at home.

15. Richard Dorson, *Folklore and Folklife: An Introduction* (Chicago: University of Chicago, 1992); Dorson, *America in Legend: Folklore from the Colonial Society to the Present* (New York: Pantheon Books, 1971); Jan Brunvand, *The Study of American Folklore* (New York: Norton, 1978); Joseph Campbell, *The Hero with a Thousand Faces* (Novato, CA: New World Library, 2011).

16. Wilson won 121 games in an eleven-year career and was a more worthy symbol for those arguing that racism contributed to Boston's baseball mediocrity. In 1962, Wilson hurled a Fenway Park no-hitter, the first since 1956. Appropriately, the previous one belonged to Mel Parnell of "Pesky's Pole" fame.

17. Jonathan Mayo, "Boston's Green: A Reluctant Pioneer," MLB.com, February 6, 2007. Retrieved August 8, 2012.

18. The minor leagues are stratified from low to high as a prospect is trained, seasoned, and prepared for the major leagues. Today, the stratification runs from A (Rookie, Short Season), A (Advanced), AA, and AAA. In Green's time, the lowest rung was Class D. One then rose to C, B (several levels), A, AA, and AAA. Oakland had been independent since 1937.

19. Howard Bryant, *Shut Out: A Story of Race and Baseball in Boston* (New York: Routledge, 2002): 9.

20. "Pumpsie Green" folder, archived in the National Baseball Hall of Fame, Cooperstown, New York (hereafter abbreviated as Baseball HOF). See also Mayo, "Boston's Green: A Reluctant Pioneer."

21. Bryant, *Shut Out*, 12.

22. Green folder, Baseball HOF.

23. Ibid.

24. Author's interview with Elijah "Pumpsie" Green, September 11, 2012.

25. Kountze's remark was quoted in an article by Michael Madden, "He Ran into a Fenway Wall," *Boston Globe*, May 28, 1993. It was found in a clipping in the Sam Jethroe File, Baseball HOF.

26. Bryant, *Shut Out*, 68–69; Jerry Gutlon, *It Was Never About the Babe: The Red Sox, Racism, Mismanagement, and the Curse of the Bambino* (New York: Skyhorse, 2009): 69–70; Richard A. Johnson and Glen Stout, *Red Sox Century* (New York: Houghton Mifflin Harcourt, 2005): 179–82. Note: The ban officially went into effect among National League teams in 1887, but it was not until two years later that the International League, then a rival major league, adopted it.

27. Bryant, *Shut Out*, 68.

28. Jules Tygiel, *Baseball's Great Experiment: Jackie Robinson and His Legacy* (New York: Oxford, 1997): 329.

29. Robert Hayden, *African-Americans in Boston: More than 350 Years* (Boston: Boston Public Library Press, 1991).

30. Zebulon Miltesky, "City of Amalgamation: Race, Marriage, Class and Color in Boston, 1890–1930" (PhD Thesis in Afro-American Studies, University of Massachusetts, Amherst 2008): 84.

31. Ronald Formisano, *Boston Against Busing: Race, Class, and Ethnicity in the 1960s and 1970s* (Chapel Hill: University of North Carolina Press, 1991).

32. Monica McDermott, *Working-Class White: The Making and Unmaking of Race Relations* (Berkeley: University of California Press, 2006).

33. Barry Bluestone and Mary Huff Stevenson, *The Boston Renaissance: Race, Space, and Economic Change* (New York: Russell Sage Foundation, 2000).

34. Ibid., 7. Bluestone and Stevenson argue that these patterns remained true long after the busing crisis subsided. In cultural terms, Boston remains a White city, whether one is speaking of popular or elite culture.

35. The Hi-Hat is now the site of the Harriet Tubman House. Information from the Sam Jethroe File, Baseball HOF.

36. Author's interview with Elijah "Pumpsie" Green, September 11, 2012. However, in the same interview, Green misremembered the timing of several events. Among the events Green misremembered is having seen an image of a White man trying to impale an African American with an American flag. He was thinking of a widely circulated image snapped by *Boston Herald American* photographer Stanley Forman. However, this occurred thirteen years after Green left Boston.

37. Bryant, *Shut Out*, 58.

38. Tygiel, *Baseball's Great Experiment*. Some minor league teams experienced increases of up to 50 percent. The usual figure given for MLB teams was around 2,500 per game.

39. Leslie Heaphy, *Negro Leagues 1869–1960* (Jefferson, NC: McFarland, 2003). There was a team called the Boston Resolutes in 1887, but this was before the Negro Leagues were organized. In 1912, there was a team called the New York Boston Giants, but it soon dropped Boston from its name.

40. In just one year were the Braves a contender, the pennant-winning season of 1948, but attendance that year was less than one might expect—just 18,901 per home contest.

41. The Braves finished fourth in 1950 and 1951, the same as they finished in 1949. The team drew just 201,279 patrons in 1952 and moved to Milwaukee in

1953. The ultimate move had no impact on 1952 attendance in Boston, as it was not announced until the offseason and Braves fans had no forewarning.

42. Baseball-Reference.com. Note: The Braves finished fourth in all three years Jethroe was with the team and were seventh (of eight) in 1950, and last in 1951 and 1952. Note: The impact of Black players on attendance is somewhat controversial. Contrary to myth, Jackie Robinson's presence on the Dodgers led to a negligible bump in attendance of just 139 patrons per game on average between 1946 and 1947, the latter year in which the team went to the World Series and one would expect an increase. Cleveland also went to the World Series during Larry Doby's first full year, which sent attendance soaring by almost fifteen thousand per game. The next year (1949), when the Indians finished third, is probably a better measure of Doby's box-office magic as that year's attendance was down from 1948, but it was still nearly ten thousand per game higher than before he arrived. Black players did not lead to big increases for the New York Giants or the St. Louis Browns; both franchises—like the Braves—soon relocated, the Browns to Baltimore in 1954, and the Giants to San Francisco in 1958.

43. Bryant, *Shut Out*; Stan Greenfield, "Keeper of Secrets," *Boston Globe*, May 26, 2013.

44. Bryant, *Shut Out*; Jackie Robinson, *I Never Had It Made* (New York: Putnam, 1972); Larry Moffi and Jonathan Kronstadt, *Crossing the Line: Black Major Leaguers 1947–1959* (Jefferson, NC: McFarland, 1994); Gutlon, *It Was Never about the Babe.*

45. Larry Whiteside, "The First to Sign," *Boston Globe*, July 22, 1979.

46. Moffi and Kronstadt, *Crossing the Line*, 7.

47. Clark Booth, "About Pumpsie Green and the Indelible Stain Yawkey-Era Racism Left on the Red Sox," *Dorchester Reporter*, July 23, 2009.

48. The term *Folk Revival* is less familiar to many. It refers to a renewed interest in American folk music—including social protest songs—that began in the 1940s and continued into the 1960s. Although many think of 1960s singers such as Bob Dylan when they think of protest music, Dylan merely rode an active and ongoing protest tradition that thrived in the 1950s. In several years, folk music also outsold rock and roll during the 1950s and early 1960s.

49. Bryant, *Shut Out*, 6.

50. Roger Birtwell, "Pumpsie Green Almost Ready," *Boston Globe*, June 16, 1958.

51. Untitled article, *Boston Globe*, March 24, 1959.

52. Milton Gross, "Green Now Used to Loneliness," *Boston Globe*, March 28, 1959; Harold Kaese, "Did Sox Give Pumpsie Green Shabby Deal?" *Boston Globe*, April 8, 1959. Note: Green occasionally went to exhibition games on a bus used by the Chicago Cubs, who had several Black players.

53. Bob Holbrook, "Red Sox Send Pumpsie Green to Minors," *Boston Globe*, April 8, 1959; "NAACP Says No Pumpsie, No Parking Lot for Sox," *Boston Globe*, April 9, 1959; "State Board to Probe Red Sox Racial Policy," *Boston Globe*, April 11, 1959; "Whole Town's Talking About the Green Boy," *Boston Globe*, April 12, 1959; Jerry Nason, "Will Yawkey Quit Boston?" *Boston Globe*, April 12, 1959; "Sox Sit Tight as Green Storm Rages," *Boston Globe*, April 12, 1959.

54. Wendell Smith, "Sports Beat," *Pittsburgh Courier*, April 25, 1959.

55. Harold Kaese, "It's Not Buddin's Fault That Green Was Shipped Out," *Boston Globe*, April 9, 1959. Note: E6 is an official scorer's designation for an error made by a shortstop. It is a form of shorthand in which player positions are numbered for easy reference: 1= pitcher, 2= catcher, 3 = first baseman, etc. The shortstop is number 6.

56. Birtwell, "Sox Recall Pumpsie," *Boston Globe*, July 22, 1959; Robert McLean, "Everyone Pleased Pumpsie Returning," *Boston Globe*, July 22, 1959; Bob Holbrook, *Boston Globe*, "Not Ready for Sox in April—Pumpsie," July 24, 1959.

57. Author's interview with Elijah "Pumpsie" Green, September 11, 2012.

58. Bobby Thomson is legendary for a home run he hit in 1951 as a member of the New York Giants. The Giants entered the summer of 1951 far behind the league-leading Brooklyn Dodgers, but they won thirty-seven of the team's last forty-four games to tie the Dodgers for first place and force a playoff for the pennant. With the Giants trailing 4–2 in the bottom of the ninth inning, Thomson hit a three-run walk-off home-run off Dodgers' pitcher Ralph Branca, which sent the Giants to the World Series. The press dubbed it the "Shot Heard Around the World" and the "Miracle of Coogan's Bluff," the latter referring to the elevated section of land along the Harlem River that rose above the Giants' home field, the Polo Grounds. Fans with sharp eyes often perched on Coogan's Bluff to watch games without paying. The playoff game took place on October 3, 1951. The Giants lost the World Series to the Yankees, four games to two.

59. "Jurges Will Try Thompson at First," *Boston Globe*, April 12, 1960.

60. Birtwell, "Jurges Defends Strategy," *Boston Globe,* April 26, 1960.

61. Shaughnessy, "Crossing the Color Line," *Boston Globe*, March 28, 1997.

62. Author's interview with Elijah "Pumpsie" Green, September 11, 2012; Clif Keane, "Harris' Side of the Story," *Boston Globe*, September 28, 1960.

63. Birtwell, *Boston Globe*, April 11, 1961.

64. "Pumpsie Undergoes Operation," *Boston Globe*, May 14, 1961; Birtwell, "Green's Slug Pct. As Pinch Batter .750," *Boston Globe*, July 31, 1961.

65. Harold Kaese, "The Buddin Story a Sad One; How Could Richards?" *Boston Globe*, November 29, 1961.

66. Hy Hurwitz, "Green Returns; Conley in NY," *Boston Globe*, July 28, 1962; Bob Holbrook, "Spur of the Moment Flight, Conley Says," *Boston Globe*, July 30, 1962; Jerry Nason, "Is Higgins Also Missing Bus in Managing Sox?" *Boston Globe*, July 29, 1962; Dan Shaughnessy, "Conley's Stories Fit to Print," *Boston Globe*, December 15, 2004.

67. Harvey Frommer, *Where Have All Our Red Sox Gone?* (Boulder, CO: Taylor Trade Publishing, 2006); see also Jerry Gutlon, *It Was Never About the Babe.*

68. Staff, "Green Broke the Last Line: Boston's," *Boston Globe*, December 23, 1997.

69. Frommer, "Pumpsie Green," http://www.travel-watch.com/pumpsegreen.htm. Accessed June 19, 2013.

70. Scott Ostler, "Green Looks Back on Breaking Barrier 50 Years Later," *San Francisco Chronicle*, July 21, 2009.

71. Frommer, *Where Have All Our Red Sox Gone?*

72. Pumpsie Green, author's interview.

73. *New York Times Magazine*, August 11, 1962.

74. "Attendance 1960–1969," mtlexpos.tripod.com/attendance/1960_1969.htm, Accessed June 3, 2013; mtlexpos.tripod.com/attendance/1950_1959.htm. Accessed June 3, 2013.

75. Bryant, *Shut Out*, 78. Demeter hit ten homers in his time with the Red Sox. Wilson, though a pitcher, hit sixteen for the Tigers.

76. ERA—the average number of runs per nine innings for which a pitcher's actions are responsible—is a better indication of a hurler's skill than wins, as those who toil on bad clubs often get very little run support.

77. Steve Fainaru, "In Racism's Shadow," *Boston Globe*, August 4, 1991.

78. The Red Sox also won the AL pennant in 1975.

79. Joanna Shepherd Bailey and George B. Shepherd, "Baseball's Accidental Racism: The Draft, African-American Players, and the Law," *Connecticut Law Review*, 44:1 (November 2011): 197–256. Note: Professional baseball rosters consist of a twenty-five-player "active" roster and a forty-player "major league roster." The active roster is the number of players each team can dress for a game. An additional fifteen players are in the minor leagues and have "options" that allow them to be elevated to the active roster if an opening occurs (injuries, roster adjustments, suspensions). Minor league players have a limited number of options, a restriction put in place to prevent teams from keeping players in the minor leagues indefinitely against their will. After a player's options are used, the parent club must either place that player on the active roster or offer him a waiver that allows other clubs to claim him.

80. These players were, in order of the year in which they debuted with the Red Sox, Reggie Smith (eight years), George Scott (nine, but in three stints, only the first lasting five years), Luis Tiant (eight), Cecil Cooper (six), Jim Rice (sixteen), Dennis Boyd (eight), and Ellis Burks (seven). Tommy Harper spent fifteen years with the Red Sox organization, but mostly as a coach. It did not get much better until the late 1990s. From 1959 to 1991, thirty-three African American players suited up for the Red Sox, of whom just nineteen played as long as four years. See Dan Shaughnessy, "Crossing the Color Line," *Boston Globe*, March 28, 1997.

81. Larry Whiteside, "Sox' Children of the 60s Look Back," *Boston Globe*, July 22, 1979. Note: *Sabermetrics* refers to use of sophisticated mathematical tools to evaluate player performances and to guide general managers (GMs) in whom they should sign. It is often credited to statistician Bill James, though this is disputed. Sabermetrics gained popularity once baseball players could become free agents and GMs had to decide whom they wished to sign to long-term contracts rather than merely rewarding good performance or docking pay for below-average performance on a yearly basis. Sabermetrics seeks to measure performance objectively and mathematically and to predict future outcomes. Peak performance is one of the latter tools. Age twenty-eight is, statistically, about the age in which superior athletes reach their prime; GMs often anticipate a five-year window of highest achievement, with twenty-eight being the average peak age. Hence, a cautious GM would seek to avoid signing long-term contracts with players who are in their mid-thirties or older.

82. Ibid.

83. Bryant, *Shut Out.*

84. Landsmark suffered a broken nose and minor injuries in the melee. He obtained a PhD from Boston University and, as of 2013, was president of Boston Architectural College. See Louis P. Mayer, *The Soiling of Old Glory: The Story of a Photograph That Shocked America* (New York: Bloomsbury Publishing, 2010).

85. Bryant, *Shut Out*, 200. Rice was criticized for being too compliant with the racist policies of the Red Sox, though Bryant notes he often spoke of being with the team as akin to a jail sentence. The infamous Margo Adams—the outed mistress of White third baseman Wade Boggs—went so far as say that Rice "wanted to be White" (201). Rice's six years remark to Burks refers to free-agency rules. In 1972, the US Supreme Court ruled against African American player Curt Flood's lawsuit challenging a team's right to own players in perpetuity, but in 1975 two players refused to sign contracts and were declared "free agents" and allowed to negotiate with new teams after playing one year without a signed contract. Management and the players' union eventually negotiated an agreement that allowed any player to become a free agent once he had played in MLB for at least six years.

86. Ibid., vii–viii. For the 1975 Cincinnati Reds, six of their starting eight position players were Black or Latino, as were another four bench players and pitchers. The Red Sox started only Jim Rice and Cecil Cooper (when they could use a designated hitter). Although Luis Tiant led the staff, just three other Black or Latino players were on the roster.

87. Jackie Robinson, *I Never Had It Made*, 10.

88. Bryant, *Left Out*; Dan Shaughnessy, "Crossing the Color Line," *Boston Globe*, March 28, 1997.

89. McDermott, *Working-Class White*, 151.

90. "Ten at UMass Injured in Fights After Series Game," *Boston Globe*, October 29, 1986; "World Series Touches Off Racial Clashes," *Harvard Crimson*, November 15, 1986; Steve Curwood, "Barrett, Wilson Talk at UMass on Series Fracas," *Boston Globe*, November 22, 1986; Allan Gold, "Cordiality and Racial Anger Mix in Massachusetts U. Protest," *New York Times*, February 16, 1988; Wornie Reed, "Commentary: The Role of Universities in Racial Violence on Campuses," *Trotter Review* 3:2 (1989); "The 1986 World Series Riot," albarossumi.livejournal.com/358418.html (November 1, 2007 reprint of 1986 log). Retrieved September 5, 2012.

91. For examples of their attacks on Red Sox management, see: Harold Kaese, "The Demise of the Red Sox: Something Has to Give—Soon," *Boston Globe*, August 23, 1970; Mike Barnicle, "Red Sox—Color Blind," *Boston Globe*, March 19, 1974; Larry Whiteside, "Sox and Minorities; Figures Say It All," July 22, 1979; Steve Fainaru, "In Racism's Shadow Red Sox Working to Shed Longtime Image, but Blacks In and Out of Baseball Still Uneasy," *Boston Globe*, August 4, 1991; Gordon Edes, "Roster Is a Bit Weak in One Area," *Boston Globe*, February 18, 2003.

92. For a typical McDonough denial, see "Sox Racist? Says Who?" *Boston Globe*, April 17, 1986. In this piece, McDonough made the incredible claim that Tommy Harper's 1985 MCAD complaint against the team was frivolous because the Elks Club in Winter Haven, Florida, was a dump unworthy of a complaint. He wrote, "If Harper felt left out, that's his problem." The MCAD disagreed and found in favor of

Constructing Legends 175

Harper on July 2, 1986. Peter Gammons wrote a withering retort to McDonough's insensitive remarks. See Gammons, "Baseball," *Boston Globe*, January 5, 1986.

93. Bryant, *Shut Out*, 248–52. Bryant details that Vaughan did, indeed, experience racial discrimination in Boston, but Vaughan's clashes with Red Sox management before his departure were also complicated by money. Vaughan was at the height of his productivity when he came up for free agency and signed a six-year eighty-million-dollar contract with Anaheim. This was much more than the Red Sox wanted to spend for a thirty-one-year-old outfielder; history vindicated the Red Sox. His production declined dramatically from 1999 onward, and Vaughan missed the entire 2001 season with injuries. He was traded to the New York Mets in December of 2001, where he spent two mediocre, injury-plagued years before another injury forced him to retire in 2003.

94. Smith quoted from Tygiel, *Baseball's Great Experiment*, 222.

95. Quoted from Frommer, "Pumpsie Green."

96. Gordon Edes, "Pumpsie Green Red Sox Pioneer," *Boston Globe*, February 23, 1997.

97. Dan Shaughnessy, "Crossing the Color Line," *Boston Globe*, March 28, 1997.

98. Joan Vennochi "Squeeze Play," *Boston Globe*, May 8, 1998.

99. Gordon Edes, "Roster Is Rather Lacking in This Area," *Boston Globe*, February 18, 2003.

100. Mike Petraglia, "Pumpsie Green Throws Out First Pitch," MLB.com, April 17, 2009; Dan Shaughnessy, "An Old Towne Toast," *Boston Globe*, April 21, 2012; Green interview.

101. "Race and Racism," clipping file, Baseball HOF.

102. Lawrence Baldassaro and Richard A. Johnson, eds. *The American Game: Baseball and Ethnicity* (Carbondale: Southern Illinois University Press, 2002): xiii, 4.

103. Incidents gathered from the "Race and Racism" file, Baseball HOF.

104. Juan Williams, "The Red Sox and Racism," National Public Radio, October 11, 2002.

105. Richard Stalker, "Bruins Fans Flood Twitter with Racist Remarks," www.webpronews.com/bruins-fans-flood-twitter-with-racist-remarka-2012-04. Retrieved August 31, 2012.

106. Sean Newell, "Carl Crawford Called Racial Slur," *Boston Globe*, July 7, 2012. Note: Many individuals, including team officials, insist that Crawford was traded because he underperformed after signing a lucrative free agent contract with Boston after the 2010 season. There is merit to that assertion, but the fact that racism could be raised as a motive for dumping Crawford remains a testament to ongoing ethnic tension within the Red Sox organization.

107. Fainaru, "In Racism's Shadow," *Boston Globe*, August 4, 1991. When Fainaru asked Black sports fans if they went to Fenway, most responded that the racism in the stands was more than they wished to endure. One remarked incredulously, "Are you kidding me?" It would take three days before they [the White crowd] would let you out!" For more on the play *Johnny Baseball*, see Ed Siegel, "A Grand Slam on the Sox's Real Curse," *Boston Globe*, June 12, 2010, and Dan Shaughnessy, "An Old

176   *Robert E. Weir*

Towne Toast," *Boston Globe*, April 21, 2012; for non-Sox fans in Greater Boston, see Russell Contreras, "Where Yankees Fans Thrive," *Boston Globe*, September 25, 2008.
  108. Bryant, "No Honor in Red Sox Anniversary," ESPN.com, July 21, 2009.

BIBLIOGRAPHY

Bailey, Joanna Shepherd, and George B. Shepherd. "Baseball's Accidental Racism: The Draft, African-American Players, and the Law." *Connecticut Law Review* (Volume 44, Number 1), 2011.

Baldassaro, Dan, and Richard A. Johnson, eds. *The American Game: Baseball and Ethnicity.* Carbondale: Southern Illinois University Press, 2002.

Barnicle, Mike. "Red Sox—Color Blind." *Boston Globe*, March 19, 1974.

Birtwell, Roger. "Pumpsie Green Almost Ready." *Boston Globe*, June 16, 1958.

Bluestone, Barry, and Mary Huff Stevenson. *The Boston Renaissance: Race, Space, and Economic Change.* New York: Russell Sage Foundation, 2000.

Booth, Clark. "About Pumpsie Green and the Indelible Stain Yawkey-Era Racism Left on the Red Sox." *Dorchester Reporter*, July 23, 2009.

Brunvand, Jan. *The Study of American Folklore.* New York: W. W. Norton, 1978.

Bryant, Howard. "No Honor in Red Sox Anniversary." ESPN.com, July 21, 2009.

Bryant, Howard. *Shut Out: A Story of Race and Baseball in Boston.* New York: Routledge, 2002.

Campbell, Joseph. *The Hero with a Thousand Faces.* Novato: New World Library, 2011.

Coffin, Tristram. *The Old Ball Game: Baseball in Fiction and Folklore.* New York: Herder & Herder, 1971.

Contreras, Russell. "Where Yankees Fans Thrive." *Boston Globe*, September 25, 2008.

Curwood, Steve. "Barrett, Wilson Talk at UMass on Series Fracas." *Boston Globe*, November 22, 1986.

Dorson, Richard. *America in Legend: Folklore from the Colonial Period to the Present.* New York: Pantheon, 1971.

Dorson, Richard. *Folklore and Folklife: An Introduction.* Chicago: University of Chicago, 1992.

Edes, Gordon. "Roster Is a Bit Weak in One Area." *Boston Globe*, February 18, 2003.

Fainaru, Steve. "In Racism's Shadow." *Boston Globe*, August 4, 1991.

Formisano, Ronald. *Boston Against Busing: Race, Class, and Ethnicity in the 1960s and 1970s.* Chapel Hill: University of North Carolina Press, 1991.

Frommer, Harvey. *Where Have All Our Red Sox Gone?* Boulder: Taylor Trade Publishing, 2006.

Gammons, Peter. "Baseball," *Boston Globe*, January 5, 1986.

Gold, Allan. "Cordiality and Racial Anger Mix in Massachusetts U. Protest." *New York Times*, February 16, 1988.

Greenfield, Stan. "Keeper of Secrets." *Boston Globe*, May 26, 2013.

Gross, Milton. "Green Now Used to Loneliness." *Boston Globe*, March 28, 1959.

Constructing Legends 177

Gutlon, Jerry. *It Was Never About the Babe: The Red Sox, Racism, Mismanagement, and the Curse of the Bambino.* New York: Skyhorse, 2009.

Guttman, Allen. *From Ritual to Record: The Nature of Modern Sports.* New York: Columbia University, 2012.

Hayden, Robert. *African-Americans in Boston: More than 350 Years.* Boston: Boston Public Library Press, 1991.

Heaphy, Leslie. *Negro Leagues, 1869–1960.* Jefferson, NC: McFarland, 2003.

Holbrook, Bob. "Red Sox Send Pumpsie Green to Minors." *Boston Globe*, April 8, 1959.

Holbrook, Bob. "Spur of the Moment Flight, Conley Says." *Boston Globe*, July 30, 1962.

Holbrook, Bob. "Not Ready for Sox in April—Pumpsie." *Boston Globe*, July 24, 1959.

Hurwitz, Hy. "Green Returns; Conley in NY." *Boston Globe*, July 28, 1962.

Johnson, Richard A., and Glen Stout, *Red Sox Century.* New York: Houghton Mifflin Harcourt, 2005.

"Jurges Will Try Thompson at First." *Boston Globe*, April 12, 1960.

Kaese, Harold. "Did Sox Give Pumpsie Green Shabby Deal?" *Boston Globe*, April 8, 1959.

Kaese, Harold. "It's Not Buddin's Fault That Green Was Shipped Out." *Boston Globe*, April 9, 1959.

Kaese, Harold. "The Buddin Story a Sad One; How Could Richards?" *Boston Globe*, November 29, 1961.

Kaese, Harold. "The Demise of the Red Sox: Something Has to Give—Soon." *Boston Globe*, August 23, 1970.

Keane, Clif. "Harris' Side of the Story." *Boston Globe*, September 28, 1960.

Madden, Michael. "He Ran into a Fenway Wall." *Boston Globe*, May 28, 1993.

Mayer, Louis. *The Soiling of Old Glory: The Story of a Photograph That Shocked America.* New York: Bloomsbury Publishing, 2010.

Mayo, Jonathan. "Boston's Green: A Reluctant Pioneer." MLB.com. February 6, 2007.

McDermott, Monica. *Working-Class White: The Making and Unmaking of Race Relations.* Berkeley: University of California Press, 2006.

McDonough, Sean. "Sox Racist? Says Who?" *Boston Globe*, April 17, 1986.

McLean, Robert. "Everyone Pleased Pumpsie Returning." *Boston Globe*, July 22, 1959.

Miltesky, Zebulon. "City of Amalgamation: Race, Marriage, Class and Color in Boston, 1890–1930." PhD Dissertation, University of Massachusetts, Amherst 2008.

Moffi, Larry, and Jonathan Kronstadt. *Crossing the Line: Black Major Leaguers, 1947–1959.* Jefferson, NC: McFarland, 1994.

"NAACP Says No Pumpsie, No Parking Lot for Sox." *Boston Globe*, April 9, 1959.

Nason, Jerry. "Is Higgins Also Missing Bus in Managing Sox?" *Boston Globe*, July 29, 1962.

Nason, Jerry. "Will Yawkey Quit Boston?." *Boston Globe,* April 12, 1959.

Newell, Sean. "Carl Crawford Called Racial Slur." *Boston Globe*, July 7, 2012.

Ostler, Scott. "Green Looks Back on Breaking Barrier 50 Years Later." *San Francisco Chronicle*, July 21, 2009.

Petraglia, Mike. "Pumpsie Green Throws Out First Pitch." MLB.com, April 17, 2009.

"Pumpsie Undergoes Operation." *Boston Globe*, May 14, 1961.

"Red Sox Home Opener." *Boston Globe*, April 17, 1998.

Reed, Wornie. "Commentary: The Role of Universities in Racial Violence on Campuses." *Trotter Review* (Volume 3, Number 2), 1989.

Robinson, Jackie. *I Never Had It Made.* New York: Putnam, 1972.

Shaughnessy, Dan. "An Olde Towne Toast." *Boston Globe*, April 21, 2012.

Shaughnessy, Dan. "Conley's Stories Fit to Print." *Boston Globe*, December 15, 2004.

Shaughnessy, Dan. *The Curse of the Bambino.* London: Penguin Books, 1991.

Siegel, Ed. "A Grand Slam on the Sox's Real Curse." *Boston Globe*, June 12, 2010.

Smith, Wendell. "Sports Beat." *Pittsburgh Courier*, April 25, 1959.

"Sox Sit Tight as Green Storm Rages." *Boston Globe*, April 12, 1959.

Staff, "Green Broke the Last Line: Boston's." *Boston Globe*, December 23, 1997.

"State Board to Probe Red Sox Racial Policy." *Boston Globe*, April 11, 1959.

"Ten at UMass Injured in Fights After Series Game." *Boston Globe*, October 29, 1986.

Tygiel, Jules. *Baseball's Great Experiment: Jackie Robinson and His Legacy.* New York: Oxford, 1997.

Vennochi, Joan. "Squeeze Play," *Boston Globe*, May 8, 1998.

Whiteside, Larry "The First to Sign." *Boston Globe*, July 22, 1979.

Whiteside, Larry. "Sox and Minorities; Figures Say it All," July 22, 1979.

Whiteside, Larry. "Sox' Children of the 60s Look Back." *Boston Globe*, July 22, 1979.

"Whole Town's Talking About the Green Boy." *Boston Globe*, April 12, 1959.

"World Series Touches Off Racial Clashes." *Harvard Crimson*, November 15, 1986.

Chapter 9

A Seasoned Rookie

Veteran Sam Jethroe Joins the Boston Braves

Stephanie Liscio

On April 18, 1950, Sam Jethroe stepped to the plate against the New York Giants at the Polo Grounds, ready for his first regular season at-bat as a Boston Brave. After six and a half seasons in the Negro Leagues and a year and a half in the minor leagues, Jethroe finally got the call to the big show. Even though he'd been repeatedly scouted and had several "tryouts" during the 1940s, the slow pace of the major leagues' reintegration meant that he had to wait until later in his career for an opportunity. The 1950 season eventually cemented his place in the history books, as he became the oldest Braves player to win the Rookie of the Year award. Jethroe spent his Negro League career with the Cleveland Buckeyes, winning a World Series in 1945 and playing in the East-West All Star Game five different times. He participated in two major league tryouts during the 1940s, both of which selected no African American players. By the time he finally donned a major league uniform, he was entering the twilight of his career. An aging body and vision issues eventually led him to exit the majors just shy of four years' service, the minimum requirement to qualify for a major league pension. By the 1990s, toward the end of his life, Jethroe led the charge to change that rule, eventually earning his own hard-fought pension.

Born in East St. Louis on January 20, 1918, Jethroe spent his early life developing as an athlete. He loved playing baseball as a child, as well as basketball, football, and boxing. His parents separated when he was young, and his mother raised five children during the Great Depression. As a youth, Jethroe worked as a laborer in a glass factory in East St. Louis, and in his spare time, he played sandlot baseball. He eventually made it to the semi-professional East St. Louis Colts, where he was initially spotted by Ernie Wright Jr., owner of the Negro League's Cleveland Buckeyes.[1] Jethroe first drew the attention of the White major leagues during his first season with the team, 1942.

Jethroe played in both East-West games held that year, the first in Chicago at Comiskey Park on August 16, 1942, and the second at Municipal Stadium in Cleveland on August 18. The East-West Classic originated in 1933 to showcase the finest Negro League players in an annual all-star event. Throughout the 1942 season, the *Cleveland Call and Post* pushed the Cleveland Indians to offer a tryout to three Buckeyes players—Jethroe, Parnell Woods, and Eugene Bremer. All three of these men happened to be on the roster for the East-West Game at Municipal Stadium, and all three had one of their worst games of the season. Playing centerfield, Jethroe reportedly committed the "prize error of the game" when he misjudged a long fly ball and dropped it. Indians team owner Alva Bradley said he was not interested in the three players based on their lackluster performance during the all-star game. "We have scouted these men . . . , we saw them play at the Stadium on the night of August 18th, and frankly, Mr. (John) Fuster (*Call and Post* sports editor), they are not big-league material. Why, not one of them got a hit . . . and the pitcher, Bremer, was knocked out of the box. They just don't stack up as material for the Indians."[2] It is unclear whether Bradley was ever truly serious about signing the players, or if he happened to see an opportunity for an iron-clad excuse to reject integrating the roster, as well as an excuse to swat down future talk of integration.

In April 1945, Jethroe was again tapped for a major league tryout, this time with the Boston Red Sox, on a damp and drizzly day that was, coincidentally, the same day that President Franklin D. Roosevelt died. Jethroe, along with Jackie Robinson and Marvin Williams, traveled to Fenway Park in what was later called a "political tryout" as much as it was a tryout based on baseball talent alone. Boston city councilman Isadore Muchnick had pressured the Red Sox to consider integration, with the threat of withholding a waiver that allowed the team to play on Sundays. Muchnick worked with Wendell Smith of the *Pittsburgh Courier*, who, along with other members of the Black press, pushed to reintegrate major league baseball in the 1940s. The players were instructed to wear uniforms for the tryout, but they were not provided with Red Sox uniforms; Jethroe wore his Buckeyes uniform, and Robinson wore his Kansas City Monarchs uniform. When Jethroe discussed the tryout in 1993, the possibility of playing in the major leagues was not what dominated his memories of the event. Even though he said, "I knew if I was given the opportunity, I could play in the big leagues," Jethroe most vividly recalled the three men walking down the street in their civilian clothes following the

Figure 9.1. Sam "The Jet" Jethro began his playing career in the Negro Leagues with the Cleveland Buckeyes in 1942. He later joined the Boston Braves as the first African American baseball player in Boston in 1950. During his inaugural year with the Braves, Jethro won Rookie of the Year honors at age 32. In 1945, he participated in an ill-fated tryout with the Boston Red Sox alongside Jackie Robinson and Marvin Williams. Credit: National Baseball Hall of Fame and Museum, Cooperstown, N.Y.

tryout, discussing the death of the president. He remembered thinking, "I can still have my fun in the Negro Leagues," even though the mood of the day was heavy, and the nation was mourning.[3]

The 1947 season was the last full season that Jethroe played in the Negro Leagues. The Buckeyes returned to the Negro League World Series that season, after winning it all in 1945. However, in the team's last hurrah, they lost to the New York Cubans. Jethroe was offered a "fat salary" to play in Mexico in 1948, but instead he chose to return to the Buckeyes prior to the start of the 1948 campaign.[4] After several years of consideration from the major leagues, and two dead-end tryouts, it looked like Jethroe finally would get his shot to play in Major League Baseball. Midway through the 1948 season, Branch Rickey and the Brooklyn Dodgers made a play for the outfielder, signed him, and assigned him to their Montreal farm club of the International League— the same minor league club where Jackie Robinson played his 1946 season.

Clay Hopper, skipper of the Montreal Royals, managed both Jethroe and Robinson in their time with the team and discussed the differences and similarities between the two men. Hopper said, "Speedy Sam Jethroe has more natural ability as a baseballer than Jackie Robinson!" He added that Jethroe had greater speed and would likely set a new all-time mark in stolen bases (he did set an International League record with Montreal in 1949). In fact, Hopper thought Jethroe was the fastest man he had ever seen. When it came to hitting ability, Hopper said that he thought Jethroe would be Robinson's equal at the plate, and that even if Jethroe didn't lead the league in batting, he would still be close to the top of the pack. Hopper said the only way Robinson was better than Jethroe was due to "his flaring competitive spirit." He added, "Jethroe is not accused of taking things too easily. He just does not show it as Robinson does."[5] This was a common theme for Jethroe—constant comparisons to Robinson, as he played for Montreal and later Boston. Even an article talking about Jethroe's strengths eventually devolved into some comparison of how those skills compared to Robinson's abilities.

Another theme about Jethroe that persisted among journalists is that somehow he was either lazy or just did not have the "fire" of other players (again, a comparison to Robinson). Unfortunately, this issue persists today—when African American or Latino players struggle on the field, there is persistent use of the negative stereotype that it is happening because they are "lazy." Jethroe was once reprimanded and fined for "loafing." He told Sam Lacy, of the *Baltimore Afro-American*, that "I think I got a rough deal." It all started when Hopper, Montreal's manager, accused Jethroe of "not hustling," and that sparked the larger disagreement. Jethroe said, "Nobody, not even Commissioner Chandler, can say I'm not hustling when I'm in a ball game. That is, they can't say it without a snap-back by me." The speedy outfielder committed an error on a drive to center field, and this was what appeared to provoke Hopper's anger. The manager "rapped the player in a meeting in the club-house and Jethroe answered back. . . . A charge of insubordination grew out of the affair and Jethroe was fined and suspended indefinitely."[6] This was certainly not the first time that Jethroe struggled defensively in the outfield; however, it was the first time those struggles were painted as a lack of effort, rather than a simple misjudgment or mistake.

While Jethroe played for Montreal in 1948, the team played host to a special guest: Barney Ewell, a sprinter just returned from winning a gold medal in the one-hundred-meter dash at the London Olympics. The two men raced each other in front of a crowd of 17,500, a figure that then–Montreal general manager Buzzy Bavasi said was a large group for a Monday night. Ewell wore track spikes while Jethroe wore baseball spikes; people on and around the team placed bets on the contest. In the end, Jethroe beat Ewell "by inches." Bavasi said that after his defeat to Jethroe, "Ewell wanted a return race, but there was none." Writing in the *Philadelphia Tribune*, Claude Harrison Jr. noted, "Sam can lay claim to being baseball's fastest man and the oldest rookie of the year."[7]

As rumors continued to swirl about Jethroe leaving Montreal to play in the major leagues, there was also a lot of speculation and discussion connected to the amount of money Jethroe would be paid. There was conjecture that Branch Rickey was asking for exorbitant fees from teams interested in acquiring Jethroe, somewhere around two hundred fifty to three hundred thousand dollars.[8] Jethroe's contract was eventually sold to the Boston Braves prior to the 1950 season for around one hundred thousand dollars, although the salary that Jethroe himself received was estimated to be less than ten thousand dollars. The speedy Jethroe set an International League record in 1949, stealing eighty-nine bases for the Royals, drawing the attention of many teams, and driving the price of his contract and buyout higher.[9]

Jethroe had a slightly rocky start to his time as a Brave—after a rough spring training, local media referred to him as the "$100,000 lemon" before he even played a regular season game. They did not discuss how it might be premature to judge a player based on preseason exhibition games. After Jethroe got off to a hot start early in the 1950 regular season, many of those writers quickly changed their tune.[10] Not every account of Jethroe was negative prior to the season; one writer pointed out that he might prove to be an attendance draw on top of helping the team. And while Jethroe's base running and batting skills were often lauded, there were always concerns about his defensive abilities. One, more positive account noted, "He's no DiMaggio afield, but he's more than adequate."[11]

The hot start was also important in establishing fans' first impressions of Jethroe. One news article described it by saying, "Most important development of the first week from Jethroe's point of view was the unanimous manner in which Boston baseball fans accepted the rookie outfielder. From the very first time he stepped on the field in Braves' regalia, he was cheered. Braves followers understand the pressure that was on this newcomer from the very start, and they admired him for his genuine comeback effort after being written off as a flop in spring training. Jethroe didn't let them down either." Another description noted, "In six games Sam Jethroe has proven he can play major league baseball. His progress this spring has been nothing short of amazing. The question being asked in Boston now is how much more will speedy Sam continue to improve; the Braves players think it will be considerable."[12]

By June the "$100,000 lemon," as he'd been called in the spring articles, was doing well enough that he received what was believed to be a roughly $2,500 raise. Even though the Braves paid that one-hundred-thousand-dollar price tag to Rickey, it was believed that Jethroe only saw around $7,500, or the minimum league salary at the time. The raise meant he was likely making close to ten thousand dollars just under two months into the season. At the time Jethroe was the only Braves player hitting above .300 and was tied for the National League lead in triples with three, was tied for second in runs scored with twenty-five, and had hit five home runs and stole five bases.[13]

By the end of August 1950, Jethroe was called "perhaps the biggest individual player surprise in the major leagues this season." Referencing the difficult spring Jethroe experienced, he was described as "Sad Sam Jethroe" and that he "was the despair of the Braves' camp through the five and a half weeks of spring training." As for Jethroe's high price tag, it was noted that "it appeared that the Boston Nationals had tossed $125,000 down the Branch Rickey drain after purchasing the center fielder from the Brooklyn club's Montreal farm. Jethroe bore no resemblance to a hitter. He couldn't bunt or drag, lacked power." Author Ralph Warner argued that Jethroe was also unimpressive in the field as he misjudged fly balls and botched fielding ground balls. Jethroe's biggest asset was his speed, but he never got to showcase it since he was unable to get on base. Veterans supposedly said he was "the worst ball player ever to appear in a major league camp." Braves manager Bill Southworth was the one person who did not give up on him. Southworth supposedly pleaded with baseball writers to exhibit patience and give Jethroe a chance. Later, Southworth noted that Jethroe was pressing during spring training, but he was much more relaxed once the regular season started. Exhibition games were supposedly more stressful to him than the regular season contests.[14]

Jethroe cooled off in the second half of the season following an injury; it was reported that he "never quite regained his early stride." He still managed to steal thirty-five bases that season, although twenty-four of those came in the first half of the season prior to his injury. He finished with a .273 average and 159 hits, including eighteen home runs and fifty-eight RBIs. The campaign was enough to earn him Rookie of the Year honors, making him, at the age of thirty-two, the oldest player ever to receive the award. That record still stands, although Kazuhiro Sasaki, playing with the Mariners, came close in 2000, as he was just a bit younger than Jethroe had been during the 1950 season. The twenty-four-man Baseball Writers Association panel gave Jethroe eleven first-place votes, six more than his closest competitor. One article noted that even though the Braves gave Rickey a decent sum for Jethroe's contract, Jethroe "proved that the abilities he displayed at Montreal were of major league caliber."[15]

After that first season, Jethroe sat down with Sam Lacy of the *Baltimore Afro-American* to discuss his thoughts on the major leagues and his own abilities. Jethroe said, "People often ask me what I consider to be the most important thing in baseball. And when they do that, it always causes me to look at them in surprise, and to ask, 'Are you kidding?' Anyone should know my legs are most important to me 'cause I make a business of running. I can run fast and I know it. May the Lord help me when I can't run anymore!"[16] Jethroe said he was not regarded as a pushover at the plate and that his fielding was stronger than the credit he received. "But when it comes to a real showdown, it's the pair of good legs I was lucky enough to draw that makes my major league baseball life a success."[17] Jethroe also noted that he was more than willing to take chances on the base paths, as he said, "If the other guy bobbles the ball, I'm gone, and he's got to throw me out. In a close game, if an outfielder holds his head down on a ground ball just a second longer than I think he should, I'm going to make him throw me out 'cause I ain't stopping!"[18]

During the 1951 season, Jethroe had a bit of a sophomore slump. One thing that seemed to deteriorate was his already-suspect defense in the outfield. A decline at the plate led to a look at other factors that could explain this overall drop in production. By mid-June 1951, Jethroe returned to the lineup sporting glasses. By August of that season, Jethroe started to steal bases at a greater rate than he had at any point so far during the 1951 season. However, the increase in base thefts was not credited to any kind of physical issue (like recovery from an injury), but instead a strategy from the Braves' new manager, Tommy Holmes. One article described it by saying that "Jethroe's running again, and there's hell to pay," adding, "That means there are tough days for opposing catchers because when the Boston Braves flash really starts to shake his heels on those basepaths there's trouble in store for someone."[19]

After Charlie Grimm took over managerial duties for the 1952 season, there were rumors that Jethroe might have been on the trading block. Jethroe was described as "an average fielder and a poor thrower, but a dangerous man with a bat and a holy terror once he got on base." However, it was rumored that Grimm said Jethroe was not "his type of player."[20] There was not much elaboration about what type of player Grimm preferred, but it was clear that between his age and eyesight issues, Jethroe's best years were likely behind him. He hit just .232 in 151 major league games in 1952, which was a steep decline over Jethroe's regular numbers. After the Braves made their move to Milwaukee in March 1953, Jethroe was sent to their American Association farm team in Toledo. He still managed to do well in Toledo during the 1953 season, where he hit .309 and led the American Association with 137 runs, 109 walks, and 120 strikeouts. However, he stole just twenty-seven bases, his lowest total since he'd played in the Negro Leagues.[21] Jethroe was the only player ever to hit a ball over the 472-foot left field fence at Swayne Field in Toledo; the ball traveled as far as the coal piles of the neighboring Red Man Tobacco Factory.[22]

In December 1953, the Braves sent six players and an undisclosed amount of cash to the Pittsburgh Pirates for Danny O'Connell. In some ways, Jethroe's time in the major leagues had come full circle—the man who had originally sold his Montreal contract to the Braves, Branch Rickey, was the man who now acquired him for the Pirates. When his new club considered the cause of Jethroe's struggles at the major league level, they once again turned to his eyesight. As a result, Jethroe was given a new prescription for his glasses in January 1954.[23]

Unfortunately, his time with the Pittsburgh Pirates pretty much ended before it started. Jethroe played just two games at the major league level with the team, as "he was not a part of the team's youth movement." In early May, he was released to the Toronto team, a member of the International League. One article noted, "The major league career of Sam Jethroe appeared to be at its end."[24] He remained in the International League until his retirement in 1958.

By the late-1940s/early-1950s, Jethroe and four other former members of the Cleveland Buckeyes—Walter Crosby, Willie Grace, Lovell "Big Pitch" Harden, and George Jefferson—had moved to Erie, Pennsylvania, at the urging of team owner, Ernie Wright Sr., who was from Erie. Jethroe was the only one of the men to make it to the major leagues before the end of his professional playing days. The five men joined Erie's recreational Glenwood League in 1960, and Jethroe played in that until he was forty-nine years old. It was said that "Despite his age . . . Jethroe was still able to thrill local baseball fans with his speed, his hitting and his showmanship."[25] He also occasionally played in the annual old-timers' game between the Braves and the Cardinals.[26]

Jethroe lived a quiet life after his retirement, running Jethroe's Bar on 15th Street in Erie. However, by the 1990s, his life became somewhat turbulent. His Erie home burned in 1994, forcing him to sleep at his bar, although he did eventually end up receiving help from the Baseball Assistance Team, a group that provides aid to former players in need. The hardships he faced led Jethroe to sue both Major League Baseball and the Major League Players Association for a pension in 1994. Jethroe did so reluctantly, saying that he did not want to sue anyone and was not "bitter with baseball"—he still loved the game—but he desperately needed the pension benefits, and the only option he believed he had was litigation. "I love the game. It's been a big part of my life," Jethroe said. "No, I don't want to sue them, but how else can I get the benefits that I need? If there was another way to get the benefits that I need, fine. But there doesn't seem to be another way."[27]

The suit focused on Jethroe's 1945 "tryout" with the Red Sox, arguing that he was denied a contract because he was African American. "They told us that we had the ability, but that it wasn't the right time," Jethroe said. "We went through all of the drills at the tryout, hitting, fielding, and what have you. There wasn't any question, at least in my mind, that we weren't good enough to play in the Major Leagues."[28] There were stories at the time that a racial slur was hurled at the players while they were on the field, which some thought originated with Red Sox manager Eddie Collins. Jethroe's lawyers, John L. Puttock and David H. Patterson, said they believed Jethroe should get credit toward his pension for his time with the Buckeyes, and for the time he spent in the minor leagues while under contract with the parent club, the Braves. Due to baseball's unspoken Jim Crow ban on African American players, his lawyers argued, Jethroe's civil rights were violated. Puttock said that he just wanted to help Jethroe, and "When I heard about the problems that Sam was having, that he and his wife (of fifty years, Elsie) don't have medical coverage and they're not in the best of health, I felt that baseball owed him something." He also said, "Here is an outstanding player from the past, and he's not being treated fairly by a game that he devoted much of his life to. Had it not been for Sam Jethroe and others like him, players wouldn't be drawing the salaries that they're drawing today."[29]

Jethroe faced another personal tragedy not long after the house fire, when in October 1995, his sixteen-year-old grandson, Sam Jethroe Jr., was fatally injured by a drunk driver as he was riding his bicycle to a corner store to buy soda. The case was settled out of court with the driver serving nine years in prison. Jethroe Jr. had lived with his grandfather since he was just one year old, and the two had traveled to baseball card shows throughout the United States. The elder Jethroe was understandably heartbroken and said that his grandson "was just beginning to live."[30]

Jethroe's suit against the major leagues was dismissed on October 4, 1996, by US district judge Sean McLaughlin in Baltimore. Despite this fact, major league baseball reversed course and provided Jethroe and dozens of other Negro League players pensions in 1997. At the time, a player needed four years of service to qualify for the pension, and Jethroe had spent a total of three years and seventeen days with the Braves and Pirates, leaving him just short of eligibility. Under Major League Baseball's agreed-upon plan, the former Negro League players would receive about ten thousand dollars per year if they'd played at least four years combined in the Negro Leagues and the major leagues.[31] Jethroe collected a pension for several years before he died of a heart attack in 2001.

It is unclear what type of career Jethroe would have had if he was allowed into Major League Baseball from the start. But it is fair to guess that his career could have lasted at least a decade or maybe more if he had remained healthy. When his professional career started, he was kept out of Major League Baseball due to segregation; by the end of his career, the majors still were not fully integrated. After the Braves left Boston, the city would not see another African American player until 1959, when Pumpsie Green joined the Boston Red Sox. The team was the last of the sixteen original franchises to integrate, twelve years after the American League was integrated by Larry Doby. While Jethroe played an important role in the reintegration of the game, change still happened at a snail's pace. More than forty years after Jethroe retired, he was finally able to receive the pension that he'd earned, and that he should have received his entire life. Even though this wrong was righted, Jethroe only got to enjoy the benefits for a few short years before he passed away. As with his playing career, he missed out on crucial time that he would never get back.

NOTES

1. Ron Wasielewski, "After Leaving Professional Baseball, Jethroe Played in Erie's Glenwood League," *Erie Times-News*, 18 June 2001, 1; Sam Jethroe and Willie Grace, Interview by Jamar Doyle, *In Their Own Words—An Oral History Project*, MS4746, Western Reserve Historical Society, Cleveland, Ohio, 1996; Mike Carlson, "Obituary: Sam Jethroe: Black Baseball Ace Fighting For Recognition in a Segregated Sport," *Guardian (London),* 17 July 2001, 18.

2. "Indians Turn Thumbs Down," *Call and Post*, 12 September 1942, 11.

3. Michael Madden, "He Ran Into a Fenway Wall; After Sox Tryout Jethroe Became First Black Boston Player—As Brave," *Boston Globe*, 28 May 1993, 29.

4. Wendell Smith, "Sports Beat," *Pittsburgh Courier*, 21 February 1948, 16.

5. Sam Maltin, "Montreal Pilot Rates Jethroe Over Jackie," *Pittsburgh Courier*, 6 August 1949, 23.

6. Sam Lacy, "Sam Jethroe Fined $100," *Baltimore Afro-American*, 27 August 1949, 1.

7. Claude Harrison Jr., "Even in Baseball Shoes, Sam Jethroe Was Faster Than Barney Ewell," *Philadelphia Tribune*, 13 March 1962, 11.

8. Vernon Jarrett, "Rickey Reported Asking Sox $300,000 For Sam Jethroe," *New York Amsterdam News*, 27 August 1949, 24.

9. Sam Lacy, "Sam Jethroe Sold To Braves For $100,000," *Baltimore Afro-American*, 8 October 1949, 15.

10. "Sam Jethroe, $100,000 Spring Lemon, Gets $2,500 Increase for Good Work," *New York Amsterdam News*, 3 June 1950, 25.

A Seasoned Rookie 189

11. Arthur Daley," Sports of the Times—Brave Hopes for the Braves," *New York Times*, 14 March 1950, 30.

12. "Boston's Sam Jethroe Answering Critics With Base Hits: Jet Standing Up Under Pressure," *Pittsburgh Courier*, 29 April 1950, 23.

13. "Sam Jethroe, $100,000 Spring Lemon, Gets $2,500 Increase for Good Work," *New York Amsterdam News*, 3 June 1950, 25.

14. Ralph Warner, "Sam Jethroe Owes Bill Southworth Debt For Brushing Off Early Season Faults," *Terre Haute Star*, 25 August 1950, 30.

15. "Jethroe of Braves Named Best Rookie," *New York Times*, 10 November 1950, 44.

16. Sam Lacy, "Running Is My Business," *Baltimore Afro-American*, 24 March 1951, 16.

17. Sam Lacy, "Running Is My Business," *Baltimore Afro-American*, 24 March 1951, 16.

18. Sam Lacy, "Running Is My Business," *Baltimore Afro-American*, 24 March 1951, 16.

19. "Jethroe's Running Again And There's Hell To Pay," *New York Amsterdam News*, 18 August 1951, 17.

20. "Sam Jethroe May Be Sold," *Atlanta Daily World*, 7 December 1952, 7.

21. "Jethroe of Braves Farmed To Toledo," *New York Times*, 14 April 1953, 32; "Braves Trade Six To Get O'Connell," *New York Times*, 27 December 1953, S1.

22. Glenn C. Smith, "Sam 'The Jet' Jethroe, One of First Blacks in Majors, Dies," *Los Angeles Sentinel*, 21 June 2001, B1.

23. "New Specs Ordered for Sam Jethroe, *Baltimore Afro-American*, 16 January 1954, 17.

24. "Sam Jethroe sent to Toronto club," *Baltimore Afro-American*, 8 May 1954, 16.

25. Ron Wasielewski, "After Leaving Professional Baseball, Jethroe Played in Erie's Glenwood League," *Erie Times-News*, 18 June 2001, 1.

26. "Touching Base With Memories," *New York Times*, 29 October 1983.

27. Daryl Bell, "Ailing ex-Negro and Major League star considers suing Major League," *Philadelphia Tribune*, 29 July 1994, 6C.

28. Daryl Bell, "Ailing ex-Negro and Major League star considers suing Major League," *Philadelphia Tribune*, 29 July 1994, 6C.

29. Daryl Bell, "Ailing ex-Negro and Major League star considers suing Major League," *Philadelphia Tribune*, 29 July 1994, 6C.

30. Ed Palattella, "Plea Expected In Death Of Jethroe Youth," *Erie Times-News*, 23 February 1996; Ron Wasielewski, "After Leaving Professional Baseball, Jethroe Played in Erie's Glenwood League," *Erie Times-News*, 18 June 2001, 1.

31. Murray Chass, "Pioneer Black Players To Be Granted Pensions," *New York Times*, 20 January 1997, C9.

BIBLIOGRAPHY

Bell, Daryl. "Ailing ex-Negro and Major League Star Considers Suing Major League," *Philadelphia Tribune*, 29 July 1994.

"Braves Trade Six To Get O'Connell," *New York Times*, 27 December 1953.

Carlson, Mike. "Obituary: Sam Jethroe: Black Baseball Ace Fighting For Recognition in a Segregated Sport," *Guardian (London)*, 17 July 2001.

Chass, Murray. "Pioneer Black Players To Be Granted Pensions," *New York Times*, 20 January 1997.

Daley, Arthur." Sports of the Times—Brave Hopes for the Braves," *New York Times*, 14 March 1950.

Harrison, Claude. "Even in Baseball Shoes, Sam Jethroe Was Faster Than Barney Ewell," *Philadelphia Tribune*, 13 March 1962.

"Indians Turn Thumbs Down," *Call and Post*, 12 September 1942.

Jarrett, Vernon. "Rickey Reported Asking Sox $300,000 For Sam Jethroe," *New York Amsterdam News*, 27 August 1949.

"Jethroe of Braves Farmed To Toledo," *New York Times*, 14 April 1953.

"Jethroe of Braves Named Best Rookie," *New York Times*, 10 November 1950.

"Jethroe's Running Again And There's Hell To Pay," *New York Amsterdam News*, 18 August 1951.

Lacy, Sam. "Running Is My Business," *Baltimore Afro-American*, 24 March 1951.

Lacy, Sam. "Sam Jethroe Fined $100," *Baltimore Afro-American*, 27 August 1949.

Lacy, Sam. "Sam Jethroe Sold To Braves For $100,000," *Baltimore Afro-American*, 8 October 1949.

Madden, Michael. "He Ran Into a Fenway Wall; After Sox Tryout Jethroe Became First Black Boston Player—As Brave," *Boston Globe*, 28 May 1993.

Maltin, Sam. "Montreal Pilot Rates Jethroe Over Jackie," *Pittsburgh Courier*, 6 August 1949.

"New Specs Ordered for Sam Jethroe, *Baltimore Afro-American*, 16 January 1954.

Palattella, Ed. "Plea Expected In Death Of Jethroe Youth," *Erie Times-News*, 23 February 1996.

"Sam Jethroe, $100,000 Spring Lemon, Gets $2,500 Increase for Good Work," *New York Amsterdam News*, 3 June 1950.

"Sam Jethroe and Willie Grace," Interview by Jamar Doyle, *In Their Own Words—An Oral History Project*, MS4746, Western Reserve Historical Society, Cleveland, Ohio, 1996.

"Sam Jethroe May Be Sold," *Atlanta Daily World*, 7 December 1952.

"Sam Jethroe Sent to Toronto club," *Baltimore Afro-American*, 8 May 1954.

Smith, Glen. "Sam 'The Jet' Jethroe, One of First Blacks in Majors, Dies," *Los Angeles Sentinel*, 21 June 2001.

Smith, Wendell. "Sports Beat," *Pittsburgh Courier*, 21 February 1948.

"Touching Base With Memories," *New York Times*, 29 October 1983.

Warner, Ralph. "Sam Jethroe Owes Bill Southworth Debt For Brushing Off Early Season Faults," *Terre Haute Star*, 25 August 1950.

Wasielewski, Ron. "After Leaving Professional Baseball, Jethroe Played in Erie's Glenwood League," *Erie Times-News*, 18 June 2001.

Chapter 10

Staying East of the Mississippi

Reengaging with Rodeo's
Diverse History and the New
England Connection

Tracey Owens Patton

In a Pace Picante Salsa commercial from 1993, a group of White American cowboys sitting around a campfire discover they are out of Pace Picante, their favorite thick and chunky salsa. Jake, one of the cowboys, has the audacity to offer a different brand of salsa made in New York City. Unlike the inferior brand, Pace is made in San Antonio, Texas, once one of the hallowed locations in the United States for all things cowboy and rodeo. In one version of this 1993 commercial, the other cowboys threaten Jake (the cowboy who deigned to suggest a salsa made in the Northeast) with a branding iron stoked in the fire to brand him with a *P* for *Pace*. Another version of the Pace commercial ends with one of the other cowboys saying, "Get a rope." None of these versions features a Black American cowboy or a cowboy of color, and none featured cowgirls, but two of these commercials invoked branding and lynching—artifacts of terrorism that were used against Black people in the United States.

Connecticut is not New York City, but in terms of its place in cowboy culture, it might as well be. When it comes to the historical, assumed, and imagined places that cowboys and rodeo inhabit, New York City and Connecticut never register on the radar. Traditionally, rodeo culture is associated with Western and Midwestern states like Arizona, California, Colorado, the Dakotas, Kansas, Montana, New Mexico, Nebraska, Oklahoma, Oregon, Texas, Utah, and Wyoming.

Figure 10.1. Steve Robinson represents a long history of African American cowboys and rodeo athletes. This photo, taken in Texas in 1911, captures the traditional image of the Black cowboy. Robinson embodies the newer East Coast version. Born in New Haven, Connecticut, Robinson spent summers as a youngster in Massachusetts training horses. He competed in amateur rodeos since he was 15 years old and later became a professional participating in the Cowboys of Color circuit. Credit: Erwin E. Smith Collection of the Library of Congress on Deposit at the Amon Carter Museum of American Art, Fort Worth, Texas, LC.S611.015."

Rodeo is found in all fifty states and enjoys vast national and international appeal. Despite the White, American-centered way in which it has been promoted, the origins of rodeo are international and racially diverse. Rodeo is also a sport that includes cowboys and cowgirls, but often, White cowgirl achievements and achievements by cowboys and cowgirls of color are erased in favor of White Western myths about cowboys.

The first half of this essay explores the history and mythology of the White American West through Paul Connerton's research on erased memory and the common themes of erasure, invisibility, and racism woven into cowboy culture. The second half of this essay centers on Connecticut cowboy Steve Robinson, who benefits from rodeo's diverse beginnings and finds his place in the rodeo arena. In using Robinson as an exemplar, this chapter illuminates two areas commonly erased in rodeo culture, which contributes to our cultural understanding of the sport of rodeo generally: 1) a regionally known Black cowboy from the East Coast is discussed, and 2) a refocusing of rodeo's gaze from the West Coast to the East Coast is conducted. Rodeo is and always has been a racially and ethnically diverse sport, and Robinson highlights this fact while adding to the narrative of Black American cowboys on the East Coast, thus challenging the long-held belief that rodeo solely found its home in the Western portion of the United States.

THE PURPOSE AND FUNCTION OF MYTHS: A THEORETICAL AND METHODOLOGICAL PERSPECTIVE

Theoretical Perspective

The sport of rodeo is enveloped in cultural memory and myth, which makes it an ideal lens through which to examine what a culture chooses to remember or ignore, erase, and marginalize, and this speaks volumes about the act of memory and commemoration. Cultural memory, as scholar Paul Connerton noted, is not a truth, but rather it engages in an act of remembering *and* forgetting that shapes any cultural narrative. Connerton's "Seven Types of Forgetting" focuses on 1) repressive erasure, 2) prescriptive forgetting, 3) forgetting that is constitutive in the formation of a new identity, 4) structural amnesia, 5) forgetting as annulment, 6) forgetting as planned obsolescence, and 7) forgetting as humiliated silence.[1] For the purposes of this chapter, forgetting as "repressive erasure" guides the sport of rodeo, and "prescriptive forgetting" illuminates the career of New England cowboy Steve Robinson.

As Connerton noted, repressive erasure is not only about its most violent interpretation (e.g., genocide, war), but it can also be seen through artwork and visual erasures. "Consider . . . the way in which the spatial disposition of the modern art gallery presents the visitor with nothing less than an iconographic program and a master historical narrative; by walking through the museum the visitor will be prompted to internalize the values and beliefs written into the architectural script."[2] Similarly, through a critical analysis of the myth of Manifest Destiny and the myth of the White West, Black Americans, Chinese and Chinese Americans, Latinx, and Native Americans were generally written out of their roles in the construction of the West. In the sport of rodeo in particular, White cowboy culture learned the sport from Black American, Latinx, and Native American cowboys, took that knowledge, and largely shut them out of the arena. Repressive and racist laws like Jim Crow closed the arena gates on them and constructed White racist, mythic narratives that were designed to silence the diversity within rodeo. Through repressive erasure, there was a silent, visual, rhetorical display of White dominance in the West and in rodeo, which was later furthered in dime novels, films, posters, and

196   *Tracey Owens Patton*

the arenas themselves. This kind of repressive erasure in forgetting led to Connerton's prescriptive forgetting.

Prescriptive forgetting allows a new identity to take hold, which is seen as a positive, because it is a gain and not a loss. In rodeo culture, to begin anew, with the false ideal of Manifest Destiny and White mythic narrative tropes, allows the transition of the West and the sport of rodeo as diverse to simply be erased. This type of erasure is seen with novels like *The Virginian* (1902) and paintings by Frederick Remington (both of which erased ethnic diversity in the West in their respective works), because "not to forget might . . . provoke too much cognitive dissonance."[3] In the claiming of a mythic identity through erasure, cowboys of color, like Steve Robinson, after seeing the visual displays of largely White cowboys written into rodeo from arenas to the screen, wrote themselves into a culture and a sport that marginalized and erased such inclusion. Robinson likely saw his inclusion in rodeo and cowboy culture as a positive, because rather than only define his *exclusion* by the color of his skin, he wrapped himself in U.S. mythic ideals that were larger than the confines of race and racism—e.g., freedom and space, which ultimately challenged the stagnant border of memory and made cultural memory, even one as fixed as the West and the cowboy culture dynamic.

Methodological Perspective

The theoretical foci of repressive erasure and prescriptive forgetting allow the methodology of critical rhetoric to emerge. A critical rhetorical methodology involves understanding the meaning derived, and looking for deeper messages coded in the text, which include both overt and covert meanings from words and visual images. Through a critical investigation of both language and symbols, we gain a deeper understanding of how meaning-making functions, how cultural myths can be better understood, and how the power of their communicative act is illuminated. Exploring the function of myth through a critical rhetorical lens allows for an examination of how Robinson found space for himself in a sport that erased its diverse foundations in favor of visual myths and erasures like that of the mythic White cowboy, the White Western tropes of Manifest Destiny, and the Marlboro Man.

THE WHITE WEST AND MANIFEST DESTINY AS IMAGINED FICTION AND ERASURE

The idea of the American West and the country's expansion westward is almost synonymous with ideologically dominant Euro-American culture. The concept of a Western United States devoid of Black Americans, Latinx,

Staying East of the Mississippi 197

and Native Americans is one that fulfills White supremacist myths. Yet the West was built on rich multicultural traditions. People of color have been co-collaborators in the construction of the West, including the culture and sport of rodeo. Even the most famous campfire song about cowboy culture and wide-open spaces, "Home on the Range," was stolen, erased, and attributed to a White man, when in reality it came from a Black American cook on the frontier. "Country music publisher John A.Lomax collected his most famous song, 'Home on the Range,' not from a golden-haired prairie Galahad but from a Black cook, who once worked a chuck wagon on a Texas cattle trail, in a 'low drinking dive' of San Antonio . . . [Lomax] consistently obscured Black collaboration."[4] Famous writer Owen Wister, who wrote *The Virginian* (1902), spent time in the West, where he knew of the existence of Black American, Latinx, and Native American cowboys and cooks on the cattle runs, yet he followed other contemporaries of his era and erased their contributions to the American West as well as their active role in cowboy culture.

The fact that rodeo and cowboy culture has been imagined as White is problematic, given that rodeo culture has part of its heritage in Africa, but this fact has long been forgotten or buried. The iconic longhorns of Texas trace back to "the plains of northern Africa and Andalucía," where the Moors (Black people) raised them and tended to them for a thousand years.[5] Christopher Columbus "using the equestrian knowledge from the Moors, introduced cattle and reintroduced the horse on his second voyage," then took this African knowledge to Spain, which eventually made its way to Hispaniola (today's Dominican Republic and Haiti) and up through the Americas. Cowboys of color participated in the major cattle drives, where, before the turn of the century, over forty thousand cowboys were employed. Of that number, between 25 and 30 percent of the cowboys were Black American, Native American, or Latinx.[6] Historians estimated that between five and six thousand Black American cowboys participated in cattle drives.[7] Yet the myth of Manifest Destiny whitewashes this history.

The myth of the West, which not only lives in the minds of Americans, but also has long extended across the Atlantic, began with the idea of Manifest Destiny, westward expansion, and the settling of a so-called uninhabited locale (referred to by Lomax as a "still unpeopled west"). Manifest Destiny (1812–1860) was a concept used to rationalize population expansion over North America to the Pacific Ocean and to acquire California, Oregon, and the Southwest—one justification for the US–Mexican War. The place and space imagined for White people, settler colonial societies that took up space on Native land, established genocidal territorial strongholds through the myth of the so-called vanishing Indian, the myth of the space as empty wilderness to be conquered and tamed, and the White supremacist myth that the taking of the land was ordained.[8] Public relations campaigns promoting "westward expansion were popularized in paintings and books, despite erasure, genocide, and the dire loss of land for African, Black American, and Native Nations."[9] In partnership with the development of the young United States painter Fredrick Remington, former US President Theodore Roosevelt, historian Frederick Jackson Turner, and author Owen Wister promoted White westward expansion as an individual identity trait involving cultural values of courage, hard work, and individualism, which justified the displacement and genocide of Native people.[10] Dime novels, too, popularized the adventures of pioneering frontiersmen Daniel Boone and Davy Crockett. Former president Roosevelt romanticized the myth of the West as one of a simpler time with plenty of land for White men to claim, in juxtaposition to the heavily populated East Coast, which made the West all that much more desirable to possess. In truth, the "simpler time" was a White mythic ideal that disappeared with technological progress like barbed-wire fencing, law enforcement, and railroad tracks. Gone were the western cattle drives; the wide-open spaces were, in fact, enclosed. None of these facts mattered, since the myth of the West was marketed to Easterners who could only imagine the possibility being marketed to them.

Tall tales spun through art, cowboys, dime novels, and stories perpetuated myths about the American West that no longer existed. These cultural narratives regarding expansionism were so wildly popular in the East "that over 50,000 Americans in the early 1840s took to the Oregon Trail and migrated west."[11] In 1883, the sport of rodeo, and the concept of cowboy culture, exploded, with popular Wild West shows spotlighting feats of skill and bravery accomplished by cowgirls and cowboys of color in the arena (e.g., Annie Oakley, Florence Hughes Randolph, Lillian Smith, Bill Pickett, "Chief Sitting Bull of the Oglala Hunkpapa, Brave Chief, Chief of the Witehitos, Chief Irontail, and Black Elk").[12] The lore and lure of the West became so ingrained and connected with identity that the Johnson County War in Wyoming in April 1892 (aka the War on Powder River) showed how far people would go to protect their slice of mythic western America. The war highlighted a clash between cowboys who still rode, homesteaders, and large ranch corporations run by big cattlemen. Cowboys found themselves "forced to homestead"[13] due to "the explosion of small ranches, and the larger ranches run by big cattlemen were upset by the number of new ranches that had sprung up there."[14] The war between all these entities "resulted in a gun fight and a two-day standoff between the ranchers, hired guns, and law enforcement. Eventually, the U.S. Cavalry, Wyoming Senators, an acting Wyoming Governor, and U.S. President Benjamin Harrison were dispatched to stop the fighting."[15]

The westward expansion "promoted the cult of Anglo-Saxon masculinity by romancing the cowboy. . . . [T]he winning of the American West . . .

had become a permanent part of American culture."[16] Dime novel narratives and paintings glorifying White male accomplishments and erasing people of color fit well with US policy of that time. With the power of his pen and the popularity of his novel, Wister was complicit in erasing the racial diversity that existed in the West in favor of a White reimagining of place, space, and territory. "In Wister's revisionist telling of the 'wild West' he recounts and admires only the hard, industrious work of white men."[17] In *The Virginian*, Wister makes invisible the widely known and respected group of Buffalo soldiers who were a prominent feature of the West. Black American cavalry units and infantry regiments served in Arizona, the Dakota Territory, Kansas, Montana, New Mexico, Nebraska, Oklahoma, Texas, Utah, Wyoming, and as far south as Mexico following the Civil War and before the Spanish-American War. The Buffalo soldiers helped make the cattle expansion possible and a career as a cowboy a reality.[18] Racist White supremacist laws, from enslavement to Black Codes to Jim Crow, made it so that all aspects of US American life were locked into the imaginary narrative of White exceptionalism, and White-only spaces made the fictionalized beliefs of the West as a place for reimagined White beginnings to seem true. For example, those in cowboy and cowgirl culture encountered signs that read "No dogs, no Negroes, no Mexicans."[19] As Jim Perry, a Black American cowboy, roper, and cook who worked for twenty years on the XIT Ranch in Texas in the late 1800s, said of the impact of racism, "If it weren't for my damned old black face, I'd have been boss of one of these divisions long ago."[20] Perry could not get beyond the "for Whites only" mandate that relegated him to cowboy, roper, and cook, but never the foreman despite twenty years of experience.

What is ironic is that Black American cowboys changed the sport of rodeo, in the same way that Black Americans changed the face of the West. In the sports arena, "because Jim Crow laws relegated African Americans to second-class citizenry, few blacks were permitted to participate in white-promoted rodeos."[21] As George B. Kirsch, Othello Harris, and Claire E. Nolte noted, the Professional Rodeo Cowboy Association (formerly the Rodeo Cowboys Association) "never formally excluded blacks [but] prior to the 1960s[,] racism and the lack of the blacks among professionals . . . effectively kept them out of the white competitions."[22] Racism coupled with Jim Crow laws had one of the largest effects on Black Americans not only in the West, but also in the arena and rodeo culture generally. The repressive erasure during this era is telling because there is a near-universal absence of cowboys of color in favor of a myth of a White-only cowboy culture. In an era of prescriptive forgetting, how do cowboys like Steve Robinson see the rodeo arena as a place of possibility, despite the relative absence of Black cowboys, and make the once-invisible iconic Black cowboys of the past visible once again?

MARKETING THE WHITE WEST
AND RODEO CULTURE

So, how did rodeo develop in the East when the rhetoric, advertising, and marketing behind rodeo was to find oneself in the openness of vast spaces of land—spaces that did not exist on the East Coast and were not part of East Coast rodeo culture? Marketing impacted rodeo in the past, and it was equally persuasive with Robinson in the present. Traveling back in time, even former president Teddy Roosevelt extolled the health benefits of going West, as well as the freedom of space, freedom from the overcrowded East Coast, and freedom of movement for White bodies, particularly White male bodies.

However, Robinson's great-grandfather, William Foster Robinson, thought differently. In echoing the language of Roosevelt, who saw only the West as a place of health and space and not the East Coast, W. Robinson "had been diagnosed with black lung disease, which was common among coal miners. . . . He bought . . . land in search of a place to live where he could breathe fresh air."[23] The place where W. Robinson found health, land, place, and space was on the East Coast, not in the West. The question becomes, why would W. Robinson ignore the media's marketing of the West as a place of opportunity? The development of rodeo on the East Coast likely began with Black Americans who experienced the imagined promise of an open and welcoming West as hollow and isolating.

In 1946, Era Bell Thompson, a Black American Western pioneer, noted in her autobiography, *American Daughter*, that initially she thought Black people were welcome in the West. However, Thompson and her family learned that the move West was not the utopia they'd been sold. As Michael K. Johnson wrote in *Hoo-Doo Cowboys and Bronze Buckaroos*, they and other Black pioneers in the West:

> left behind black communities to become part of a strange white frontier world, which offers greater opportunity for landownership, less (but not a complete lack of) racism, a degree of safety from the antiblack violence erupting throughout much of early twentieth-century America, and escape from the corrupt Jim Crow culture of segregation and second-class citizenship. That escape, however, comes at the cost of separation from African American culture and community. Is it preferable to remain isolated from "our people" in the relative safety of the frontier or to risk the dangers of antiblack violence in the civilized metropolis?[24]

The question that Johnson advances about racism, safety, and violence in the West would become a concern for Black Americans, particularly after some territories and states opened doors for Black American migration westward, as with the Exodusters in Kansas in the late 1870s. As Black pioneer Mifflin

Wistar Gibbs wrote in his autobiography, "With thrift and a wise circumspection financially, their opportunities were good; from every other point of view they were ostracized, assaulted without redress, disenfranchised and denied their oath in a court of justice."[25] With this marginalization and overt racism, coupled with the effects of Jim Crow, the West was crafted as a "white space." Until 1927, when the law was repealed, the state of Oregon banned Black people from moving to and living in the state. The ripple effects of this racist legacy live on today: only 2 percent of Oregon's population is Black.[26] More broadly, fewer Black Americans live in the West today than in the Eastern and Southern areas of the country.

Although rodeo began with Latinx, Native Americans, and Black Americans "teaching White men how to rope, work cattle, and set the foundation of rodeo, White men eventually commercialized the sport and made rodeo what it is today, sans the participation" of people of color. Despite its diverse beginnings, there are significantly fewer Black American, Native American, and Latinx people in the sport today than there are White people.[27] The numbers of cowboys of color in rodeo in the United States "have dwindled since the days of the open frontier and the cattle drives," despite their iconic contributions to the sport itself. For example, in his book, *The Life and Adventures of Nat Love* (1907), the famous Black cowboy also known as "Deadwood Dick," catalogued his "wild west adventures," writing of his life on a slave plantation, to Kansas, to life with Native American people.

Bill Pickett, a Black American cowboy from Taylor, Texas, is credited with the invention of "bulldogging," a popular rodeo event commonly known as steer wrestling, which is still in practice today, including by Steve Robinson. Until he became a celebrity for his trademark bulldogging technique, Pickett was forced to dress as a Mexican toreador in the rodeo arena because rodeos did not admit Black contestants.[28] In 1920, a newspaper reporter crowned Jesse Stahl, a Black American cowboy who became famous for his saddle bronc-riding abilities, as the "best wild horse rider in the west."[29]

The effects of direct and indirect discrimination against cowboys of color are clearly seen in media depictions that reinforce the racism of the sport. "It is bitterly ironic that white patriarchy appropriated ethnic skills and knowledge that helped create the rodeo in the first place."[30] Racism and discrimination in rodeo forced the creation of segregated rodeo communities for cowboys of color like the All Indian Rodeo Cowboys Association, the Bill Pickett Invitational Rodeo Circuit (BPIR), the Indian National Finals Rodeo (INFR), the Canadian Indian Finals Rodeo (CIFR), the Okmulgee Invitational (started in 1956, the longest running Black rodeo in the United States, on Muscogee Nation, Oklahoma), the Southwestern Colored Cowboys' Association, and the Soul Circuits.[31] Robinson was one cowboy who participated in segregated rodeo events, because that was the easiest way to ride before he was a PRCA

(Professional Rodeo Cowboys Association) member. However, this forced racial segregation perpetuated the myth that Western spaces like rodeo were all White, and that the West was, too.[32]

Through images, narratives, and the law, the identity of who *was* the West and who *built* the West was fully imagined. The White Western male was the stereotype of what could be achieved through hard work, a six-shooter, and traditional gender roles. These tropes of masculinity transcend the confines of the West and are found all over the country and world thanks to mediated formats like art, dime novels, posters, radio, and television. Television and film are particularly effective tools with which to disseminate dominant tropes that rhetorically and visually perpetuate the myth of the White West. Surprisingly, it was televisual media that allowed the rodeo gates to open and for Robinson, engaged in prescriptive forgetting, to find his place within the sport. Examining cowboy culture and rodeos challenged the stereotypes and placed people of color at the center of the narratives of the West. Cowboy culture is a lived experience that the media narrates through film to continue a White Western myth that never existed. Engaging in repressive erasure, the media reified rodeo as the embodiment and performance of the myth of conquering the West.

The media's misrepresentation of people of color has become commonplace. The collusion of White Western myth, the historical erasure of people of color, and a sport glorifying individual achievement all evolved to support a false narrative of something all White and all male that reflected and replicated racial and racist angst. As Connerton said, repressive erasure can be employed to "deny the fact of a historical rupture as well as to bring about a historical break."[33] This means that even when mediated representations of Black people in rodeo and cowboy and cowgirl culture appear, it can still be within the confines of White racism and White hegemonic power. For example, "in westerns of the [early] era, black actors sometimes appear as entertainers . . . but more commonly these characters are associated with domestic spaces or duties, appearing as cooks, maids, servants, and/or as messengers, and they most often function in comic roles."[34] Films like *Cimarron* (1930), which won the Oscar for Best Picture in 1930, had an African American cast as a servant, or *Man of the Frontier* (1936) where the Black American cast had to dance in the saloon for White people.

While there were early films that challenged White depictions of Black Americans in the West, these did not have the power to trump the tropes. The list of trope examples is long: *The Homesteader* (1919), *The Exile* (1931), *Haunted Gold* (1933), *Riders of the Black Hills* (1938), *Harlem on the Prairie* (1937), *Two-Gun Man from Harlem* (1938), *Harlem Rides the Range* (1939), and *The Man Who Shot Liberty Valance* (1962).[35] Even the real-life Bass Reeves, aka, the Lone Ranger, was the famed and feared Black

American U.S. marshall in what is now the state of Oklahoma.[36] The Lone Ranger is one of the most popular movie and television characters. Yet loathe to challenge the tropes of Whiteness with this iconic character, Hollywood panders its investment in valorizing Whiteness, as seen most recently with the 2013 *The Lone Ranger* film where the Lone Ranger was still played by a White actor, and not by a Black actor, which would have been historically accurate.[37] It is this same film and televisual mediated format that provided the space for Black youth–turned–Black cowboys to reimagine their place in rodeo, and this included Robinson. Through the absence of seeing themselves visually represented, they engaged in prescriptive forgetting and mapped onto themselves the artifacts and generic rodeo marketed tropes of adventure, athleticism, freedom, and horses.

Hollywood actor James Pickens Jr., known to many as Dr. Richard Webber on *Grey's Anatomy*, is one of those children who, regardless of mediated erasure, could find himself in the sport of rodeo. As a steer roper, he participates in team penning, and is a member of the United States Team Roping Championships, and regularly participates in the nation's only touring African American rodeo, the Bill Pickett Invitational Rodeo. Pickens was influenced by media when it came to his love of cowboy culture.[38] "I'm a child of the fifties," Pickens told a writer for *Black Enterprise*, "and my father was a big fan of TV westerns. Back then each network had at least ten or eleven westerns, and my brother and I would try to watch all of them. The horse has always been my favorite animal. It's so beautiful and powerful. There's something about them that epitomizes freedom."[39] Pickens, like so many other cowboys of color, was not only enamored with rodeo culture, but he also used media (advertising, marketing, and television) as a vehicle to challenge the White-only line demarking rodeo and write himself into the space in a similar way that Black icons of the sport like Nat Love, Bill Pickett, and Jesse Stahl have. Connecticut cowboy Steve Robinson's love of rodeo was stoked by television too. "(As a child), everybody wanted to play army, and I wanted to play cowboys and Indians. The cowboys from TV became my heroes."[40]

CONNECTICUT COWBOY STEVE ROBINSON

When I searched the internet for "what is Connecticut known for," *rodeo* did not make the list. Rather, things like ESPN Sports Center, fall foliage, the first hamburger (1895), the Polaroid camera (1934), the first helicopter (1939), and Yale University were the offered results. I imagine that Steve Robinson was mesmerized by rodeo culture through mediated representations in film and television, much like steer roper Pickens described, despite the fact that he was not visually represented in the sport except through segregated rodeos and stereotypical images. Black American cowboys were and are forced to endure racism that the PRCA passively and actively supported in the 1950s and 1960s. The racism of the past in the sport has ripple effects, and Black American bull rider Abe Morris estimated in 2005 that the PRCA is made up of about 97 percent White cowboys.[41] Perhaps it is the common, mythic ideal of space and freedom of movement that created the allure for Robinson.

Like Connerton's "prescriptive forgetting," forgetting how media wrote him and other cowboys of color out of the arena was a gain for Robinson because it enabled him to write himself into the sport he loves and revitalize his connection to rodeo through other cowboys of color—greats who might otherwise remain confined to the forgotten past. In the common refrain of "if you can see it, you can be it," Robinson was able to reengage with the rodeo arena as a cowboy who happened to be Black because of the prescriptive forgetting in which he engaged, and through those icons who came before him (e.g., Bill Pickett, Jesse Stahl, Myrtis Dightman).

Once a New Haven Connecticut firefighter, Robinson had been a "part-time professional cowboy since he was seventeen," competing as a calf roper, team roper, and steer wrestler, yet he did not have a direct mentor to guide him through the sport. As Robinson stated, "I think I could've been a champ if I'd had a mentor when I was young. . . . How many African-Americans own ranches? A horse is a luxury in this part of America."[42] Robinson, however, was one of those lucky people whose family owned a ranch, since Robinson's great-grandfather on his patriarchal side, William Foster Robinson, "bought [a] ranch for $900 in 1906, and since then it has never left the family's control."[43] In creating a space for imagining, Robinson's mother enabled him to participate in the sport he loved. "When I was a baby, I would get excited when I saw a horse. My mother was the facilitator of our dreams. She bought my brother and me saddles. We didn't even have horses at the time."[44] It is interesting that two people in Robinson's life helped him facilitate his dream of being a cowboy, first a great-grandfather who likely had experienced the immediacy of a post-enslaved United States and knew the meaning and value of land and control of that land, and second, his mother. As it relates to both people, they would have had difficulty finding a home in cowboy culture and rodeo at that time, due to race and gender, but they would have known the value of instilling possibility in Robinson. Through helping Robinson attain his dreams, both his great-grandfather and his mother opened the arena door to prescriptive forgetting and possibility. Neither his great-grandfather nor his mother were in rodeo, but they allowed Robinson to dream through and beyond the barriers the rodeo arena had erected long ago. Through providing land and a subscription to *Western Horseman*, these became rhetorical artifacts and a vehicle through which Robinson could take the first step into

Staying East of the Mississippi   205

writing himself into rodeo and overtly challenging White mythic rodeo history merely through his presence.

For example, Robinson pored over magazines like *Western Horseman*, saved up money from summer jobs to secure a contractor's estimate, and purchased the materials necessary to build a horse barn on the family's property in 1972, when he was sixteen years old.[45] Including cultural artifacts like horses, a barn, and even rodeo magazines reflects Robinson's work in developing a greater understanding of what one needs on a practical and cultural level to be part of the sport of rodeo. To create an identity is a moment of action, and one cannot say they are truly a cowboy or cowgirl and part of the culture without the cultural artifacts (barn, horse, land) and without skill. The artifacts and the skill become the visual record that make it that much more difficult for assumed insiders in the community (in this case, White cowboys) to deny that Robinson belongs in that world. Reading an iconic magazine like *Western Horseman* developed Robinson's language and cultural knowledge, which allowed him to seamlessly fit into the rodeo community beyond purchasing horses and building a barn. Robinson's love of horses was so famous in Connecticut that he was known as "that kid from Connecticut who was crazy enough to get on hard-to-handle horses," and he spent time doing so with his great-grandfather in rural Beckett, Connecticut.[46] In Beckett, Robinson had the privilege of growing up on his family's farm (where he was able to practice the skills required in the rodeo arena), as well as access to a rural space that provided him with additional cultural knowledge and the ability to hone his skills. Even though Robinson might not have had a mentor, he had the daily life of working on a ranch and learning about horses. Therefore, much like the West, where rodeo reigns supreme, Connecticut, too, has the wide-open spaces that allowed Robinson to receive a cowboy education.

I also argue that modern civil rights pioneers in the sport, like Myrtis Dightman, also moved Robinson. A famed cowboy, Dightman popularized the sport for many, but particularly for Black cowboys, and he was referred to as the Jackie Robinson of rodeo. Dightman was the first African American bull rider to qualify for the PRCA National Finals Rodeo in 1967 and 1968, and the first serious contender of color for the world title.[47] In the 1960s, when he asked what it would take for him to win the world title, he was told to keep riding a bull like he had been—and to turn White.[48] In his research, Demetrious Pearson found in post-1965:

> On several occasions, African American cowboys recalled incidents in which they were not welcomed at some of the mainstream rodeos. Several recounted incidents in which they were required to ride before the fans had entered the arena, while others competed after they had left. Incidents of unfair judging and the refusal to pay individuals for winning or placing were also mentioned. These

and other incidents were among the reasons given for the formation of ethnic rodeos, riding clubs, and associations.[49]

Despite the overt and covert forms of racism that Dightman and other cowboys of this era endured, this barrier-breaking cowboy inspired many Black American boys, teens, and men to enter the arena.

In fact, in referring to Robinson's statement about being a professional cowboy if only he had a mentor, perhaps in the mid-1960s, 1970s, and 1980s, Dightman cast a long shadow in rodeo, as did a few other cowboys of color. In making space for some cowboys of color nationally, there were those like Charles Sampson, who began his rodeo career at the age of twelve, after meeting Myrtis Dightman. Sampson became the first African American PRCA Rodeo World Champion bull rider in 1982.[50] Fred Whitfield began his rodeo career at the age of seven with calf roping and eventually became a PRCA member in 1990. Whitfield competed in team roping and calf tying, winning over eight World Titles at PRCA Finals, three National Final Rodeo (NFR) aggregate titles, and two prestigious awards at the PRCA in calf roping and the coveted All-Around Cowboy title, the first for an African American cowboy in 1999.[51] Through the inclusion and visibility of some cowboys of color, the naturalized Whiteness of cowboy and rodeo culture was pushed to provide avenues for inclusion even if the notion of Black cowboys provided visual cognitive dissonance in terms of how the sport of rodeo was marketed.

However, Robinson would make his mark regionally, making space not only for himself, but also for the state of Connecticut as a place for rodeo culture. Robinson had roper Bud Bramwell, a Black cowboy from suburban Stamford, Connecticut, to look up to, and model his regional career after. Robinson's admiration for Bramwell allowed him to disrupt the narratives of rodeo and cowboys as White, and as Western. Bramwell was an All-Around Cowboy at Oklahoma State University and cofounder of the American Black Cowboy Association, which existed from 1968 to 1973.[52] Following in Bramwell's footsteps, Robinson participated in rodeo at Oklahoma State University, where he eventually earned his PRCA card, but by keeping a foothold in hometown segregated Black rodeos (e.g., Okmulgee Invitational Rodeo), Robinson had to "write a letter to the PRCA competition department asking for permission to compete in his hometown rodeo."[53] The PRCA does not recognize non-sanctioned rodeos, in which the majority of people of color in rodeo participate. The practice of only recognizing PRCA events gives power back to an organization that once closed its arenas to Black American, Latinx, and Native cowboys and, thus, on its diverse beginnings. As Connerton noted, forgetting is an act of power, and it is "better to consign some things to a shadow world" to avoid uncomfortable truths.[54]

However, today, rodeo markets itself as a more diverse and inclusive space to a wide variety of communities of color, and audiences see this diversity in events like the Bill Pickett Invitational Rodeo, which traveled to thirty-seven cities in 2021 to introduce the sport to youth who live in densely populated areas; the Soul Circuit. which became the Southwestern Colored Cowboys Association and still exists today; the Compton Cowboys, which brings farming and horsing experiences to the city; and the Yeehaw Agenda, which centers on women in rodeo and encourages their participation. Further, Hollywood celebrities have become involved in rodeo—for example, steer roper James Pickens Jr.; Lil Nas X, who entered into cowboy culture with his outfits, and in particular, with his huge 2019 hit, "Old Town Road"; Megan Thee Stallion, who wore bedazzled chaps in 2019 and a rhinestone cowgirl bodysuit in 2021, which pays homage to the rich culture of cowgirls and rodeo queens; and Beyoncé who released her chart-topping country album, "Cowboy Carter," in 2024.

The participation in rodeo of cowboys like Dightman, Sampson, Whitfield, and Robinson broadens Black American participation in a sport that is often stereotyped as something for White men only, and something that is only found west of the Mississippi River. Robinson's role in rodeo requires a reexamination of what we think we know about the positionality of rodeo being rooted in the West, and so we have turned our gaze to the East Coast and Black American influence within the sport there. As an exemplar of rodeo on the East Coast, Robinson forced rodeo to reimagine itself beyond narrowly defined and mediated tropes of White cowboys only, as well as rodeo being confined to the Western portion of the United States. Steve Robinson, the Connecticut rodeo cowboy, provides a counternarrative to what we think we know about rodeo and where we regionally place the sport as it exists in the United States.

NOTES

1. See Paul Connerton, "Seven Types of Forgetting," *Memory Studies* 1, no. 1 (2008).

2. Connerton, "Seven Types of Forgetting," 60.

3. Connerton, "Seven Types of Forgetting," *Memory Studies* 1, no. 1 (2008), 63.

4. Cantwell, Robert, *When We Were Good: The Folk Revival* (Cambridge: Harvard University Press, 1996), 72.

5. Frantz, Joe B., and Julian Ernest Choate Jr., *The American Cowboy: The Myth and the Reality* (Norman: University of Oklahoma Press, 1955), 20.

6. See Bob Jordan, *Rodeo History and Legends* (Montrose, CO: Rodeo Stuff, 1993).

7. Dwayne Mack, "The Black West," in *Making of the American West: People and Perspectives*, ed. Benjamin H. Johnson, *Perspectives in American Social History* (Santa Barbara, CA.: ABC-CLIO, 2007), 135–60.

8. For more detail on settler colonialism, see Jodi A. Byrd, *The Transit of Empire: Indigenous Critiques of Colonialism* (Minneapolis, MN: University of Minnesota Press, 2011); Roxanne Dunbar-Ortiz and Dina Gilio-Whitaker, *"All the Real Indians Died Off": And 20 Other Myths About Native Americans* (Boston, MA: Beacon Press, 2016); and Shari M. Hundorf, *Going Native: Indians in the American Cultural Imagination* (Ithaca, NY: Cornell University Press, 2015).

9. Tracey Owens Patton, "Obscured Collaboration: African American Presence in the Myth of the White West." In H. G. Ruffin II and D. A. Mack (eds.), *Freedom's Frontier: African*

Americans in the West from Great Migration to Twenty First Century (Norman, OK: University of Oklahoma Press, 2018), 323.

10. See Tracey Owens Patton, "Obscured Collaboration."

11. Tracey Owens Patton, and Sally M. Schedlock, *Gender, Whiteness, and Power in Rodeo: Breaking away from the Ties of Sexism and Racism* (Lanham, MD.: Lexington Books, 2012), 4.

12. Patton and Schedlock, *Gender, Whiteness, and Power in Rodeo*, 167.

13. Patton and Schedlock, *Gender, Whiteness, and Power in Rodeo*, 5.

14. Patton and Schedlock, *Gender, Whiteness, and Power in Rodeo*, 5.

15. Patton and Schedlock, *Gender, Whiteness, and Power in Rodeo*, 5.

16. Joan Burbick, *Rodeo Queens: On the Circuit with America's Cowgirls* (New York: Public Affairs, 2002), 21.

17. Tracey Owens Patton, and Sally M. Schedlock, *Gender, Whiteness, and Power in Rodeo: Breaking away from the Ties of Sexism and Racism* (Lanham, MD.: Lexington Books, 2012), 5–6.

18. Patton and Schedlock, *Gender, Whiteness, and Power in Rodeo*, 158.

19. Patton and Schedlock, *Gender, Whiteness, and Power in Rodeo*, 164; Paul Wachter, "Fred Whitfield and the Black Cowboys of Rodeo: The Champion Calf-Roper is a Legend and an Outlier," *Andscape*, 2016, https://andscape.com/features/fred-whitfield-and-the-black-cowboys-of-rodeo/.

20. Richard W. Slatta, *Cowboy: The Illustrated History* (New York: Sterling, 2006), 75.

21. Demetrious W. Pearson, "Shadow Riders of the Subterranean Circuit: A Descriptive Account of Black Rodeo in the Texas Gulf Coast Region," *Journal of American Culture* 27, no. 2 (June 2004), 192.

22. Quoted in Patton and Schedlock, *Gender, Whiteness, and Power in Rodeo, Breaking away from the Ties of Sexism and Racism* (Lanham, MD.: Lexington Books, 2012), 164. Also see Michael Allen, *Rodeo Cowboys in the North American Imagination* (Reno: University of Nevada Press, 1998), 243; George B. Kirsch, Othello Harris, and Claire E. Nolte, *Encyclopedia of Ethnicity and Sports in the United States* (Westport, Ct.: Greenwood Press, 2000), 390.

23. Keith Ryan Cartwright, *Black Cowboys of Rodeo: Unsung Heroes from Harlem to Hollywood and the American West* (Lincoln, NE: University of Nebraska Press, 2021), 251.

24. Michael K. Johnson, *Hoo-Doo Cowboys and Bronze Buckaroos: Conceptions of the African American West* (Jackson: University Press of Mississippi, 2014), 83.

25. Mifflin Wistar Gibbs, *Shadow and Light: An Autobiography* (1902), excerpts, National Humanities Center Resource Toolbox, http://nationalhumanitiescenter.org/pds/maai/identity/text4/gibbs.pdf.

26. Census data do not provide statistics on those who may have selected more than one racial box (e.g., being biracial, tri-racial, etc.), where at least one race chosen was Black.

27. Tracey Owens Patton, and Sally M. Schedlock, *Gender, Whiteness, and Power in Rodeo: Breaking away from the Ties of Sexism and Racism* (Lanham, Md.: Lexington Books, 2012), 180.

28. Demetrious W. Pearson, "Shadow Riders of the Subterranean Circuit: A Descriptive Account of Black Rodeo in the Texas Gulf Coast Region," *Journal of American Culture* 27, no. 2 (June 2004), 192.

29. Philip Durham, and Everett L. Jones, *The Adventures of the Negro Cowboys* (New York: Bantam, 1969), 107.

30. Tracey Owens Patton, and Sally M. Schedlock, *Gender, Whiteness, and Power in Rodeo: Breaking away from the Ties of Sexism and Racism* (Lanham, Md.: Lexington Books, 2012), 180.

31. As Demetrious Pearson noted, Soul Circuits had been around since the 1940s in Southern rural communities and were "unsanctioned weekend competitions close to home. None of these rodeos on the Soul Circuit was sanctioned by the PRCA, the largest national and international governing body of professional rodeo. Although these rodeos are viable professional competitions, the payouts are nominal and exposure is minimal; therefore, they rarely enhance the marketability of the rodeo athlete" (196). It is believed that Soul Circuits transformed into the Southwestern Colored Cowboys' Association (SCAA), where famed cowboy Myrtis Dightman rode (see Tracey Owens Patton, and Sally M. Schedlock, *Gender, Whiteness, and Power in Rodeo: Breaking away from the Ties of Sexism and Racism* [Lanham, MD.: Lexington Books, 2012]).

32. Tracey Owens Patton, "Obscured Collaboration: African American Presence in the Myth of the White West." In H. G. Ruffin II and D. A. Mack (eds.), *Freedom's Frontier: African Americans in the West from Great Migration to Twenty First Century* (Norman, OK: University of Oklahoma Press, 2018), 326.

33. Paul Connerton, "Seven Types of Forgetting," *Memory Studies* 1, no. 1 (2008), 60.

34. Michael K. Johnson, *Hoo-Doo Cowboys and Bronze Buckaroos: Conceptions of the African American West* (Jackson: University Press of Mississippi, 2014), 103–04.

35. Tracey Owens Patton, "Obscured Collaboration: African American Presence in the Myth of the White West." In H. G. Ruffin II and D. A. Mack (eds.) *Freedom's*

Frontier: African Americans in the West from Great Migration to Twenty First Century (Norman, OK: University of Oklahoma Press, 2018), 331.

36. Art Burton, *Black Gun, Silver Star: The Life and Legend of Frontier Marshal Bass Reeves* (Lincoln: University of Nebraska Press, 2006).

37. In 2023, Paramount+ aired the show, *Bass Reeves: Lawman*, which stared Black British actor David Oyelowo as Bass Reeves.

38. "About the Sports of Team Penning and Ranch Sorting," United States Team Penning Association, http://www.ustpa.com/index.php?cat=what.

39. Latoya M. Smith, "Backtalk with James Pickins, Jr.," *Black Enterprise*, July 2009, 96.

40. Roberta McCulloch-Dews, "Keep Vision Alive," *Berkshire Eagle*, March 22, 2012, para. 9, https://www.berkshireeagle.com/archives/keep-vision-alive/article _54d5c630-a33e-571b-a126-8335f304b953.html.

41. Pamela Lepore, "ON THE RODEO Cowboys of Color Gather to Sing 'Home on the Bronx' in Crotona Park Horse Feast," *New York Daily News*, August 19, 2000, 24.

42. Lepore, "ON THE RODEO Cowboys of Color gather," 24.

43. Roberta McCulloch-Dews, "Keep Vision Alive," *Berkshire Eagle*, March 22, 2012, para. 6, https://www.berkshireeagle.com/archives/keep-vision-alive/article _54d5c630-a33e-571b-a126-8335f304b953.html.

44. McCulloch-Dews, "Keep Vision Alive," para. 9.

45. See Keith Ryan Cartwright, *Black Cowboys of Rodeo: Unsung Heroes from Harlem to Hollywood and the American West* (Lincoln, NE: University of Nebraska Press, 2021), 252; see Keith Ryan Cartwright, "Celebrating Black Cowboys of Rodeo: The East Coast," *Wrangler Network*, February 8, 2021, para. 10, https:// wranglernetwork.com/news/celebrating-black-cowboys-of-rodeo-the-east-coast/.

46. Keith Ryan Cartwright, *Black Cowboys of Rodeo: Unsung Heroes from Harlem to Hollywood and the American West* (Lincoln, NE: University of Nebraska Press, 2021), 253.

47. George B. Kirsch, Othello Harris, and Claire E. Nolte, *Encyclopedia of Ethnicity and Sports in the United States* (Westport, Ct.: Greenwood Press, 2000), 390.

48. Andy Smith, "Bull Rider Paved Way for Blacks in Rodeo Arena," in *Conroe (Tex.) Courier*, November 11, 1997.

49. Pearson, "Shadow Riders of the Subterranean Circuit," 197.

50. "2003 Hall of Fame Inductee, Charles Sampson," National Multicultural Western Heritage Museum and Hall of Fame, http://www.cowboysofcolor.org/profile.php ?ID=3; Professional Rodeo Cowboys Association, http://www.prorodeo.com/.

51. "Biography," Fred Whitfield: The Official Website, http://www.fredwhitfield .com/index.php?option=com_content&view=article&id=51&Itemid=5.

52. See Keith Ryan Cartwright, "Celebrating Black Cowboys of Rodeo: The East Coast," *Wrangler Network*, February 8, 2021, para. 5, https://wranglernetwork.com/ news/celebrating-black-cowboys-of-rodeo-the-east-coast/.

53. Keith Ryan Cartwright, *Black Cowboys of Rodeo: Unsung Heroes from Harlem to Hollywood and the American West* (Lincoln, NE: University of Nebraska Press, 2021), 257.

Staying East of the Mississippi 211

54. Paul Connerton, "Seven Types of Forgetting," *Memory Studies* 1, no. 1 (2008) 63.

BIBLIOGRAPHY

"2003 Hall of Fame Inductee, Charles Sampson," National Multicultural Western Heritage Museum and Hall of Fame, http://www.cowboysofcolor.org/profile.php ?ID=3; Professional Rodeo Cowboys Association, http://www.prorodeo.com/.

"About the Sports of Team Penning and Ranch Sorting," United States Team Penning Association, http://www.ustpa.com/index.php?cat=what.

Allen, Michael. *Rodeo Cowboys in the North American Imagination.* Reno: University of Nevada Press, 1998.

Burbick, Joan. *Rodeo Queens: On the Circuit with America's Cowgirls.* New York: Public Affairs, 2002.

Burton, Art. *Black Gun, Silver Star: The Life and Legend of Frontier Marshal Bass Reeves.* Lincoln: University of Nebraska Press, 2006.

Byrd, Jodi. *The Transit of Empire: Indigenous Critiques of Colonialism.* Minneapolis: University of Minnesota Press, 2011.

Cantwell, Robert. *When We Were Good: The Folk Revival.* Cambridge: Harvard University Press, 1996.

Cartwright, Keith Ryan. "Celebrating Black Cowboys of Rodeo: The East Coast," *Wrangler Network*, February 8, 2021, para. 10 https://wranglernetwork.com/news/ celebrating-black-cowboys-of-rodeo-the-east-coast/.

Cartwright, Keith Ryan. *Black Cowboys of Rodeo: Unsung Heroes from Harlem to Hollywood and the American West.* Lincoln: University of Nebraska Press, 2021.

Connerton, Paul. "Seven Types of Forgetting." *Memory Studies* (Volume 1, Number 1), 2008.

Dunbar-Ortiz, Roxanne, and Gilio-Whitaker, Dina. *"All the Real Indians Died Off": And 20 Other Myths About Native Americans.* Boston: Beacon Press, 2016.

Durham, Philip, and Everett L. Jones. *The Adventures of the Negro Cowboys.* New York: Bantam, 1969.

Frantz, Joe B., and Julian Ernest Choate Jr. *The American Cowboy: The Myth and the Reality.* Norman: University of Oklahoma Press, 1955.

Gibbs, Mifflin Wistar. *Shadow and Light: An Autobiography* (1902), excerpts, National Humanities Center Resource Toolbox, http://nationalhumanitiescenter.org /pds/maai/identity/text4/gibbs.pdf.

Hundorf, Shari. *Going Native: Indians in the American Cultural Imagination.* Ithaca: Cornell University Press, 2015.

Johnson, Michael. *Hoo-Doo Cowboys and Bronze Buckaroos: Conceptions of the African American West.* Jackson: University Press of Mississippi, 2014.

Jordan, Bob. *Rodeo History and Legends.* Montrose: Rodeo Stuff, 1993.

Lepore, Pamela. "ON THE RODEO Cowboys of Color Gather to Sing 'Home on the Bronx,'" in Crotona Park Horse Feast," *New York Daily News*, August 19, 2000, 24.

Mack, Dwayne. "The Black West," in *Making of the American West: People and Perspectives*, ed. Benjamin H. Johnson, *Perspectives in American Social History*. Santa Barbara: ABC-CLIO, 2007.

McCulloch-Dews, Roberta. "Keep Vision Alive," *Berkshire Eagle*, March 22, 2012, https://www.berkshireeagle.com/archives/keep-vision-alive/article_54d5c630 -a33e-571b-a126-8335f304b953.html.

Morris, Abe. *My Cowboy Hat Still Fits: My Life as a Rodeo Star*. Greybull: Pronghorn Press, 2005.

Patton, Tracey Owens, and Sally M. Schedlock. *Gender, Whiteness, and Power in Rodeo: Breaking away from the Ties of Sexism and Racism*. Lanham: Lexington Books, 2012.

Patton, Tracey Owens, "Obscured Collaboration: African American Presence in the Myth of the White West." In H. G. Ruffin II and D. A. Mack, eds. *Freedom's Frontier: African Americans in the West from Great Migration to Twenty First Century.* Norman: University of Oklahoma Press, 2018.

Pearson, Demetrious. "Shadow Riders of the Subterranean Circuit: A Descriptive Account of Black Rodeo in the Texas Gulf Coast Region," *Journal of American Culture* (Volume 27, Number 2), 2004.

Slatta, Richard. *Cowboy: The Illustrated History.* New York: Sterling, 2006.

Smith, Andy. "Bull Rider Paved Way for Blacks in Rodeo Arena," in *Conroe Courier*, November 11, 1997.

Smith, Latoya. "Backtalk with James Pickins, Jr.," *Black Enterprise* (July 2009).

Wachter, Paul. "Fred Whitfield and the Black Cowboys of Rodeo: The Champion Calf-Roper Is a Legend and an Outlier," *Andscape*, 2016, https://andscape.com/ features/fred-whitfield-and-the-black-cowboys-of-rodeo/.

Chapter 11

Boom Boom Barbosa to Jair

Boston's Minor-League, Major-League Soccer and Black Identity

Steven Apostolov

Until the late 1990s, the history of association football in the United States—or "soccer," as the game is known to most Americans—was not a common topic among historians, sociologists, anthropologists, or other researchers. It was not a subject of much discussion among soccer aficionados, either, as most fans were interested in stories about soccer from countries with deep traditions in the game. Outside of the United Kingdom, there are very few places in the world where soccer existed prior to its codification as a modern sport in 1863. This was perhaps only the case in ancient, medieval, and modern Greece and Italy.

In Massachusetts, during the early seventeenth century, archaic kicking games were played by English colonists and Native Americans in Boston and surrounding areas. Later, during the mid-nineteenth century, the Boston Game, a premodern sport containing elements of what would later become rugby and soccer, became the favorite activity of children of the Bostonian elite, the so-called Brahmins, who founded the Oneida Football Club. Many members of the Oneida Football Club studied at Harvard, where, from the late 1860s to the early 1870s, they transmitted their passion for the Boston Game to their peers.[1]

During the 1890s, soccer fascinated many workers at the numerous textile mills, shipyards, and factories around New England. After the death of the short-lived American League of Professional Football Clubs (ALPFC) in 1894, soccer was practiced as a semiprofessional activity at many industrial plants. Many amateur teams and leagues coexisted alongside the

213

factory-sponsored teams. First, the Boston and District League, an amateur league in Massachusetts, was mainly comprised of Anglo-Scottish teams. By the second decade of the twentieth century, the British teams were joined by many other ethnic teams. In fact, at that time, amateur and semiprofessional soccer was better developed in some regions of the United States than in the countries now considered superpowers of the game. As a result, in 1921 the American Soccer League (ASL), a fully professional sports enterprise, fielded a dozen teams, mostly in the Northeast. Some of the best professional players from Great Britain, Austria, Hungary, and Czechoslovakia, to name a few countries leading in soccer at the time, crossed the Atlantic to join teams in Massachusetts, Rhode Island, Connecticut, New York, New Jersey, and Pennsylvania, attracted by the higher salaries the American team owners offered. In 1924, the United States fielded a team of amateurs, as was required by the organizers, to represent the country during the Olympic Games in Paris. George Collins, who had a dual role as an Olympic soccer coach and a reporter for the *Boston Globe*, made an interesting observation: "In what other country of the world will you find such a heterogenous mass playing soccer or any other sport? In the Boston district alone there are Irish, English, Scots, Swedes Norwegians, Armenians, Turks, Welsh, Portuguese, Canadians, South Africans, Chinese and Germans, not to forget our own boys who of late years have been fast picking up the soccer game."[2] It is obvious from this comment and other historical research that ethnicity played a crucial role in the development of soccer in the United States. However, except for a few Asian amateur teams, soccer teams were predominantly Caucasian. Were there any African American or Black players involved?

This chapter will first analyze the literature and historiography of American soccer. It will then focus on the role of ethnicity and the participation of Black players in soccer in America and around the world, outlining the involvement of the few Black players in minor- and major-league soccer in the Boston area from the 1960s until the late 1990s. Finally, the piece will conclude with a discussion of what American soccer would have looked like with more African American players involved in the game.

EXCEPTIONALISM AND NATIVISM IN THE
HISTORIOGRAPHY OF AMERICAN SOCCER

There are no better words to describe the development of soccer in the United States than soccer historian David Kilpatrick's: "amnesia and antagonism." Kilpatrick, a professor at Mercy University, noted that "the inferiority complex that plagues the game is to no small degree rooted in the sense that the sport is considered by some as 'new,' compared with other, more established 'major league' sports, such as baseball, basketball, and gridiron."[3] Until the 1990s, most of soccer historiography focused on countries and regions where the sport was well-established. Andrei Markovits, a professor of political science and German studies at the University of Michigan, was among the few academically trained scholars who attempted to explain the "failure" of American soccer, although several self-educated historians and journalists tackled the topic as well. In terms of academic scholarship, Markovits was followed by other writers who argued that American nativism halted the development of soccer.

According to proponents of American exceptionalism in sports history, soccer's place in American society was "overcrowded" by baseball from below and American football from above. Once American football and baseball filled the gap, the increasing popularity of basketball and ice hockey made soccer's development impossible.[4] This social model was built upon a theory implying that just as America has never developed a large socialist movement, it has also never accepted soccer. The exceptionalist theory also suggests that the space for sports in any given society is limited, and once that space is taken, it will be impossible for a new sport to gain popularity.

Claiming that soccer is as American as baseball and as popular as American football would be an exaggeration. However, underestimating the importance of American soccer and ignoring its episodes of popularity would overlook important aspects of the American sporting and popular culture experience. Certainly, the game was marginalized by baseball, but soccer was not "crowded out" by all American sports simply because baseball, gridiron, basketball, and ice hockey did not develop with the same velocity or on the same timeline. While baseball has been deeply rooted in American society since the mid-nineteenth century, basketball was first a women's sport, and then an ethnic sport.

In the 1920s, basketball became popular with the children of Jewish immigrants, who played it in many cities of the Northeast. Many of basketball's early stars were Jews.[5] It would take several decades for African Americans to get involved and for the NBA to become a successful sports enterprise. And while the sport of ice hockey enjoyed popularity in the American Northeast and Canada, it was not until the early 1990s that its popularity expanded.

At the turn of the twentieth century, the future of American football was still obscure. An extremely violent sport that produced a significant number of injuries and a high death toll among college students, American football was prohibited by President Theodore Roosevelt in 1905.[6] It was not until the mid-1920s that football became a professional sport. Was it then a threat to soccer, which became a professional sport following the establishment of the American Soccer League in 1921; did football "overcrowd" soccer from above, as proponents of exceptionalism in American sports have attempted to persuade us?

These first discrepancies in the exceptionalist theory are followed by others. By exclusively focusing his research on the popularity of baseball, football, basketball, and ice hockey, Markovits underestimated the enormous wave of immigrants (several million at the turn of the twentieth century) that impacted American society. Predominantly Anglo-Scottish immigration gave way to immigration from Ireland, as well as from Southern, Central and Eastern Europe. The newcomers did not follow American sports upon arrival (much of which they probably did not understand), but rather they played and followed European sports, with soccer being the most prevalent. The new patterns of immigration impacted and reshaped American society. Several million immigrants arrived at the turn of the century and therefore provided additional "space" for sports. Some of that "space" was occupied by soccer—the world's most popular sport.

Markovits was not the only scholar who attempted to explain the failure of soccer in the United States without fully researching all aspects of the game. Sugden and Tomlinson explained the failure of American soccer as due to nativist feelings. According to Sugden, "soccer has been and continues to be viewed by the mass of the American public as (an) essentially foreign game," and the un-American aspects of the sport prevented it from fascinating native-born sports fans.[7]

In sharp contrast to that statement, soccer veteran Walter Bahr said that "soccer was considered an American game during my childhood [1920s–1930s]." Bahr was a member of the 1950 US National Team, which defeated England during the World Cup in Brazil. Born and raised in Philadelphia, he learned how to play soccer with thousands of other kids at a sports club called the Lighthouse.[8] John Souza, a teammate of Bahr's on the national team, had a similar experience growing up in Fall River, Massachusetts, during the 1920s. "Each section of the city had a team, sometimes multiple teams. We played the Irish, we played the French, we played against everybody," said Souza.[9]

The debate over the un-American aspect of soccer raises a pertinent question: What is American, and what is un-American? And that question has also a diachronic aspect, or a second part: If something was considered un-American at the turn of the twentieth century, was it still perceived in the same way by society in the 1950s or at the turn of the millennium? Certainly, at the turn of the twentieth century, some Americans who were probably influenced by popular nativist propaganda of the time despised many foreign customs. A Bostonian Protestant "Brahmin" would never have marched on Saint Patrick's Day alongside an Irish immigrant, whereas nowadays, the 17th of March—an ethnic holiday—has become a day of celebration for all Boston residents, as well as leaders of the city and state. This is a perfect example of an event that was once considered un-American but that became perfectly American over the course of a century and is currently observed nationwide.

The same could be said for food. A respectable businessman from New York City would never have consumed a bagel or *knish* at a Jewish deli on the Lower East Side at the turn of the century. Today, bagels are considered as American as apple pie, not only in the United States, but around the world. American fast-food chains have adopted them, and in this way, they have spread around the world as American cuisine. Bagels are also on the menu at many trendy cafés in London, Paris, and other European capitals, and if any of these Europeans are asked to explain where they come from, they might mention America and not give credit to the Eastern European Jews who brought the recipe with them while immigrating to the New World.

Another vivid example can be found in American political life. When Al Smith was defeated in the 1928 presidential election, it was largely due to his religion, which generated anti-Catholic attacks from political interests, including the Ku Klux Klan. Several decades later, John F. Kennedy was not crippled by his Irish Catholicism and managed to defeat Richard Nixon. In 2002, the fact that Al Gore chose an Orthodox Jew for his running mate was not the reason George W. Bush defeated him.

Let us go back to the "un-American character of soccer," as debated by Sudgen and Tomlinson. Even if at some point during the twentieth century, soccer might have been considered un-American—that could have been the case in the 1960s and 1970s, when the North American Soccer League (NASL) fielded entire teams comprised of foreign athletes—soccer has slowly but surely become a fundamental part of the fabric of American society.

The assumption that American soccer was never successful because its place was already taken by other sports is not convincing because, again, the four major American team sports did not develop simultaneously. Until the early 1920s, the only true professional team sports in the United States were baseball and soccer. If nativism was deeply rooted in American society at the turn of the twentieth century, that is no longer true. American society from the early twentieth century forward has very little in common with post–World War II America. And US society today is totally different from either era. If soccer was considered un-American because some of the ASL and most of the NASL players were foreigners, today's Major League Soccer (MLS) players are, by contrast, predominantly American and college educated. Evidently the un-Americanism that could have crippled the ASL or the NASL, if anything like that happened at all, is no longer applicable to MLS.

The following part of the chapter will shift the focus to ethnicity and the involvement of Black players in soccer.

DISCUSSION ABOUT ETHNICITY AND
INVOLVEMENT OF BLACK PLAYERS IN SOCCER

The ethnic aspect of soccer in the United States is an important one. At the end of the nineteenth century, soccer teams and leagues were homogenous. They fielded predominantly English and Scottish players. Just as they did around the world, the English and Scots spread the gospel of soccer in Massachusetts, as well as other parts of the nation. The homogeneity of soccer teams could have been a reason for the decline of some teams in Western Massachusetts. Historian Brian Bunk has argued that one of the reasons for the failure of the Holyoke Falcons Football Club was its homogeneous British identity.[10] During the second part of the twentieth century, most leagues and teams in Eastern Massachusetts became more ethnically diverse, with the massive involvement of Irish, Canadians, Portuguese, Swedish, Norwegian, German, Armenian, American, and Chinese players.[11] But were there any African American or Black players?

When asked if the United States would ever become a superpower in world soccer, Harry Keogh, another veteran of the 1950 US World Cup team that defeated England in Brazil in 1950, answered, "I don't see why not. But we need to attract a greater percentage of natural athletes, and *some* Black players, too. We need to get them into soccer earlier and develop their skills. If we don't do this, we will fail short."[12] Keogh accomplished an outstanding career as a varsity soccer coach at St. Louis University. He personally scouted, coached, and developed a lot of players. Not many of them were Black or African American. Ironically, his teammate who scored the winning goal against England in 1950 was Black, although not African American. Joe Gaetjens was born in Port-au-Prince, Haiti, on March 19, 1924. He grew up in a well-to-do family. By the age of fourteen, he was already one of the star players of L'Etoile Haitienne—one of the most popular soccer teams in the Haitian capital in the 1940s. In the closing stages of World War II, he moved to New York City to enroll at Columbia University. During his college studies in accounting, he also worked at a restaurant and played for the Brookhattan Galicia—an ethnic, semiprofessional soccer club affiliated with the second American Soccer League (ASL).[13] He earned a reputation as a solid and intelligent player, scoring some uncanny goals.[14] As a permanent resident of the United States, he qualified to try out for Team USA and was selected. He scored the only goal during the game between the United States and England. It was certainly the biggest upset in the history of the World Cup, a battle between David and Goliath on the soccer pitch. Prior to the tournament, England had defeated some of the strongest national teams, and many anticipated that the "cradle of soccer" would capture the 1950 Jules Rimet trophy.

Assuming there had been a mistake in transmitting the information over cable, some news outlets printed the final score as ten to one for England. In fact, the match ended up 1–0 for the United States. The year after that memorable victory, Gaetjens moved to Paris, where he spent a few years playing for the Racing Club de Paris. It was the first and last time he played purely professional soccer, as very few players made a living playing for the semi-professional ASL in the United States. After his stay at *la ville de lumière*, he went back to Haiti, where he started a family and opened a dry-cleaning business. In the early 1960s, the notorious Tonton Macoute death squads of dictator François Duvalier kidnapped him. He disappeared and was never seen again.[15] In the 1970s, official requests for details about his disappearance from Brazilian soccer legend Pelé and even former US secretary of state Henry Kissinger remained unanswered. As of today, people still speculate on how he was killed and where.

Joe Geatjens was not the only Black player on the Brookhattan Galicia team. Pito Villanon, a Cuban-born Black player, competed with Geatjens for the top goal scorer's position in the second ASL.[16] Gilles Heron, another Black player of Jamaican origin, joined the Detroit Wolverines in 1946 and led the North American Soccer Football League (NASFL) with fifteen goals. He was spotted by a foreign scout and, like Geatjens, went to play in Europe. His career in the Celtic FC was limited to the reserve team, where he scored fifteen goals in fifteen games. According to sportswriter Frank Dell'Apa, he then played for Third Lanark in Scotland and the Kidderminster Harriers in England before returning to the Detroit Corinthians in 1954.[17] Although some Black players began to emerge on the American soccer pitches in the late 1940s and early 1950s, they were mostly of Caribbean origin, and their numbers were extremely limited. In the early years of soccer, administrators, coaches, and players of Northern European descent dominated the game in most countries, including the United States.[18] In Brazil, for example, soccer in the early years was practiced and enjoyed at exclusive private clubs. British expats and the local White bourgeoisie kept it segregated and completely White for a while. Spectators, among them elegantly dressed ladies and gentlemen, celebrated the ends of matches with toasts of gin and whiskey to the British monarch. It would be pertinent to note that the Brazilian National Team's performance during the initial tournaments of the World Cup was mediocre. It was not until the inclusion of Leonidas da Silva, Domingos da Guia, and a few other players of color during the 1938 World Cup tournament that *la Seleçao* became more successful—finishing with a respectable 2–1 loss in the semifinal to the Italians, who became World Cup champions. During the 1960s and 1970s, the number of Black players in top-level professional soccer increased but remained small. They played mainly in countries like France and Portugal, which still had strong colonial ties with Africa. However, things changed significantly when Jean-Marc Bosman, a Belgian professional player, filed a claim against his club, the Royal Football Club of Liege, at the European Court of Justice, and won the case. The case became known as the Bosman Ruling. It allowed players to sign up with a new club after the expirations of their contracts, preventing their previous club from requesting a transfer fee. The Bosman Ruling removed obstacles to players' mobility within the European Union and gave them free agency. Suddenly, the elite clubs of the big four European leagues—the English Premier League (EPL), *La Liga* in Spain, *Bundesliga* in Germany, and *Seria A* in Italy—enticed the top players of the other European Leagues with more limited financial resources. That caused considerable financial disparity between clubs and created a demand for players in less-affluent leagues and clubs whose players had departed for better paychecks with the big four European soccer leagues. Deepening financial inequality between European leagues and clubs boosted the demand for cheap labor from Africa and Latin America.[19] The following part of the chapter will document the role of some Black players in minor-league soccer in Boston and the surrounding areas during the late 1960s and early 1970s.

"BOOM BOOM" BARBOSA AND MINOR-LEAGUE SOCCER IN THE BOSTON AREA DURING THE 1960S AND 1970S

Brazilian immigrants have settled in large numbers in several cities in the United States. They are well represented in Atlanta, Boston, Miami, and New York City. Brazilians adore soccer: it is part of their culture. Considering their passion for soccer, there is no doubt that wherever Brazilians settle, sooner or later they will get involved in soccer—playing it or watching it from the stands or on television screens. In the 1970s, at a well-known Jewish resort in upstate New York that employed hundreds of Brazilians as dishwashers, busboys, waiters, and housekeepers, "there were even Brazilian soccer teams from the various hotels that competed with each other," observed American anthropologist Maxine Margolis.[20]

According to another scholar, sociologist Ana Christina Braga Martes, the same type of work-related soccer activities was documented even earlier in Massachusetts, where "in the 1960s, an American businessman organized a soccer team in Lowell, Massachusetts. About 20 Brazilians from Belo Horizonte were hired by the businessman. They later decided to remain in the city and help other family members to follow them."[21] Braga Martes, however, was wrong about a few minor details—the businessman who had brought the Brazilians to Massachusetts was not American, and he personally helped more than one hundred Brazilian players to come to Massachusetts.

Boom Boom Barbosa to Jair 221

John Bertos, a Greek immigrant who owned a janitorial company employing some two hundred workers, was so passionate about soccer that he invested a considerable amount of money in a semiprofessional team affiliated with the second ASL. Bertos acquired the Boston Astros in 1968. From 1968 until the mid-1970s, he made multiple trips to Belo Horizonte and personally recruited players from Atletico Mineiro and other professional teams of the State Minas Gerais. Upon his arrival, he would help players to find housing and even employ some in his company if they were unable to find work elsewhere. They would work during the week and play for the Astros on the weekend.[22] Bertos paid his players between one hundred and three hundred dollars per match. When the Astros were based in Lowell, the team played games before one thousand people at the local municipal stadium. When they moved to Fall River, Massachusetts, the average crowd attending games was between four and five thousand. When the Astros played in Boston, Nickerson Field often had capacity crowds of about 12,500 per game. With such attendance, the Astros outshined their competition from the major league—the New England Tea Men, affiliated with the North American Soccer League (NASL). The Tea Men played at Boston College and Shafer Stadium: they struggled to gather good attendance and moved in the late 1970s to Jacksonville, Florida. "One spectator more for us meant one spectator less for them [the New England Tea Men]," explained Bertos. "The Portuguese of Fall River loved us. Spectators were waiting for our bus in front of the stadium. Fans hugged us, kissed us, we were treated like celebrities," remembered Wagner Leao, who played for the Astros from 1968 until 1972.[23]

The Astros were a predominantly Brazilian team during most of their existence. In 1973, for instance, nine of the eleven players of the Astros were recent Brazilian immigrants, and some of them were Black. "I had a few black players, but none of them was American," said Bertos.[24] Helio Barbosa, nicknamed "Boom Boom" Barbosa because of his rare ability to dribble and shoot with both feet, became one of the fans' favorites. He also had a tremendous facial resemblance to Pelé. Barbosa was born on September 25, 1940, in Nova Lima, Brazil. He was an orphan. Later, a poor family adopted him, but they could not provide him with much education. By the late 1960s, he had already become an established soccer professional, wearing the colors of Vila Nova Atletico Clube (not to be confused with the much younger Vila Nova Futebol Clube from the neighboring state of Goias). Vila Nova AC was founded in 1908 by English expats, working as foremen in mining and manufacturing. It became known as the first club from Minas Gerais to have players selected to represent the country at the international level. Peracio, a player of Vila Nova AC, played for Brazil alongside Leonidas during the World Cup in 1938, putting three goals in the nets of his country's opponents. Nova Lima AC plunged into obscurity throughout most of the 1950s and

 THE 1973 BOSTON ASTROS SOCCER TEAM

Standing: (L to R)-Gustavo Carias, Tony Soares, Ernie Gomes, Carl Benedito, Joe Reis, Arthur Dessimone, Jerry Souza.
Front: (L to R) - Joe Santos, Luis Oliviera, Helio Barbosa, Eddie Braga, (Capt.) Itamar Alves.

Figure 11.1. The 1973 Boston Astros Soccer Team (Helio Barbosa is in front, holding the ball). During his six years in the American Soccer League, Barbosa was one of the best forwards. Image provided by Steven Apostolov.

1960s. But in 1971, the team again earned a promotion to the top level of Brazilian professional soccer.[25] Barbosa fascinated John Bertos with his skills during one of his visits to Brazil to recruit players. In 1972, Bertos assisted "Boom Boom" in moving to the Boston area, just as he had done before with many other Brazilians. "Barbosa became instantly one of the fans' favorites, especially among the kids," remembered publicist David Pickett, who attempted to digitize some of the Astros' archival materials and maintains a website dedicated to the team.[26] "The Astros would organize many soccer clinics during the 1970s and many young children attended them. I remember during one of them, an Astros player was taking corner kicks and Barbosa would take turns to blast the ball in the net with his left foot, his right and would also do headers," shared Joe Pickett, David's older brother who volunteered as a water boy when the Astros played at Boston University's stadium.[27] When he grew up, Joe married a Brazilian woman from Minas Gerais. Since then, he has been traveling constantly to Minas Gerais. During one of his visits in 2015, he met "Boom Boom" Barbosa in Nova Lima, which is a municipality located about ten miles south of Belo Horizonte—the capital of the state of Minas Gerais. The former water boy spent some time with one of the heroes from his childhood. "Everybody seemed to know Helio, he is very well respected in Nova Lima," David Pickett wrote.[28]

The Boston Astros folded in 1975. Their owner, Jon Bertos, could not keep up financially with the owner of the New England Tea Men, who was an oil executive with much deeper pockets. Bertos was a successful small business owner, but by the mid-1970s, running even a semiprofessional team became extremely expensive. It was certainly beyond his means, and he almost went bankrupt. To recover his losses, he transferred some of his players to professional soccer teams of the NASL and his native Greece. He even sold a player who became a placekicker in the NFL's Green Bay Packers.

Many of the Brazilians who were hired by Bertos stayed in the United States. It is interesting to note, however, that their social backgrounds were not homogeneous. Some of them were from the middle class. "My brother Alan and I come from a middle-class, well-to-do family. Our father was a lawyer and didn't want us to play soccer for the junior team of Atletico Mineiro," remembered Wagner Leao.[29] In the United States, the Leao brothers were able to practice their favorite sport away from their unhappy father, but what brought food to the table was their white-collar jobs—Leao retired as a manager of a scientific laboratory. Just like most players of the second ASL, he supplemented his income as a soccer player. A few of the Astros came from Brazil with only soccer skills. Some of them married American women and stayed in the United States, supporting their families as unskilled workers. Some others, who were from underprivileged social backgrounds, found it difficult to support themselves by playing only semiprofessional soccer and had to return to Brazil after minor-league and major-league professional soccer in the United States started to experience problems in the late 1970s. One of them was Helio "Boom Boom" Barbosa. He returned to his native Nova Lima, where he coached Vila Nova AC and briefly became president of the club.[30] The following part of the chapter will shift the focus to illustrate the development of amateur and major-league soccer in the Boston area during the 1990s.

"JAIR" AMATEUR AND MAJOR LEAGUE SOCCER IN THE 1990S

The Luso American Soccer Association (LASA) was founded in 1973. Only a few years later, the number of affiliated teams grew to twenty. LASA benefited from a sophisticated structure and solid fundraising, based on the traditional club system of Portugal. Each season, distinguished clergy such as Archdiocese of Boston, Bishop Sean Patrick O'Malley (now Cardinal

O'Malley), and dignitaries such as the Portugal consul general attended the league's annual fundraising dinners.[31]

In addition to the annual dinner, during which the league generated significant donations from companies, religious organizations, and foreign governments, LASA benefited from highly structured local fundraising from small and mid-sized local companies. Small companies, such as Da Sá Fish Market, Carmelo's Auto Body, Terra Nostra Restaurant, Oliveira Imports Co., Mario Fonseca Pest Control, to name just a few, supported one or several teams. Most of these companies still exist. The Lusitanos of Lowell, Massachusetts, were sponsored by Friend's Pizza Restaurant & Lounge. Massachusetts& Gift Shop, which is still run by and employs Portuguese Americans in Fall River, Massachusetts, has always supported Fall River Sports FC. The name of this supermarket was therefore displayed on the shirts of the players. Continental Market, another Portuguese supermarket in Fall River, supported the biggest rivals of Fall River Sports FC—Associação Académica de Fall River. Most LASA teams were also associated with Portuguese social clubs, which were affiliated with professional soccer teams from Portugal. Tony Frias, who directly sponsored LASA's Hudson Benfica FC, often invited and covered the expenses of famous Portuguese powerhouses, such as SL Benfica, Sporting CP, and Mira Mar SC. Games would usually be organized during the offseason of the Portuguese professional league. Major Portuguese newspapers and TV stations covered the team tours in detail.

Between three and five thousand spectators regularly attended LASA games. Certain teams collected considerable funds from gate receipts. Advertising local businesses and companies on the teams' shirts was also very common, and that was another source of revenue for these "amateur" teams. Tony Frias, a wealthy Portuguese American businessman and owner of S&F Concrete Inc., spent a lot of money on his team. One of his former players admitted to receiving one thousand dollars per game from him. Later, the same player refused a professional contract from Major League Soccer (MLS). His earnings as an IT entrepreneur and the supplement from Hudson Benfica quadrupled the offer from MLS: "I was in love with my wife, I had a great income from my own business, and Tony was generous to me, he appreciated my talent and treated me like his own son."[32] Other players were also paid. None of them, however, enjoyed remunerations as large as those received by Murphy. Sean Carrey, a former midfielder for the Lowell Lusitanos, earned seven hundred dollars per match at the peak of his LASA career. Luis Cerqueira, a young Portuguese immigrant, earned one hundred dollars per match during his year of playing for Lowell United. "It was great money for a high school student at the time," shared the former LASA player.[33] Anselmo "Jair" Ribeiro, a former professional player of Sporting CP, SC Olhanese and PFC CSKA Sofia, New England Revolution,

Boom Boom Barbosa to Jair 225

San Jose Clash, and Tampa Bay Mutiny, cut his teeth in soccer as a LASA player.[34] While in high school, he earned between $100 and $120 per match. Although the league and its officials claimed to be amateurs, most LASA players were paid. Younger players received about one hundred dollars per game, while the remuneration for some adults ranged from $150 to $300 per game. In a few exceptional cases, extremely talented players made more. All LASA players and their families were treated free at the restaurants and bars of the social clubs associated with their soccer teams—and most LASA teams had one.

Anselmo "Jair" Ribeiro was nicknamed "Jair," after the famous Brazilian player Jair da Rosa Pinto, who played alongside Pelé and even coached him for a while. "Jair" was born on the Cape Verdean Islands, an archipelago of volcanic islands located off the coast of West Africa. In 1988, his mother came to work for an airline in Boston, and Jair followed her. He had three brothers and two sisters. One of his brothers became a professional soccer player, joining the Sporting CP in Portugal, but an injury prematurely ended his career. Jair enrolled at Madison Park Technical Vocational High School when he was fourteen. "We had a great soccer team at Madison Park, mostly kids from my country. We qualified for the state championship. We lost in the final, but it was a great experience. It helped me develop as a player, playing with talented high school kids after school and on weekends playing with grown men in LASA, and even making a few bucks," remembered Jair.[35]

Jair graduated from high school before the foundation of MLS. His only option to play top-level professional soccer was to move to Europe. He signed up with the legendary Portuguese team Sporting CP. He seldom saw any playing time there as he was competing for the same playing spot as Krassimir Balakov, a Bulgarian player who was one of the best attacking midfielders in the world during the mid-1990s. Sporting loaned Jair to SC Olhanese, where he met and befriended another Bulgarian, Stoitcho Mladenov, who assisted his transfer to the most successful Bulgarian soccer team, PFC CSKA Sofia. In 1997, Jair captured both—the Bulgarian Cup and the trophy of the Bulgarian Professional Soccer League, becoming one of the fans' favorites. By that time, MLS had already fielded ten teams and they needed more players than the American colleges could provide. Jair was getting married to a woman from Boston and felt it was the right time and opportunity to transfer to the New England Revolution.

There is a large Cape Verdean community in Massachusetts. It is difficult to determine their number exactly, as some Cape Verdeans kept their Portuguese passports after the country earned its independence. However, scholars generally agree there are about fifty thousand Cape Verdeans who live in the Greater Boston Area. By the late 1990s, LASA had become a predominantly Cape Verdean league, and just like other Portuguese speakers, Cape Verdeans adore soccer—it is an inseparable part of their culture. Jair had an outstanding stint with the Revs, playing twenty-nine games and scoring four goals. "Every time I played," the veteran recalled, "there were a couple of thousand Cape Verdeans at Gillette Stadium, wearing Rev's shirts adorned with my name, singing traditional Cape Verdean songs and chanting my name after I scored." It was a surprise when the Revs traded him to the San Jose Clash. He later played for another MLS team—the Tampa Bay Mutiny, before finishing his professional career in 2003, playing minor-league soccer for the Western Mass Pioneers. While his career achievements are impressive, many others with whom he played soccer in high school and for LASA teams did not have the same opportunities he enjoyed. "It was very difficult to develop as a professional soccer player in the United States during the early 1990s," he said. "I had to go to Europe to become a pro because we didn't have a professional league here. I remember a few African American kids on my high school team who were very talented athletes, but they switched to other sports because there was no future in professional soccer at that time in the United States."[36]

CONCLUSION

As previously noted, the Brazilian National team became more successful in 1938 than in previous tournaments with the inclusion of Leonidas and some other Black players. With the exception of France and Portugal, very few countries had any Black players in the early stages of soccer. Most European teams remained all White for a while. In 1978, the Netherlands reached the World Cup final and lost to their Argentinian hosts in a dramatic way. The 1978 Dutch team fielded eleven Caucasian players. However, with the inclusion of some Black players in the 1980s and 1990s, their style became even more sophisticated, and Ruud Gullit, Clarence Seedorf, Edgar Davids, and Frank Rijkaard helped their national team win the European crown in 1988, and afterward paved the way to another World Cup final in 2010. The same could be said about the German National Team. It remained exclusively White even longer than the Dutch team. In 2014, Germany won its fourth World Cup title having multiple Black players on its roster.

DaMarcus Beasley is certainly one of the most accomplished American soccer players so far. He was born in a middle-class African American family in Fort Wayne, Indiana. After a promising initial career with MLS's Chicago Fire, he transferred to PSV Eindhoven of the Dutch first division. For three seasons, he played fifty-six games and scored ten goals. He then moved to the English Premier League, arguably the strongest and wealthiest professional soccer entity, where he played for a season for Manchester City, scoring three goals and assisting a few. After that he moved to the Scottish power-house team, Rangers FC. After a short stint with Hanover 96 of the German *Bundesliga*, he moved to Puebla FC in Mexico, where he played ninety-two games, scoring twelve goals. He came back to MLS to finish his professional career as a player for Huston Dynamo FC.

Beasley was recently interviewed by MLS's news outlet for a piece on Black History Month. "When you're young, you never look at it as you're the only black person playing soccer. I just wanted to have fun with my friends. When we started traveling around Indiana, Michigan, and Ohio to play differ-ent teams, we were the diversity! You would rarely see other Black players in the Midwest, and you could count on one hand the number of Black kids on my high school team."[37] The situation has certainly improved since Beasley's childhood and initial days as a professional. We can see that reflected in the rosters of MLS. Until recently, most soccer players of color in the United States were not African American, but foreigners. Some of the veterans inter-viewed for this chapter (Harry Keogh, John Bertos, and Jair) emphasized the importance of involving African American players for the future development of soccer in the United States. Soccer has been growing, slowly and surely. And what a thrill, what an absolute enrichment to the game it would be, to have more African American youths—not only from the middle class, but from urban backgrounds as well—involved in the game, just as they are in football, basketball, and baseball. And if that happens, and America plays one day on the same level with the best in the world, can we dream and look forward to a World Cup final featuring the United States?

NOTES

1. Between 2007 and 2011, Steven Apostolov conducted original archival research on the Oneida Football Club and the history of the Boston/Harvard Game. In 2011, using previously unexplored primary sources, Apostolov's PhD dissertation docu-mented the biographies of several Oneida FC players and explained how they trans-mitted the Boston Game to their peers at Harvard University. It further explored how the last surviving Oneida team members commemorated the Boston/Harvard Game by erecting a monument on the Boston Common, and the monument's complicated history. See Apostolov, "*Les hauts et les bas du soccer professionnel aux Etats-Unis à partir du cas du Massachusetts* [The Ups and Downs of Professional Soccer in the United States from the Perspective of Massachusetts,]" (PhD diss., University of Paris VIII, 2011), 30–82. In 2016, the author expanded his original research by analyz-ing why the premodern Boston/Harvard Game was abandoned in favor of rugby in 1874. See Apostolov, "Native Americans, Puritans and 'Brahmins': genesis, practice and evolution of archaic and premodern football in Massachusetts," *Sport in Society*,

20, no. 9, (2017): 1259–70. Kevin Tallec-Marston and Mike Cronin examine the same archival sources and reach similar conclusions in their recent work on the Oneidas.

2. George M. Collins, "German Sport Club Latest in Soccer Field Hereabouts," *Boston Globe*, 5 March 1924.

3. David Kilpatrick, "Amnesia and Animosity: An Assessment of Soccer in the States," *Sport in Society*, 20, nos. 5/6 (2017): 627–40.

4. Andrei Markovits, "The Other American Exeptionalism: Why is there no Soccer in the United States?" *International Journal of the History of Sport*, vol. 2, issue 7, (1990): 230–60. See as well Andrei Markovits and Steven Hellerman, *Offside: Soccer and American Exceptionalism* (Princeton: Princeton University Press, 2001).

5. Douglas Stark, *When Basketball was Jewish: Voices of Those Who Played the Game* (Lincoln: University of Nebraska Press, 2017).

6. Paul Dietschy, *Histoire du Football*. (Saint-Amand-Montrond: Editions Perrin, 2010), 492.

7. John Sugden, "USA and the World Cup: American Nativism and the Rejection of the Peoples Game," 222, in John Sugden and Allan Tomlinson, eds. *Hosts and Champions: Soccer Cultures, National Indentities and the USA World Cup* (Brookfield: Ashgate, 1994).

8. Walter Bahr, in discussion with the author.

9. John Souza, in discussion with the author.

10. Brian Bunk, "The Rise and Fall of Professional Soccer in Holyoke Massachusetts, USA," *Sport in History*, vol. 31, no. 3 (2011): 283–306.

11. Steven Apostolov, "Soccer Ethnicity, and Shipbuilding in Industrial Quincy, Massachusetts during the Early Twentieth Century," in Chris Bolsmann and George Kioussis, eds. *Soccer Frontiers: The Global Game in the United States, 1863–1913* (Knoxville: The University of Tennessee Press, 2021), 60–61.

12. Harry Keogh, email correspondence with the author, dated 01 February 2002. The author is tremendously grateful to Keogh for introducing him to the other four surviving at the time members of team USA 1950.

13. It should be noted that after the original and fully professional American Soccer League (ASL) folded in 1933, ASL II continued to exist mainly in the Northeast of the United States, but as a semiprofessional league. With the exception of John Souza, very few players were able to make a living by playing in the ASL II.

14. Lesly Gaetjens, *The Shot Heard Around the World: The Joe Gaetjens Story* (Middletown: Privately Published, 2021), 1–16.

15. *Ibid.*, 38–39.

16. David Wangerin, *Soccer in a Football World: The Story of America's Forgotten Game* (Philadelphia: Temple University Press, 2008), 103–04.

17. Frank Dell'Apa, "Heron the Forgotten Pioneer of US Soccer," February 12, 2007, on www.espn.com [site accessed on September 3, 2022].

18. *Ibid.*

19. Peger Alegi, *African Soccerscapes: How a Continent Changed the World's Game* (Athens: Ohio University Press, 2010), 97–98.

20. Maxine Margolis, *Little Brazil: Ethnology of Brazilian Immigration in New York City* (Princeton: Princeton University Press, 1994), 12.

21. Ana Christina Braga Martes, *Brasileiros nos Estados Unidos: Un Estudio Sobre Imigrantes em Massachusetts* (Sao Paulo: Paz e Terra), 61–62.

22. John Bertos (owner of the Boston Astros), in discussion with the author, May 19, 2009, in Lowell Massachusetts. Mr. Bertos welcomed warmly the author and introduced him to former players and volunteers of the Boston Astros. Bertos provided his own archive and facilitated interviews with many of the Astros' players. He followed up with many emails and phone calls even at the time of writing of this piece—the spring and summer of 2022. The author was therefore able to document some of the history of the team, especially the involvement of Brazilians and Black players.

23. Wagner Leao (midfielder for the Boston Astros 1968–1972), in discussion with the author, June 26, 2009, in Lowell Massachusetts. Just like Bertos, Leao was very helpful with many follow up emails and phone interviews, the last of which took place at the time of writing of this chapter—the spring and summer of 2022.

24. Bertos.

25. Bianchini Barbosa (son of Helio Barbosa), in discussion with the author, November 29–December 31, 2021. Helio Barbosa suffers from Alzheimer's disease. All details about him were gathered from his son, teammates, officials, and water boys of the Boston Astros.

26. David Pickett (water boy for the Astros during the 1970s, also currently in charge of the Astros' archives and their website www.bostonastros.com), in discussion with the author, October 3, 2021.

27. Joe Pickett (water boy for the Astros during the 1970s), in discussion with the author, October 13, 2021.

28. Joe Pickett, email correspondence with the author, December 28, 2015.

29. Leao.

30. Barbosa.

31. Steven Apostolov, "Everywhere and Nowhere: The Forgotten Past and Clouded Future of American Professional Soccer from the Perspective of Massachusetts," *Soccer & Society*, vol. 13, no. 4 (2012), 526.

32. Ronald Murphy (former player of Hudson Benfica of the LASA), in discussion with the author, January 20, 2009.

33. Luis Cerqueira (former player of Lowell United of the LASA), in discussion with the author, May 19, 2009.

34. Anselmo "Jair" Ribeiro (former player of Sporting CP, SC Olhanese, PFC CSKA Sofia, New England Revolution, and Tampa Bay), in discussion with the author, January 3, 2010. "Jair" has always dedicated time for interviews and follow-ups. His interviews were initially utilized in 2011 in the PhD dissertation of Apostolov. Subsequent interviews were conducted in May and June of 2021.

35. *Ibid.*

36. *Ibid.*

37. DaMarcus Beasley, "DaMarcus Beasley: How a Fort Wayne Kid Broke Barriers and Reached Soccer's Peak," February 14, 2022, https://www.mlssoccer.com/news/damarcus-beasley-how-a-fort-wayne-kid-broke-barriers-and-reached-soccer-s-peak [accessed September 9, 2022].

BIBLIOGRAPHY

Alegi, Peger. *African Soccerscapes: How a Continent Changed the World's Game.* Athens: Ohio University Press, 2010.

Apostolov, Steven. "Everywhere and Nowhere: The Forgotten Past and Clouded Future of American Professional Soccer from the Perspective of Massachusetts." *Soccer & Society* (Volume 13, Number 4), 2012.

Apostolov, Steven. "Native Americans, Puritans and 'Brahmins': Genesis, Practice and Evolution of Archaic and Pre-modern Football in Massachusetts." *Sport in Society* (Volume20, Number 9), 2017.

Apostolov, Steven. "Soccer Ethnicity, and Shipbuilding in Industrial Quincy, Massachusetts during the Early Twentieth Century," in Bolsmann, Chris and George Kioussis, eds. *Soccer Frontiers: The Global Game in the United States, 1863–1913.* Knoxville: The University of Tennessee Press, 2021.

Beasley, DaMarcus. "DaMarcus Beasley: How a Fort Wayne Kid Broke Barriers and Reached Soccer's Peak." February 14, 2022, https://www.mlssoccer.com/news/damarcus-beasley-how-a-fort-wayne-kid-broke-barriers-and-reached-soccer-s-peak.

Braga Martes, Ana Christina. *Brasileiros nos Estados Unidos: Un Estudio Sobre Imigrantes em Massachusetts.* Sao Paulo: Paz e Terra, 2012.

Bunk, Brian. "The Rise and Fall of Professional Soccer in Holyoke Massachusetts, USA." *Sport in History* (Volume 31, Number 3), 2011.

Collins, George. "German Sport Club Latest in Soccer Field Hereabouts." *Boston Globe*, 5 March 1924.

Dell'Apa, Frank. "Heron the Forgotten Pioneer of US Soccer." February 12, 2007, www.espn.com.

Dietschy, Paul. *Histoire du Football.* Saint-Amand-Montrond: Perrin, 2010.

Gaetjens, Lesly. *The Shot Heard Around the World: The Joe Gaetjens Story.* Middletown: Privately Published, 2020.

Kilpatrick, David. "Amnesia and Animosity: An Assessment of Soccer in the States." *Sport in Society* (Volume 20, Numbers 5/6), 2017.

Margolis, Maxine. *Little Brazil: Ethnology of Brazilian Immigration in New York City.* Princeton: Princeton University Press, 1994.

Markovits, Andrei, and Steven Hellerman, *Offside: Soccer and American Exceptionalism.* Princeton: Princeton University Press, 2001.

Markovits, Andrei. "The Other American Exeptionalism: Why is there no Soccer in the United States?" *International Journal of the History of Sport* (Volume 2, Number 7), 1990.

Stark, Douglas. *When Basketball Was Jewish: Voices of Those Who Played the Game.* Lincoln: University of Nebraska Press, 2017.

Sugden, John. "USA and the World Cup: American Nativism and the Rejection of the Peoples Game," in Sugden, John and Allan Tomlinson, eds. *Hosts and Champions:*

Soccer Cultures, National Identities and the USA World Cup. Brookfield: Ashgate, 1994.

Wangerin, David. *Soccer in a Football World: The Story of America's Forgotten Game.* Philadelphia: Temple University Press, 2008.

Chapter 12

Fighting for Recognition

The Almost-Legendary Career of Medina Dixon

Donna L. Halper

As a high school freshman in 1978, Medina Dixon said she wanted to be "the best girls basketball player who ever lived."[1] One must leave it to others to debate whether she achieved that goal, but she certainly achieved many others: a record-setting high school career, leading her college team to a national championship, and playing on amateur teams that won numerous awards and medals. Sportswriters of her time said she was among the best players they ever saw, male or female, yet Dixon never became a household name. In fact, to this day, many basketball fans have probably never heard of her. In some ways, that is not surprising; Americans acknowledge female athletes less than their male counterparts.

While women's sports have benefited from the implementation of the 1972 Education Amendments Act, Title IX, challenges remain. Title IX recognized gender equity in education as a civil right and led to more investment in athletic programs for girls and women. More young women now excel in high school and college basketball than at any time previously, and since the 1996 inception of the WNBA, women's basketball has been professionalized. Still, the attention paid to men's basketball—both college and professional— is far greater than that paid to the women's game. Consider. Historically, the media has almost obsessively covered "March Madness," the Men's Division I college basketball tournament, while, until recently, the women's college tournament has either been downplayed or ignored. Not until 2003 did ESPN begin nationally televising the entire women's tournament, having broadcast as few as seven of the tournament games in years past.[2] The media provides prime-time coverage of the annual NBA draft, during which the best male college players are selected by NBA teams, but it rarely does the same for the WNBA draft, nor do they cover WNBA games to the same degree as the NBA.

On occasion, individual female athletes do receive as much attention as an equally popular male star. Tennis player Serena Williams and gymnast Simone Biles carry star power that garners consistent global media attention. Sometimes a women's team does something no other American team, male or female, has done, and the public takes notice. The US Women's National Soccer Team is notoriously more popular than the men's team. Since the 1990s, they have been so successful on the world stage that they attract large audiences. As a result, the media notices them more than most women's teams. They remain the exception rather than the rule. Moreover, despite winning four Women's World Cups and four Olympic gold medals, the players on the Women's National Soccer Team received substantially less pay than their male counterparts, which changed only quite recently. In 2019, they filed and won a gender-discrimination lawsuit against the United States Soccer Federation (USSF). In that suit, the players stated that the Federation "has paid only lip service to gender equality and continues to practice gender-based discrimination against its champion female employees on the [women's national team], in comparison to its less successful male employees on the [men's national team]."[3] The US women's soccer team stands as an anomaly in women's sports, a position for which they had to massively self-advocate in order to gain.

When Dixon was born in 1962, Title IX did not exist, relegating female athletes to a place out of the sports spotlight. The question of whether women should participate in athletics, and if so, how much, was still being debated. Most major sports were still gendered masculine, and thus, it was considered unsuitable (and unfeminine) for a young woman to play them. There was a lingering cultural belief that women were inherently fragile, and if they engaged in too much exercise (which included playing sports), they could become infertile.[4] If they were to participate in sports, women often had to play by different rules than men. For most of the twentieth century, standard practices in women's basketball exemplified the myth that females were "the weaker sex," lacking the stamina to participate in anything as strenuous as running up and down the court as men did. Women's teams "played a type of half-court game with three forwards and three guards on each side who could not cross the center line, could have only two dribbles, and had three seconds to pass or shoot the ball."[5] These official rules were not changed until the early 1970s.

Dixon learned to love sports from her family. One of fourteen children born to Claudia and Herb Dixon, she had two sisters and eleven brothers.[6] Several of her brothers had successful collegiate and professional athletic careers.[7] As

Fighting for Recognition 235

a young girl, she enjoyed watching her brothers play, but she was not content to just watch; she wanted to join them. She was especially drawn to basketball, which she learned to play by men's rules. Her brothers encouraged her, and she took to the game almost immediately. She was soon displaying moves on the court that were not expected from girls. In fact, as her brother Rob recalls, she grew so confident in her abilities that she even engaged in "trash talk"—she would block a shot and then taunt the player who had tried to score.[8]

Dixon was raised in Mattapan, by then a Black neighborhood of Boston, where she faced the personal implications of the city's evolving relationship with systemic racism. Decades earlier, it had been home to many European Jewish immigrants, but as population patterns shifted and White residents of the city moved to the suburbs, parts of Boston became *de facto* segregated. This included Mattapan, Dorchester, and Roxbury, all of which were predominantly Black. Meanwhile, neighborhoods like South Boston, Charlestown, and West Roxbury were overwhelmingly White. The Boston Public School Committee was also overwhelmingly White, and by the mid-1960s, advocates for Black students were calling attention to what they saw as an overt effort to give more resources to majority-White schools, while ignoring the needs of majority-Black schools. Subsequently, the NAACP accused the School Committee of resisting any efforts to address racial imbalance in the schools.[9] This eventually led to a landmark 1974 ruling by US district judge W. Arthur Garrity, who stated that the Boston Public Schools were, for all intents and purposes, racially segregated. He mandated a controversial plan of busing students from majority Black schools into schools that were majority White to achieve racial balance. In her first year of high school, Dixon was among the first Black students who were bused to a majority-White school: the newly built West Roxbury High School.

She joined the girls' basketball team at West Roxbury and made an immediate impact, averaging thirty-five points and twenty rebounds during her first year.[10] At six-feet-two, Dixon was much taller than her teammates, but her height was not her only advantage. She was a versatile player who could block shots, steal the ball, or make clutch baskets. Given her talent, New England Junior Olympics coach Don Fay chose her for his twelve-member girls basketball team, the Boston Blazers. What they did not get, however, was much press attention. Even when the Blazers won their first game in impressive fashion, with Dixon scoring twenty-one points, only the *Quincy Patriot Ledger* covered it thoroughly.[11] They were about to compete in the national AAU tournament in Tullahoma, Tennessee, the first time a New England team had ever participated.[12] Although the Blazers did not win the championship, they earned respect for how well they played, and they received valuable experience competing at a higher level.[13] Major newspapers like the *Boston Globe* only gave the win passing mention, and although the *Boston Herald American* had a page devoted to women's sports, nothing about the Blazers' victory was on it. When they were eliminated, Dixon and the Blazers returned home, gratified to win a game in a national tournament, but disappointed with how things ended.

Perhaps the lack of media interest simply reflected the culture's continuing ambivalence about girls who played sports. Although attitudes were beginning to change by the 1960s, it was still an era when girls who followed sports were considered unusual (according to myth, girls only liked sports if their brothers or boyfriends were playing). Female sports fans were advised to avoid looking or acting "mannish," and being called a "tomboy" was not a compliment. As for girls who wanted to play, they were advised to make sure they dressed in a feminine manner when not competing, wear makeup, and always have an attractive hairstyle.[14]

Many of these cultural norms of traditional femininity were derived from how White middle- and upper-class women were expected to act, but the situation for Black girls was even more complicated. They not only had to navigate a terrain that was rife with sexist stereotypes, but they frequently encountered racist stereotypes as well. For example, White women from the upper social strata were often portrayed as delicate and genteel, a civilizing influence on a coarse society, while Black women were depicted quite the opposite—as loud, immoral, and aggressive, incapable of acting in a ladylike manner.[15] Thus, the trash talk that was such a part of the men's game, which Dixon picked up, would have reinforced the stereotype of Black people as low-class and ill-mannered. (Even years later, trash-talking Black female players recalled how they were considered "ghetto," while White female players who did the same thing were described as "passionate about playing the game.")[16]

In fairness, playing hard and showing emotion also created problems for White female athletes. They not only had to contend with the stereotype suggesting their behavior was unladylike, but they also faced the myth that playing sports was dangerous for their social life—allegedly, women athletes were unappealing to men.[17] Many magazines of that era advised young women that if they were good at sports like tennis or bowling, they should downplay their abilities or even intentionally lose when playing against a guy. I can still recall being told repeatedly that guys did not like it if a girl was better at something than they were. Or, as the popular television character Dobie Gillis suggested to teenage girls, if you want to get a boyfriend, don't be too athletic: "a boy wants a girl, not an opponent."[18]

Even more worrisome to the predominantly conservative-minded culture was the lingering belief that playing sports might cause otherwise-heterosexual

Fighting for Recognition 237

women to become lesbians. Some sociologists have posited that myths like this were used to frighten young women so they would not deviate from the long-standing norms of traditional femininity.[19] Meanwhile, Black female athletes encountered two contradictory stereotypes that their White teammates did not—the myth that Black people were lazy and uneducated, which Dixon saw firsthand while she played overseas basketball after college; and the myth that Black people were naturally athletic, thus their athletic accomplishments were not the result of hard work or effort but good genes.[20] In other words, a talented Black female athlete like Dixon could easily be dismissed as *nothing special*, since she was supposedly born with athletic ability. Otherwise, the dominant White society saw her as problematic—someone who was not as intelligent or as competitive as her White teammates, someone who required more attention from her coach to insight her highest ability.[21]

Some of Dixon's fondest childhood memories involved playing basketball with her brothers until all hours, while likely unaware that she would not have the same opportunities as them. She grew to understand this disparity, and thus worked hard to prove herself. In middle school, she played on the boys' basketball team because the school did not have one for girls. Eager to become an excellent player, she was fortunate to find a female mentor who saw her talent and helped her to develop it. Alfreda Harris ran the basketball program at the Shelburne Community Center in nearby Roxbury, where she coached the girls' team. A combination of disciplinarian, motivator, and teacher, she held to the motto: "Education through Recreation." Harris was an inspirational figure, a role model for many young women in Boston's Black neighborhoods.[22] She heard about Dixon from a friend, who told her there was a young girl who "plays [basketball] with the guys. She's really good." Harris arranged a meeting. Immediately aware of the then-fifteen-year-old's potential, she persuaded her to come to Shelburne and join their team, where she soon became a star player. Harris nicknamed Dixon "Ice" because she was so confident and cool, even when playing under pressure.[23]

After Dixon's freshman year, her parents decided she would be better off enrolling in a different school system. Boston was becoming increasingly chaotic: Black students bused to White neighborhoods were being taunted and insulted. Some of the schools, including the one she attended, had violent incidents, plus her parents felt she was not learning enough in her classes.[24] Then an off-ramp presented itself: Dixon was recruited by two influential members of the athletic department at Cambridge Rindge and Latin School (CRLS)—Mike Jarvis, the coach of the boys' basketball team, and JoAnn O'Callaghan, who coached the girls' team. CRLS had a very successful basketball program, as well as a good reputation for its academics. Cambridge, which was only a few miles from Boston, was supposed to be a much safer city. Her parents "signed some papers" and enrolled her there

238   *Donna L. Halper*

for her sophomore year.[25] This would later become a problem, but according to Dixon, her family was unaware at the time that there was anything wrong with what they did. They were simply trying to provide her with a better opportunity.

In her first year at CRLS, she almost immediately became a star player. Playing center, she averaged nineteen points and fifteen rebounds a game and led her team to the Division 1 state championship. When Dixon was named to the 1979 *Boston Globe* All-Scholastic Girls' Basketball Team, her coach called her "the finest high school athlete I've seen" and predicted a bright future for her. Never one for false modesty, Dixon spoke about her ability to make things happen on the court, stating, "No girl in the world can stop me when I'm hot"; and sportswriters who had seen her making big plays all season had to agree.[26] Meanwhile, on the boys' team, there was a seven-foot center named Patrick Ewing, and he, too, was turning into a star player. In fact, just as Dixon was a big reason the girls team did so well, Ewing was a major factor in the CRLS boys' team winning the state championship that year. The two became friends and played against each other during physical education classes. Dixon enjoyed the challenge of playing against him, and she recommended that other female players play against the men. She believed that doing so helped her to improve her game.[27]

Dixon's accomplishments helped to elevate media coverage of girls' basketball at CRLS. One local newspaper editorial said, "The girls, long working in the shadow of their male counterparts, have played the part of unsung heroines for too long." While crediting good coaching and players who never gave up, the newspaper went on to credit "the visible and powerful symbols of Pat Ewing and Medina Dixon" for how well the boys' and girls' teams did in 1979.[28] As for Ewing, he was so impressed with Dixon's skills that he suggested she try out for the boys' team. Coach Jarvis gave the idea some serious thought, but as he later said, "Back then, girls didn't play on boys' teams." He was certain, however, that if any girl could have done it, Dixon was the one. "She was that good," he said.[29] Dixon also had her doubts and decided not to try out. She thought it would be perceived as "a real slap in the face" to the girls' program, stating, "It would have been great publicity for me but . . . it would not have been a cool thing to do." So, she remained with the CRLS girls' team.[30] However, she would periodically tell reporters that one day, she hoped to try out for the National Basketball Association.[31]

Unfortunately, a January 1980 investigation into the eligibility of a CRLS transfer student, who had played four games on the boys' team, led to a similar investigation into Dixon's eligibility. Actions taken by her recruiter—including going to her home and soliciting her for the team—were possible rules violations. The more serious question rested on whether she was a Cambridge resident, which would have relegated her as legally allowed to attend CRLS.

Fighting for Recognition 239

As with most school districts, including Boston and Cambridge, if you did not officially live in the district, you were not allowed to enroll, let alone play sports. Dixon lived in Mattapan, yet a petition submitted on her behalf to the Middlesex County Probate Court said her mother had died, and Dixon was now living in Cambridge with her guardian, who happened to be Coach Jarvis's sister-in-law. Dixon's mother, however, was very much alive, and said she was puzzled as to why there was a guardianship petition or why the document claimed she had died.[32] The petition's ultimate purpose was to render Dixon a resident of Cambridge and eligible to play, but neither of Dixon's parents said they'd agreed to sign any documents that made false statements.

The Massachusetts Interscholastic Athletic Association (MIAA) met to decide on both cases, and their decision outraged many people. The MIAA found recruiting and eligibility violations in both programs but issued no penalty against the boys' team (even though evidence suggested that a second player had lived elsewhere during part of the season), while finding Dixon ineligible and ordering the girls' team to forfeit its entire season. The MIAA also stripped the girls' team of its state title. The *Boston Globe* was among the newspapers that found this decision both inconsistent and unfair to the players on the girls' team, none of whom had done anything wrong, and to Dixon, who was "thrown into [the situation] not by her own doing but by the actions of adults."[33] She was barred from playing for a year and felt like she had been "used, big-time . . . just so I could win a state title for Cambridge."[34] She remained upset about it for years. Because of complaints from athletic directors in the Suburban League, where the CRLS boys' team played, the MIAA reconsidered their decision in late February 1980. They decided that the boys' team was not allowed to compete in the upcoming state championship tournament.[35] The girls' team's punishment, however, was still far harsher.

After sitting out the 1979–1980 season, Dixon returned to the CRLS girls' basketball team in time for the 1980–1981 season to raving success. Everyone was glad to have her back. There was a different coach, Terri Riggs, and some new players, but the team picked up where it left off. In her senior year, Dixon averaged twenty points and seventeen rebounds a game. Her team nearly won the state championship, but they lost the final playoff game and finished second. Dixon won numerous awards, including CRLS's female athlete of the year and *Parade* magazine's girls' All-American team. Her friend Patrick Ewing was named male athlete of the year and selected for the boys' team. Ewing had another impressive year, and many colleges were eager to recruit him. (He decided to play at Georgetown University in Washington, DC.) Because he was arguably the best male high school basketball player in the country, there were many sports stories written about him.

A growing number of publications, including the *New York Times*, not known for covering sports at the time, began paying attention to Dixon's exploits. Of course, men's college basketball still had more status than the women's game did, and although Dixon was now getting more coverage than other local female athletes, it still paled in comparison to that of Patrick Ewing. Sportswriters wondered which college Dixon would choose, since many scouts said she was "the best prospect in women's basketball."[36] When she made her decision, there was no fanfare and no media event announcing the choice, as there was for Ewing. She admitted to a reporter that it bothered her, since she had worked hard to earn her reputation as a star player. But she acknowledged the lack of attention was just "the way it is sometimes."[37] And she hoped to do her part to change it.

By now, at least in theory, male and female athletes had equal rights, thanks to Title IX, but they did not have equal opportunities. As Dixon's coach told a reporter, in most cases, "The girls have to pay their own transportation when they visit various schools, unlike men's sports where the athletic department [of a college] pays to have top prospects visit their school." This meant Dixon's final choice might be decided because of financial reasons—how many campus visits she could afford to make.[38] Other factors that mattered to her were the school's Black population size, their academic reputation (she planned to study computer science), and—since she came from a large family—available scholarship amounts.[39] In the end, she decided on the University of South Carolina. Her decision was not treated as major news in the Boston media; most local papers just gave it a passing mention, and sports-talk radio seldom if ever mentioned girls' sports. *Sports Illustrated* did write about her success, endorsing her as important enough for the largest sports magazine to take notice. Coach Pam Parsons sang her praises, convinced that Dixon would help lead the Gamecocks to a national title. Parsons had recruited several other outstanding high school players, but she told reporters, "Medina is the best incoming freshman I've ever seen."[40]

Just as the mainstream media failed to discuss how Black players from Boston were enduring racial taunts when they played against White suburban teams, they also rarely discussed why the best women players in general, and Black players in particular, were not heavily recruited by any of Boston's major universities. In 1984, Boston College's women's basketball coach Margo Plotzke seemed to acknowledge this, noting that schools in greater Boston were losing out to the top-rated colleges in other states, especially in the Midwest and South, where women's basketball was building a following. "We lose so many talented prospects—just look at Medina."[41] Black players from Boston, who loved the city but had to attend schools in other states, agreed. Looking back on her high school experience, Robin Christian, a star at Jamaica Plain High School (among the many young women mentored by Alfreda Harris), observed, "People from Boston just didn't care about women's basketball. I didn't even know what a real crowd looked like until I

Fighting for Recognition 241

got to college . . . " She also claimed that a prevailing stereotype led people to believe that Black students were less intelligent and less academically prepared than their White counterparts and contributed to the lack of access granted to Black athletes. "You had [Boston College] and [Boston University] right there, and no one was interested [in us]," she said. "It was almost as if they didn't think we could cut it at their school."[42] So, Christian played for the University of Iowa, and Dixon played for South Carolina.

At first, it seemed Dixon was well on her way to having a successful college basketball career, averaging sixteen points a game, and fitting in well. But then everything fell apart, through no fault of her own. Coach Parsons was a controversial figure known for creating winning teams, but also for being temperamental and sometimes emotionally explosive toward players. Parsons faced a scandal involving recruiting violations—accusations that she allowed certain players to accept cash payments. Even more problematic were rumors that Parsons was having a sexual relationship with a member of her team, something she later acknowledged.[43] The coach was asked to resign, and Dixon did not get along well with her replacement. After talking it over with her family, she decided to transfer to another school with a successful women's basketball program, Old Dominion University (ODU) in Norfolk, Virginia. Marianne Stanley, her new coach, was delighted to have her on the team. "I enjoy working with Medina. She is pleasant, funny, and really enthusiastic."[44]

As a transfer student, Dixon had to wait a few months until she was eligible to play. Once she was in the lineup, she adapted well to being on a team where she was not the only good player; she did not need to do it all herself.[45] What she accomplished was impressive. Playing forward, she consistently led the Lady Monarchs in scoring, rebounding, assists, steals, and free throws. At the end of the 1984 season, she was named the team's most valuable player, averaging nearly twenty-one points and ten rebounds a game. "Medina is one of the best players in the country right now," Coach Stanley said. "She has incredible instincts for the game."[46] Unfortunately, the Lady Monarchs were upset in the Eastern Regional finals, but with most of the players returning, Dixon was hopeful that in 1985, the team would reach the NCAA Final Four.

They did that and more. The Lady Monarchs went all the way to a national championship. As one local reporter recalled, while there were other good players on the Lady Monarchs, it was Dixon who was "the emotional force behind a team, led by a demanding coach in Marianne Stanley, that constantly overperformed. . . . [Medina] was brilliant, unpredictable and absolutely driven. And I saw few players with more drive and determination."[47] Dixon did not play well in the first half of the championship game—a rare occurrence for her—but teammate Tracy Claxton was having none of it. She gave Dixon some advice in a fiery speech. Dixon said it could not be quoted, since

Figure 12.1. Medina Dixon is a basketball icon in Boston, but she holds an equally impressive standing as a national and international champion. During the 1990s, the Boston born Dixon captured a bronze medal in the 1992 Olympics and another Bronze in the Pan American Games. A graduate of Cambridge Rindge and Latin School, she entered college as the nation's top women's basketball prospect. She attended Old Dominion University and led the team to the 1984–85 National Championship. Credit: Old Dominion Athletics.

Fighting for Recognition 243

it "had a lot of bleeps in it," but whatever Claxton told her, it worked.[48] Dixon had a dominant second half, helping ODU to come from behind and beat the University of Georgia Lady Bulldogs 70–65. She had eighteen points and fifteen rebounds in that game, but those totals did not tell the entire story of what she meant to the team. In the three seasons she played for ODU, she finished with 1,968 points, ranking her eighth in team history; she earned numerous accolades, including being named to the Kodak All-American women's team in 1985. Years later, in January 2011, the Lady Monarchs retired her #13 jersey, only the seventh time in team history that this had occurred, and proof of how much the fans still appreciated her contributions to the team's success.[49]

In 1985, the men's NCAA championship game received most of the national attention. Dixon's friend Patrick Ewing played in that game, as Villanova defeated Georgetown for the championship. Afterward, the *Newport News Daily Press* editorialized that now was a good time to "appreciate Virginia's own national basketball champs, the Lady Monarchs of Old Dominion University . . . [who] have dominated women's basketball almost as thoroughly as Georgetown has dominated the men's game."[50] It is telling that the newspaper needed to remind its readers that the achievements of the ODU's women's basketball team deserved some attention.

While some online sources say that Dixon graduated from ODU, the university registrar says she did not. She attended off and on from 1982 to 1988, majoring in Occupational and Technical Studies, which included marketing and fashion merchandising. When Dixon's playing career ended at ODU, she had few options. Unlike Patrick Ewing, who went on to fame in the NBA with the New York Knicks, there was no American women professional team where she could continue to do what she loved. So, she went overseas, as many talented female college stars did. She planned to return to the States and one day open a business: she had been studying marketing and thought she might open a chain of shoe stores for women who wore larger sizes.[51]

Dixon played in Milan, Italy, for a year, then spent seven years in Japan; she was well-paid there, and even rose to the position of assistant coach. She had an endorsement contract with sporting goods giant Mizuno. The downside of living in a country with so few people of color was too much for her, however; she was regarded as a curiosity amongst the natives. She recalls children running after her and trying to touch her to "see if the black would rub off."[52] In 1993, when Japanese basketball voted to no longer allow foreign players, she ended up playing in Russia. She had not expected to go there, but she received a lucrative offer from Centralnyi Sportivnyi Klub Armi (CSKA). In some ways, she was a pioneer. Only a few years earlier, Russia had been the enemy, but now relations between the United States and the former USSR had improved, and American players were being welcomed. Dixon played in Russia for several years.

During her overseas adventures, there were other noteworthy milestones. In 1990, Dixon was chosen for the US Women's National Team to compete in the Goodwill Games in Seattle, where they defeated the Soviet Union 82–70 for the championship. Then, in 1992, she was chosen for the US women's Olympic team, which once again included some of the best-known and most-talented American female players. Dixon tried out for the Olympic team in 1984 but failed to make the cut. This time, at the age of twenty-nine, she was selected by Rutgers University Coach Theresa Grentz for the Barcelona games. Grentz was already familiar with Dixon, having coached her during the Goodwill Games. She had confidence in Dixon's skills, stating that "Medina is a tremendous offensive rebounder," and adding, "her passing game has really improved. She made some passes during the [Olympic] trials that were really scintillating."[53]

The US women's team was widely favored to win a gold medal. Many on the team hoped this would reinvigorate interest in women's basketball, and maybe even lead to a US professional league.[54] Unlike what took place in the Goodwill Games, however, there was a stunning upset. The Russian Unified team outplayed the Americans and defeated them 79–73. Dixon had a good Olympics overall, scoring a team-high seventy-nine points. But what mattered most to her was winning, and she was extremely disappointed about not bringing home the gold for the United States. Still, winning the bronze medal was a great honor, even if it felt like a major letdown at the time, and it was another of her many accomplishments.[55]

After her playing career ended, she returned to the United States around 1997, and was once again living in Boston by 2000. Some people did not know that she had been diagnosed with epilepsy, and later, diabetes. She was still eager to give back to the community where she was raised. In 2006, she got involved with the Violence Free Zone Initiative and agreed to run a summer women's basketball league, serving as a mentor to the girls as Alfreda Harris had done for her years earlier. Even when playing ball overseas, Dixon had periodically returned to Boston to visit her family or participate in a community event like the 1994 Alfreda Harris Women's Invitational tournament.

In addition to not talking much about her health at that time, Dixon also seems to have kept her personal life private. As mentioned earlier, there was a stereotype that equated female athletes with lesbians, at a time when the culture was still overtly anti-gay. Lesbian athletes tried to keep anyone from knowing, for fear that it would harm their careers. If Dixon ever spoke publicly about her sexuality, those interviews would be difficult to find. Perhaps, having endured both racism and sexism during her athletic career, she was not eager to invite homophobia too. But we do know that while playing in

Fighting for Recognition 245

Japan, she met a woman named Hiroyo ("Yoyo"), and they fell in love. When Dixon came back to the United States, Hiroyo came with her, and they eventually married.

In 2018, Dixon's health worsened. She was diagnosed with pancreatic cancer. She fought it courageously, encouraged by some of her former ODU teammates with whom she had kept in touch. When she grew too weak to travel, her friends held Zoom sessions with her. She died on November 8, 2021, with her wife and their daughter by her side.[56] She was only fifty-nine. After her passing, tributes poured in from people who had either played alongside her in high school or watched some of her amazing exploits on the court.

Posthumously, Boston mayor Michelle Wu and the City of Boston Parks & Recreation Department renamed the neighborhood basketball courts at Mattapan's Walker Playground, the same courts where she used to practice as a child, as the Medina Dixon Basketball Courts. It became the first outdoor basketball court in Boston named after a woman. Family members and friends attended the renaming ceremony, and while they appreciated the honor, her brother Zachary commented, "Nothing against Boston, but I always ask why it took so long for her to be remembered. . . . She was in the Olympics, and she was an NCAA National Champion. What more could she have done? I do have to say, though, that we are grateful that we're doing this now."[57]

When Thomas (Tom) Arria, director of athletics at Cambridge Rindge and Latin School, hosted an event in May 2021 to induct Dixon into the CRLS Hall of Fame and retire her #44, he referred to her as "arguably the greatest female basketball player to play in the state of Massachusetts." Others who knew her continued to sing her praises. Alfreda Harris said, "We can thank Medina Dixon and Cambridge Rindge and Latin for putting women's basketball on the map." Former ODU teammate and later WNBA star Nancy Lieberman stated, "She would have been a superstar in the WNBA."

Dixon was a transitional figure in women's sports. She attracted more media attention for women's high school basketball, and she earned a large following when she played college ball. But because women's professional basketball had not yet taken hold in the United States, many of her accomplishments occurred overseas. Because her high school and college achievements took place at a time when women's sports were rarely broadcast on radio or television, only a limited audience knew how good she really was. Today, though Boston media outlets pay more attention to women's sports than ever before, the lion's share of the coverage still overwhelmingly goes to men's pro sports. As a sports fan and a media historian, I regret that nobody called Dixon to my attention in the 1980s. I'm sure I would have enjoyed watching her. I hope her memory will inspire other young women and girls to play sports, and I hope the media will give those talented female athletes the coverage Dixon never received—but should have.[58]

NOTES

1. Karen Roth, "Dixon Is Center of Attention on Olympians," *Boston Herald American*, May 10, 1978, 26.

2. Jim Sarni, "CBS Still Exploring Options for War," *(Ft. Lauderdale) South Florida Sun-Sentinel*, March 17, 2003, 2D.

3. Alaa Abdeldaiem, "USWNT Players File Gender Discrimination Lawsuit Against U.S. Soccer," *Sports Illustrated*, March 8, 2019, https://www.si.com/soccer /2019/03/08/uswnt-players-sue-us-soccer-gender-discrimination-lawsuit.

4. Jess Romeo, "Policing the Bodies of Women Athletes Is Nothing New," *JSTOR Daily*, August 12, 2021, https://daily.jstor.org/policing-the-bodies-of-women-athletes -is-nothing-new/.

5. Amy Lifson, "When Iowa Girls' Basketball Ruled the Courts," *HUMANITIES*, Spring 2019, Volume 40, Number 2, https://www.neh.gov/article/when-iowa-girls -basketball-ruled-courts.

6. Bob Snyder, "Gal Cager Eyes Male $$," *Syracuse, New York Herald-Journal*, July 25, 1981, B-3.

7. Dick Trust, "Dixon Dossier: Can Do Anything," *Quincy Patriot Ledger*, January 30, 1979, 18.

8. "At long last, Medina Dixon's Legacy Is Put on the Record," *Dorchester (Massachusetts) Reporter*, August 24, 2022, https://www.dotnews.com/2022/long-last -medina-dixon-s-legacy-put-record.

9. More about this period of time, the legal cases, and various other documents related to the busing crisis can be found at the Archives and Public History Project of the University of Massachusetts/Boston. This link is about the often-heated reactions to the Racial Imbalance Act of 1965: https://bosdesca.omeka.net/exhibits/show/racial -imbalance_bps/reactions-and-opinions; and this link is about how *de-facto* segregation in the schools led to Judge Garrity's order to implement busing: https://www .archivespublichistory.org/?p=1277.

10. Karen Roth, "Dixon Is Center of Attention on Olympians," *Boston Herald American*, May 10, 1978, 26.

11. Dick Trust, "Dixon Injures Vols," *Quincy Patriot Ledger*, June 21, 1978, 36.

12. Dick Trust, "12 Girls, History in Making," *Quincy Patriot Ledger*, May 16, 1978, 26.

13. Dick Trust, "Fay Papile Win Respect," *Quincy Patriot Ledger*, July 3, 1978, 36.

14. Robert E. Washington and David Karen, "Sport and Society," *Annual Review of Sociology*, Vol. 27 (2001), 198–99.

15. Jenny Lind Withycombe, Intersecting selves: African American female athletes' experiences of sport, *Sociology of Sport Journal*, Vol. 28, #4, (2011), 479–81.

16. Mia Berry, "Angel Reese, Caitlin Clark and the Trash Talk Drawing Attention to Women's Basketball," Andscape, April 7, 2023, https://andscape.com/features/angel-reese-caitlin-clark-and-the-trash-talk-drawing-attention-to-womens-basketball/.

17. Pamela Grundy and Susan Shackelford, *Shattering the Glass: The Remarkable History Of Women's Basketball*, New York: New Press, 2005: 2.

18. Enid A. Haupt, "How to Win Dates and Influence the Dobie Gillis Type," *TV Guide*, December 5, 1959, 22.

19. Elaine M. Blinde, and Diane E. Taub, "Women Athletes as Falsely Accused Deviants: Managing the Lesbian Stigma," *Sociological Quarterly*, Vol. 33, No. 4 (Winter 1992): 521–22.

20. Debbie Becker, "From Stocks to Steals, USA's Dixon Makes All the Right Moves," *USA Today*, August 3, 1992, 3E.

21. Manuel R. Zenquis, and Munene F. Mwaniki, "The Intersection of Race, Gender, and Nationality in Sport: Media Representation of the Ogwumike Sisters," *Journal of Sport and Social Issues*, Vol. 43, #1, January 13, 2019, 23.

22. Mark Murphy, "For Harris, Discipline is Key," *Boston Herald*, May 21, 1989: B17.

23. Julian Benbow, "Cambridge Basketball Icon Medina Dixon Was a Local Treasure, a Transformative Talent, and a Special Friend," *Boston Globe*, November 12, 2021, C1, C5.

24. Richard J. Connolly, "False Recruit Data Stirs Cambridge Row," *Boston Globe*, January 31, 1980, 1, 18.

25. Jackie MacMullan, "It's Becoming Her Dominion: Controversy over Medina Dixon Starts Anew," *Boston Globe*, February 6, 1983, 59.

26. Ann McGrath, "Globe All-Scholastic Basketball Team," *Boston Globe*, April 10, 1979, 40.

27. Jim Kelley, "Ewing's 'Teammate' Steals Festival Show," *Buffalo News*, July 25, 1981, SM 5.

28. "Champions of the Universe . . . Why Not?" *Cambridge, Massachusetts Chronicle*, March 22, 1979, 4.

29. Julian Benbow, "Cambridge Basketball Icon Medina Dixon Was a Local Treasure, a Transformative Talent, and a Special Friend," *Boston Globe*, November 12, 2021, C1, C5.

30. David Aldridge, "Women's Dream Team Wins 111–55 Runaway," *Washington Post*, July 31, 1992, D1.

31. John O'Donnell, "Scholastic Cage Stars have Eye Toward Future," *Watertown, New York Daily Times*, July 25, 1981, 15.

32. Richard J. Connolly, "False Recruit Data Stirs Cambridge Row," *Boston Globe*, January 31, 1980, 1, 18.

33. Larry Ames, "MIAA A Model of Inconsistency," *Boston Globe*, February 2, 1980, 22.

34. Jackie MacMullan, "It's Becoming Her Dominion: Controversy over Medina Dixon Starts Anew," *Boston Globe*, February 6, 1983, 59.

35. Ellen Ruppel Shell, "Hoop Squad Forfeits Season," *Cambridge Chronicle*, February 21, 1980, 1.

36. Jim Benagh, "Sports World Specials: Pressure Defense," *New York Times*, March 16, 1981, C2.

37. Joe Concannon, "Dixon Steals Thunder at Sports Festival," *Boston Globe*, July 29, 1981, 64.

38. Dennis Danheiser, "Dixon Leads Warrior Cagers," *Cambridge Chronicle*, February 5, 1981, 8.

39. Myra Precourt Bauer, "Recruiting Taking Turn for Worse?" *Philadelphia Daily News*, February 4, 1981, 52.

40. Roger Jackson, "Two Born Winners," *Sports Illustrated*, November 30, 1981, https://vault.si.com/vault/1981/11/30/two-born-winners-if-their-bloodlines-mean-a -thing-evelyn-johnson-and-medina-dixon-will-make-south-carolina-a-top-contender -for-the-ncaa-womens-title.

41. David Ruben, "Medina Dixon's still shooting for the top," *Cambridge Chronicle*, January 12, 1984, 6.

42. Jackie MacMullan, "Traveling Call," *Boston Globe*, April 2, 2006, E1.

43. Liz Chandler, "Spotlight to Shadow: Parsons Looks Back," *Charlotte Observer*, March 30, 1996, 1A, 12A.

44. Jackie MacMullan, "It's Becoming Her Dominion: Controversy over Medina Dixon Starts Anew," *Boston Globe*, February 6, 1983, 59.

45. Lynne E. Farrell, "Medina Dixon Goes Out on Top," *Boston Globe*, March 31, 1985, 52.

46. David Ruben, "Medina Dixon's Still Shooting for the Top," *Cambridge Chronicle*, January 12, 1984, 6.

47. Harry Minium, "ODU's 1985 National Championship Team Came Together to Comfort Medina Dixon," *Old Dominion University Athletics*, July 14, 2022, https: //odusports.com/news/2022/7/14/womens-basketball-minium-odus-1985-national -championship-team-came-together-to-comfort-median-dixon.aspx.

48. "Lady Monarchs Take Throne," *Newport News Daily Press*, April 1, 1985, C1, C3.

49. Melinda Waldrop, "ODU Great Dixon to Join Select Club," *Newport News Daily Press*, January 28, 2011, B3.

50. "Lady Monarchs Rule," *Newport News Daily Press*, April 2, 1985, 4.

51. Lynne E. Farrell, "Medina Dixon Goes Out on Top," *Boston Globe*, March 31, 1985, 52.

52. Linda Robertson, "Is There Life After College Basketball? Women Bounce Overseas to Find Dreams," *Salt Lake Tribune*, July 11, 1993, D4.

53. Dave Johnson, "Summer Olympics: Ex-ODU Star Wants Gold," *Newport News Daily Press*, July 24, 1992, 2.

54. Bob Gillespie, "At a Loss," *(Columbia, South Carolina) The State*, August 6, 1992, 1C, 7C.

55 Bob Ryan, "Unified Team Hits Its Target—Gold Medal," *Boston Globe*, August 8, 1992, 64.

56. Harry Minium, "ODU's 1985 National Championship Team Came Together to Comfort Medina Dixon," *Old Dominion University Athletics*, July 14, 2022, https:

//odusports.com/news/2022/7/14/womens-basketball-minium-odus-1985-national
-championship-team-came-together-to-comfort-median-dixon.aspx.

57. "At Long Last, Medina Dixon's Legacy Is Put on the Record," *Dorchester (Massachusetts) Reporter*, August 24, 2022, https://www.dotnews.com/2022/long -last-medina-dixon-s-legacy-put-record.

58. There are a series of YouTube videos that were made about Dixon's life in 2020. Her voice is weak, because she is fighting cancer, but the videos are a fascinating glimpse into her life: https://www.youtube.com/@medinadixon7608. NBC Sports Boston's Tom E. Curran also did a tribute YouTube video about her, in 2022: https: //www.youtube.com/watch?v=omNtXHNM0wk. The ceremony when her high school jersey was retired can be found here: https://www.youtube.com/watch?v =mQEDd4sJLII.

BIBLIOGRAPHY

Abdeldaiem, Alaa. "USWNT Players File Gender Discrimination Lawsuit Against U.S. Soccer." *Sports Illustrated*, March 8, 2019, https://www.si.com/soccer/2019 /03/08/uswnt-players-sue-us-soccer-gender-discrimination-lawsuit.

Aldridge, David. "Women's Dream Team Wins 111–55 Runaway." *Washington Post*, July 31, 1992.

Ames, Larry. "MIAA: A Model of Inconsistency." *Boston Globe*, February 2, 1980.

"At long last, Medina Dixon's Legacy Is Put on the Record." *Dorchester (Massachusetts) Reporter*, August 24, 2022, https://www.dotnews.com/2022/long -last-medina-dixon-s-legacy-put-record.

Bauer, Myra Precourt. "Recruiting Taking Turn for Worse?" *Philadelphia Daily News*, February 4, 1981.

Benagh, Jim. "Sports World Specials: Pressure Defense." *New York Times*, March 16, 1981.

Benbow, Julian. "Cambridge Basketball Icon Medina Dixon Was a Local Treasure, a Transformative Talent, and a Special Friend." *Boston Globe*, November 12, 2021.

Berry, Mia. "Angel Reese, Caitlin Clark and the Trash Talk Drawing Attention to Women's Basketball." Andscape, April 7, 2023, https://andscape.com/features/angel-reese-caitlin-clark-and-the-trash-talk-drawing-attention-to-womens -basketball/.

Blinde, Elaine M., and Diane E. Taub, "Women Athletes as Falsely Accused Deviants: Managing the Lesbian Stigma." *Sociological Quarterly* (Volume 33, Number 4), 1992.

"Champions of the Universe . . . Why Not?" *Cambridge, Massachusetts Chronicle*, March 22, 1979.

Chandler, Liz. "Spotlight to Shadow: Parsons Looks Back." *Charlotte Observer*, March 30, 1996.

Concannon, Joe. "Dixon Steals Thunder at Sports Festival." *Boston Globe*, July 29, 1981.

Connolly, Richard. "False Recruit Data Stirs Cambridge Row." *Boston Globe*, January 31, 1980.

Danheiser, Dennis. "Dixon Leads Warrior Cagers." *Cambridge Chronicle*, February 5, 1981.

Farrell, Lynne. "Medina Dixon Goes Out on Top." *Boston Globe*, March 31, 1985.

Gillespie, Bob. "At a Loss." *(Columbia, South Carolina) The State*, August 6, 1992.

Grundy, Pamela, and Susan Shackelford. *Shattering the Glass: The Remarkable History of Women's Basketball*. New York: New Press, 2005.

Haupt. Enid. "How to Win Dates and Influence the Dobie Gillis Type," *TV Guide*. December 5, 1959.

Jackson, Roger. "Two Born Winners." *Sports Illustrated*, November 30, 1981, https://vault.si.com/vault/1981/11/30/two-born-winners-if-their-bloodlines-mean-a-thing-evelyn-johnson-and-medina-dixon-will-make-south-carolina-a-top-contender-for-the-ncaa-womens-title.

Johnson, Dave. "Summer Olympics: Ex-ODU Star Wants Gold." *Newport News Daily Press*, July 24, 1992.

Kelley, Jim. "Ewing's 'Teammate' Steals Festival Show." *Buffalo News*, July 25, 1981.

"Lady Monarchs Rule." *Newport News Daily Press*, April 2, 1985.

"Lady Monarchs Take Throne," *Newport News Daily Press*, April 1, 1985.

Lifson, Amy. "When Iowa Girls' Basketball Ruled the Courts." *HUMANITIES*, Spring 2019 (Volume 40, Number 2), https://www.neh.gov/article/when-iowa-girls-basketball-ruled-courts.

MacMullan, Jackie. "It's Becoming Her Dominion: Controversy Over Medina Dixon Starts Anew." *Boston Globe*, February 6, 1983.

MacMullan, Jackie. "Traveling Call." *Boston Globe*, April 2, 2006.

McGrath, Ann. "Globe All-Scholastic Basketball Team." *Boston Globe*, April 10, 1979.

Minium, Harry. "ODU's 1985 National Championship Team Came Together to Comfort Medina Dixon." *Old Dominion University Athletics*, July 14, 2022, https://odusports.com/news/2022/7/14/womens-basketball-minium-odus-1985-national-championship-team-came-together-to-comfort-median-dixon.aspx.

Murphy, Mark. "For Harris, Discipline is Key." *Boston Herald*, May 21, 1989.

O'Donnell, John. "Scholastic Cage Stars Have Eye Toward Future." *Watertown, New York Daily Times*, July 25, 1981.

Robertson, Linda. "Is There Life After College Basketball? Women Bounce Overseas to Find Dreams." *Salt Lake Tribune*, July 11, 1993.

Romeo, Jess. "Policing the Bodies of Women Athletes Is Nothing New." *JSTOR Daily*, August 12, 2021, https://daily.jstor.org/policing-the-bodies-of-women-athletes-is-nothing-new/.

Roth, Karen. "Dixon is Center of Attention on Olympians." *Boston Herald American*, May 10, 1978.

Ruben, David. "Medina Dixon's Still Shooting for the Top." *Cambridge Chronicle*, January 12, 1984.

Fighting for Recognition   251

Sarni, Jim. "CBS Still Exploring Options for War." *(Ft. Lauderdale) South Florida Sun-Sentinel*, March 17, 2003.

Shell, Ellen Ruppel. "Hoop Squad Forfeits Season." *Cambridge Chronicle*, February 21, 1980.

Snyder, Bob. "Gal Cager Eyes Male $$." *Syracuse, New York Herald-Journal*, July 25, 1981.

Trust, Dick. "Dixon Dossier: Can Do Anything." *Quincy Patriot Ledger*, January 30, 1979.

Trust, Dick. "Dixon Injures Vols." *Quincy Patriot Ledger*, June 21, 1978.

Waldrop, Melinda. "ODU Great Dixon to Join Select Club." *Newport News Daily Press*, January 28, 2011.

Washington, Robert, and David Karen. "Sport and Society." *Annual Review of Sociology* (Volume 27), 2001.

Withycombe, Jenny Lind. "Intersecting Selves: African American Female Athletes' Experiences of Sport." *Sociology of Sport Journal* (Volume 28, Number 40), 2011.

Afterword

(Re)centering Boston Sport History

A Biographical Glimpse of Seven African American Female Athletes Who Are Shaping Boston Sport

Eileen Narcotta-Welp

Boston is a city that loves sport. While shopping at Faneuil Hall or strolling through Harvard Square, any out-of-towner will hear the low tones of Bostonians chatting about the Red Sox, Patriots, Celtics, or Bruins. One might hear disdainful rumblings of "Yankees suck," or overzealous fanaticism for Boston legends such as Bill Russell, Larry Bird, Ted Williams, David Ortiz, Bobby Orr, or Tom Brady. Growing up just south of the "hub of the universe," as my father still fondly refers to our home city, sport became and still remains a part of my and many others Bostonian's sociological imagination—entrenched in the identity of who and what it means to be from Massachusetts, and ultimately, New England. However, the "history" of Boston sport focuses on normative assumptions: White, male professionals that overshadows historically marginalized athletes and sports. Beyond the confines of what the media chooses to represent, Boston has a richer sport history that lies in wait to be revealed. In this chapter, it is my privilege to center the experiences and accolades of seven Black female athletes who have lived in and/or competed for the city of Boston.

BLAKE BOLDEN—*ICE HOCKEY—BOSTON COLLEGE EAGLES AND BOSTON BLADES*

A city that was once an engine of the Industrial Revolution, but hollowed out by an ever-evolving capitalist economy, Cleveland embodies the notion of loss. This history of loss is also embedded in the history of the city's professional sport franchises. Ice hockey, then, is not the first sport that comes to mind when Cleveland is discussed, but it should be. Born on March 10, 1991, Blake Bolden is a ceiling-breaking ice hockey player who spent much of her childhood in Cleveland on ice. Along with a storied playing career at the collegiate, international, and professional levels, the National Hockey League (NHL) Los Angeles Kings hired Bolden as the first Black female scout in February 2020.[1]

Raised in Stow, Ohio, a predominantly White suburb of thirty thousand people, Bolden's childhood dreams centered around architecture or being president of the United States.[2] A life in sport took hold when she stumbled across the game of ice hockey at the age of six. Her mother's boyfriend, who was a police officer and worked part-time as a security guard at Gund Arena, began taking Bolden to Cleveland Lumberjack games. At those games, Bolden got to see a behind-the-scenes version of the game, while running around in the locker rooms and meeting the players.[3] However, a real passion for the game was stoked when she watched the United States Women's National Hockey team win gold in the 1998 Nagano Winter Olympics. After that game, she said to herself and others: "I think I want to be a professional ice hockey player. I want to make that come true."[4] Her journey began in minor youth hockey for the International Hockey League (IHL) Cleveland Barons and the Ohio Flames, and it continued at the Northwoods School, a private boarding school in Lake Placid, New York, where she was able to hone her skills on the ice. While at the Northwoods school, USA Hockey identified Bolden as having national team talent. In 2008 and 2009, she competed for the United States at the U18 World Championships, winning gold in both tournaments.[5]

Bolden's ice hockey career started heating up when she arrived in Boston in 2009. She chose Boston College (BC), a premier hockey and academic school in the well-to-do suburb of Chestnut Hill, over other top-ten programs such as those at the University of Minnesota and the University of Wisconsin. Bolden had high hopes for winning at BC: "I was like, okay . . . we're going to win Hockey East, we're going to win Beanpots, we're going to win [the National Championship], we're going to win it all, and it's going to be great!"[6] The shock of a losing season her first year at BC provided the dose of reality that she needed to commit to her craft. As one of the best offensively minded defensive players in the country, Bolden helped the Boston College women's ice hockey team achieve three National Collegiate Athletic Association (NCAA) Frozen Fours, amassing a stunning eighty-two points in 139 games. In her senior year, she was named team captain and earned Hockey East's Defensive Player of the Year and NCAA All-American honors.

While Bolden did not make the cut for the 2014 Sochi Olympics, her professional career was just beginning. In 2013 the Canadian Women's Hockey League (CWHL) Boston Blades selected her fifth overall, making her the first Black player to earn this honor. Bolden recalled, "That is when I said, 'My job isn't done, I love this game . . . '"[7] Good thing she was not done; Bolden was named to the CWHL All-Star team and helped the Boston Blades win a Clarkson Cup in 2015. On October 11, 2015, Bolden became the first Black woman to compete in the upstart National Women's Hockey League (now the Professional Women's Hockey League) when she signed with the Boston Pride. In 2016, she helped the Pride win the Isobel Cup with an 80 mph slapshot, one of the fastest in women's hockey.[8] Over the next few years, Bolden's hockey career took her to Switzerland and Buffalo, New York, making lasting impacts on HC Lugano and the Beauts, respectively, as she was named NWHL's Defensive Player of the Year in 2019.

In 2020, Bolden retired from playing, but not from the game, as she wants to continue to be a role model for young women who play hockey.[9] She created "EmBolden Her," an online mentorship program, where young girls between the ages of thirteen and sixteen hear Bolden and other ice hockey players discuss setting goals and how to manage their time, as well as hockey techniques and strategies.[10] Bolden's advocacy for young Black women in hockey led to her meeting Los Angeles Kings president Luc Robitaille at a sport conference. Robitaille was impressed with Bolden's résumé, and he developed a position for her in the Kings organization. She is the first Black woman to hold the position of NHL scout, and she has helped to diversify interest in hockey in Los Angeles as the Kings' growth and inclusion specialist.[11] Bolden's exceptional play on the ice and committed work to growing the game off of it is an example of the progress the NHL is trying to achieve. Jeff Scott, the NHL's vice president of community development and growth, believes Bolden's legacy is galvanizing: "What Blake's been able to do as a player and being able to bridge that in a post career is inspirational."[12] For now, we can only wait to see what "first" Bolden will conquer next.

ALIYAH BOSTON—*BASKETBALL—*
WORCESTER ACADEMY

Aliyah Boston adjusted quickly to the harsh New England winters, eventually calling Massachusetts "my second home."[13] In the summer of 2014, Boston (age twelve) and her older sister Alexis (age fourteen) relocated 1,700 miles to Worcester, Massachusetts, from the island of St. Thomas, US Virgin Islands, when their family sent them to the mainland to pursue a dream of a debt-free college education. While they were in Massachusetts, that dream expanded to playing basketball at the highest level of the National Collegiate Athletic Association (NCAA) and professionally in the Women's National Basketball Association (WNBA).[14]

Born on December 11, 2001, Boston idolized her sister and, like her, started playing basketball at the age of ten.[15] Playing basketball on the sun-kissed outdoor courts of St. Thomas might seem like a dream come true, but opportunities to face the level of competition needed for the sisters to reach their potential were limited. While it was a difficult decision for Cleone Boston to send her young daughters to live with their aunt Jenaire Hodge in Worcester, she notes, 'They were . . . big fish in a small pond, (and) they had to find a bigger pond," and for Aliyah, moving to Massachusetts allowed her to "have bigger dreams."[16] While Boston attributes her easy adjustment to Massachusetts to the fact that "she was still young and 'learning to grow up,'" she felt as if she had "a Caribbean parent living with her."[17] The Caribbean was never far away, as her aunt sprinkled Boston's mainland life with a bit of home in the form of curry chicken and fried plantains.[18]

Sherry Levin, head coach for Worcester Academy, realized early on that Boston's "ceiling is really high."[19] The six-foot-four forward won Gatorade Massachusetts Player of the Year honors in 2017, 2018, and 2019. As a senior, she averaged 17.3 points, 10.6 rebounds, and 3.2 blocks per game, helping her team to two straight New England Prep School Athletic Council Class A Championships and earning her a consensus All-American selection, as well as invites to the McDonald's All-American Game and the Jordan Brand Classic.[20] All that success on high school courts caught the attention of USA Basketball. Boston has represented the United States and won gold at the 2017 International Basketball Federation (FIBA) Under-16 Women's Americas Championship (named Most Valuable Player), 2018 Summer Youth Olympics, 2018 FIBA Under-17 Women's Basketball World Cup, 2019 FIBA Under-19 Women's Basketball World Cup, and most recently at the 2021 FIBA Women's AmeriCup.[21] In 2019, for her hard work and dedication to the game, *HoopGurlz Recruiting Rankings* assessed Boston as the third-highest-ranked high school player in the nation. She chose the University of South Carolina

Gamecocks over historically top-seeded schools such as Connecticut and Notre Dame because "South Carolina just felt like home."[22]

There is no place like home for Boston, as she crushed records and brought a NCAA championship to the Columbia campus. Over the course of her four years, she became the most decorated player in program history, averaging 14.1 points, 10.9 rebounds, and 2.4 blocks per game. For her individual efforts she was named National Freshman of the Year (2020), National Defensive Player of the Year (2022, 2023), Honda Cup Winner (2022), Academic All-America Team Member of the Year (2022), and Women's Basketball Academic All-American of the Year (2021, 2022). Those individual awards also turned into team results: three regular South Eastern Conference (SEC) Season Championships (2021, 2022, 2023), three SEC Tournament Titles (2021, 2022, 2023), and three NCAA Final Four appearances (2021, 2022, 2023), including a National Championship in 2022. She helped her team to a 129-9 record during her career, achieving a number-one ranking in the Associated Press Poll for thirty-eight straight weeks. Over those thirty-eight weeks, her team became the third NCAA basketball program to hold the number-one spot in the AP Poll in consecutive seasons.[23] While there was the potential for Boston to play a fifth year in Columbia (due to a COVID waiver) and bring a second NCAA championship home to Columbia, she instead declared for the WNBA draft on April 1, 2023. Nine days later, on April 10, 2023, she was chosen by the Indiana Fever as their first-ranked overall pick.[24] Fever general manager Lin Dunn was ecstatic on draft night, noting that selecting Boston with the number-one pick "'sends a message that we're serious about reestablishing the Indiana Fever as a championship caliber program.'"[25]

In her first season with the Fever, Boston is living up to the hype. She is the Fever's second-leading scorer with 14.7 points per game, while averaging 7.9 rebounds and 2.6 assists in 28.3 minutes of play.[26] According to *ESPN Stats & Info,* she is not only the first player in Fever history, but also the youngest player in league history, to score twenty points on 75 percent shooting, gather ten rebounds, and dish five assists in a game. Unsurprisingly, Boston has been named to the 2023 WNBA All-Star Team, and she will be the first rookie player to start an All-Star game since 2014.[27] It looks as though Boston has made another home for herself in the cornfields of Indiana, and the rest of us are lucky to witness her ability to adapt and thrive in new spaces.

SIKA HENRY—*TRACK AND FIELD AND TRIATHLONS—TUFTS UNIVERSITY*

Sika Henry's journey to become the first African American women to qualify for her professional card in the triathlon in 2021 is not an illustrious affair. For Henry, there is no anecdotal story about her immediate success in track and field or long-distance running. In fact, her first experience with track at age eleven in predominantly White Montclair, New Jersey, was a distinctly negative experience: "The first day, they tried to make me do the hurdles, and I'm really clumsy, so I never went back."[28] Instead, she focused her efforts on the historically White-dominated sport of swimming, where she competed on the varsity squad at Mount Saint Dominic Academy, and she fully intended to compete in the sport in college.

Reevaluating her athletic future during the last few months of her senior year of high school, Henry had the novel idea that she would run and jump for the track-and-field team at Tufts University in Medford, Massachusetts.[29] She believed her "genetics" were better suited for athletics as she "had long legs, [her] Grandpa played football, ran track and long jumped for Alabama, and [her] Dad could dunk and played football for Michigan State."[30] Henry walked onto the Tufts University track-and-field team in 1999, and by her junior year, she was jumping over a five-foot-five bar and running a fifty-eight-second four-hundred-meter leg with the four-by-four-hundred-meter relay team, earning her and her teammates All-American status.[31] But running long distances was never at the forefront of Henry's mind; if anything, any distance over a mile seemed "long and painful."[32]

After college, Henry moved back to Montclair and worked in Manhattan's financial district, where she fell out of shape due to the demands of her job. Wanting a physical challenge back in her life, Henry signed up for an Atlantic City marathon in 2008. She admits that the experience was a "hot mess" of "walking and puking," but somehow she broke the four-hour mark and figured if she trained properly, she might "be okay at this."[33] In 2013, after a move to Virginia and a tough breakup that left her seeking a distraction, Henry signed up for a local spring triathlon, consisting of a half-mile swim, a 12.4-mile bike, and a 3.1-mile run.[34] Competing in that first triathlon, she noticed the lack of diversity: "I'm pretty sure I was the only Black woman that day." She became curious as to why there were so few people of color participating.[35] For Henry, her presence was needed so that other athletes of color could see themselves in her triumph or defeat in a White-dominated sport.

Over the next four years, Henry dedicated herself to the sport and leaned into her training. As her times ticked down and her personal records stacked up, Henry, still working full-time, focused on obtaining professional status.

For triathletes to gain a pro card, an individual needed to finish as either a top-ten amateur at a World Championship event, place in the top five at a USA Triathlon Age Group National Event, or finish as a top-three amateur at another qualifying race.[36] An individual who gained a pro card was eligible for professional pool prize monies and sponsorships that helped financially support athletes in training. Henry is a steel-nosed competitor, but in 2019, she almost quit the sport completely. During the Ironman 70.3 Galveston race, she was in a horrific cycling crash. Swerving out the way of another rider who had merged into her lane without looking, Henry slammed into a roadside barricade and hit the ground at 25 mph. The crash rendered her unconscious and left her with a broken nose and teeth, gashes on her head that required over thirty stitches, and road rash all over her body.[37] Henry regained her strength and courage, and within six months after her crash, she competed in the Ironman 70.3 in Augusta, Georgia. Two years later, in May 2021 at the Challenge Cancun, she finished third overall in the amateur bracket, becoming the first African American woman and the second African American ever to receive a professional card for triathletes.[38]

In September 2021, Henry raced as a professional for the first time. The moment overwhelmed her as she confessed the race "was one of her worst," and that there was a steep learning curve racing as a professional as compared to an amateur.[39] Henry notes that "chasing after my pro card was a very self-absorbed endeavor,"[40] but she is "grateful for what I have accomplished, that I have more of a platform to get my story out more."[41] While she will continue to race as a professional, her focus can now turn to raising awareness and "visibility" on the international stage for people of color to gain more access to endurance races and their community.

BIANCA SMITH—*BASEBALL—RED SOX*

Bianca Smith's conscious memory has always included a love of baseball. Her mother, Dawn Patterson, a devoted New York Yankees fan (Red Sox fans can forgive this personal blemish), introduced her to the game at the age of three. Born in 1991, she grew up during the television craze of *Barney & Friends*, *Rugrats*, and *The Magic School Bus*, but Smith's attention centered on baseball and, in particular, Yankees Hall of Fame shortstop Derek Jeter.[42] Baseball has a long history of segregation, both by gender and by race. Smith, then, never played baseball growing up; instead, at the age of twelve, she picked up a softball and competed for Colleyville Heritage High School (Colleyville is a suburb of Dallas, Texas), and she continued to play at Dartmouth College, in Hanover, New Hampshire. Even though she was not initially recruited to play for the Ivy League school, Smith worked with the Dartmouth baseball team for two years. When Smith bumped into the softball coach in the halls of Dartmouth's athletic facility one day, the softball coach asked Smith to try out for the team. As a junior, Smith walked onto the softball team and became a two-year varsity letter winner as an out-fielder.[43] While playing for the Big Green, Smith, a sociology major, consid-ered a career in baseball management. This might seem like a difficult path for most, let alone a woman in a male-dominated sport, but her perseverance has led to a number of distinctions in her young career.

Smith jumped from Dartmouth College to Case Western Reserve University (CWRU) in Cleveland, Ohio, to pursue a master's degree in business admin-istration. While most college baseball coaches were hesitant to give Smith a role in any aspect of team management, Matthew Englander, CWRU head baseball coach, was excited about Smith's potential. After their first meeting on a campus tour, Englander notes that Smith "impresses you immediately. She's smart, she's humble, she's genuinely a good person."[44] Immediately, Englander offered Smith the role of the team's first director of baseball opera-tions. With no hesitation, Smith accepted.[45] In this new role, she organized fundraisers, started an alumni newsletter, managed travel itineraries, sched-uled meals for the team, created social media accounts, and even dabbled in team and player analytics.[46] The versatility of her skills on the field and in the office has earned her the respect of the CWRU coaching staff and play-ers. CWRU's athletic director, Amy Backus, notes that "[Smith] is a woman in baseball, and guys respect her because she knows the game."[47] In the classroom at CWRU, Smith earned both a master of business administration (MBA) degree and a doctor of law (JD) degree in 2017. With this kind of experience and education, Smith seems as if she would be a shoo-in for any position at any level in baseball.

After graduating from CWRU, Smith participated in the Major League Baseball's (MLB) inaugural Take the Field program, intended to place women in coaching and scouting opportunities at the professional level.[48] This pro-gram allowed her to gain access to and obtain two prestigious internships with the Texas Rangers and the Cincinnati Reds. Even with a growing résumé, however, Smith, as a woman of color in a field dominated by White men, continued to experience barriers to access in the sport she loves. For example, she emailed over one hundred NCAA Division I institutions regard-ing coaching positions. She heard back from twenty-six, but only one offered her a position, and that one did not pay enough for her to accept the job.[49] In 2019, Smith finally landed at Carroll University in Waukesha, Wisconsin, as an assistant athletic director for compliance and administration and assis-tant coach and hitting coordinator for the baseball team. Carroll University catcher T.J. Pfaffle notes that someone of Smith's pedigree is usually reserved for more popular sports, such as basketball and football. Hiring Smith was "the first real step outside of that."[50]

Within a year of being hired at Carroll University, Smith received an email from the Boston Red Sox. Red Sox management had seen her résumé and thought she would be a good candidate for a major-league coaching position. The hiring of the first African American woman to a major league club is historic, especially for an organization that has a checkered past regarding segregation.[51] Even more momentous for Smith was gaining employment with a team her mother despised. Smith believes her late mother, who passed away from cancer in 2013, would be proud of her, but that "(she) is going to haunt me for the rest of my life."[52] In her first year as a Red Sox, Smith spent most of her coaching energy on fielding and base running. With that experience, Smith became more involved with hitting and working with manager Jimmy Gonzalez, and she even coached third base a few times.[53] In 2023, Smith declined a multiyear offer from the Red Sox to continue coaching in their system. Smith notes, "[The offer] was still a coaching position; it just wasn't where I wanted to be . . . I absolutely loved my time there . . . I would love to come back if the position was a good fit."[54] As of now, Smith is looking to pursue different opportunities to further her career. Maybe someday she will be back in the Red Sox organization, this time as general manager.

CHANTÉ BONDS, ADRIENNE SMITH, AND WHITNEY ZELEE—*FOOTBALL—BOSTON RENEGADES (BOSTON MILITIA)*

For many in New England, football success is connected to the New England Patriots. However, tucked away in the North Shore community of Revere, Massachusetts, another football team rivals the Patriots' legacy of winning. The Boston Renegades are a premier women's tackle football team that competes in the Women's Football Alliance (WFA). Formerly known as the Boston Militia, the Boston Renegades are committed to winning and encouraging women and girls to break barriers through the game of football.[55] Erin Baumgartner, former player and partial owner of the Renegades, eased any concerns over the relaunched organization in 2015: "It's going to be a different team now, but with the same total commitment to kicking ass."[56] With a history of winning championships, the Renegades have not disappointed. As of the summer of 2022, the Renegades have won seven WFA Championships—four in a row (2018–2022; 2020 was cancelled due to COVID-19)—and they boast a thirty-one-game winning streak.[57] This team is a dynasty, but a dynasty does not exist without exceptional players. The following is a short biography of three exceptional African American players who have all donned the Renegades jersey and solidified the legacy of this team.

Chanté Bonds

A Brockton, Massachusetts, native, Chanté Bonds's love for sport started early as she played basketball competitively and football around the neighborhood. She became a star basketball player for Brockton High School, leading her team to a state title in 2001. She played collegiately at Bentley College in Waltham, Massachusetts, where she helped the women's basketball team reach the Division II Final Four in 2003, and she was named Northeast 10 Conference Defensive Player of the Year.[58] She went on to coach basketball at Fairleigh Dickinson University, the College of Holy Cross, and the University of Massachusetts, Boston.[59] After retiring from coaching, Bonds was named head of the math department at a public school in Boston.[60]

Figure A.1. Brockton born, Chanté Bonds, achieved an impressive array of athlete and academic accomplishments. As a basketball standout, she led Bentley College to an appearance in the NCAA Division II final four. She later coached basketball at Bentley, and other nearby schools including UMass Boston, UMass Lowell, and Holy Cross. She realized her dream to become a professional football player in 2009 when she joined the New York Sharks and then the Boston Renegades of the Women's Football Alliance. Her stellar career as a Renegade earned her Boston's prestigious Football Legacy Award in 2023. Image provided by Robert Mara.

Bonds's childhood fondness for the game of football never left her, however, and she began to play with various teams in the WFA starting in 2010. She is a versatile player who plays on both sides of the ball; she is a cornerback and a wide receiver, but she has played as quarterback, kick returner, and running back when needed.[61] She is called the "Swiss Army Knife" of women's professional football.[62] For her usefulness, Bonds earned the 2017 WFA Defensive Player of the Year award, and in 2018, she was named both the WFA's season and national championship game Most Valuable Player.[63] Bonds's experience in football has moved beyond our national borders. In 2022, she participated on the US Women's Tackle National Team, which won gold, defeating Great Britain 28–10 at the International Federation of American Football (IFAF) Women's Tackle World Championship in Vantaa, Finland.[64]

Adrienne Smith

Enamored by the National Football League (NFL), Smith would set up her teddy bear, Ginger, and use the stuffed animal as a tackling pad while her parents watched their hometown team, the Washington Commanders. When she was seven years old, her father purchased her a football and taught her how to throw and tackle in order to compete against the boys in her Alexandria, Virginia, neighborhood.[65] As there was no institutional support for girls' football in the 1980s, Smith competed in softball and basketball.[66] A focus on education was crucial for Smith; both of her parents were academics, and they instilled in her the importance of education and a strong work ethic. Smith notes, "My parents told me an education is power and the way to get up and out in this world."[67] Her work ethic paid off with an undergraduate degree from Washington University in St. Louis, Missouri, and a master's of business administration from Columbia School of Business in New York City. The work ethic she learned from her parents has transferred onto the football field.[68]

In 2006, shortly after Smith's mother's passing, a friend politely nudged her to try out for the New York Sharks.[69] She made the team, eventually moving to the Boston Militia in 2010, and she has continued to compete for the Boston Renegades. In her fourteen professional seasons, Smith has garnered a list of accomplishments and honors: two gold medals with the US Women's Football National Team (scoring the first touchdown in IFAF history), four WFA Championships, and nine WFA All-Star appearances.[70] In 2022, she notched her most recent accolade, surpassing Jeanette Gray of the Chicago Force on the WFA's all-time receiving yard list on May 21, 2022, against the DC Divas.[71] Smith's career is by no means slowing down. In 2013, she started Gridiron Queendom, a company that promotes and supports women and girls who play—and love—the game of football.[72] She is the creator of Blitz Champz, a football-themed card game for kids and families that won a National Parenting Product Award. And in 2021, she joined with the American Flag Football League (AFFL) to lead its new Women's Division, overseeing operations and sponsorships.[73] Flag football makes its Olympic debut in 2028, and Smith has no doubt, at that time, she will be putting another medal around her neck.[74]

Whitney Zelee

A dancer must develop grace and a kinesthetic awareness of their body to flawlessly move through space. A skilled soccer player needs to be quick with an attacking mindset to be productive on the field. Whitney Zelee, a Boston native, developed all these skills while competing on soccer fields and in the dance studio as a young athlete.[75] Zelee captained her soccer team at Winsor School, graduating in 2006, and she moved on to the College of Holy Cross to finish her studies. She graduated from Holy Cross in 2010 with a bachelor of science degree in psychology, completing the premed program.[76]

After not competing in athletics for five years, Zelee had no dreams of athletic stardom. But after watching a friend play a men's semipro football game, her interest in tackle football was sparked. Zelee tried out for and made the Boston Militia in 2011. When combined, the skills she'd honed through soccer and dance as an adolescent were exactly the competencies she needed to be a successful running back. Zelee made an immediate impact for the team, helping them win a WFA National Championship in 2011 and 2014, and she was named Most Valuable Player of the 2011 WFA National Championship game.[77] In 2013, Zelee became a breakout star, running 2,832 yards over the course of an eleven-game season. Sports author Neal Rozendaal summed up Zelee's 2013 campaign as "the most dominant season by any running back in women's football history."[78] The 2014 campaign marked a different point in her career, however, as she began to feel the effects of playing a violent game. Over a three-year period, she tore her labrum in both shoulders, broke her ankle, and tore the meniscus in her knee.[79] Regardless of her injuries, she continued to outpace her competitors, amassing 7,266 yards and 121 touchdowns on 674 carries in forty-eight games.[80] After a loss in the WFA National Championship game in 2017, Zelee retired from the Boston Renegades.

Typically, an athlete's story ends after four surgeries, but Zelee could not stay away from the game. In 2018, she stepped into a coaching role for the Renegades, but she could not continue because she found it "too difficult emotionally."[81] Amazingly, in 2023, after finally recovering from her injuries, Zelee decided to lace her football cleats again, this time on the defensive side of the ball. As a defensive lineman, she is now responsible for preventing running backs from gaining yardage—an ironic situation not lost on Zelee.

The Boston Renegades, with Zelee back in the fold, won their eighth WFA national championship in Canton, Ohio, against the St. Louis Slam, on July 22, 2023.[82]

NOTES

1. Kristen Anderson, "Kings' Scout Blake Bolden Happy to Play the Role of Trailblazer," *thehockeynews.com*, 8 March 2021, https://thehockeynews.com/news/kings-scout-blake-bolden-happy-to-play-the-role-of-trailblazer, last accessed on June 1, 2023; Scott Procter, "Blake Bolden Helping Cultivate Next Generation of Diverse Hockey Stars," *bvmsports.com*, 25 February 2022, https://bvmsports.com/2022/02/25/blake-bolden-helping-cultivate-next-generation-of-diverse-hockey-stars/, last accessed on June 1, 2023.

2. United States Census Bureau, "Quick Facts: Stow City, Ohio; United States, *census.gov*, 2022, https://www.census.gov/quickfacts/fact/table/stowcityohio,US/PST045222, last accessed on June 1, 2023; National Hockey League, "Blake Bolden Discusses Her Journey in Hockey," 2021, *youtube.com*, https://www.youtube.com/watch?v=RiDMsNjVZzw, last accessed on June 1, 2023.

3. Bryna Jean-Marie, "Blake Bolden Continues to Break the Ice," 4 November 2021, *si.com*, https://www.si.com/nhl/2021/11/04/los-angeles-kings-blake-bolden-100-influential-black-women, last accessed on June 1, 2023.

4. National Hockey League, "Blake Bolden Discusses."

5. "Blake Bolden: About," *blakebolden.com*, 2023, https://www.blakebolden.com/about-me, last accessed June 10, 2023.

6. Maithri Harve, "'I Want to Go to BC, I Want to Help Change a Program': An Interview with BC WIH Alum Blake Bolden," *bcinterruption.com*, 11 May 2021, https://www.bcinterruption.com/2021/5/11/22427671/i-want-to-go-to-bc-i-want-to-help-change-a-program-an-interview-with-bc-wih-alum-blake-bolden, last accessed June 2, 2023, para. 15, brackets original.

7. Procter, "Blake Bolden Helping Cultivate," para. 5.

8. Branson Wright, "Kings Scout Blake Bolden Want to Inspire the Next Wave of Black Women in Hockey," *andscape.com*, 25 April 2022, https://andscape.com/features/kings-scout-blake-bolden-wants-to-inspire-the-next-wave-of-black-women-in-hockey/, last accessed on June 2, 2023.

9. Matt Larkin, "Blake Bolden Q&A: On Mentoring Women and the Secret to Scouting," *thehockeynews.com*, 31 January 2021, https://thehockeynews.com/news/blake-bolden-q-a-on-mentoring-women-and-the-secret-to-scouting, last accessed June 3, 2023.

10. Julian McKenszie, "Blake Bolden Discusses EmBolden Her, a 6-Month Mentorship Program for Aspiring Female Hockey Players," *theathletic.com*, 3 November 2021, https://theathletic.com/2908772/2021/11/03/blake-bolden-discusses-embolden-her-a-6-month-mentorship-program-for-aspiring-female-hockey-players/, last accessed on June 2, 2023.

11. Branson Wright, "Kings Scout Blake Bolden."

12. Ibid., para. 39.

13. Greg Levinsky, "How Worcester Played an Important Role in Aliyah Boston's Path to Women's Basketball Stardom," 31 December 2021, *bostonglobe.com*, https://www.bostonglobe.com/2021/12/31/sports/how-worcester-played-an-important-role-aliyah-bostons-path-womens-basketball-stardom/, last accessed on June 3, 2023, para. 3.

14. Tara Sullivan, "'There is No Ceiling for Her': South Carolina's Aliyah Boston, Who Grew Up in Mass., is the Face of Women's College Basketball," *bostonglobe.com*, 10 February, 2023, https://www.bostonglobe.com/2023/02/10/sports/aliyah-boston-south-carolina/, last accessed on June 2, 2023.

15. ibid.

16. Levinsky, "How Worcester Played," para. 6.

17. Hunter Simpson, "Aliyah Boston Reflects on Upbringing in USVI and Encouraging Young Female Athletes," *stthomassource.com*, 25 June 2022, https://stthomassource.com/content/2022/06/25/aliyah-boston-reflects-on-upbringing-in-usvi-and-encouraging-young-female-athletes/, last accessed June 3, 2023, para. 9; Levinsky, "How Worcester Played," para. 11.

18. Levinsky, "How Worcester Played."

19. Walter Villa, "Where Will Aliyah Boston Take Her Two Gold Medals Next?," *espn.com*, 27 September 2018, https://www.espn.com/espnw/sports/story/_/id/24811694/elite-prospect-aliyah-boston-strikes-gold-usa-basketball-leaving-paradise-behind#, last accessed on June 3, 2023, para. 7.

20. "Aliyah Boston," *gamecocks.com*, 2023, https://gamecocksonline.com/sports/wbball/roster/season/2020-21/player/aliyah-boston/, last accessed on June 3, 2023.

21. "Women's All-Time Roster: USA Basketball History," *usab.com*, 2023, https://www.usab.com/about/competitive-history-stats, last accessed on June 3, 2023.

22. "Aliyah Boston," *espn.com*, 2023, https://www.espn.com/high-school/girls-basketball/recruiting/player/_/id/224799/aliyah-boston, last accessed June 3, 2023; Walter Villa, "No. 3 Prospect Aliyah Boston Joins the Talented Crowd Headed to South Carolina," *espn.com*, 21 November 2018, https://www.espn.com/espnw/sports/story/_/id/25331760/no-3-prospect-aliyah-boston-joins-talented-crowd-heading-dawn-staley-south-carolina-gamecocks, last accessed on June 3, 2023, para. 3.

23. "Aliyah Boston," *gamecocks.com*; Brad Muller, "Aliyah Boston Has Done it All, and Now She Wants More," *gamecocksonline.com*, 5 October 2022, https://gamecocksonline.com/news/2022/10/05/aliyah-boston-has-done-it-all-and-now-she-wants-more/, last accessed on June 3, 2023; Jeff Schwartz and Brian Alden, "Corey Kispert of Gonzaga, Aliyah Boston of South Carolina Lead Academic All-American® Division I Men's & Women's Basketball Teams," *academicallamerica.com*, 28 March 2021, https://academicallamerica.com/documents/2021/5/28//2020_21_DI_Basketball_AAA.pdf?id=3177, last accessed June 3, 2023.

24. Scott Horner, "LIVE: Indiana Fever Pick Aliyah Boston, Grace Berger in WNBA Draft," *indystar.com*, 10 April 2023, https://www.indystar.com/story/sports/basketball/wnba/fever/2023/04/10/wnba-draft-2023-indiana-fever-have-the-no-1-overall-pick-aliyah-boston/70098520007/, last accessed on June 3, 2023; Alexa Philippou, "South Carolina Star Aliyah Boston Declares for WNBA Draft," *espn.com*,

1 April 2023, https://www.espn.com/womens-college-basketball/story/_/id/36031545/south-carolina-star-aliyah-boston-declares-wnba-draft, last accessed on June 3, 2023.

25. Brian Haenchen (@Brian_Haenchen), "Fever GM Lin Dunn on drafting Aliyah Boston." This "sends a message that we're serious about re-establishing the Indiana Fever as a championship caliber program," Twitter, 10 April 2023, 6:25 p.m., https://twitter.com/Brian_Haenchen/status/1645568685409697793?ref_src=twsrc%5Etfw%7Ctwcamp%5Etweetembed%7Ctwterm%5E1645568685409697793%7Ctwgr%5E3b68d325b1aa7377cac9c68afe061763bc21e69e%7Ctwcon%5Es1_&ref_url=https%3A%2F%2Fwww.indystar.com%2Fstory%2Fsports%2Fbasketball%2Fwnba%2Ffever%2F2023%2F04%2F10%2Fwnba-draft-indiana-fever-select-aliyah-boston-with-no-1-overall-pick%2F70088084007%2F.

26. Annie Costabile, "Fever Rookie Aliyah Boston is Making WNBA History," *chicago.suntimes.com*, 15 June 2023, https://chicago.suntimes.com/chicago-sky-and-wnba/2023/6/15/23762647/fever-rookie-aliyah-boston-making-wnba-history, last accessed July 2, 2023.

27. Lauren Campbell, "Aliyah Boston Named to WNBA All-Star Game; First Rookie Starter Since 2014," *masslive.com*, 25 June 2023, https://www.masslive.com/sports/2023/06/aliyah-boston-named-to-wnba-all-star-game-first-rookie-starter-since-2014.html, last accessed July 2, 2023.

28. Allison Torres Burka, "Sika Henry," *startingling1928.com*, 22 June 2023, https://www.startingline1928.com/pioneerstories, last accessed July 3, 2023, para. 2.

29. Sika Henry, "Why Am I Not Getting Any Faster," *why-i-run.blogsport.com*, 24 July 2012, http://why-i-run.blogspot.com/2012/07/, last accessed on July 3, 2023.

30. ibid., para. 2.

31. Alanis Thames, "'I Can't Just Quit': Sika Henry is the First African American Woman to be Recognized as a Pro Triathlete. But a Horrible Bicycle Crash in 2019 Nearly Thwarted Her Dream," *nytimes.com*, 23 November 2021, https://www.nytimes.com/2021/11/23/sports/sika-henry-triathlon.html, last accessed on July 3, 2023; Henry, "Why Am I Not."

32. Thames, "'I Can't Just Quit,'" para. 8.

33. Diego Jesus Bartesaghi Mena, "Montclair Native Sika Henry is First U.S.'s First Pro Black Female Triathlete," *montclairlocal.new*, 7 June 2021, https://montclairlocal.news/montclair-native-sika-henry-is-first-u-s-s-first-pro-black-female-triathlete/, last accessed on July 3, 2023, para. 11.

34. Thames, "'I Can't Just Quit.'"

35. Torres Burtka, "Sika Henry," para. 5.

36. Thames, "'I Can't Just Quit.'"

37. George Banker, "Resilience, Grit, Determination Define Sika Henry," *runners-gazette.com*, 22 February 2022, https://runnersgazette.com/2022/02/22/resilience-grit-determination-define-sika-henry/, last accessed on July 4, 2023; Thames, "'I Can't Just Quit.'"

38. Niamh Lewis, "Sika Henry: USA's First Black Female Pro Triathlete on How Community Support After Horror Accident Stopped Her from Quitting," *espn.com*, 5 October 2021, https://www.espn.com/olympics/triathlon/story/_/id/31597228/usa

-first-black-female-pro-triathlete-how-community-support-horror-accident-stopped
-quitting, last accessed on July 4, 2023.

39. Thames, "'I Can't Just Quit,'" para. 38.

40. ibid., para. 40.

41. Lewis, "Sika Henry," para. 26.

42. Adrienne Frank, "Blazing a New Trail to the Ballpark: CWRU Provided a Springboard for Alumna Bianca Smith's Pioneering Move to Coaching Professional Baseball," *case.edu*, Spring 2021, https://case.edu/think/spring2021/blazing-new-trail .html, last accessed on July 5, 2023; Greg Joyce, "Derek Jeter Finally Inducted into Baseball Hall of Fame: 'Heartbeat of a Yankees Dynasty," *nypost.com*, 8 September 2021, https://nypost.com/2021/09/08/yankees-derek-jeter-inducted-into-baseball-hall -of-fame/#, last accessed July 5, 2023.

43. Branson Wright, "Red Sox Coach Bianca Smith Has Spent Career Proving She Belongs," *andscape.com*, 12 January 2021, https://andscape.com/features/red-sox -coach-bianca-smith-has-spent-her-career-proving-she-belongs/, last accessed on July 5, 2023; "2012 Softball Roster: Bianca Smith," *dartmouthsports.com*, 2012, https:// dartmouthsports.com/sports/softball/roster/bianca-smith/8107, last accessed on July 5, 2023.

44. Puneet Bansal and Nathan Lesch, "Bianca Smith: From the Spartans to the Red Sox," *observer.case.edu*, 5 February 2021, https://observer.case.edu/bianca-smith -from-the-spartans-to-the-red-sox/, last accessed on July 5, 2023, para. 2.

45. Frank, "Blazing a New Trail."

46. Bansal and Lesch, "Bianca Smith."

47. Wright, "Red Sox Coach," para. 27.

48. Frank, "Blazing a New Trail"; Juliet Macur, "If Mom Could See Her Now," *nytimes.com*, 3 March 2021, https://www.nytimes.com/2021/03/03/sports/baseball/ bianca-smith-red.html, last accessed July 5, 2023.

49. ibid.

50. Ian Browne, "Red Sox Hire Smith, First Black Female Coach," *mlb.com*, 5 January 2021, https://www.mlb.com/news/red-sox-hire-bianca-smith-first-black-female -baseball-coach, last accessed July 5, 2023; Wright, "Red Sox Coach," para. 39.

51. Julian McWilliams, "Red Sox Hiring Bianca Smith as Minor League Coach, Making Her First Black Woman to Coach in Pro Baseball History," *boston.com*, 5 January 2021, https://www.boston.com/sports/boston-red-sox/2021/01/04/red-sox -bianca-smith/, last accessed on July 5, 2023.

52. Macur, "If Mom Could See,"Her Now," para. 8

53. Browne, "Red Sox Hire Smith."

54. Alex Speier, "Bianca Smith, the First Black Woman Hired as a Coach by an MLB Team, Leaves Red Sox Organization," *msn.com*, 27 January 2023, https://www .msn.com/en-us/sports/mlb/bianca-smith-the-first-black-woman-hired-as-a-coach-by -an-mlb-team-leaves-red-sox-organization/ar-AA16OIKc, last accessed on July 5, 2023, para. 3, brackets original.

55. Shira Springer, "For Renegades, a Name Change and a Mission to Keep Dynasty Alive," *bostonglobe.com*, 7 February 2015, https://www.bostonglobe.com/

sports/2015/02/07/local-women-tackle-difficult-task-keeping-their-football-dynasty
-alive/pFrPziOI2T58f86sAwamdL/story.html, last accessed on July 7, 2023, para. 6.

56. Springer, "For Renegades, a Name," para. 6.

57. Hayden Bird, "Boston Renegades Win Fourth Straight Title, Backup Quarter-back Named MVP: It's the Seventh Championship in Team History," *boston.com*, 11 July 2022, https://www.boston.com/sports/morning-sports-update/2022/07/11/boston-renegades-football-championship-win/, last accessed on July 7, 2023.

58. The Sports Museum, "Boston vs. Bullies All-Star: Chante Bonds," *sports-museum.org*, 2023, https://www.sportsmuseum.org/boston-vs-bullies/about-us/all-stars/chante-bonds/, last accessed on July 7, 2023.

59. Endia Berger, "U.S. National Team Alumni Spotlight: Chanté Bonds," *blogs.usafootball.com*, 16 December 2022, https://blogs.usafootball.com/blog/8508/u-s-national-team-alumni-spotlight-chante-bonds, last accessed on July 7, 2023.

60. She Plays, "She Plays Team of the Month," *bostonrenegadesfootball.org*, 11 October 2022, https://www.bostonrenegadesfootball.org/bonds-and-renegades-spotlighted-in-she-plays-womens-sports-magazine/, last accessed on July 7, 2023.

61. Sunday Night Football on NBC, "On Her Turf Presents Football Is Female: Chante Bonds," *facebook.com*, 18 October 2018, https://www.facebook.com/watch/?v=1901936199904198, last accessed on July 7, 2023.

62. Kat Hasenauer Cornetta, "Boston Renegades Again the Best in Women's Football, Win Fourth Straight Championship," *bostonglobe.com*, 10 July 2022, https://www.bostonglobe.com/2022/07/10/sports/boston-renegades-again-best-womens-football-win-fourth-straight-championship/, last accessed on July 7, 2023, para. 1.

63. Boston Renegades, "Player Information: Chante Bonds, #21," *bostonren-egadesfootball.org*, 2023, https://www.bostonrenegadesfootball.org/player/bonds-chante/, last accessed July 7, 2023.

64. Berger, "U.S. National Team Alumni."

65. Aryanna Prasad, "Adrienne Smith is Chasing Excellence and Equality," *fansided.com*, 15 August 2022, https://fansided.com/2022/08/15/adrienne-smith-boston-renegades-nfl-allies/, last accessed on July 8, 2023; Female First, "Boston Ren-egades' Adrienne Smith Talks about Breaking the Women's Football Alliance All-Time Record," *femalefirst.co.uk*, 9 June 2022, https://www.femalefirst.co.uk/features/boston-renegades-adrienne-smith-breaks-football-alliance-record-1354830.html, last accessed on July 7, 2023.

66. Taylor Kujawa, "Adrienne Smith: The Rise of Women's GridIron Football (Part One)," *herfootballhub.com*, 10 February 2022, https://herfootballhub.com/adrienne-smith-and-the-rise-of-womens-gridiron-football-part-one/, last accessed July 7, 2023.

67. Jiji Ugboma, "Adrienne Smith, The 5-Time WFA Champion and Harlem Hip-Hop Tours Founder, Eyes Empowerment for Women in Sports and Business," *vibe.com*, 12 July 2022, https://www.vibe.com/features/digital-covers/adrienne-smith-wfa-football-champion-empowers-women-1234676699/, last accessed on July 7, 2023, para. 5.

68. ibid.

69. Aaron Rottenberg, "Adrienne Smith, a 5-Time WFA Champion and Harlem Hip-Hop Tours Founder, Eyes Empowerment for Women in Sports and Business," *list23.com*, 12 July 2022, https://list23.com/961061-adrienne-smith-a-5-time-wfa-champion-and-founder-of-harlem-hip-hop-tours-believes-in-women-s-empower/, last accessed on July 7, 2023; Boston Renegades, "Player Information: Adrienne Smith, #10," *bostonrenegadesfootball.org*, 2023, https://www.bostonrenegadesfootball.org/player/smith-adrienne/, last accessed on July 8, 2023.

70. Senita Brooks, "Adrienne Smith is Leading the Way for Women in Football: The Boston Renegades's Star Wide Receiver is a Tireless Advocate for Her Sport, Committed to Creating Awareness and Tackling Existing Stereotypes," *si.com*, 2 June 2022, https://www.si.com/more-sports/2022/06/02/adrienne-smith-boston-renegades-womens-football, last accessed on July 8, 2023.

71. Prasad, "Adrienne Smith Is Chasing"; Mark Simon, "Smith Breaks WFA All-Time Receiving Yards Record," *bostonrenegadesfootball.org*, 24 May 2022, https://www.bostonrenegadesfootball.org/smith-breaks-wfa-all-time-receiving-yards-record/, last accessed on July 7, 2023.

72. Joyce Bassett, "All In-Column: Athlete, Actress Adrienne Smith the Face of Women in Football," *timesunion.com*, 6 June 2021, https://www.timesunion.com/sports/article/Athlete-actress-Adrienne-Smith-the-face-of-women-16228329.php, last accessed on July 7, 2023; Ugboma, "Adrienne Smith."

73. Mark Simon, "Adrienne Smith Head Up American Flag Football League's New Women's Division," *bostonrenegadesfootball.org*, 22 March 2021, https://www.bostonrenegadesfootball.org/adrienne-smith-heads-up-american-flag-football-leagues-new-womens-division/, last accessed July 7, 2023.

74. Ugboma, "Adrienne Smith."

75. Boston Renegades, "Player Information: Whitney Zelee, #33," *bostonrenegadesfootball.org*, 2023, https://www.bostonrenegadesfootball.org/player/zelee-whitney/, last accessed July 8, 2023.

76. "Whitney Zelee: Chief Administrative Officer," *trilliuminvest.com*, 2023, https://www.trilliuminvest.com/team/whitney-zelee, last accessed July 8, 2023.

77. Mark, Staffieri, "Whitney Zelee Emerging as the Finest Running Back in All of Women's Football," *bleacherreport.com*, 18 June 2013, https://bleacherreport.com/articles/1675886-whitney-zelee-emerging-as-the-finest-running-back-in-all-of-womens-football, last accessed on July 8, 2023; Russ Crawford, "Whitney Zelee (Football)," *ussporthistory.com*, 2 November 2017, https://ussporthistory.com/2017/11/02/top-ten-historically-significant-women-athletes-part-i/, last accessed July 8, 2023.

78. Neal Rozendaal, "The Greatest Players in Women's Football History: Part 3," *nealrozendaal.com*, 2017, https://nealrozendaal.com/womensfootball/greatest-players-history-2017-part-3/, last accessed on July 8, 2023, para. 24.

79. Hannah Lichtenstein, "Loving and Leaving the Grind of Being a Football Player with Whitney Zelee," 11 February 2021, *Run Along*, podcast, MP3 audio, 21:45, https://www.podbean.com/pu/pbblog-fhr8r-4447d1.

80. Boston Renegades, "Player Information, Whitney Zelee."

81. Lichtenstein, "Loving and Leaving."

82. Boston Renegades, "Schedule (2023)," *bostonrenegadesfootball.org*, 2023, https://www.bostonrenegadesfootball.org/schedule-2023/, last accessed on July 8, 2023.

BIBLIOGRAPHY

"Aliyah Boston," *espn.com*, 2023, https://www.espn.com/high-school/girls-basketball/recruiting/player/_/id/224799/aliyah-boston.

Anderson, Kristen. "Kings' Scout Blake Bolden Happy to Play the Role of Trailblazer," *thehockeynews.com*, 8 March 2021.

Banker, George. "Resilience, Grit, Determination Define Sika Henry," *runnersgazette.com*, 22 February 2022, https://runnersgazette.com/2022/02/22/resilience-grit-determination-define-sika-henry/.

Bansal, Puneet, and Nathan Lesch. "Bianca Smith: From the Spartans to the Red Sox," *observer.case.edu*, 5 February 2021, https://observer.case.edu/bianca-smith-from-the-spartans-to-the-red-sox/.

Bassett, Joyce. "All In-Column: Athlete, Actress Adrienne Smith the Face of Women in Football," *timesunion.com*, 6 June 2021, https://www.timesunion.com/sports/article/Athlete-actress-Adrienne-Smith-the-face-of-women-16228329.php.

Berger, Endia. "U.S. National Team Alumni Spotlight: Chanté Bonds," *blogs.usafootball.com*, 16 December 2022, https://blogs.usafootball.com/blog/8508/u-s-national-team-alumni-spotlight-chante-bonds.

Bird, Hayden. "Boston Renegades Win Fourth Straight Title, Backup Quarterback Named MVP: It's the Seventh Championship in Team History," *boston.com*, 11 July 2022, https://www.boston.com/sports/morning-sports-update/2022/07/11/boston-renegades-football-championship-win/.

"Boston Renegades' Adrienne Smith Talks about Breaking the Women's Football Alliance All-Time Record," *femalefirst.co.uk*, 9 June 2022, https://www.femalefirst.co.uk/features/boston-renegades-adrienne-smith-breaks-football-alliance-record-1354830.html.

Brooks, Senita. "Adrienne Smith is Leading the Way for Women in Football: The Boston Renegades's Star Wide Receiver is a Tireless Advocate for Her Sport, Committed to Creating Awareness and Tackling Existing Stereotypes," *si.com*, 2 June 2022, https://www.si.com/more-sports/2022/06/02/adrienne-smith-boston-renegades-womens-football.

Burka, Allison Torres. "Sika Henry," *startingline1928.com*, 22 June 2023, https://www.startingline1928.com/pioneerstories.

Campbell, Lauren. "Aliyah Boston Named to WNBA All-Star Game; First Rookie Starter Since 2014," *masslive.com*, 25 June 2023, https://www.masslive.com/sports/2023/06/aliyah-boston-named-to-wnba-all-star-game-first-rookie-starter-since-2014.html.

Cornetta, Kat Hasenauer. "Boston Renegades Again the Best in Women's Football, Win Fourth Straight Championship," *bostonglobe.com*, 10 July 2022, https://www

.bostonglobe.com/2022/07/10/sports/boston-renegades-again-best-womens-football-win-fourth-straight-championship/.

Costabile, Annie. "Fever Rookie Aliyah Boston is Making WNBA History," *chicago.suntimes.com*, 15 June 2023, https://chicago.suntimes.com/chicago-sky-and-wnba/2023/6/15/23762647/fever-rookie-aliyah-boston-making-wnba-history.

Crawford, Russ. "Whitney Zelee (Football)," *ussporthistory.com*, 2 November 2017, https://ussporthistory.com/2017/11/02/top-ten-historically-significant-women-athletes-part-i/.

Frank, Adrienne. "Blazing a New Trail to the Ballpark: CWRU Provided a Springboard for Alumna Bianca Smith's Pioneering Move to Coaching Professional Baseball," *case.edu*, Spring 2021, https://case.edu/think/spring2021/blazing-new-trail.html.

Greg Joyce, "Derek Jeter Finally Inducted into Baseball Hall of Fame: 'Heartbeat of a Yankees Dynasty," *nypost.com*, 8 September 2021, https://nypost.com/2021/09/08/yankees-derek-jeter-inducted-into-baseball-hall-of-fame/#.

Harve, Maithri. "'I Want to Go to BC, I Want to Help Change a Program': An Interview with BC WIH Alum Blake Bolden," *bcinterruption.com*, 11 May 2021. https://www.bcinterruption.com/2021/5/11/22427671/i-want-to-go-to-bc-i-want-to-help-change-a-program-an-interview-with-bc-wih-alum-blake-bolden.

Henry, Sika. "Why Am I Not Getting Any Faster," *why-i-run.blogsport.com*, 24 July 2012, http://why-i-run.blogspot.com/2012/07/.

Horner, Scott. "LIVE: Indiana Fever Pick Aliyah Boston, Grace Berger in WNBA Draft," *indystar.com*, 10 April 2023, https://www.indystar.com/story/sports/basketball/wnba/fever/2023/04/10/wnba-draft-2023-indiana-fever-have-the-no-1-overall-pick-aliyah-boston/70098520007/.

Ian Browne, "Red Sox Hire Smith, First Black Female Coach," *mlb.com*, 5 January 2021, https://www.mlb.com/news/red-sox-hire-bianca-smith-first-black-female-baseball-coach.

Jean-Marie, Bryna. "Blake Bolden Continues to Break the Ice," 4 November 2021, *si.com*, https://www.si.com/nhl/2021/11/04/los-angeles-kings-blake-bolden-100-influential-black-women.

Kujawa, Taylor. "Adrienne Smith: The Rise of Women's GridIron Football (Part One)," *herfootballhub.com*, 10 February 2022, https://herfootballhub.com/adrienne-smith-and-the-rise-of-womens-gridiron-football-part-one/.

Larkin, Matt. "Blake Bolden Q&A: On Mentoring Women and the Secret to Scouting," *thehockeynews.com*, 31 January 2021, https://thehockeynews.com/news/blake-bolden-q-a-on-mentoring-women-and-the-secret-to-scouting.

Levinsky, Greg. "How Worcester Played an Important Role in Aliyah Boston's Path to Women's Basketball Stardom," 31 December 2021, *bostonglobe.com*, https://www.bostonglobe.com/2021/12/31/sports/how-worcester-played-an-important-role-aliyah-bostons-path-womens-basketball-stardom/.

Lewis, Niamh. "Sika Henry: USA's First Black Female Pro Triathlete on How Community Support After Horror Accident Stopped Her from Quitting," *espn.com*, 5 October 2021, https://www.espn.com/olympics/triathlon/story/_/id/31597228/usa-first-black-female-pro-triathlete-how-community-support-horror-accident-stopped-quitting.

Lichtenstein, Hannah. "Loving and Leaving the Grind of Being a Football Player with Whitney Zelee," 11 February 2021, *Run Along*, podcast, MP3 audio, 21:45, https://www.podbean.com/pu/pbblog-fhr8r-4447d1.

Macur, Juliet. "If Mom Could See Her Now," *nytimes.com*, 3 March 2021, https://www.nytimes.com/2021/03/03/sports/baseball/bianca-smith-red.html.

McKenszie, Julian. "Blake Bolden Discusses EmBolden Her, a 6-Month Mentorship Program for Aspiring Female Hockey Players," *theathletic.com*, 3 November 2021, https://theathletic.com/2908772/2021/11/03/blake-bolden-discusses-embolden-her-a-6-month-mentorship-program-for-aspiring-female-hockey-players/.

McWilliams, Julian. "Red Sox Hiring Bianca Smith as Minor League Coach, Making Her First Black Woman to Coach in Pro Baseball History," *boston.com*, 5 January 2021, https://www.boston.com/sports/boston-red-sox/2021/01/04/red-sox-bianca-smith/.

Mena, Diego Jesus Bartesaghi. "Montclair Native Sika Henry Is First U.S.'s First Pro Black Female Triathlete," *montclairlocal.new*, 7 June 2021, https://montclairlocal.news/montclair-native-sika-henry-is-first-u-s-s-first-pro-black-female-triathlete/.

Philippou, Alexa. "South Carolina Star Aliyah Boston Declares for WNBA Draft," *espn.com*, 1 April 2023, https://www.espn.com/womens-college-basketball/story/_/id/36031545/south-carolina-star-aliyah-boston-declares-wnba-draft.

Prasad, Aryanna. "Adrienne Smith is Chasing Excellence and Equality," *fansided.com*, 15 August 2022, https://fansided.com/2022/08/15/adrienne-smith-boston-renegades-nfl-allies/.

Procter, Scott. "Blake Bolden Helping Cultivate Next Generation of Diverse Hockey Stars," *bvmsports.com*, 25 February 2022, https://bvmsports.com/2022/02/25/blake-bolden-helping-cultivate-next-generation-of-diverse-hockey-stars/.

Rottenberg, Aaron. "Adrienne Smith, a 5-Time WFA Champion and Harlem Hip-Hop Tours Founder, Eyes Empowerment for Women in Sports and Business," *list23.com*, 12 July 2022, https://list23.com/961061-adrienne-smith-a-5-time-wfa-champion-and-founder-of-harlem-hip-hop-tours-believes-in-women-s-empower/.

Rozendaal, Neal. "The Greatest Players in Women's Football History: Part 3," *nealrozendaal.com*, 2017, https://nealrozendaal.com/womensfootball/greatest-players-history-2017-part-3/.

Schwartz, Jeff, and Brian Alden. "Corey Kispert of Gonzaga, Aliyah Boston of South Carolina Lead Academic All-American® Division I Men's & Women's Basketball Teams," *academicallamerica.com*, 28 March 2021, https://academicallamerica.com/documents/2021/5/28//2020_21_DI_Basketball_AAA.pdf?id=3177.

"She Plays Team of the Month," *bostonrenegadesfootball.org*, 11 October 2022, https://www.bostonrenegadesfootball.org/bonds-and-renegades-spotlighted-in-she-plays-womens-sports-magazine/.

Simon, Mark, "Adrienne Smith Head Up American Flag Football League's New Women's Division," *bostonrenegadesfootball.org*, 22 March 2021, https://www.bostonrenegadesfootball.org/adrienne-smith-heads-up-american-flag-football-leagues-new-womens-division/.

Simpson, Hunter. "Aliyah Boston Reflects on Upbringing in USVI and Encouraging Young Female Athletes," *stthomassource.com*, 25 June 2022, https://stthomassource

.com/content/2022/06/25/aliyah-boston-reflects-on-upbringing-in-usvi-and-encouraging-young-female-athletes/.

Speier, Alex. "Bianca Smith, the First Black Woman Hired as a Coach by an MLB Team, Leaves Red Sox Organization," *msn.com*, 27 January 2023, https://www.msn.com/en-us/sports/mlb/bianca-smith-the-first-black-woman-hired-as-a-coach-by-an-mlb-team-leaves-red-sox-organization/ar-AA16OIKc.

Springer, Shira. "For Renegades, a Name Change and a Mission to Keep Dynasty Alive," *bostonglobe.com*, 7 February 2015, https://www.bostonglobe.com/sports/2015/02/07/local-women-tackle-difficult-task-keeping-their-football-dynasty-alive/pFrPziOI2T58f86sAwamdL/story.html.

Staffieri, Mark. "Whitney Zelee Emerging as the Finest Running Back in All of Women's Football," *bleacherreport.com*, 18 June 2013, https://bleacherreport.com/articles/1675886-whitney-zelee-emerging-as-the-finest-running-back-in-all-of-womens-football.

Sullivan, Tara. "'There is No Ceiling for Her': South Carolina's Aliyah Boston, Who Grew Up in Mass., Is the Face of Women's College Basketball," *bostonglobe.com*, 10 February, 2023, https://www.bostonglobe.com/2023/02/10/sports/aliyah-boston-south-carolina/.

Thames, Alanis. "'I Can't Just Quit': Sika Henry is the First African American Woman to Be Recognized as a Pro Triathlete. But a Horrible Bicycle Crash in 2019 Nearly Thwarted Her Dream," *nytimes.com*, 23 November 2021, https://www.nytimes.com/2021/11/23/sports/sika-henry-triathlon.html.

The Sports Museum, "Boston vs. Bullies All-Star: Chante Bonds," *sportsmuseum.org*, 2023, https://www.sportsmuseum.org/boston-vs-bullies/about-us/all-stars/chante-bonds/.

Ugboma, Jiji. "Adrienne Smith, The 5-Time WFA Champion and Harlem Hip-Hop Tours Founder, Eyes Empowerment for Women in Sports and Business," *vibe.com*, 12 July 2022, https://www.vibe.com/features/digital-covers/adrienne-smith-wfa-football-champion-empowers-women-1234676699/.

United States Census Bureau, "Quick Facts: Stow City, Ohio; United States, *census.gov*, 2022, https://www.census.gov/quickfacts/fact/table/stowcityohio,US/PST045222.

Villa, Walter. "Where Will Aliyah Boston Take Her Two Gold Medals Next?," *espn.com*, 27 September 2018, https://www.espn.com/espnw/sports/story/_/id/24811694/elite-prospect-aliyah-boston-strikes-gold-usa-basketball-leaving-paradise-behind#.

Walter Villa, "No. 3 Prospect Aliyah Boston Joins the Talented Crowd Headed to South Carolina," *espn.com*, 21 November 2018, https://www.espn.com/espnw/sports/story/_/id/25331760/no-3-prospect-aliyah-boston-joins-talented-crowd-heading-dawn-staley-south-carolina-gamecocks.

Wright, Branson. "Kings Scout Blake Bolden Want to Inspire the Next Wave of Black Women in Hockey," *andscape.com*, 25 April 2022, https://andscape.com/features/kings-scout-blake-bolden-wants-to-inspire-the-next-wave-of-black-women-in-hockey/.

"Whitney Zelee: Chief Administrative Officer," *trilliuminvest.com*, 2023, https://www.trilliuminvest.com/team/whitney-zelee.

Wright, Branson. "Red Sox Coach Bianca Smith Has Spent Career Proving She Belongs," *andscape.com*, 12 January 2021, https://andscape.com/features/red-sox-coach-bianca-smith-has-spent-her-career-proving-she-belongs/.

Index

Aaron, Hank, 103, 162
Adventures of Huckleberry Finn (Twain), 41
AFFL. *See* American Flag Football League
African Methodist Episcopal Church (AME Church): Charles Street, 56–57; founding of, 9
Albion Cycle Club, 91–93
Ali, Muhammad, 103
"All Coons Look Alike to Me," 97
All Indian Rodeo Cowboys Association, 201
Almy, "Doc," 80
Alvarado, Luis, *165*
AME Church. *See* African Methodist Episcopal Church
American Academy of Dental Science, 40
American Daughter (Thompson, E. B.), 200
An American Dilemma (Myrdal), 160–61
American Flag Football League (AFFL), 263–64

The American Game (Baldassaro & Johnson), 162

American Medical College (Philadelphia), 36
American Revolution, 3
American Soccer League (ASL), 214, 215
American West: as imagined fiction, 196–99; tropes, 202–3; Wister's revisionism of, 199. *See also* Manifest Destiny
Anderson, Robert, 101
Anderson Street Church, 9
Annual Women's Indoor Track and Field Championships 1934, 112
anti-draft riots, 53
anti-Irish prejudice, 37
Aparicio, Luis, *165–66*
Aponte, Luis, *166–67*
Aquatic Club of Georgia, 4; establishment of, 3
Arden, Alice, 112
Armaindo, Louise, 69n34
Armas, Tony, *167*
Arria, Tom, 245
A.S.C., 55
Ashe, Arthur, 102, 103
ASL. *See* American Soccer League
assimilation, 65
Attucks, Crispus, 53, 67n8
Austin, Sam, 80

278 *Index*

Avila, Bobby, *164*
Aviles, Ramon, *166*
Azcue, Joe, *165*

Babcock, J. C., 16
Backus, Amy, 260
Bahati, Rahsaan, 103
Bahr, Walter, 216
Bailey, Frances B., 37
Balakov, Krassimir, 225
Bald, Eddie, 94
Baldassaro, Lawrence, 162
Baltimore Afro-American, 41, 101, 182
Banneker, Benjamin, 40
Barbosa, Helio, 221, *222*; Pickett, D.,
    on, 222–23
Barnes, S. W., 22n5
basketball, 256–57; gender myths,
    234; popularity of, 215; women's
    rules, 234
Baumgartner, Erin, 261
Bavasi, Buzzy, 183
Baylor, Don, *167*
Bay State Golf Association, 44
Bearings, 57–58
Beasley, DaMarcus, 226–27
Becker, William, 96
Bene, 55
Benevolent Fraternity of Coachmen's
    ball, 55
Beniquez, Juan, *165–66*
Berry, Robert, 11
Bertos, John, 222–23; Brazilians
    recruited by, 221
Bicycle Racing Stars of the Nineteenth
    Century, 100
The Biglin Brothers Turning the Stake
    (Eakins), 2
Bill Pickett Invitational Rodeo Circuit
    (BPIR), 201, 207
Binghamton (NY) Daily Times, 5
Blackburn, Jack, 78
Black Christian Church, 43
Black cowboys, 199; Pearson on, 205–
    6. *See also Specific Black cowboys*

Black cyclists: Boston Wheelman ban,
    60; Company L, 55; Elliott on, 66;
    Handy on, 60; LAW ban, 56–57, 91;
    Riverside Cycle Club, 56. *See also
    Specific Black cyclists*
Black Eagles, 130
Black soccer players, 218–20. *See also
    Specific Black soccer players*
"Black *vs.* White" race, 63
Blitz Champz, 263
Bluestone, Barry, 147
Bolden, Blake: advocacy of, 255; career
    of, 254–55; early life of, 254
Bonds, Chanté, 259, 262;
    accomplishments of, *262*, 263
Booth, Clark, 117
Bosman, Jean-Marc, 220
Bosman Ruling, 220
Boston, Aliyah: achievements of,
    257; early life of, 256; high school
    ranking of, 256
Boston Against Busing (Formisano), 147
Boston Astros, 221, *222*; folding of, 223
Boston Common, access to, 37, 145
Boston Confronts Jim Crow
    (Schneider), 66
Boston Evening Transcript, 2
Boston Globe: on Franklin Park, 44; on
    Grant, G. F., 41; on Johnson, F., 12,
    18–20
Boston Journal, 60, 62
Boston Massacre, 53, 67n8
Boston Music Hall, 12
Boston Post: on Knox, K., 61, 63; on
    Taylor, M., 95
Boston Pursuit team, 61
Boston Renegades, 261–64
Boston *vs.* Philadelphia race, 95
Boston Wheelmen Club, 60
Boyd, Dennis, *166–67*
The Boy in Blue (film), 21
BPIR. *See* Bill Pickett Invitational
    Rodeo Circuit
Bradley, Alvin, 180
Braga Martes, Ana Christina, 220

Index 279

Bramwell, Bud, 206
Braves, 148–49; Jethroe debut, 179, 183–84
Bray, Henry T., 72n86
Brazilian immigrants, 220–21; Bertos recruiting, 221
Breaking Away (film), 104
Bressoud, Eddie, 153
British Heavyweight Championship, 81
Brock, Sam, 94
Brookhattan Galicia, 218
Brookline Country Club, 39
Brooklyn Daily Eagle, 94
Brown, Burt, 11
Brown, Walter: Camp on, 16; sliding seat invented by, 15–17
Brown v. Board of Education, 141
Brunvand, Jan, 139
Bryant, Howard, 141, 156–57; on Green, 142–43, 163–64
Buckner, Bill, 159
Buddin, Dan, 152, 153
bulldogging, 201
Bunk, Brian, 218
Bureau of Refugees, Freedmen, and Abandoned Lands, 6–7
Burks, Ellis, 158, *167*
Burns, Tommy, 79–80
Burr, Aaron, 3
Burrell, Martha, 79
Butler, Benjamin, 7
Butler, Frank, 92, 95
Butler, Jay, 45
Butler, Nat, 61, 63, 95
Butler, Ned, 92
Butler, Tom "T.C.," 10, 96–97

Cage, Nicholas, 21
Calumet Cycle Club, 93–94
Camp, Walter, 16
Campanis, Al, 162
Campbell, Joseph, 142
Canadian Indian Finals Rodeo (CIFR), 201
Carew, Mary, 110

Carrey, Sean, 224
CCC. *See* Consolidated Cycling Clubs of Boston
census records: on Johnson, F., 8–9; on Knox, K., 53; Mulatto category, 67n4; slavery and, 5; on Watts, 8
Century Road Club of America (CRCofA), 60; Percival on, 61
Cepeda, Orlando, *166*
Cerqueira, Luis, 224
Chandler, Ned, 103
Charles Street AME Church, 56; Douglass and, 57; Garrison and, 57; Truth and, 57
Chautauqua Lake Fizzle: anticipation for, 14; calling off, 14; *Cincinnati Daily Gazette* on, 19–20; Johnson, F., on, 14; *New York Herald* on, 15; parody of, 20; prize money at, 13; *Rochester Democrat and Chronicle* on, 13–14; rowing profession ended by, 15
cholera, 8
Christian, Robin, 240–41
Christopher, Joe, *165*
CIFR. *See* Canadian Indian Finals Rodeo
Cincinnati Daily Gazette, 19–20
Civil Rights Act, 90
Civil War, 6, 19; Fort Monroe history museum of, 7
Claflin, Larry, 151, 156
Claxton, Tracy, 241–43
Claypoole, Elizabeth, 22n14
cleft palate, 37
Cleveland Museum of Art, 22n5
Coachman, Alice, 109
Cobb, Ty, 144
Cohan, George M., 97
Coker, Daniel, 40
Collins, Bud, 151
Collins, George, 214
Colored Heavyweight Champion, 81
Colored National League, 57
Colored Women's Bowling League, 113

The Coming Woman, 72n86

Committee on Fair Employment Practice, 141

Commonwealth (VA) vs. Frenchy Johnson (colored), 7–8

Company L, Sixth Massachusetts Volunteer Militia, 55

competitive shooting: Johnson, F., and, 18–19; targets, 18; traps, 18

Compton Cowboys, 207

Conley, Gene, 153

Connerton, Paul, 195

Consolidated Cycling Clubs of Boston (CCC), 57

consumption. *See* tuberculosis

contrast, 65

Cooper, Cecil, *165–66*

Cote, Joe, 100, 103

Courtney, Charles: on Johnson, F., 10; *New York Herald* on, 13; on sliding seat, 17

Crawford, Carl, 163

CRCofA. *See* Century Road Club of America

Crisis, 43

Crystal Lake Park, 93

Cuffee, Paul, 40

Cullen, Countee, 43

cultural memory, 195

Currie & Ives, 20

cycling craze, 55–56; end of, 63

cycling season 1895, 57–59

Darktown Comic Series, 20

Darwin, Bobby, *166*

Davis, Piper, 150

Deadwood Dick, 201

Dedham Cycle Club, 92–93

Dell'Apa, Frank, 219

Delmont, Al, 80

Delowry, Michael, 10

Demeter, Don, 156

Dempsey, Jack, 83

Devil's Darning Needle (boat), 4

dialect stereotypes, 29n184; Johnson, F., and, 21

Dickerson, William F., 9

Didrikson, Babe, 111

Dightman, Myrtis, 205–6

distance, 65

Dixon, George, 42

Dixon, Medina: Arria on, 245; college decision of, 240; early life of, 234–38; health problems of, 244–45; international career of, 243–44; investigation into, 238–39

Dobie, Gil, 125

Dobson, Oliver, 68n22

Donovan, Karen Brown, 64

Dorson, Richard, 137

Dottin, Jazz, 65

double consciousness, 53

double-V campaign, 169n13

Douglass, Frederick, 53; Boston arrival of, 54; Charles Street AME Church and, 57

Driscoll, Jeremiah, 2

Du Bois, W. E. B., 38, 55; on double consciousness, 53; on passing, 62; on Reconstruction, 63; on Talented Tenth, 71n85

dugout canoes, 4

Dunn, Jerry, 101

Dunn, Lin, 257

Eakins, Thomas, 2

Earth Day 1970, 101

Easler, Mike, *167*

East-West Classic, 180

Education Amendments Act, Title IX, 233

Eliot, Charles W., 38

Elliott, Sterling, 59; on Black cyclists, 66

Elston, Howard, *165*

Emancipation Proclamation, 3, 6–7

EmBolden Her, 255

Englander, Matthew, 260

erased memory, 194

Index 281

ethnicity, soccer and, 218–20
Ethnicity, Sports, Identity (Ritchie), 64
Evans, Dwight, 158
Ewell, Barney, 183
Ewing, Patrick, 238–40, 243
exceptionalism, soccer and, 214–17

Fairmont Athletic Club, 82
Fall River (MA) Daily Herald, 19
Faulkner, George, 11
Fay, Don, 235
feathering the spruces, 6
Fifty-Fifth Massachusetts Infantry, 53
Fifty-Fourth Massachusetts Infantry, 19, 53
Fizzell, Mildred, 112
Fleischer, Nat, 77, 84
Flood, Curt, 162
folk revival, 171n47
foot stretcher, 15
Forbes, George Washington, 35, 40; on Grant, G. F., 41
Forest and Stream, 11
Forman, Stanley, 157
Formisano, Ronald, 147
Fort Monroe, Virginia, 8; Civil War history museum at, 7; Johnson, F., at, 7
Fort Wagoner, South Carolina, 19
Fourth of July rowing regatta 1878, 1–3
Foy, Joe, *165*
Francis, Herb, 103
Franklin Park, 39; *Boston Globe* on, 44
Fraser, Wilfred R., Sr., 114
Frazee, Harry, 168n9
free agency, 158
Freedmen's Bureau, 6; Johnson, F., and, 7–8; List of Colored Persons Sent North, 8
Frias, Tony, 224
Frommer, Harvey, 154
Fugitive Slave Act of 1850, 53, 145

Gaetjens, Joe, 218–19
Gammons, Peter, 151

Gans, Joe, 78
Garrison, William Lloyd, 53; Charles Street AME Church and, 57
Garrity, W. Arthur, 235
Gates, Henry Louis, Jr., 163
George Appold (ship), 24n59; Johnson on, 8
George Street Bike Challenge for Major Taylor, 102
Gibbs, Mifflin Wistar, 200–201
glass balls, 18
Glory (film), 19
Goddard, William, 71n78
Goddess of Liberty (boat), 4
golf: expansion of, 40; premodern, 37; racist caricatures and, 41–42; White privilege and, 36, 40–41
golf tee: Grant, G. F., inventing, 35, 40–41; Lowell inventing, 41; natural, 40; Nigger Head, 41–42; patents for, 41; Reddy, 41
golliwog pins, 41
Gonzalez, Adrian, 163
Gonzalez, Jimmy, 261
Goodman, Teddy, 94
Goodreault, Gene, 126
Good Roads, 56, 66
Grand Order, 71n76
Grange, Red, 6
Grant, George Franklin: Boston arrival of, 36; *Boston Globe* on, 41; career of, 38–39; clientele of, 38; death of, 40, 43–44; Demonstrator of Mechanical Dentistry promotion of, 37; early life of, 36; family of, 37; Forbes on, 41; golf tee invented by, 35, 40–41; harassment of, 44; Harvard acceptance of, 37; legacy of, 44–45; obituaries of, 40–41; oblate palate prosthetic invented by, 38; parents of, 36; politics of, 42–44; resignation of, 38; salary of, 38; social networks of, 42; *Washington Post* on, 40
Grant, Tudor E., 36

Green, Elijah, 137, *138*; Boston arrival of, 147–48; Bryant on, 142–43, 163–64; debut of, 142; NAACP and, 143; on racism, 154; Red Sox debut of, 143, 152; retirement of, 154; statistics of, 140–41, 152–53
Greenquist, Walter, 100
Gregory, Ann, 44
Grentz, Theresa, 244
Gridiron Queendom, 263
Grimké, Angelina Weld, 43
Grimké, Archibald, 39; NAACP cofounding by, 43; Washington, Booker T., protest of, 42–43
Grimm, Charlie, 185
Gutierrez, Jackie, *167*
gutta percha resin, 40

Hagen, Walter, 41
Hague, William, 81
Hall, A. M., 72n86
Hall, Charles, 60
Halstat, Ida, 60
Handy, William, 63–64; on Black cyclists ban, 60
Hanlan, Edward "Ned," 21; *New York Herald* on, 13
Hannibal Athletic Club, 69n32
Hard Road to Glory (Ashe), 102
Harlem Renaissance, 43
Harper, Tommy, 160, *166*
Harrington, Ethel, 111
Harris, Alfreda, 237
Harrison, Claude, Jr., 183
Hart, Albert Bushnell, 38
Hart, Frank, 11
Harvard Echo, 11
Harvard University: Dental Alumni Association, 38; Department of Mechanical Dentistry, 37; Grant, G. F., accepted into, 37; Odonatological Society, 38; 250th anniversary celebration, 35
Harvard-Yale Boat Race 1852, 4
Hasenfus, Olive, 110, 112

Hatcher, Billy, *167*
Haynes, Klondike, 81
Hedstrom, Oscar, 92
Hemings, Sally, 62
Hendee, George, 92
Hendee Manufacturing Co., 91
Henderson, Dave, *167*
Henning, Harold, 44
Henry, Sika, 259; early life of, 258
Herman, Billy, 156
Hernandez, Ramon, *166*
Heron, Gilles, 219
Higgins, Marguerite, 150
Higgins, Pinky, 150–54
Hill, Frank, 3
Hill, Georgine Russell, 45
Hogan, Eddie, 97
Hogan, Ernest, 71n73
Holmes, Joseph Gardner, 64, 68n22
Holmes, Tommy, 185
Holovak, Mike, 126; on Montgomery, 129
Holyoke Falcons Football Club, 218
Hoo-Doo Cowboys and Bronze Buckaroos (Johnson, M. K.), 200
HoopGurlz Recruiting Rankings, 256
Hopper, Clay, 182
Horn, Sam, *167*
Hosmer, George, 10–11
Hovland, Car, 65
Humphreys, Bill, 101
Hunter tandem bicycle, 70n62
Hurst, Frederick, 159
"Hushed by the Hands of Sleep" (Grimké, A. W.), 43

ice hockey, 254–55
identity creation, 205
IHL. *See* International Hockey League
Improvement in Seats for Row Boats patent, 15–17
Indiana Fever, 257
Indianapolis Freeman, 51–52, 63
Indian National Finals Rodeo (INFR), 201

Index

283

Instruction and Hints on Rowing, 22n5
International Hockey League (IHL), 254
International Order of Odd Fellows, 71n76
interracial marriage, legalizing, 53
Irvington-Milburn race, 93
Isham, John, 62–63
Isham's Octoroons, 62–63
Iver Johnson Arms and Cycle Works, 91

Jackie Robinson Day, 137, 140
Jackson, Charles H., 42
James Michael Curley Cup, 110
James Robertson and Sons, 41
Jarvis, Mike, 237
Jeanette, Joe, 83; Langford fighting, 79; retirement of, 84
Jefferson, Thomas, 62
Jenkins, Ferguson, *166*
Jeter, Derek, 259
Jethroe, Sam, 141, 146, 148–49; Braves debut, 179, 183–84; contract of, 183; early life of, 179–80; first impressions of, 183–84; Harrison on, 183; Hopper on, 182; lawsuit of, 186–88; retirement of, 186; Rookie of the Year honor, 184–85
job discrimination, 37
Johnny Baseball, 163
Johnson, Frenchy: acclaim for, 3, 11; as America's First Black Sports Star, 21; arrest of, 8; bear shot by, 18; *Binghamton (NY)Daily Times* on, 5; birth of, 6; Boston arrival of, 8–9; *Boston Evening Transcript* on, 2; *Boston Globe* on, 12, 18–20; census records on, 8–9; on Chautauqua Lake Fizzle, 14; *Cincinnati Daily Gazette* on, 19–20; competitive shooting career of, 18–19; conduct of, 12; Courtney on, 10; death of, 20; dialect stereotypes and, 21; first race of, 10; *Forest and Stream* on, 11; at Fort Monroe, 7; on fouling, 3; Freedmen's Bureau report on, 7–8; on *George*

Appold, 8; *Harvard Echo* on, 11; last interview with, 19–20; last race of, 17–19; legacy of, 20–21; name origin of, 5; *New York Times* on, 12; nicknames for, 6; obituary for, 20; occupation of, 9; physical description of, 11; popularity of, 12–13; racist caricatures of, 20; respect for, 21; Rickords' marriage to, 9; Ross, W., fighting, 17; rowing career of, 10–11; in Shaw Guards, 18–19; sickness of, 17–19; on slavery, 4–5; in volunteer militia, 18–19
Johnson, Jack, 75–77, 103; Burns fighting, 79–80; Langford fighting, 79; Mann Act violation of, 83
Johnson, Michael K., 200
Johnson, Richard, 162
Joiner, Florence Griffith, 109
Joyner-Kersee, Jackie, 109
Jurges, Billy, 153

Kaese, Harold, 152
Kemble, Edward, 41
Kennedy family, 44
Keogh, Harry, 218
Kerr, George, 122, 125
Ketchel, Stanley, 75, 77; murder of, 76, 82
Kilpatrick, David, 214–15
Kilrain, Jake: boxing career of, 12–13; racing career of, 12
Kirkwood, Joe, 41
Kittie Knox Days, 64
Knox, John H., 52; Boston arrival of, 53–54; death of, 67n9
Knox, Kittie, 91; acclaim for, 61–62; background of, 51–53; birth of, 54; *Boston Journal* on, 60, 62; *Boston Post* on, 61, 63; Boston return of, 59–61; census records on, 53; death of, 64, 71n78; father of, 52–53; *Indianapolis Freeman* on, 51–52, 63; League of American Wheelmen and, *52*, 56–59; legacy of, 64–65;

284   *Index*

mother of, 53; Mulatto label of, 53; *New York Times* on, 58; as pacesetter, 60; *Salem Gazette* on, 61–62; social dances attended by, 55–56, 59, 61, 63–64; *Southern Cycler* on, 51, 58; *Worcester Spy* on, 60
Kountze, Mabray, 143, 151

L39ion of Los Angeles, 103
Labor Day *Boston Herald* Bicycle Parade, 62
Lacy, Sam, 144, 182
Lady Monarchs, 241–43
Landsmark, Ted, 157
Lane, George, 2
Lang, Bill, 82
Langford, Sam, 42; in Australia, 83; background of, 77–78; Boston arrival of, 77; as Colored Heavyweight Champion, 81; death of, 85; first heavyweight fight, 79; Fleischer on, 77, 84; Gans fighting, 78; Hague fighting, 81; Haynes fighting, 81; Jeanette fighting, 79; Johnson, J., fighting, 79; Lang fighting, 82; Lumley on, 78; marriage of, 79; McVea fighting, 82, 84; in Mexico, 84; nickname for, 76, 78; rediscovery of, 85; reputation of, 78; Smith, James, fighting, 80; Thorne fighting, 80; vision restoration of, 84; Walcott fighting, 78; worst performance of, 75–77
Lanouette, William, 22n13
LASA. *See* Luso American Soccer Association
LAW. *See* League of American Wheelmen
League Ball, 59
League of American Bicyclists, 64
League of American Wheelmen (LAW), 51; Black membership ban, 56–57, 91; Knox, K., and, 52, 56–59; on women's racing, 58
Leahy, Frank, 125–28

Leao, Wagner, 221, 223
Lee, Howard, 39
The Legacy of Slavery at Harvard, 38
legends, 139, 168n2
leisure, 37; racist caricatures and, 42
Lenox Athletic Club, 77
Levin, Sherry, 256
Lewis, William Henry, 42, 44
The Life and Adventures of Nat Love (Deadwood Dick), 201
Lincoln, Abraham, 6–7
Lincoln University, 9
Lomax, John A., 197
Lonborg, Jim, 156
Lone Ranger, 203
Louis, Joe, 6
Lowell, William, 41
Lower Creek Boat Club, 4
Loyalist Canadian settlements, 77
Lucchino, Larry, 140, 155
Lumley, Arthur, 78
Luso American Soccer Association (LASA), 226; attendance for, 224; earnings from, 224–25; founding of, 223; fundraising for, 224
Lynch, Michael, 2
Lynn, Fred, 158
Lynn Central Sportsmen's Club, 18

Madeira, Pansy, 110
Madison, James, 3
Madison Square Garden, 84, 94
Major Knox Adventures, 65
Major League Soccer (MLS), 217
Major Motion, 101–2
Major Taylor Association, 102
Major Taylor Cycling Club, 102
Major Taylor Velodrome, 102
Manifest Destiny, 195; as imagined fiction, 196–99
Mann Act, 83
Mantilla, Felix, *164*
Manzanillo, Josiah, *167*
March Madness, 233
marginal adaptation, 148

Index 285

Margolis, Maxine, 220
Marichal, Juan, *166*
Markovits, Andrei, 215
Martin, Oliver, 103
Massachusetts Classic, 44
Massachusetts House of
  Representatives, 37
Massasoit, 67n6
Massasoit Guard, 53
Mass-Bike, 64, 65
Massie, Giddeon, 103
Mauch, Gene, 151
Mays, Willie, 150
McDermott, Monica, 159
McDonough, Will, 149
McDuffee, Eddie, 63, 95, 97
McFarland, Floyd, 95
McGlothen, Lynn, *166*
McIntosh, High D., 82–83
McLaughlin, Sean, 187
McQuillan, J., 80
McVea, Sam, 83; death of, 84; Langford
  fighting, 82, 84
Mearls, Katherine, 110
Mejias, Roman, *164*
Merchants and Miners Transportation
  Co., 24n59
Metcalfe, Ralph, 100
Miletsky, Zebulon, 146
Mladenov, Stoitcho, 225
MLS. *See* Major League Soccer
Montgomery, Lou, *118*; Booth on, 117;
  family of, 117; final high school
  game of, 121; Holovak on, 129;
  O'Rourke on, 129; retirement of,
  130–31; Roberts on, 121; tributes
  to, 132
Morehouse, Henry Lyman, 71n85
Morehouse College, 71n85
Moret, Roger, *165–66*
Morris, Abe, 204
Morris, Evan, 2
Morris, Robert, 37
Moses, Edwin, 103
Mott, Albert, 97

Mount Auburn Cemetery, 64
Muchnick, Isadore, 180
Mulatto category, 53, 67
Munger, Louis, 89
Munz, F. A., 94
Murphy, Isaac, 3
Murrow, Edward R., 150
Myrdal, Gunnar, 160–61

NAACP. *See* National Association for
  the Advancement of Colored People
Nagano Winter Olympics, 252
NASL. *See* North American Soccer
  League
National Association for the
  Advancement of Colored People
  (NAACP), 39; Green and, 143;
  Grimké, Archibald, cofounding, 43
National Athletic Club Philadelphia, 82
National Conference of Colored Women
  of America, 57
National Cycling Association, 98
National Negro Business League, 43
nativism, soccer and, 214–17
NBA draft, 234
Negro Election Day, 37
Negro National Bowlers Association
  (NNBA), 113
New England Cycling Coalition for
  Diversity, 64
New England Tea Men, 221
New Era Club, 57
new journalism, 150–51
New York Clipper, 20
New York Herald: on Chautauqua Lake
  Fizzle, 15; on Courtney, 13; on
  Hanlan, 13; on sliding seat, 16
New York Times: on, Johnson, F., 12; on,
  Knox, K., 58
Nigger Head golf tee, 41–42
NNBA. *See* Negro National Bowlers
  Association
North American Soccer League
  (NASL), 217

Oak Bluffs on Martha's Vineyard, 44
Oakhurst Links, 39
Oakland Oaks, 142
oars, 2
oblate palate prosthetic, 38
O'Callaghan, JoAnn, 235
O'Connell, Danny, 186
Oglivie, Ben, *165–66*
Okmulgee Invitational, 201
O'Malley, Sean Patrick, 223–24
O'Neil, Peter, 159
Opportunity, 43
Oregon racial bans, 201
Orient cycles, 91
O'Rourke, Charlie, 126; on
    Montgomery, 129
Ortiz, David, 140
Oswego Public Library, 36
Owens, Jesse, 103; nicknames for, 6

Pace Picante Salsa, 193
Pacific Coast League (PCL), 142
Parnell, Mel, 139, 168n6
Parsons, Pam, 240–41
passing, 62
Patterson, Dawn, 259
PCL. *See* Pacific Coast League
Pearson, Demetrious: on Black
    cowboys, 205–6; on Soul Circuits,
    209n31
Pena, Tony, *167*
Pennsylvania Colored Wheelmen's
    Association, 94
Percival, Charles, 52; on Century Road
    Club of America, 61; on, Knox,
    K., 58
Perez, Tony, *166–67*
Perkins, George, 56; on, Knox, K., 59
Perry, Jim, 199
Pesky, Johnny, 137, 139, 154
Pfaffle, T. J., 260
Phillips, Helen, 112
Phillips, Wendell, 53
Pickens, James, Jr., 203
Pickett, Bill, 201

Pickett, David, 222–23
Pickett, Joe, 222
Pickett, Tidye, 109, 111
Pierce, Burns, 61, 92, 94–95
pigeons, 18
Pitt, Phyllis, 36
Pizarro, Juan, *165*
plantation mentality, 144
Player, Gary, 44
Plays-in-Place, 65
Pleck, Elizabeth, 68n12
Plessy v. Ferguson, 57, 91
Plotzke, Margo, 240
Pollard, Fritz, 103
Ponkapoag Golf Course, 44
Pope Manufacturing Co., 91
Premier Hockey Federation, 255
prescriptive forgetting, 195–96, 204
Press Cycle Club, 59
Professional Rodeo Cowboy
    Association, 199
public transit segregation, 53

Quaine, William H., 110
Quinones, Rey, *167*
Quintana, Carlos, *167*

Race for Change, 104
racial eugenics, 38
racism: dialect stereotypes, 21, 29n184;
    Green on, 154; Rock on, 37; Taylor
    on, 95–96
racist caricatures: golf and, 41–42; of
    Johnson, F., 20; leisure and, 42
racist lithographs, 20
racist sheet music, 63
Rakes, Joseph, 157
Randolph, Willie, 157
RCC. *See* Riverside Cycle Club
Reasons, George, 101
Reconstruction, 56–57; Du Bois on, 63
Reddy Tee, 41
Red Sox, 257–59; Green debut for, 143,
    152; Impossible Dream season of,
    156; minority players 1933–1992,

164–67; plantation mentality of, 144; tryouts, 149, 180–81, 187
Reed, Wornie, 41
Remington, Frederick, 198
repressive erasure, 195
Republican Party, 42
Ribeiro, Anselmo, 224–26
Rice, Jim, 158, *166–67*
Richardson, Sha'Carri, 109
Richt, F. A., 94
Rickard, Ted, 84
Rickey, Branch, 183–84
Rickords, Theresa, 9
Riggs, Terri, 239
Ring (magazine), 77
Ritchie, Andrew, 64, 102
Rivera, Luis, *167*
Riverside Cycle Club (RCC), 51–52, 91; Black cyclists, 56; members of, 68n22
Roberts, Dave, 168n7
Roberts, E. Marion, 119–20; on Montgomery, 121
Robinson, Floyd, *165*
Robinson, Jackie, 103, 124; debut of, 141
Robinson, Jeanine, 70n69
Robinson, Steve, *194*, 201–7
Robinson, William Foster, 200, 204
Robitaille, Luc, 255
Rochester Democrat and Chronicle, 13–14
Rock, John S.: clientele of, 36; on job discrimination, 37; public writings of, 37; on racism, 37
Rocker, Joe, 162
rodeo: African heritage of, 197; cultural understanding of, 194–95; marketing, 200–203; theoretical perspective on, 195–96. *See also* American West; Black cowboys
Romero, Ed, *167*
Romo, Vicente, *165*
Roosevelt, Theodore, 43, 104, 107n51, 198

Ross, Betsy, 3, 22n14
Ross, Wallace, 11; Johnson, F., fighting, 17
rowing, 1–2; Chautauqua Lake Fizzle ending professional, 15; examples of interest in, 22n14; machine exhibition, 26n101; popularity of, 3; slavery and, 3–4; society intersecting with, 22n13
Roxbury Wheelmen, 60
Rozendaal, Neal, 264
Rudolph, Wilma, 109
Ruffin, Josephine St. Pierre, 57, 62, 64, 70n66
Russell, Bill, 148, 157
Ruth, Babe, 6
Ryder, Clement, 72n86

Saba, Frank, 119–20
sabermetrics, 173n80
Saint-Gaudens, Augustus, 67n6
Salem Gazette, 61–62
Sampson, Charles, 206
Santiago, Jose, *165*
Sasaki, Kazuhiro, 185
Saunders, Nathan, 68n22
Schilling, Chuck, 153
Schneider, Mark, 66
school desegregation, 37
Schott, Marge, 162
Schwinn, Frank, 100
Scott, George, 155, 157, *165–66*
Scott, Jeff, 255
sculling: nineteenth-century manual on, 22n5; sweeping compared with, 2
See-Saw Club, 92
Segui, Diego, *166*
Separate Car Act 1986, 91
Sharp, Becky, 4
Shaughnessy, Dan, 140, 168n9, 168n11
Shaw, Robert Gould, 18–19, 53
Shaw Guards, 18–19
Shawmut Rowing Club, 12
shells, 1–2
Sherif, Muzafer, 65

shoplifting, 13
Shut Out (Bryant), 142–43, 156–57
Silver Lake Regatta, 11, 21
Sinnette, Calvin, 39
Six-Day Race, 94
slavery: abolishment of, 3, 53; Butler, B., on, 7; census records and, 5; Johnson, F., on, 4–5; rowing and, 3–4
sliding seat: Brown, W., inventing, 15–17; Camp on, 16; Courtney on, 17; history of, 16; leg muscles and, 15; *New York Herald* on, 16; patent, 15–17
Smith, Adrienne, 261–62; career of, 263–64
Smith, Al, *164*
Smith, Albert, 36
Smith, Bianca, 259–61
Smith, George, *165*
Smith, Gerrit, 36
Smith, James "Tiger," 80
Smith, John Jay, 37
Smith, Lee, *167*
Smith, Reggie, 155, 157, *165–66*
Smith, Robert, 64
Smith, Tommie, 103
Smith, Wendell, 101, 161
Sneed, Thomas, 162
soccer: Bahr on, 216; Black players in, 218–20; Brazilian, 219–21; crowded out, 215; ethnicity and, 218–20; exceptionalism in, 214–17; failure of, 215–16; Keogh on, 218; Kilpatrick on, 214–15; nativism in, 214–17; as un-American, 216–17
Social History of the Bicycle (Smith, Robert), 64
Soul Circuits, 201, 207; Pearson on, 209n31
Southern Cycler, 51, 58
Southwestern Colored Cowboys' Association, 201, 207
Southworth, Bill, 184
Souza, John, 216

Spanish-American War, 107n51
spectacle racing, 69n34
spoons, 6; examples, 23n40
A Square Deal for Every Man (Roosevelt), 104
Stahl, Jesse, 201
stake turns, 2
Stanley, Marianne, 241
stationary plank seats, 16
Stearns bicycle company, 93
Stephen Greene Press, 101
Stevenson, Mary Huff, 147
Stokes, Louise: American Olympic team selection of, 109, 111; bowling career of, 113; death of, 114; early life of, 109–10; marriage of, 114; running retirement, 113; tributes to, 114
Stone, I. F., 150
Stout, Glenn, 122–23
Sullivan, David, 64
Sullivan, John L., 13, 81–82
summer complaint, 8
Sumner, Charles, 90
sweep rowing: nineteenth-century manual on, 22n5; sculling compared with, 2

Taconic Golf Club, 44
Talented Tenth, 55, 71n85; Du Bois on, 71n85
Tartabull, Jose, *165*
Tarver, LaSchelle, *167*
Tasby, Willie, *164*
Taylor, Marshall "Major," 3, 42, 59, 63, 65–66; achievements of, *90*; autobiography of, 99–101; background of, 89; *Boston Post* on, 95; *Brooklyn Daily Eagle* on, 94; as colored champion of America, 94; death of, 100; first European tour of, 98; historical articles about, 101; house purchase of, 98; isolating, 95–96; no-Sunday-racing clause, 96; obituary of, 100; professional career of, 94; race record of, *99*; on racism,

Index

95, 96; reputation of, 93; retirement of, 99; tributes to, 103; world record setting of, 93
Taylor, Otis, 103
Teamoh, Robert, 56–57, 91
Tewksbury Almshouse, 8
Thames Grove Regatta, 17
Thompson, Era Bell, 200
Thomson, Bobby, 172n57
Thorne, Geoff, 80
Tiant, Luis, *165–66*
tokenism, 155
Tonton Macoute death squads, 219
Towle, Katherine, 53
track and field, 258–59
traps, 18
trash talk, 236
Trask, Mary, 149
triathlons, 258; pro card, 259
The Triumph of the Amateurs (Lanouette), 22n13
Trotter, James Monroe, 40; Washington, Booker T., protest of, 42–43
Troy, Willis, 96
Truth, Sojourner, 57
tuberculosis, 17–19
Turner, Frederick Jackson, 198
Tuskegee Institute, 42
Twain, Mark, 41

un-American: food, 217; politics, 217; soccer as, 216–17
Unbound Gravel ride, 104
Underground Railroad, 36
Union Black Cycle Club of Louisville, 56
United States Golf Association (USGA), 35
University of Massachusetts Amherst riots, 159–60
Urban League, 43
USGA. *See* United States Golf Association
US Women's National Soccer Team, 234

Vails, Nelson, 103
Valdez, Julio, *166–67*
Van Courtlandt Park, 39
vaudeville, 62–63
Vaughan, Mo, 160, *167*
Veale, Bob, *166*
Vennochi, Joan, 162
Vila Nova AC, 221
Villanon, Pito, 219
Violence Free Zone Initiative, 244
The Virginian (Wister), 197, 199
Vreeland, George, 111

Walcott, Joe, 78
Walker, Ben, 92
Walker, Chico, *166–67*
Walker, David, 40, 42, 145
Walker, Edwin, 42
Walker, Moses Fleetwood, 3
Wallace, Mike, 150
Walsh, Stella, 112–13
Waltham Cycle Park, 58
Waltham Manufacturing Company, 91
Ward, Joel, 163
"The Warmest Baby in the Bunch," 97
War on Powder River, 198
Washington, Booker T., 38–39; Grimké, Archibald, protesting, 42–43; Trotter protesting, 42–43
Washington, Kenny, 103
Washington, Porter, 42
Washington, Richard, 62
Washington Post, 40
Watson, Bobby, 103, *166*
Watts, Anna, 5; Census data on, 8
Watts, Francis J., 5; death of, 8
West End, 55
Western Horseman, 205
Weymouth Falls, Nova Scotia, 77
WFA. *See* Women's Football Alliance
whaling industry, 54
Wheaton, Horace, 68n22
Wheaton, Viola, 51–52
White flight, 147, 157
White privilege, 36, 40–41

290   *Index*

Whitfield, Fred, 206
Willard, Jess, 83
Williams, Juan, 163
Williams, Justin, 103
Williams, William T., 43
willow dippers, 6
Wills, Harry, 83, 84
Wilson, Butler, 39
Wilson, Earl, 142, 155–56, *164–65*
Wilson, Mary, 13
Wister, Owen, 197; American West revisionism by, 199
Women's Football Alliance (WFA), 261–64
women's racing: *Bearings* on, 57–58; costume contest, 58; LAW on, 58; opposition to, 57–58

Woodall, Larry, 150
Woodman, Joe, 77–78
Worcester Cycle Club, 100
Worcester Spy, 60
Wright, Ernie, Jr., 180
Wu, Michelle, 245
Wyatt, John, *165*
Wynn, Earl, 152

Yale, Her Campus, Class-Rooms, and Athletics (Camp), 16
Yawkey, Bill, 144
Yawkey, Tom, 143–44, 149
Yeehaw Agenda, 207

Zelee, Whitney, 261–63; injuries of, 264
Zimmerman, Arthur, 59

About the Editors and Contributors

ABOUT THE EDITORS

Robert Cvornyek is professor emeritus of history at Rhode Island College. He currently serves as an assistant teaching professor at Florida State University, Panama City, where he specializes in sports history. He received his PhD in history from Columbia University. Robert has written extensively on the intersection of race, sports, and cultural expression, and recently, he edited the autobiography of baseball Hall-of-Famer Effa Manley. He is currently working on a documentary film that explores the "money game" in New England African American baseball. Robert also codirects the program *It Don't Mean a Thing If It Ain't Got That Swing: Baseball, Jazz, and Black Cultural Expression.*

Douglas Stark focuses on making history more engaging, relevant, and accessible to a diverse audience. His experience includes strategic planning, fiscal management, project management, facility development, historic preservation, collections care, content and exhibition development, branding and messaging, product development, programming and outreach, and audience engagement. He served as museum director at the International Tennis Hall of Fame in Newport, Rhode Island, for thirteen years. He also worked at the Naismith Memorial Basketball Hall of Fame and the US Golf Association. He is the 2016 recipient of the International Sports Heritage Association's W. R. "Bill" Schroeder Distinguished Service Award. He is the past president of the New England Museum Association (NEMA), and he received a NEMA Excellence Award in 2021. Douglas is a graduate of Brandeis University, where he received his BA in American history with a minor in the history of art. He pursued graduate studies at New York University, where he earned an MA in American history with dual certification in museum studies, and archival management, historical society administration, and historical editing. He holds an MBA with a concentration in nonprofit management from the

University of Massachusetts at Amherst. He is also the author of five books on basketball.

ABOUT THE CONTRIBUTORS

Steven Apostolov earned a PhD in 2011 from the University of Paris. Since then, Apostolov has taught social history and sports management and administration classes at multiple colleges and universities in New England and New York. He currently teaches French for Newport Public Schools. Apostolov's research interests focus on US sport, economic, social and cultural history. Apostolov resides in South Kingstown, Rhode Island. In his spare time, he likes to ski, play tennis, scuba dive, ride his motorcycle, and travel around the world.

Lane Demas is professor of history at Central Michigan University, where he specializes in African American history. He is the author of two books: *Game of Privilege: An African American History of Golf* (University of North Carolina Press, 2017) and *Integrating the Gridiron: Black Civil Rights and American College Football* (Rutgers University Press, 2010). His media contributions include interviews for outlets such as the *New York Times*, the *Chicago Tribune*, the *Boston Globe*, and *CNN.com*, radio interviews for *National Public Radio* and BBC World *Service*, and interviews for *ESPN* television documentaries. Professor Demas has earned awards from the National Endowment for the Humanities (NEH), the Fulbright Program, the United States Golf Association (USGA), and the North American Society for Sport History (NASSH). He is also editor of the *Michigan Historical Review*, the only scholarly publication devoted to Michigan history.

Lorenz J. Finison is a public health consultant and bicycling historian who researches issues of race, class, and gender. He received his PhD in social psychology from Columbia University. His bicycling history publications include *Boston's Cycling Craze, 1880–1900: A Story of Race, Sport, and Society* (2014); *Boston's 20th Century Bicycling Renaissance: Cultural Change on Two Wheels* (2018); and *Bicycling Inclusion and Equity: Histories of New England and Beyond* (2022, forthcoming). He is a founding member of Cycling Through History and the Friends of the Bicycling History Collections at University of Massachusetts-Boston. Most recently, he is a founding member of the New England Cycling Coalition for Diversity.

Donna L. Halper is associate professor of communication and media studies at Lesley University in Cambridge, Massachusetts. A widely quoted media

About the Editors and Contributors 293

historian with expertise in the history of broadcasting, she is the author of six books (including *Invisible Stars: A Social History of Women in American Broadcasting* and *Boston Radio—1920–2010*); she has also written numerous book chapters, as well as freelance articles for magazines and journals. When not researching radio and TV history, she writes about baseball, focusing on Negro Leagues history, baseball "firsts," and biographical sketches of early sportswriters. A former radio deejay and music director, credited with having discovered the rock band Rush, Dr. Halper reinvented herself and attained her PhD at the age of sixty-four.

Leslie Heaphy, PhD, is associate professor of history at Kent State University at Stark. She is the author/editor of six books and numerous articles on the Negro Leagues, women's baseball, and the New York Mets. She also serves as vice president of SABR and is on the board of the International Women's Baseball Center. Dr. Heaphy is also the editor of *Black Ball*, an annual, peer-reviewed journal on the Negro Leagues and Black baseball. She also served on two National Baseball Hall of Fame Committees that elected a total of nineteen Negro League players, owners, and pioneers to the Hall.

Edward H. Jones is a retired attorney living in Pittsburgh, Pennsylvania. He is a former club rower who learned the sport on Pittsburgh's Allegheny River, the same body of water where his subject, professional rower Frenchy Johnson, won a single-sculls boat race a century earlier in 1879. Jones's research interest lies with chronicling the struggles and triumphs of lesser-known African American sports figures.

Stephanie Liscio is the author of *Integrating Cleveland Baseball: Media Activism, the Integration of the Indians, and the Demise of the Negro League Buckeyes*, and she is currently the director of prospect research at Hiram College in Hiram, Ohio. Stephanie earned her PhD in history from Case Western Reserve University, her MA in applied history from Shippensburg University, and her BA in English writing and history from the University of Pittsburgh. Her research has focused on Negro League baseball and public stadiums following World War II; she has also written about the Cleveland Indians/Guardians for a number of publications. When she's not watching or complaining about baseball, Stephanie likes to spend time with her husband, John, and Shih Tzu, Izzy.

Susan A. Michalczyk is professor at Boston College in the Morrissey College of Arts and Sciences. Born in Boston, she completed her undergraduate degree at Boston College and her doctoral work at Harvard University. In her work as author and documentary filmmaker, Michalczyk focuses on

294   *About the Editors and Contributors*

the autobiographical narrative/memory experience as it relates to film and literature. Her most recent publications and documentaries revolve around historical, sociopolitical, and ethical issues of racism and antisemitism. She has been a partner with her husband, John J. Michalczyk, in both teaching and film production for over twenty-five years, focusing on issues of social justice and human rights. Coproducer and scriptwriter, her works include *Lou Montgomery: A Legacy Restored*; *Killing Silence: Taking on the Mafia in Sicily*; *Writing on the Wall: Remembering the Berlin Wall*; and *Nazi Law: Legally Blind*. Her most recent book, coauthored with her husband, is *Costa-Gavras: Encounters with History*.

Eileen Narcotta-Welp is associate professor in the Department of Exercise and Sport Science at the University of Wisconsin—La Crosse. She earned her PhD in health and sport studies from the University of Iowa in 2016. As a feminist cultural studies scholar, Narcotta-Welp's research interests include intersections of race, class, gender, and sexuality in regard to high-performance women's sport in both the US and transnational contexts. Her work appears in the *Journal of Sport History*, *Sport in Society*, and *Soccer and Society*, as well as in multiple edited book collections.

Tracey Owens Patton is professor in the Department of English and adjunct professor in African American & Diaspora Studies in the School of Culture, Gender, and Social Justice at the University of Wyoming. She also served as the director of the African American & Diaspora Studies Program from 2009 to 2017 at the University of Wyoming. She earned her PhD in communication at the University of Utah. Her area of specialization is critical cultural rhetorical studies and communication, critical media studies, feminist and womanist theory, and transnational studies. She has published numerous journal articles, published a coauthored book titled *Gender, Whiteness, and Power in Rodeo: Breaking Away from the Ties of Sexism and Racism* (2012), and has a forthcoming book entitled *A Nation's Undesirables: Mixed-Race Children and Whiteness in the Post-Nazi Era*.

Andrew Smith is dean of the College of Professional Studies at Millikin University. He earned a PhD in History from Purdue University, where he began writing about the history of boxing and race in the United States. His work appears in the *Journal of Sport History* and *International Journal of the History of Sport*, as well as edited collections including *A Companion to American Sport History, American National Pastimes—A History,* and *Philly Sports: Teams, Games, and Athletes from Rocky's Town*. Smith is the author of "No Way But to Fight: George Foreman and the Business of Boxing" and

About the Editors and Contributors 295

has appeared on media outlets like ESPN Radio, Fox Sports, National Public Radio, and Sirius XM.

Lynne Tolman is president of the Major Taylor Association, Inc. Her journalism career has included thirty-five years as a reporter, cycling columnist, and editor at *The Worcester Telegram & Gazette*, after stints at *The Boston Globe* and other daily newspapers. Her writing has appeared in *VeloNews*, *The Ride*, *Bike Culture*, *USA Cycling*, *Bike Racing Nation*, *The Wheelmen*, *Podium Cafe*, *The Boneshaker*, and other cycling media. At the 1996 Olympics, she was press information manager for road and track cycling for the Atlanta Committee for the Olympic Games. She holds a bachelor's degree from the Medill School of Journalism at Northwestern University.

Robert E. Weir, PhD, is a former senior Fulbright scholar to New Zealand and retired history professor who most recently taught at the University of Massachusetts-Amherst. He has published scores of articles and eleven books. His latest is *The Marx Brothers and America: Where Film, Comedy and History Collide*. He has also written a guide to unusual and overlooked sites in Western Massachusetts entitled *Who Knew? Roadside Revelations in Western Massachusetts*. He lives in Northampton, where he hangs out with friends at a coffee shop, does volunteer work, roots for the Yankees, and dabbles in freelance photography and journalism.